Politeness in Language

W
DE
G

Politeness in Language

Studies in its History, Theory and Practice

Second revised and expanded edition
With a new introduction by Richard J. Watts

Edited by
Richard J. Watts
Sachiko Ide
Konrad Ehlich

Mouton de Gruyter
Berlin · New York

Mouton de Gruyter (formerly Mouton, The Hague)
is a Division of Walter de Gruyter GmbH & Co. KG, Berlin.

The first edition was published in 1992 as volume 59
of the series *Trends in Linguistics. Studies and Monographs.*

⊗ Printed on acid-free paper which falls within the guidelines
of the ANSI to ensure permanence and durability.

Library of Congress Cataloging-in-Publication Data

Politeness in language : studies in its history, theory, and prac-
tice / with a new introduction by Richard J. Watts ; edited by
Richard J. Watts, Sachiko Ide, Konrad Ehlich. − 2nd rev. and
expanded ed.
    p. cm.
  Includes bibliographical references and index.
  ISBN 3-11-018549-0 (hardcover : alk. paper) −
  ISBN 3-11-018300-5 (pbk. : alk. paper)
  1. Politeness (Linguistics)   I. Watts, Richard J.   II. Ide,
Sachiko, 1939−   III. Ehlich, Konrad, 1942−
  P299.H66P6   2005
  306.44−dc22
                                              2005023519

ISBN 3 11 018549 0 hc.
ISBN 3 11 018300 5 pb.

Bibliographic information published by Die Deutsche Bibliothek

Die Deutsche Bibliothek lists this publication in the Deutsche Nationalbibliografie;
detailed bibliographic data is available in the Internet at <http://dnb.ddb.de>.

Preface

This book has been long in the making, and without an enormous amount of devoted hard work by a team of assistants at the English Department of the University of Berne it might never have seen the light of day. A more explicit expression of our thanks to that team will be given shortly. Beforehand, however, it may be of interest to readers to know something of the genesis of this collection of papers on aspects of politeness in language.

At the Annual Meeting of the Societas Linguistica Europæa in Freiburg i. Br., Germany, in July 1988, a workshop was held on linguistic politeness. It was organised by the three editors of this volume and participants included five other contributors, Shoshana Blum-Kulka, Gudrun Held, Florian Coulmas, Konrad Werkhofer and Richard Janney.

Looking back over time at that workshop, we believe that it was a resounding success, so much so that despite certain healthy differences of opinion on terminology and method it was felt that the papers should be published and other initiatives such as establishing a communicative network of researchers into linguistic politeness and forming an international research group should be launched. As so often happens, little has so far come of the last two aims, not because of a lack of enthusiasm on the part of the initiators but because of the vagaries of life beyond the groves of academe. In particular, two of the central figures in the group became seriously ill and had to undergo surgery.

Priorities therefore had to be set, and the first priority was the publication of the proceedings of the Freiburg workshop. It was felt that the eight papers by the participants in the workshop should form the backbone of the book and that other researchers should be invited to participate. The idea was to give a view of politeness that was not centred on research being carried out in the United States or Britain, and to focus on four areas, the historicity of the concept of politeness and the history of politeness research in Europe and elsewhere, the fundamental theoretical problems of a notion of linguistic politeness, examples of the kind of empirical research being carried out within the framework of a notion of politeness, and examples of some of the theoretical and empirical problems in a non-Western oriented conceptualisation of politeness. The rationale behind the structure of the book is presented in the introductory chapter.

Without the patience of the contributors in the face of a seemingly endless stream of problems and their willingness to deal with the demands made on them by the editors there clearly would have been no book, and our thanks go to all those who contributed and to those involved in the behind-the-scenes work at their end of the line.

Our greatest thanks, however, must go to the team of assistants in Berne, first and foremost to Daniela Kessler. Daniela has been in charge of the practical problems involved in typing in manuscripts, writing to contributors and to the publishers, formatting all the texts and entering all the corrections (if there are any mistakes still in the text fault must be found with Richard Watts for not being a careful enough proofreader, and not to Daniela) and, last but not least, compiling the index. Without Daniela's care and persistence there truly would have been no book.

However, she has been very ably and loyally assisted at various times by Ursula Krähenbühl, Franz Andres, Daniel Stotz, Julie Diamond, Josef Troxler and Yves Robert. To all of them we owe a debt of thanks.

None of the shortcomings of this collection, whether technical or in terms of content, may be laid at anyone's door but our own, and we, the editors, accept full responsibility for any mistakes or weaknesses still remaining in the text.

Contents

Part 3: Politeness in a Non-Western Cultural Setting

Contributors

Shoshana Blum-Kulka
Hebrew University, Jerusalem

Florian Coulmas
German Institute of Japanese Studies, Tokyo

Konrad Ehlich
University of Munich

Gudrun Held
University of Salzburg

Sachiko Ide
Japan Women's University, Tokyo

Richard W. Janney
University of Munich

Annelie Knapp
University of Siegen

Manfred Kummer

Roger D. Sell
Abo Akedemi University, Finland

Judith Stalpers

Renate Valtin
Humboldt University, Berlin

Sabine Walper
University of Munich

Richard J. Watts
University of Berne

Konrad T. Werkhofer
Berlin

Linguistic politeness research: *Quo vadis?*

Politeness in Language in retrospect

> Nothing will ever fix the reference of "politeness"
> to human behaviour once and for all.
> Roger Sell, p. 113

Why republish, as a second edition, a collection of articles on linguistic politeness that appeared in 1992? Is it not the case that research has progressed well beyond the issues in linguistic politeness that were uppermost in our minds in the late 1980s and early 1990s? Surely a second edition can only have historical value at most?

If the answers to the second two questions were an unequivocal "yes", there would indeed be little reason to republish the contributions. As matters stand, however, research into linguistic politeness has not progressed much further than the euphoric acclaim accorded to Penelope Brown and Stephen Levinson's *Politeness: Some Universals in Language Usage* (1987) and the flood of empirical research that it inspired. True, there have been bold and notable attempts to reach out beyond the confines of Brown and Levinson's work, and I shall return to some of these during this new introductory chapter. But those who had been working in the field prior to 1987 had already begun to criticise various aspects of Brown and Levinson's work. It had, after all, been available since 1978 as a long article entitled "Universals in language usage: Politeness phenomena" in a collection edited by Esther Goody (*Questions and Politeness: Strategies in Social Interaction*), and Brown and Levinson deal with much of the criticism that had ensued in the intervening years in their 54-page introduction to the 1987 reprint.

Between 1978 and 1987 and immediately after the reprint in 1987 opposition was raised against Brown and Levinson's conceptualisation of politeness as the realisation of face threat mitigation. Their approach did not seem to account for ways in which politeness had been understood in the English-speaking world prior to the late twentieth century, nor did it seem to account for ways in which related lexemes in other languages were used to refer to equivalent aspects of social behaviour.

There was a certain uneasiness about the rationalist, individualistic approach to politeness which saw it as a set of strategies to achieve social goals with a minimum of social friction. In a 1980 review of Esther Goody's book, Richard Schmidt says of Brown and Levinson's concept of politeness that it is "an overly pessimistic, rather paranoid view of human social interaction" (1980: 104). For those who had read their Goffman, it was clear that Brown and Levinson had interpreted his concept of face selectively and had adapted it to their own purposes. In particular, they had transformed a social understanding of face into an individualistic one.

There were of course other alternative approaches to linguistic politeness on the market, notably Robin Lakoff (1973, 1977) and Geoffrey Leech (1983), but these leaned too heavily on Grice while remaining essentially rationalist in orientation. A third alternative approach to Brown and Levinson (Fraser and Nolen 1981) focused on the notion of the Conversational Contract, which maintains that every individual, on entering a social interaction, must recognise a set of rights and obligations which determine how s/he is meant to behave. But nothing is said about how those rights and obligations come to be fixed in the first place. Are they socially predetermined in some way, and how does the individual learn of their "existence"?

At the International Pragmatics Association meeting in Antwerp, 1987, a group of scholars who held such critical views of the canonical approaches to linguistic politeness (Richard J. Watts, Shoshana Blum-Kulka, Gudrun Held, Sachiko Ide) met informally and decided to coordinate their efforts for presentation of the issues at the 1988 annual meeting of the Societas Linguistica Europeæ in Freiburg im Breisgau, Germany. During the intervening year Konrad Ehlich, Richard Janney, Konrad Werkhofer and Florian Coulmas were contacted and agreed to participate in Freiburg. The contributions by what was loosely called the 'Politeness Research Group' were enriched by invited articles by Roger Sell, Annelie Knapp-Potthoff, Judith Stalpers, Sabine Walper and Renate Valtin, and Manfred Kummer, thus making up *Politeness in Language: Studies in its History, Theory and Practice.*

It is in the nature of such edited volumes that the contributions are in many ways arbitrary. *Politeness in Language* was no exception, and this made a division into sections difficult. However, the first six contributions in *Part 1: The Theory and History of Linguistic Politeness,* which with the exception of the invited contribution by Roger Sell

were all from core members of the group, as well as three contributions in *Part 3: Politeness in a Non-Western Cultural Setting* by core
members Shoshana Blum-Kulka, Sachiko Ide (and the research team
associated with her), and Florian Coulmas hang together remarkably
well. It is here that we can discern the beginnings of new approaches
to the study of linguistic politeness. Blum-Kulka and Arndt and Janney
were developing a cross-cultural framework in which to look at politeness phenomena; Watts was looking critically at the assumptions of
universality when applied to language usage and was developing his
alternative notion of politic behaviour; Ide was challenging what she
saw (and still sees) as a Eurocentric (Western-based) approach to politeness that was incompatible with Asian (and not just Asian!) conceptualisations; Werkhofer was reaching out to establish a social psychological approach, but particularly towards the understanding of politeness as "a socially and historically constituted, powerful symbolic
medium" (p. 159); Ehlich was concerned to make us aware of the historical relativity inherent in conceptualisations of politeness, which
motivates against rationalist explanations of universality. All of these
criticisms, suggestions and hypotheses, some of them tentative, others
forceful, point towards radical new ways of thinking about linguistic
politeness. Above all, they reveal – with hindsight – the first tentative
signs of *postmodernist* thinking about politeness, as I hope to show in
this introductory chapter.

I shall refrain from summarising the contents of the chapters here.
Instead I shall use quotations from different points in the book to
structure the indications of alternative thinking about politeness that
are to be found in it and to show how we might construct a postmodernist approach to the subject.

We can start with the quotation by Sell heading this section. Sell's
statement indicates that politeness will always be a slippery, ultimately
indefinable quality of interaction which is subject to change through
time and across cultural space. There is, in other words, no stable referent indexed by the lexeme *polite*, which indicates that *Politeness in
Language* was venturing into unexplored territory in 1992. The ex-
ploratory nature of the book is expressed by the following quotation
from the "Introduction" by Watts, Ide and Ehlich:

> It is not our purpose to solve the problems of linguistic politeness, but rather
> to highlight the many problems which exist and which need to be addressed
> from the comparative, cross-cultural perspective, from the empirical perspec-

tive and from the theoretical perspective. (p. 16)

This calls for problems to be addressed rather than solved. It is clear on reading the book that several problems are there to be solved and that, far from representing a fixed paradigm within which instances of verbal interaction can be analysed in terms of politeness parameters, Brown and Levinson's model raises a wide range of problems that also need to be addressed.

This new introductory chapter is organised as follows: first, I shall tackle the issues arising from attempts to define politeness and from the assumption of its universality. I shall then move on to consider the important question of first-order and second-order politeness, which was explicitly expressed in this volume for the first time. After that I shall focus on the cultural and historical relativity of politeness and the problem of ethnocentricity, moving on from there to a discussion of the notion of face and to criticisms of Brown and Levinson's model. This will be followed by criticism of pragmatic approaches to linguistic politeness. Politeness as a social phenomenon will then be tackled, followed by some of the consequences of adopting a first-order approach to politeness. This will lead to a serious consideration of lay persons' evaluations of polite behaviour and thence to a postmodernist, discursive focus on linguistic politeness. All of these issues are to be found in the book, although obviously not in fully developed form. But they are there nevertheless, which is reason enough for publishing a second edition of *Politeness in Language*.

Definitions of politeness and the universality problem

> A main problem, we suggest, is the lack of agreement
> among investigators about how politeness
> should be defined as an object of study.
> (Richard Janney and Horst Arndt, p. 22)

> [...] it is our intention with this volume of papers on linguistic
> politeness to deepen the research perspectives within this field
> by questioning more profoundly what polite linguistic
> behaviour actually is and what grounds there
> might be for claims of universality.
> (Richard J. Watts, Sachiko Ide and Konrad Ehlich, p. 2)

The second lead quotation at the head of this section is taken from the

"Introduction" and is programmatic. Two principal issues emerge as desiderata for the whole volume,

a) there is a need to question "more profoundly" what we should understand by the term "politeness", and

b) there is likewise a need to investigate the claim that, whatever it is, politeness is a universal feature of human social interaction.

The expression "more profoundly" implies that the editors were not happy with the ways in which politeness had hitherto been defined. They were likewise not happy with terms such as "universals of language usage". Indeed, in my own contribution to the volume I tackle this problem head-on. The difficulty is that it is pointless making claims about universality if researchers are not in agreement about what politeness actually *is*. The lead quotation from Janney and Arndt's contribution given at the head of this section also highlights the need to focus on what the "object of study" actually is. So before before we move on to consider more substantive issues that are raised in the book, let us start by taking a look at some of the definitions of politeness given in the literature.

In Watts (2003: 50–53) I discuss some of the definitions given by Sifianou (1992a) from the literature on linguistic politeness. Lakoff (1975a), for example, suggests that "… politeness is developed by societies in order to reduce friction in personal interaction", which implies that friction is undesirable and that societies, in some mysterious way, "invent" politeness to prevent, or at least minimise it. But this still doesn't tell us what politeness is. Leech (1980: 19) defines it as "strategic conflict avoidance" and the establishment and maintenance of comity, and he suggests that it "can be measured in terms of the degree of effort put into the avoidance of a conflict situation". This turns politeness into a set of strategies for the avoidance of conflict, but it tells us nothing about what those strategies are.

The term "conflict avoidance" is similar to that of the "reduction of friction". It is even more similar to Brown and Levinson's definition of politeness as rational behaviour aimed at the strategic softening (or mitigation) of face-threatening acts (1978, 1987). The focus in their definition is clearly on the speaker, but as I point out in Watts (2003: 51), in this case "we cannot know how the hearer … will react". In a discursive approach to politeness, which I will argue for during the course of this introductory chapter, we need to access the hearer's reaction to evaluate whether the utterance has been interpreted as an act of politeness or not. Indeed, as Werkhofer points out in this volume, if Brown and Levinson and those who follow their lead are taken seriously, they have gravely misinterpreted the purpose of Grice's Cooperative Principle:

> Starting from a Gricean approach to the speaker's intentions and combining it with a notion of "face", this model presupposes a specific relationship between *ego* and *alter*, namely an antagonistic one. (p. 165–166)

Following Brown and Levinson, Kasper (1990: 194) concludes that communication should be seen as "a fundamentally dangerous and antagonistic endeavor", which brings us back to Schmidt's comment on Brown and Levinson's conceptualisation of politeness as being "an overly pessimistic, rather paranoid view of human social interaction". As with Leech, Kasper sees politeness as a set of strategies "to defuse the danger and to minimalise the antagonism". Hill *et al.* (1986) define politeness as "one of the constraints on human interaction, whose purpose is to consider others' feelings, establish levels of mutual comfort, and promote rapport". Once again, politeness is defined as behaviour which promotes such positive interactional qualities as "mutual comfort" and "rapport", disregarding the possibility that politeness could be used by the speaker to exert power over the addressee and is therefore contestable behaviour. The most enigmatic definition of all is given by Fraser and Nolen (1980), who see politeness as "a property associated with a voluntary action".

There is a degree of vagueness in all these definitions which does not augur well if we wish to claim universality for politeness. We might well agree that it is not possible to imagine a human society which does not make use of communicative strategies to avoid interpersonal friction, to avoid conflict, to minimise possible antagonism, to foster mutual comfort and promote rapport. That much would seem to be characteristic of all human societies, although Janney and Arndt are sceptical even here: "... it is doubtful ... whether techniques and strategies for signalling these feelings in different cultures are universal" (p. 29). Regardless of whether we consider such strategies universal, however, the central issue is whether or not we should call whatever it is that helps us to do these things "politeness".

In his contribution to the volume, Ehlich is particularly critical of the use of the English term "politeness" on the grounds that

[s]cientific conceptualisations make use of everyday expressions to define politeness, and they very often do so in a completely unquestioning, matter-of-fact way, in other words – unscientifically. (p. 73)

He also criticises the "unquestioning" use of the English language in creating scientific concepts, since, as we shall see in the following section, there is no guarantee that a native English speaker will understand the "scientific" term "politeness" in quite the same way as s/he would normally think of it, i.e. as an everyday term that is not all that frequently used. Things become even more complicated when we transfer the term to refer to strategies for avoiding conflict, fostering mutual comfort and promoting rapport to other social groups using other languages. This is particularly well illustrated in the contribution by Ide *et al.*, who show convincingly that the (roughly) equivalent term in Japanese, *teneina*, has very different sets of connotations associated with it from the English term "politeness".

We need to ask why Brown and Levinson's claim that the study of linguistic politeness is the study of a universal aspect of language usage has found so many adherents during the 1990s and the early years of this decade. But we also need to focus in more detail on what it is that Brown and Levinson consider "universal". The search for universals of human behaviour – and it's immaterial for the moment whether we are thinking in terms of cognitive (or what Chomsky would call biological) linguistic universals or universal modes of behaviour that seem to be valid wherever we observe human beings engaged in social practice – is an attempt to promote them to the scientific status of objects of knowledge lying outside individual experience. It is part of a modernist view of scientific endeavour that, in relation to the study of language, ultimately places both language structure and language behaviour outside human beings.

As Scannell ([1998] 2002: 262) points out, the effect of modernist views is "to establish language as an object of knowledge only by uncoupling it from praxis and being". The modernist view of scientific endeavour is a rationalist, Cartesian one, but it is the canonical (perhaps Western) view of how scientific enquiry, including social scientific enquiry, should be carried out. In this approach the *cogito* of Descartes' famous adage is taken to be the prerequisite of the fact of being, the *sum – cogito, **ergo** sum*. A modernist view of linguistic politeness thus attempts to see it as "an object of knowledge" and the only way to do this is to "uncouple it from praxis and being". A postmodernist view would see things the other way round.

At a number of points in *Politeness in Language* we can trace a distinctly questioning attitude towards uncoupling politeness from social praxis and being. In the "Introduction" Watts, Ide and Ehlich reject the idea that politeness is a "socio-anthropological given" and suggest that it emerges out of instances of social interaction:

> Politeness is thus a dynamic concept, always open to adaptation and change in any group, in any age, and, indeed, at any moment of time. It is not a socio-anthropological given which can simply be applied to the analysis of social interaction, but actually arises out of that interaction. (p. 11)

Janney and Arndt come to a very similar conclusion:

> From a sociopsychological point of view, politeness is not a static logical concept, but a dynamic interpersonal activity that can be observed, described, and explained in functional interactional terms. Within a given culture, almost any normal adult can be polite in impolite ways, or be impolite in polite ways. (p. 22)

Rather than being a "static logical concept", i.e. "an object of knowledge", politeness is a "dynamic, interpersonal activity", i.e. it is rooted in praxis and being. Ehlich also voices similar intuitions:

> Thus "politeness" is not a given, but is related to a standard that lies outside it. (p. 75)

What that "standard" is will be taken up later.

Now, it would be more than a little unfair to accuse Brown and Levinson of attempting to create "a given" which can be labelled "politeness", whether that given is taken to be sociopsychological, pragmatic or social-anthropological. It would also amount to throwing the baby out with the bath-water to deny that there is something universal about politeness. This point is fully recognised by Werkhofer despite what amounts to his virtual dismantling of the Brown and Levinson model:

> To explore such processes and differences would of course be desirable: going beyond the crude dualisms of "independent" vs. "dependent" and of social vs. individual factors, we might then begin to understand how politeness is actually constituted and used not only in terms of purportedly universal principles, but in both universal and specific terms. (p. 158)

What Brown and Levinson do contend, however, is that politeness is the functional product of strategies of face-threat mitigation. So the universal feature that they are proposing is not really politeness at all, but the notion of "face". We will defer a discussion of face until a little later when we consider Goffman's way of conceptualising it in more detail. Suffice it to say at the moment that politeness as it is perceived in instances of praxis does not always have to be connected with face-threatening. In the next section, therefore, I shall consider how the volume moves towards a postmodernist understanding of politeness by focusing on ways in which lexemes like *polite, well-mannered, impolite, rude*, etc. are used in evaluations of social interaction. This will require making a distinction between *first-order* and *second-order politeness*.

First-order and second-order politeness: Politeness as a normative, moral concept

> Our suggestion … was to lower the level of idealisation, leave the analysis of rules of politeness … to philosophers, and begin paying more systematic attention to how people actually express their feelings to each other in everyday conversation …
> (Janney and Arndt, p. 22)

For want of a clear definition of politeness in the literature Ehlich maintains that "[w]e are … forced to take as our departure the present state of affairs in lay conceptualisations of politeness and the way in which these have been transferred to the definition of the relationship between language and politeness" (p. 81). He seems to accept this point rather grudgingly, as if having to resort to lay conceptualisations of the term were not a particularly scientific step to take. On the other hand, Watts, Ide and Ehlich point out that "we ignore lay interpretations of politeness at our own peril" (p. 15). A number of tentative, and some more forceful, statements like these are made throughout the volume, and they indicate a shift of emphasis away from the attempt to construct a model of politeness which can be used to predict when polite behaviour can be expected or to explain post-factum why it has been produced and towards the need to pay closer attention to how participants in social interaction perceive politeness. The volume does not explicitly declare the development of such a paradigm change in politeness research to be one of its main aims, but at an early point in the "Introduction" we make it abundantly clear that there *is* a need to distinguish between what we call first-order and second-order politeness:

> We shall argue in this introduction that a distinction needs to be made between first-order and second-order politeness. We take first-order politeness to correspond to the various ways in which polite behaviour is perceived and talked about by members of socio-cultural groups. (p. 3)

We define second-order politeness in the "Introduction" as "a theoretical construct, a term within a theory of social behaviour and language usage" (p. 3). To rephrase Scannell's description of a modernist approach to the study of language, second-order politeness is seen "as an object of knowledge", but "only by uncoupling it from praxis and being".

Eelen (2001) takes up this distinction between first-order and second-order politeness. What he calls "politeness1" consists of lay concepts of politeness, and "politeness2" is defined as concepts of politeness central to theoretical models of politeness. The distinction is further developed in Watts (2003), where it is argued that evaluative terms related to the field of politeness such as *polite, impolite, rude,* etc. are subject to discursive dispute in that participants in social interaction are likely to differ in attributing these evaluations to individuals' contributions to the interaction. The range variation in the attribution of the terms is easily testable by getting participants to comment on how they would evaluate contributions to verbal interaction in which they were involved, or in commenting on contributions to other forms of interaction in which they were not involved. There is of course a danger of them making post factum evaluations that might not correspond to real-time evaluations by the participants themselves during the interaction (cf. the criticism of this method of procedure in Locher and Watts 2005).

The major argument against basing a theory of politeness on lay interpretations of the term – and this includes the use of any lexemes in use in other languages to refer to similar types of linguistic and non-linguistic social behaviour – is that it is impossible to operationalise those terms in empirical research. The assumption underlying this argument is – once again – that a model can only be constructed rationally, i.e. it represents the modernist approach towards scientific research. But terms like English *polite, well-mannered, rude, impolite,* etc. are by their very nature evaluative and normative. Several of the contributors to this volume openly acknowledge this and warn against the construction of an all-encompassing "non-evaluative" term "politeness". In distinguishing between ritual and politeness behaviour, Held stresses the subjective nature of the term:

> In contrast to ritual ... politeness is characterised to a far greater extent by subjective variation ... (p. 149)

Sell is particularly clear in his insistence on the subjective, moralistic aspect of politeness:

> An act performed by one person is received as impolite, whereas, performed under the same circumstances by a virtually identical person, the same act is perceived as polite. (p. 116)

He argues that, in studying literary texts, we become aware not only of the normativity of politeness evaluations, but also of the continual "flux" in those evaluations between social groups, individuals and across time:

> My main argument ... has been that by studying the politeness portrayed *in*, and the politeness expressed *by*, literary texts we come to see that human behaviour and the meaning of moral terms are for ever in flux. (pp. 128–129)

Werkhofer tentatively adds an ethical note to these perceptions of politeness:

> ... politeness may have something to do with what is considered just and right with regard to a particular social event or with the construction of social realities and with social order. (p. 172)

and then, later in his contribution, makes this point of view explicit:

> This pattern thus enables us to understand the moral and ethical connotations of politeness – connotations that would seem to follow naturally from being associated with social order. (p. 192)

So quite apart from rejecting lay conceptualisations as being "unscientific", I shall argue that it is precisely those conceptualisations which should form the rockbed of a postmodernist approach to the study of linguistic politeness, one which begins by stressing the need to take on Jacob Mey's "*general* paradox of language", i.e. "it is natural only inasmuch as the desire to communicate, and the need to express themselves, are natural for all humans" (2001: 43). I shall adopt Scannell's point that "human being is being-in-language" ([1998]

2003: 163), i.e. that being human logically entails linguistic action, or performing "being human" *in* language rather than simply *with* language. Language creates the worlds within which each of us exists, or to quote Scannell again, "[i]t brings into being the common world that is *between* the participants in the interaction. This world may be one that is literally talked into existence ..., or it may be that the talk produced is *of* a particular world (an event, a person, a place)" ([1998] 2003: 263). The worlds we create are thus fundamentally social, but, in terms of how we perceive them, they are first and foremost within ourselves. Moving out from this perspective, it is still possible for us to construct a model of linguistic politeness and, in doing so, to consider the universal nature of polite linguistic behaviour. But the model will be radically different from those at present in use in linguistic politeness research. Constructing such a model can only be done by looking more closely and more intensively at how people use the terms that are available to them in their own languages and by recognising the discursive struggle over those terms. In the postmodernist approach to politeness, first-order politeness (Eelen's politeness1) should be the starting point of such an endeavour. This is entirely in line with Ehlich's point that

> [w]e are therefore forced to take as our departure the present state of affairs in lay conceptualisations of politeness and the way in which these have been transferred to the definition of the relationship between language and politeness. (p. 81)

The cultural and historical relativity of "politeness"

> Even in the eighteenth century ... "breeding", "manners",
> and "politeness" could already carry more cynical connotations,
> connotations which clearly bore some relation
> to the way people were actually behaving.
> (Sell, p. 110)

Sell's statement that "human behaviour and the meaning of moral terms are for ever in flux" (p. 129, quoted in the previous section) implies that perceptions of politeness vary from social group to social group and from one historical period to another. This is precisely because politeness, if it refers to anything, refers to a moral concept which is subject to discursive dispute. Both Sell and Watts take their examples from the 18th century. As is clear from the lead quotation at the head of this section, 18th century conceptualisations of politeness in Britain equated it with "breeding" (by which those writers who make that comparison mean, of course, "good breeding") and "manners". In my own contribution to the volume, which argues against the Brown and Levinson hypothesis that politeness, seen as face threat mitigation, is a universal of language usage, I make the following point:

> If within the early eighteenth-century framework the same claim of univer-sality is made, we are forced to the conclusion that all speech communities have at their disposal linguistic ways and means of enhancing *ego*'s social standing, of signalling membership in a social elite, and stigmatising and/or, if need be, persecuting non-members. (p. 47)

In other words, if we take eighteenth century British conceptualisa-tions of politeness as being universal, we come to the opposite conclu-sion from Brown and Levinson. And this, of course, immediately calls into question too literal and too superficial a notion of universality.

Indeed, the term politeness as it was used in 18th century British writings occupied such a dominant position in the minds of the *classe politique* of the time (the gentry and the aristocracy) that it has become a subject of interest in its own right for social historians (cf. Langford 1989), literary critics (McIntosh 1998) and researchers within the field of cultural studies (Klein 1984, 1986, 1990, 1992, 1994; Potkay 1994). It became a subtle instrument for excluding members of the upcoming commercial middle classes from the ranks of the gentry, thus denying them access to positions of power and wealth (Watts 1999). In Watts (2002 and 2003: chapter 2) I have taken this argument further to show that politeness was a central concept in the formation of social class structure in Britain and in the development of standard English. Seen in this light, politeness became the main component of a dominant ideological discourse in Britain in the eighteenth century:

> The concept of politeness was appropriated as the basis of a hegemonic dis-course in which the ability to control a specific language variety was inter-preted as providing access to high social status from which power could be exercised. Determining who was a member of "polite society", however, was in the hands of those who had already gained access. (Watts 2003: 40)

This side of politeness is also anticipated in the original introductory chapter of *Politeness in Language*:

> A speaker for whom politeness directly or indirectly implies social stigmati-
> sation and exclusion from the institutional acquisition of status and thereby
> the ability to exercise power over others is not likely to think of [politeness]
> in positive terms. (p. 5)

The idea of an ideology of politeness is echoed by Sell in the sentence
immediately following the lead quotation:

> Clearly, too, the more unedifying operations of politeness were not confined
> to intercourse between individuals. Politeness was also part of the larger
> ideological apparatus by which the aristocratic elite of the metropolis for so
> long marginalised the Tories and maintained the Whig supremacy. (p. 110)

From the discussion of historical relativity outlined above, readers
might have erroneously assumed that contributors to the volume have
restricted themselves to eighteenth century Britain. However, the general importance of taking a historically relative perspective towards
politeness is stressed in the subtitle of the volume, *Studies in its History, Theory and Practice*, and a detailed non-British perspective is
presented in Ehlich's contribution.

Ehlich traces the beginnings of politeness in the Western world as
far back as the first shifts from nomadic to agrarian forms of existence
in the Ancient Orient (the river valleys of the Nile, the Euphrates and
the Tigris), and he links it to the socio-economic development of larger
demographic agglomerations. Like all of the contributors to the volume, he sees politeness as a product of social structure, and he bases
his arguments on "a cultural documentation of social developments
and processes in written form that reaches back over five thousand
years" (p. 83). He suggests that we can only talk about polite behaviour on the basis of a standard that has been socially set:

> Politeness is not a feature inherent to the action, but is connected with an in-
> teractional relationship which is itself transmediated by a standard. (p. 76)

The "standard" – and that standard will vary from one social group to
the next across cultures and through time – is dependent on hierarchically ordered social structures, as Held also maintains:

> The following factors are important and they reflect the transmitted value
> judgements of a hierarchically ordered society, establishing rights and privi-
> leges which are still valid today ... (p. 137)

The standard will determine for the individual that any behaviour in
excess of it will be in some sense socially marked, e.g. in displaying

deference, humility, obedience, etc. in an upward direction or mercy, demeanour, magnanimity, etc. in a downward direction. Ehlich argues that the social relationships that he outlines through history and in Near Eastern and later European societies "show very clearly how forms of politeness gradually evolve in specific social conditions" (p. 93).

Cultural, rather than historical, relativity is represented in the contributions by Arndt and Janney, Coulmas, Ide *et al.* and Blum-Kulka. The major problem with cross-cultural or intercultural approaches is, as Eelen (2001) and Watts (2003) point out, the lack of a solid and workable definition of the term "culture". This is not only a problem in politeness research, but also in anthropology itself, so I do not feel constrained to offer a definition at this juncture. Suffice it to say that we are nevertheless able to recognise "cultural" differences between groups and to pinpoint what constitutes those differences without needing to give a full definition of the term.

One of the reasons why such recognitions of cultural difference are possible is given by Arndt and Janney when they say that "[b]eing interculturally tactful ... is a complicated skill that involves much more than simply translating politeness formulas from one language into another" (p. 21). In other words, individuals have been socialised into forms of social behaviour over a long enough period of time for the observance of what Arndt and Janney call "tact" to have become automatic. On the other hand, they warn against cultural overgeneralisation:

> ... intercultural communication never takes place between idealised "members of culture" in vacuo ... but always between real people in real situations ... (p. 38)

Blum-Kulka's research into the kinds of metapragmatic definitions given by lay persons in Israel reveals that

> ... "politeness" is positively associated with tolerance, restraint, good manners, showing deference and being nice to people, but is simultaneously referred to in a negative manner as something external, hypocritical, unnatural. (p. 257)

Her extended research into social interaction within Israeli, American Jewish and American–Israeli immigrant families has led her, despite this apparent contradiction, to confirm many of the folk notions of politeness dealt with in the literature as well as the equation of politeness with interpersonal harmony and face threat mitigation. But she also stresses the fact that

> ... the attitudes expressed are deeply embedded in cultural traditions; that is why the word denoting the phenomenon under consideration carries with it slightly negative connotations. (p. 277)

Both Ide *et al.* and Coulmas deal with Japanese language and culture, but from different points of view. Ide *et al.* are interested in the degree to which the corresponding lexemes in English and Japanese (*politeness* and *teneina*) connote, in speakers' evaluations of politeness, the same range of adjectival attributions in both languages. They point out that "the equivalence across cultures of the key term itself needs to be questioned" (p. 281), and, as if to confirm this warning, the results they achieve from their empirical study are not only very revealing, but also rather sobering. Politeness in the eyes of American informants is primarily associated with notions of respect, considerateness, friendliness and appropriateness, whereas with Japanese informants, although the association with respect is, as in the case of American informants, most closely linked with politeness, pleasantness and appropriateness are far more important than considerateness, and friendliness is not linked to politeness at all. Ide *et al.* conclude that although "[c]oncepts of politeness thus defined by researchers may be applicable to any possible culture"

> ... we cannot assume that the concept of "politeness" is fully equivalent to the concepts of corresponding norms in other languages, since language itself is the door to a concept in people's minds. (p. 282)

Coulmas discusses the use of Japanese honorifics in social interaction as part of an argument which aims to separate the notions of "polite language" and "polite language usage". In line with other researchers (cf. Matsumoto 1989; Usami 2001) he concludes that the Japanese cannot *but* use various types of honorifics in virtually all forms of social interaction, but that this does not imply that the Japanese are necessarily more polite than members of other language communities:

> Whether or not the speakers of Japanese are very polite or whether politeness is highly valued in Japanese society are entirely different questions which can only be answered on the basis of a detailed analysis of social structure and conduct as well as the historical background of Japanese etiquette in the Con-

fucian ideology imported from China. (p. 321)

He refutes the argument that, because of the rich system of honorifics, Japanese culture is very polite:

> This, I think, is a rather meaningless supposition, for the simple reason that, unless the notion is watered down to something like general consideration and benevolence, politeness is necessarily defined within the framework of a given culture. (p. 321)

Politeness is, in other words, culturally as well as historically relative.

There is, then, a wealth of evidence in the contributions to this volume that all the contributors concur with the opinion that

> [n]othing will ever fix the reference of "politeness" to human behaviour once and for all. (Sell, p.117)

On the contrary, its illusive referent is constantly subject to individual, social, cultural and historical change. And since this is the case, it is rather dangerous to claim universality for the concept. We might go further and conclude, as many critics of Brown and Levinson did in the 1990s, that Politeness Theory was ethnocentric, even Eurocentric or Anglocentric. Both Ehlich and Held warn against ethnocentricity:

> ... whereas in relation to individual actions by individual actors the standard is developed by the group itself and reproduced when politeness is attributed, *the attempt to find a standard* beyond *those groups can become caught up all too easily in two different traps: in ethnocentricity or in apparent universality.* (Ehlich, p. 79, my italics)

> In line with the development of linguistic pragmatics the focal point of this research has been Anglo-Saxon, the result being that the English language is not only the primary object of research and source of data for linguistic politeness, but is also responsible, in its function as a metalanguage, for terminological concepts that are often hard to translate into other languages. (Held, p. 131, my italics)

The danger of setting up a model of politeness which works smoothly for Western societies but not for Asian and African societies appears to be built into the face-threat-mitigation interpretation offered by Brown and Levinson. In the following section I shall compare their notion of face with Goffman's and show that many of the misgivings voiced in the volume are indeed picked up in later literature on linguistic politeness.

The concept of "face" as a basis for politeness theory

> Receiving Goffman's face metaphor selectively, the authors
> of the modern view deliberately reinterpret it in unambiguously
> individualistic terms, abstracting not only from the dimension
> of ritual order, but from all kinds of social order and so ...
> they unduly favour individualistic, Gricean elements
> over the social ones taken from Goffman.
> (Werkhofer, p. 178)

Earlier in this introductory chapter I argued that the universal feature of Brown and Levinson's Politeness Theory is face rather than politeness itself. In the years between the first and second editions of *Politeness in Language* the concept of face has been debated intensively in the politeness literature and has become an area of research in its own right (cf. the references in Watts 2003). In a critical review article of the 1987 reprint of Brown and Levinson, Coupland *et al.* (1988: 255) even suggest that it might be best to abandon the search for a universal notion of politeness altogether and focus instead on "recognising overlapping sets of face-related strategies".

In the lead quotation to this section Werkhofer criticises Brown and Levinson ("the authors of the modern view [of politeness]") for deliberately, i.e. knowingly and purposely, reinterpreting Goffman's original notion of face "in unambiguously individualistic terms". As Werkhofer points out, theirs was a selective reading of Goffman, since it ignored "the dimension of ritual order", which Goffman had taken from Durkheim, and the kinds of social order which Goffman infused into his conceptualisation of the term. It is also true to say that Goffman's use of the term "face" was not new, since it had enjoyed currency in the social anthropology literature for some time prior to his social definition of it in 1955 (cf. Hu's work on "The Chinese concepts of 'face'" in 1944). Goffman's understanding of "face" is considerably richer than Brown and Levinson's individualistic interpretation as, firstly, positive face, i.e. "the individual's desire that her/his wants be appreciated and approved of in social interaction" (Watts 2003: 86), or, secondly, negative face, i.e. "the desire for freedom of action and freedom from imposition" (Watts 2003: 86).

It is not my purpose in this introductory chapter to give an interpretative analysis of Goffman's notion of face. For a detailed discussion the reader is referred to Watts (2003: chapter 5). But it is important to stress Goffman's understanding of the term as constituted in social interaction. He defines face as an image "pieced together from the expressive implications of the full flow of events in an undertaking" ([1955] 1967: 31) and as "the positive social value a person effectively claims for [her/himself] by the line others assume [s/he] has taken during a particular contact" (1967: 5). This latter quotation would appear to be the source for Brown and Levinson's positive face, but it is important to note that the individual claims a positive social value in accordance with the ways in which *others* have interpreted the line s/he is taking in the interaction. The term "line" is defined by Goffman as "a pattern of verbal and non-verbal acts by which [a participant] expresses [her/his] view of the situation and through [her/his] evaluation of the participants" (1967: 5). Face is certainly constructed individually, but only on the basis of "approved social attributes". In addition, since face is constructed and reconstructed in every instance of social interaction, an individual may be assigned an indeterminate number of faces.

More important for politeness theory, however, is the obvious fact that face must be involved in all instances of social interaction, which will include those types of social interaction in which face threatening is an integral part of the line that an individual participant is expected to adopt. We can interpret Goffman as implying that face is constructed discursively in instances of socio-communicative verbal interaction, i.e. it is constructed socially. If this is the case, we need a theory of facework rather than one of politeness, unless we are prepared to give up the notion of face threat mitigation as being the basis of politeness.

Some of the contributions to this volume express this idea explicitly. Sell, for example, suggests the following:

> ... I already differ from Brown and Levinson, in that I do not see politeness as a principle in isolation from others, and I do not see it as coming into operation only when people face-threateningly address each other, talk about other people, or make commands, requests, or enquiries. (p. 114)

Werkhofer considers strategic planning in order to mitigate a potential face-threat, which as we saw in an earlier section is the core of the Brown and Levinson approach to politeness, to be an infrequent occurrence:

> ... there may indeed be cases where the individual speaker strategically plans and generates a politely mitigated face-threatening act, thus more or less conforming to this model. But this is only a special case ... (p. 167)

In the "Introduction" we question the validity of a notion of negative face, as Brown and Levinson define it, for communities in which possessions are shared and/or in which the social constraints of the community determine a speaker's freedom of action:

> ... how is negative face to be understood in a culture in which possessions of individuals are at one and the same time possessions of the community, or in which the individual's right to act depends crucially on the consent of the community. (p. 10)

In addition, Ehlich challenges the universal nature of face if it is conceptualised as Brown and Levinson conceptualise it:

> For example, what does "face" (Brown and Levinson 1978) mean for a fully developed bourgeois society, and what does its universalisation mean, since this appears characteristic for present-day scholarly studies on politeness the world over, even though contrasting social anthropological data in ethnographic literature might yield other results (cf. Strecker forthcoming). (p. 107)

The contributions to *Politeness in Language* thus throw a considerable amount of doubt on whether the face-threat mitigation approach is valid as the basis of a Theory of Politeness, and on whether any such rational, modernist approach is appropriate at all given the normative, fluctuating evaluations of polite behaviour made by lay (i.e. non-linguist) participants in verbal interaction. Politeness is a matter of discursive dispute. As we have seen, many of the contributions begin to sound out the feasibility of bottom-up discursive approaches which will ultimately lead to a new, postmodernist view of politeness. I shall return to this point later. In the next section, however, I will explore some of the more trenchent criticism of the Brown and Levinson model in the volume.

Werkhofer's criticism of Brown and Levinson

> But polite language use has of course to do with real persons, and Brown and Levinson's model might be and has in fact been understood as explaining how they go about this task. In this chapter, then, I shall, in spite of Brown and Levinson's warnings to the contrary, take what they say about their model person literally, wondering how s/he will behave, what s/he can do and what not.
> (Werkhofer, p. 155)

Two of the contributions to *Politeness in Language*, Werkhofer and

Watts, focus quite specifically on aspects of Brown and Levinson's model of linguistic politeness, while other contributors, notably Ehlich, Held and Sell, make passing comments of a critical nature on the model. I do not reject the claim for universality outright in chapter 2, but I attempt to tease out what could be meant by the term "universal of language usage" and to suggest an alternative approach which involves restricting politeness to a narrower range of linguistic behaviour than is common in the literature. I shall return to this point in a later section. Werkhofer, on the other hand, expressly states that he intends to "critically reconstruct Brown and Levinson's model with regard to its psychological and sociological implications" (p. 155), and I shall focus largely on his critical comments in this section.

Werkhofer identifies two approaches to the study of politeness, which he calls "traditional" (by which he means primarily the study of social etiquette) and "modern" (by which he means rationalist approaches based on Gricean pragmatics). The "modern" approach in fact corresponds to what I have called in this introductory chapter the "modernist" approach, and Werkhofer appears to be trying to create a synthesis of the two in an effort to move towards a postmodernist perspective to politeness. He maintains that he wishes to "reconstruct" Brown and Levinson, which implies that he is not fundamentally against many of the assumptions which they make. In order to reconstruct the model, he first has to deconstruct it, and this he does very thoroughly.

The lead quotation to this section informs the reader that Werkhofer intends to disregard Brown and Levinson's warning not to take their Model Person (MP) too seriously and to use that fictive persona as a starting point for his criticism. He does this precisely because the MP is neither psychologically nor sociologically viable. In the first place, the very suggestion of setting up an MP represents a step towards extrapolating away from real persons and real interaction. Just as Chomsky's idealised native speaker/hearer allows him to construct an abstract model of linguistic competence, so too is the MP meant to allow Brown and Levinson to construct an abstract model of linguistic politeness. The problem is that, whereas Chomsky's idealised native-speaker/hearer does allow theoretical linguists to consider the structure of language in isolation from the contexts of language use, Brown and Levinson's Theory of Politeness sets out to be a model of language usage. This cannot but involve real speakers and real addressees in real-time situations.

Werkhofer's criticism of the MP is that it focuses too heavily on model speakers rather than on model addressees. At the same time, however, Brown and Levinson's overt commitment to the rational nature of the MP leads them into seeing what they consider politeness to be, viz. as part of a rational, goal-oriented process controlled by predefined intentions. As Werkhofer points out, this runs counter to the assumed attributes and anticipated reactions of the addressee:

> The first thing to be noted is that this model combines two quite different kinds of entities. There are, on the one hand, "intentions", "acts" or "strategies" that can clearly be identified as having to do with what the speaker thinks or does. And there are, on the other hand, notions that have to do with the addressee, as, for example, the addressee's face or the anticipated reaction of the addressee ... (p. 165)

It should also be obvious that, in real instances of verbal interaction, speakers generally act and react in accordance with the real-time constraints of ongoing interaction regardless of whether or not they originally intended to achieve certain goals. As Werkhofer points out, speakers may frequently need to revise those intentions and strategies on the basis of new information processed during the interaction:

> Why should the speaker not, in order to adapt to a situation that may already be novel as s/he enters it and that may develop and change while s/he is planning and saying what s/he has to say, constantly take in new information, thus proceeding in "real time", drawing on whatever external data may be available to her/him? (p. 168)

The major problem that Werkhofer pinpoints is the almost total disregard of the social factors within which polite behaviour emerges and from which it originates in the first place. True, Brown and Levinson do posit three socio-cultural entities which, they maintain, enter into assessments of the degree of facework (I am deliberately avoiding the term "politeness" here) that should be offered to mitigate different kinds of face-threat: the power that the addressee possesses with respect to the speaker, the social distance between the speaker and the addressee, and the degree to which the act required of the addressee is considered an imposition in the culture concerned. Quite apart from the reappearance of the ominous term "culture", the categories of power and social distance are at best static, are understood from an individualistic point of view and are, to say the least, somewhat crude. Werkhofer has the following to say about proponents of the Brown and Levinson view of politeness:

> ... all versions of this view either neglect social realities completely or, adopting a remarkably simplistic, traditional [I would prefer to say "modern-ist" – RJW] approach, reduce them to only a small set of vaguely defined dimensions which are then relegated to a secondary status, thus again emphasising individualism. (p. 157)

To make matters worse, we are given a rather dubious method of computing the degree of seriousness of the face threat (cf. Watts, Ide and Ehlich, p. 89), which determines the type of strategy chosen to mitigate it. To be fair, however, Brown and Levinson explicitly warn their readers that the formula ($W_x = D(S,H) + P(H,S) + R_x$) is only meant to spell out overtly the complex and almost instantaneous decision-making process that a speaker goes through in choosing a politeness strategy. It is not meant to be operationalised as a quantitative method to measure the degree of politeness present in an utterance. Werkhofer has the following to say about the equation:

> The role of social realities is further relativised by reducing them to numerical values on only three dimensions and by finally aggregating these into only one weightiness value. (p. 175)

> Being defined as static entities that determine polite meanings, these variables represent a narrow approach to social realities, an approach that neglects the dynamic aspects of social language use ... (p. 176)

As it is focused primarily on the concept of the Model Person, i.e. on individual speakers, and on the MP's intentions, which lead her/him to choose one out of a set of politeness strategies, Brown and Levinson's Theory of Politeness is not well adapted to exploring the sources of polite behaviour in social structure and social reproduction:

> As it is triggered by an intention of the speaker, social factors can only come in later. Thus already relegated to a secondary status, their impact is further reduced by defining them vaguely and by representing them in terms of ultimately only one quantitative value. (p. 180)

Werkhofer moves tentatively towards a social constructivist, postmodernist approach to politeness, some aspects of which I will mention later. For the moment, however, I should like to focus on criticism of the Gricean basis of the Brown and Levinson model.

The pragmatic basis of models of linguistic politeness

> Despite Lakoff's early insistence that we are dealing with
> pragmatic rules, it is clear that politeness involves
> more than just pragmatic well-formedness,
> whatever that might be.
> (Watts, Ide & Ehlich, p. 6)

The major impulse towards Werkhofer's "modern" theories of linguistic politeness was undoubtedly the appearance in print of Grice's "Logic and conversation" in 1975, although mimeograph copies of the William James lectures had been circulating among the linguistic community for at least the previous six years. In the William James lecture that formed the basis of his 1975 article – and also in other lectures, which are hardly mentioned in the literature! – Grice presents his Cooperative Principle with its four conversational maxims of quantity, quality, relation and manner, which, with the exception of the Maxim of Relation, were split into a number of submaxims. It is no exaggeration to say that Grice's CP set the study of pragmatics fully in motion when the text of "Logic and conversation" began to circulate. Until then pragmatics had largely been concerned with laborious attempts to demarcate semantics as the linguistic study of meaning from pragmatics, in which the significance of language in action and within the context of its production became as important as, if not more important than, semiotic theories of reference, denotation and connotation.

Grice also hinted in "Logic and conversation" that other maxims contributing towards conversational cooperation might be suggested, e.g. a politeness maxim. Whether Grice meant his comment seriously or whether it was merely a passing comment on his part is immaterial here, but it certainly served to revive a keen interest in the ways in which politeness, however it was to be understood, contributed towards smooth, conflict-free and cooperative communication. The pragmatic turn that Grice's CP sparked off, together with his comments on possible further maxims, promised new vistas of research into the centrality of language in human communication. Were there general principles governing the ways in which human beings communicate, as Grice suggested, and if there were, what would they be and how might we define them? In other words, were there universal principles of language usage?

In Watts (2003: chapters 3 and 4) I have dealt with what I call "pragmatic" models of politeness as presented by Lakoff (1973a, b, 1977, 1979), Leech (1977, 1980, 1983) and also by Brown and Levinson (1978). As the lead quotation to this section indicates, Lakoff (1973a) suggested the setting up of pragmatic rules, which would include rules of politeness and determine "pragmatic well-formedness":

> We should like to have some kind of pragmatic rules, dictating whether an utterance is pragmatically well-formed or not, and the extent to which it deviates if it does. (Lakoff 1973a: 296)

Again, we note the modernist, rationalist desire to create an "object of knowledge" governed by a set of pragmatic rules as well as by grammatical, phonological and semantic rules and to place human language as an autonomous object of study outside proper human control in social interaction. Leech avoids referring to "rules" when talking about linguistic pragmatics. For him, the grammatical level of linguistic structure is controlled by rules, whereas pragmatics is "principle-controlled (= rhetorical)" (1983: 5). The argument in both pragmatic approaches, however, is that polite linguistic behaviour in certain kinds of social interaction needs to be indirect. In Leech's model indirectness insures that both speaker and hearer may gain the maximum amount of benefit from an utterance with the least amount of cost. In the third model based on Grice, i.e. Brown and Levinson ([1978] 1987), indirectness is a means of achieving one's strategic goals whilst minimising potential face threats as much as possible. In her contribution to *Politeness in Language* Held stresses the central significance in the indirect speech act approach to politeness:

> It is thus evident that the indirectness approach, despite its one-sidedness, occupies a central position in accounting for politeness, since, apart from the ease with which it can be understood, it has provided definite formal and situational results. (p. 142)

It is not my purpose here to go into detail concerning the merits and demerits of Grice's CP in the study of linguistic pragmatics nor to outline the reaction to it that occurred in the late 1970s and early 1980s and resulted in Relevance Theory. I would argue, however, that Grice has been radically misinterpreted in linguistic circles, and some of those misinterpretations were taken up in *Politeness in Language* in relation to politeness theory. In order to illustrate this, I shall again focus on Werkhofer's contribution.

Clearly, Werkhofer considers Grice's side remarks on the feasibility of introducing a Maxim of Politeness into the CP as indicating a fundamental lack of interest in politeness on his part:

> Quite on the contrary, politeness is only an example here – and a significant one – of what Grice is not at all concerned with. (p. 160)

In dealing with the Gricean basis of Brown and Levinson, he suggests that the indirectness of speech acts leading to the minimisation of face-threatening is not what Grice was intending to achieve with his CP at all. This is all the more significant, since, as we've seen, this is the bedrock of the Brown and Levinson conceptualisation of politeness:

> What this theory [Brown and Levinson] is meant to explain ... is the opposite of what Grice had been aiming at: while his speaker, without literally expressing them, seeks to convey and in fact successfully does convey his true intentions, the polite speaker of the modern view will tend more or less to hide and obscure them, if necessary to the point at which they are no longer understandable. (p. 161)

There are also crucial contradictions in Brown and Levinson's statements. On the one hand they assume that Grice's theory is fundamentally correct while, on the other hand, avowing that "the Gricean postulates are '"unmarked" or socially neutral (indeed asocial)' and that they are 'of quite different status from that of politeness principles'" (Werkhofer, p. 161). As Werkhofer points out, the problem facing Brown and Levinson is to somehow square the reliance on Grice with an essentially antagonistic, and somewhat pessimistic view of social interaction.

In point of fact, the mistake often made with Grice (1975) – and Lakoff, Leech and Brown and Levinson all fall into the same trap here – is to take him as postulating a model of conversation, in which the principle of optimal cooperation is the controlling principle. What the *philosopher* Grice was attempting to set up was a way of accounting for utterer's meaning alongside utterance meaning, i.e. a way of *logically* accounting for the means by which addressees are capable of deriving unstated implications from utterances. In order to do this he created an ideal state of communicative cooperation, only to suggest that it is against this underlying principle that participants in interaction are able to evaluate deviations from that principle. In this spirit, Relevance Theory is a logical development of Gricean Pragmatics, and Grice should not be interpreted as setting up a theory of conversation. Although Werkhofer does not actually go so far as to state this, he implies very strongly that the Brown and Levinson theory of politeness founders on precisely this point:

> Starting from the premise that "Grice's theory [...] is essentially correct", Brown and Levinson reformulate this position by postulating that the intentions of the polite speaker must be face-threatening or anti-social ones. The fact that this assumption is no longer consistent with the Gricean framework can in itself hardly be criticised, but subscribing to a deliberately individualistic, in fact antisocial model of the speaker, the modern view introduces the remarkable premise that there must be, as a prerequisite for politeness to occur, a fundamental antagonism between the speaker's intentions, on the one hand, and social aspects, on the other. (p. 180)

The important point in the above quotation from Werkhofer's contribution is his conclusion that Brown and Levinson subscribe to "a deliberately individualistic, in fact antisocial model of the speaker". We now need to assess to what degree *Politeness in Language* contains the elements necessary to develop a social approach towards politeness and may thus be regarded as clearing the way towards postmodernist approaches.

Politeness as a social phenomenon

> Thus polite activity is an activity that recognises the socially
> constructed limit as being relevant to the activity itself.
> In and of itself it does not exist.
> (Ehlich, p. 78)

The "socially constructed limit" invoked by Ehlich in the lead quotation forms part of the "standard" that he mentions at other places in his contribution, and as we have seen earlier in this chapter, the limit or standard will fluctuate from social group to social group and through time. The limit as such is not empirically definable but is intuitively constructed by the social group for the whole range of social interactions in which individuals are involved. It is at all times open to reconstruction along different lines, but as long as individuals remain within the fluctuating boundaries of the limit, the limit itself will be socially reproduced and will form patterns of behaviour that seem natural and appropriate to individuals participating in social interaction. But how or where does politeness fit into this schema?

For Ehlich politeness is generated in the tension between the "socially constructed limit" and actions which go "beyond that which is socially required within the framework of these regularities [of behaviour]" (p. 74). So without the social limit politeness simply doesn't exist. On the other hand, actions that take place within the socially constructed limit are not always perceived as polite, even though, in acquiring a feel for those limits, the individual might still sense that some of the actions s/he is required to perform are unnecessary. S/he may have acquired a feel for some of those actions by being told that they are "polite", hence in some way necessary. For example, a participant in an interaction may feel that the "normal", appropriate and socially acceptable way to ask for a pen is to say something like *Could you pass me a pen?* or *Could you pass me a pen please?* rather than *Pass me a pen (please)*. On the other hand, all three (or four) utterances might seem appropriate to her/him without any of them being necessarily classified as "polite" or "impolite". Tension emerges when the participant is not sure of the socially acceptable mode of request in a specific social situation, or when s/he is sure but decides to give just a little more, e.g. *D'you think you could pass me that pen, please?* So the tension between what is and what is not considered polite is a tension between an individual and the social group:

> In the case of an individual ... an action appears polite when it displays something in addition to or beyond what is agreed upon as "normal behaviour". In this case the actor retains as an option the possibility of "it could be done differently". (Ehlich, p. 74-75)

Ehlich's idea that "an action appears polite when it displays something in addition to or beyond what is agreed upon as 'normal behaviour'" is analogous to the way in which I interpret politeness as being marked politic behaviour:

> Thus what counts as polite behaviour depends entirely on those features of the interaction which are socio-culturally marked by the speech community as being more than merely politic. (p. 51)

I shall explain how I understand the term "politic behaviour" in the following section, but it should be clear that social interaction lying within Ehlich's "socially constructed limit" is effectively "politic behaviour". The major question that will be addressed in the following section is whether or not it is necessary or even useful to "invent" a supplementary term to refer to appropriate forms of behaviour which most other researchers simply call "polite".

Werkhofer criticises the Brown and Levinson model of politeness precisely because it does not properly consider the social values that politeness instantiates. Similar to Ehlich, he argues for an approach towards the study of politeness which sees it as a mediating force between between the individual and the "social, motivating and structuring courses of action" sanctioned by society. In order to do this, he resorts to Georg Simmel's "Die Philosophie des Geldes" ['The Philosophy of Money'] (1901). Simmel maintains that money can be seen as either a public or a private good and the key to understanding it is to consider "the ways in which the individual maximises its utility as a symbolic resource in the exchange of goods" (Watts 2003: 115). Paradoxically, however, as a symbolic resource it is "a social institution and quite meaningless if restricted to one individual" (Werkhofer, p. 190), since "... economic exchange can only be performed if and insofar as the value of objects is not only subjectively held, but also socially confirmed in acts of exchange" (p. 184). Politeness can thus be seen as a form of interactional "payment" in excess of what would normally be required.

In the following section I shall discuss the idea that politeness is a marked part of politic behaviour, in other words, to maintain the comparison of politeness with money, that it is a kind of social "tip". But before I do, we need to consider the importance of socio-communicative verbal interaction for any conceptualisation of politeness, since the discursive view of politeness allows us to take a postmodernist rather than a modernist view of the subject. Janney and Arndt point out that politeness "depends on multimodal communicative skills that are learned through social interaction" (p. 25). The skills on which conceptualisations of politeness are based can only be acquired through praxis. In terms of real time social interaction Werkhofer maintains that politeness may be a quality of the interaction that is built up over several turns at talk, i.e. that it is a question of discursive negotiation rather than an individual's strategic attempts to avoid face-threatening:

> ... polite utterances may turn out typically to be developed over several turns, so that, rather than taking place only in the speaker's mind, an extended production process and a real dialogue can be shown to occur. Observations of this kind would of course still further discredit the linear, mentalistic, "within the head" approach. (p. 171).

In line with his hypothesis that politeness is a medium of social inter-action comparable to money, he goes on to suggest that "[a]s the proc-ess of constituting the medium has been a social, interactive and prac-tical one, so the process of passing it on to other users will have to be social, interactive and practical, too" (p. 194).

The more practically oriented contributions to the volume in Part 2 also recognise the importance of looking at politeness within the framework of social interaction, i.e. of taking a discursive approach. Knapp-Potthoff, for example, argues that in situations in which a me-diator in cross-linguistic communication needs to consider whether or not to translate possible politeness formulae, i.e. in cross-linguistic in-teraction, "politeness which its addressee receives only secondhand (or rather: 'second-mouth') might not be the same as that which its origi-nal producer had intended, and this for reasons of discourse structure" (p. 205). In their discussion of how children develop a feeling for the acceptability of white lies to protect the positive face of the addressee, Walper and Valtin argue that this protective mode of social behaviour is closely correlated with the context of the verbal interaction:

> … the increasingly positive evaluation of white lies is situation-specific to the extent that it does not occur for contexts of great intimacy, viz. for the child's relationship with his or her own mother. (p. 236)

Stalpers's study of interaction between Dutch and French business partners shows that the negotiation of business deals is a form of social interaction which tends to preclude extra payment in the form of po-liteness:

> They act in accordance with, and under the mutual assumption of, the princi-ple "time is money". It can be argued that this principle is at variance with the general expectation of polite conduct in discourse as it is assumed for casual conversation … (p. 230)

Politic behaviour and politeness

> Thus what counts as polite behaviour depends entirely on those features
> of the interaction which are socio-culturally marked by the speech
> community as being more than merely politic.
> (Watts, p. 51)

Since I proposed the concept of "politic behaviour" in 1988, I have frequently been asked why I consider it necessary. Surely it would be much more convenient to classify all politic behaviour, together with behaviour that is commented on explicitly or implicitly by participants as "polite", with the cover term "linguistic politeness". It is quite possible, of course, that "politic" is too close to "polite" for comfort. A number of politeness researchers have used the term "appropriate behaviour" instead (e.g. Meier 1995) or as an alternative to "politic" (Locher 2004), although Eelen (2001) has criticised "appropriateness" on the grounds that it smacks of a rationalist approach to social structure. He also rejects "politic" as not being a term in common usage and as not having a negative counterpart (cf. Locher 2004: 86).

The debate over whether or not to use the term "politic" takes us straight back to the question of first-order and second-order politeness. As we've seen above, many of the contributions to *Politeness in Language* argue, either explicitly or implicitly, that politeness research needs to take lay assessments of both verbal and non-verbal behaviour seriously. Whatever terms are used in whatever language to refer to forms of behaviour as POLITE (e.g. in English, positively evaluative lexemes like *polite, polished, courteous, well-mannered*, etc. or negatively evaluative lexemes like *standoffish, snobbish, stuck-up, priggish*, etc.), they all reveal normative, moral attitudes towards social behaviour, and they are all used by participants either during or after the social interaction. They are thus all open to discursive dispute. This by no means makes them unworthy of the attention of researchers into social interaction. Quite the contrary! What should interest us is how and when they are used, or whether, in the close analysis of verbal interaction, participants react non-verbally or verbally without making use of any of these lexemes in such a way as to suggest that they have become consciously aware of their own or a co-participant's social behaviour. In order to do this, we need to make use of some notion of social appropriateness as perceived by individual participants.

It is at this point that we notice the dialectic between the individual and the social group which helps us individually to acquire a feel for the socially constructed limits of forms of behaviour posited by Ehlich. It is the tension between the individual and the social which gives rise to perceptions of politeness and not the forms of appropriate social behaviour themselves that are internalised by the individual. In order to make this distinction between what is felt to be socially appropriate behaviour and what is perceived to be more than socially required, I have suggested the term "politic" as a second-order, i.e. theoretical, concept precisely because it is not in common usage and indexes a wide variety of forms of social behaviour that include but are broader than what might be referred to in lay terms as POLITE. I consider it adequate in a theory of social praxis, since it avoids the confusion of first-order attributions of politeness being used in a so-called second-order Theory of Politeness.

The price of taking this step is high since it would mean giving up the idea of a Theory of Politeness altogether, but it would also pave the way towards postmodernist conceptualisations of politeness. Let's return for the moment to Scannell's distinction between a modernist (hence rationalist) and a postmodernist theory of language. A modernist theory tends to isolate language from the set of language users, even in speech act theory and Gricean pragmatics, and it leads to a denaturalisation of language. A postmodernist theory starts from the assumption that language is within the individual as a social being and therefore that talk instantiates social interaction. Descartes' guiding principle can be turned on its head to read *sum, ergo cogito*, i.e. I exist (and note that I can only exist as a social being) and because of this I think. Through discourse in social interaction we create common worlds, the most significant being our interpersonal relationships with others. The interactional negotiation of these relationships has been referred to as *relational work* (Locher 2004; Locher and Watts 2005), and it involves us in social praxis.

There are two principal ways to account for the development of a set of predispositions to act in specific ways in specific situations. We can invoke the notion of *frame* (cf. Bateson 1954; Goffman 1974, 1981; Tannen 1993; Escandell-Vidal 1996; Schank and Abelson 1977), which Tannen defines as "structures of expectation based on past experience" (1993: 53). Alternatively, we can make use of Bourdieu's Theory of Practice (1990), in which the core notion is that of the *habitus*, referring to "the set of predispositions to act in certain ways, which generates cognitive and bodily practices in the individual" (Watts 2003: 149).

The discursive approach to polite behaviour sees it as part of the relational work carried out in any socio-communicative verbal interaction, which encompasses the entire continuum of verbal behaviour (cf. Fig. 1 below). Figure 1 is an attempt to represent in diagrammatic form differences along the total spectrum of relational work. The dotted line separating unmarked politic behaviour from positively marked politic behaviour that is open to interpretation as "polite" should not be taken to represent an absolute boundary between the two. It is rather a movable area in which one type of behaviour shades off into the other.

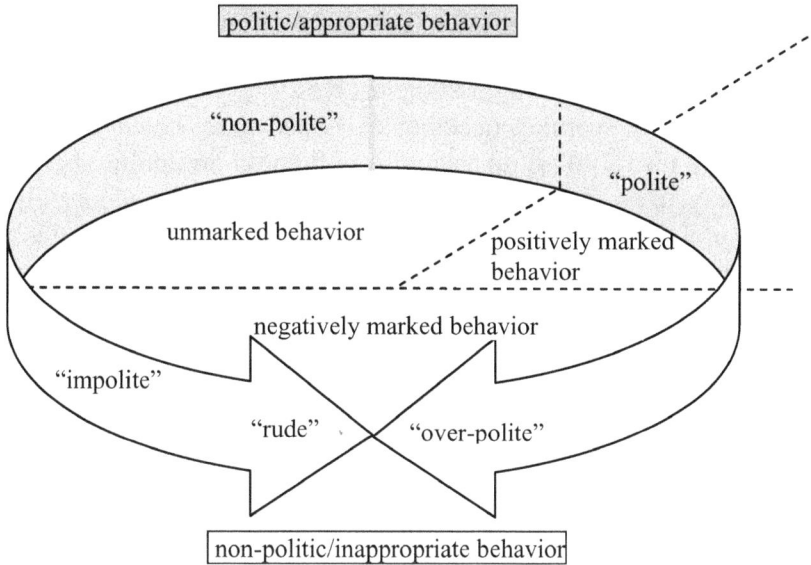

Figure 1. *Relational work*

The points at which speakers perceive politic behaviour to be "polite" may, and certainly do, vary considerably from speaker to speaker, from community of practice to community of practice and even from one situational context to another in the case of individual speakers. The variation depends on a wide range of social and contextual variables. Individual participants may sense instances of verbal interaction to be in line with the norms established in previous interactions, such that a great deal of the relational work in any interaction will be unmarked and will go unnoticed. It will be *politic* (cf. Watts 2003; Locher and Watts 2005). Positively marked politic behaviour is open to an overt interpretation as polite. Hence only a relatively small subsection of politic behaviour is likely to be explicitly evaluated by participants as 'polite'. Marked behaviour, however, can be noticed in two different ways. It may be perceived as negative either if it is open to an interpretation as impolite (or as downright rude), or if it is perceived as over-polite, i.e. both kinds of negatively marked non-politic behaviour tend towards similar kinds of affective reaction on the part of co-participants. Certain speakers consistently evaluate polite behaviour as unnecessary and offensive. The figure is thus meant to represent situations in which the communicative effects of over-polite behaviour may seem remarkably similar to those of downright rude behaviour, which is why the two ends of the spectrum are shown as turning in upon themselves.

A word of warning needs to be added here, however. While it is certainly useful to try to visualise politeness and politic behaviour in this way, it is still ultimately impossible to do so adequately in the form of a diagram. Human behaviour cannot be reduced to this form of two-dimensional representation. For example, the reader should be-ware of interpreting the white, outside surfaces of the arrows as repre-senting impolite, overpolite and rude behaviour, and the shaded, inside surface as appropriate, politic and polite behaviour – although there is a sense in which the potentiality of producing non-politic behaviour is always latently present in the production of appropriate behaviour and vice versa.

A postmodernist approach to politeness assumes that, since every individual lives in language and the creation of that individual's world involves her/him in interaction, the discursive dispute over terms like *polite, rude, impolite, brash, courteous*, etc. can only be observed by paying careful attention to instances of interaction. As Scannell puts it, "... in initiating, sustaining and disengaging from talk human beings are in the business ... of talking into being that of which they speak in the ways in which they speak of the matter(s) to hand, whatever they may be" ([1998] 2001: 263). In other words, people are engaged "in talking into being" what they take to be, among other things, polite.

Quo vadis?

> New thinking about politeness is required ...
> Konrad Ehlich, p.107

It would be inappropriate – non-politic – at this point to elaborate fur-ther on the various ways in which approaches to linguistic politeness could be made from a postmodernist rather than a modernist, rationalist perspective. For more details the reader may refer to Mills (2003), Watts (2003), Locher (2004) and some of the contributions to Christie (2004). In the intervening years between the publication of *Politeness in Language* and the present, a number of the points made in the contributions to this volume have been taken up, in many cases independent of a reading of the volume. But this certainly indicates that we were on the right track in 1992. I will therefore conclude this new introductory chapter by briefly reviewing some of those issues.

In the introduction to the 1992 volume, we noted the following:

> ... we believe that [politeness] is tied up with the most basic principles of human, socio-cultural organisation involving conceptualisations of appropriate individual behaviour, in particular linguistic behaviour, the structuring of interpersonal relationships within social groups and, above all, the nature and distribution of power. (p. 11)

At the 1997 IPrA conference in Reims a workshop was held on precisely the issue of power in the study of linguistic politeness. The proceedings of that workshop were published as a special issue of *Pragmatics* in 1999. In the intervening years between 1997 and today the link between politeness and power has been developed intensively by a research group located at Loughborough University, Nottingham Trent University, Sheffield Hallam University and the University of Leeds and has resulted in a number of interesting papers (e.g. Bargiela-Chiappini and Harris 1996; cf. also the collection of papers edited by Chris Christie in *Multilingua* 23–1/2). Work by Holtgraves (1997a, b) and Kienpointner (1997) also stresses the importance of power in argumentation and deliberate rudeness.

In Watts (2003: Chapter 6) I base my alternative model of relational work, which includes instances in which one or another participant might evaluate social behaviour as polite, on Bourdieu's theory of practice and on my own theory of emergent networks. The model takes into consideration that a viable theory of social practice should be the bedrock on which any analysis of polite behaviour should rest. The idea of emergent networks bears many similarities to that of communities of practice (cf. Wenger 1998; Eckert and McConnell-Ginet 1998) although the latter deals with communities that are constructed and repeatedly reproduced *through* practice, whereas the former refers to the *ongoing* construction of network links between interactants *in* practice. Both concepts are important in accounting for the ways in which individuals construct their social habitus.

In retrospect, it is surprising to see how frequently similar ideas are expressed in the contributions to *Politeness in Language*. Janney and Arndt see the acquisition of what they call tact (rather than politeness) as occurring in repeated instances of social interaction:

> By interacting with other members of the culture in different situations throughout their lives, people acquire broad frameworks of common knowledge, experience, expectations, and beliefs that enable them to be tactful ... (p. 30)

The "broad frameworks of common knowledge, experience, expectations, and beliefs" are equivalent to Ehlich's "socially constructed limits", and Janney and Arndt's statement comes remarkably close to expressing what Bourdieu understands by the term "habitus". The similarity is strengthened by statements such as the following in Ehlich's contribution:

> Once such assumptions are formed, they remain relatively stable and their influence on social interaction becomes almost automatic ... (p. 31)

> This advantage cannot be fully explained biologically, for it develops out of an individual's lifetime of experience with others in a group ... (p. 34)

Held also sees politeness as being regulated by social interaction, i.e. by praxis:

> Politeness is not only concerned with constantly recurring linguistic formulae but in particular with recurrent behaviour patterns, which regulate social interaction and gain their function and significance from the specific constellations for which they are obligatory. (p. 148)

And this once again echoes Bourdieu's concept of the habitus.

Werkhofer goes a little further and relates acquired social experience with cognitive structures, which indicate that repeated social praxis has become "embodied". This expresses Bourdieu's notion of the habitus as the embodiment of cognitive and bodily practices in the individual and the idea of performance in social practice which is central to the community of practice:

> ... The process of learning or acquiring politeness is one of reconstructing, cognitively and/or practically, the medium.

> ... The knowledge of the user will thus be a cognitive and practical one, too. (Werkhofer, p. 194)

Many of these ideas are now in use in recent research into politeness (cf., e.g., Mills 2003, 2004; Mullany 2004; Bargiela-Chiappini and Harris 1996), and they are a strong indication of the postmodernist turn that politeness research has taken. We have seen throughout this new introductory chapter that *Politeness in Language* prefigures these developments. It contains a number of revolutionary ideas on the study of linguistic politeness which have since been taken up and developed further. While it may not always have been the case that the researchers referred to at the beginning of this paragraph had access to *Politeness in Language*, many certainly did. So the publication of a second, paperback edition will make those ideas available to a wider audience. Obviously it's impossible to escape the impression that a second edition may appear to have merely historical value. This is unavoidable, since a collection of contributions can hardly be rewritten or changed radically from its original state. But if that historical value helps us to find our bearings more easily in the study of linguistic politeness, then it will have achieved its purpose.

Richard J. Watts
Erlach, August 2005

Introduction

Richard J. Watts, Sachiko Ide and Konrad Ehlich

Interest in the socio-cultural phenomenon of politeness and the ways in which it is realised in language usage has certainly grown since Brown and Levinson's seminal article in 1978. Evidence for this is provided in the number of publications that have appeared on the subject during the nineteen eighties, which include at least three special issues devoted to the topic in international journals, and more particularly to the republication of the article in book form in 1987 with a 54 page introduction surveying research in the field in the intervening nine-year period.

Questions about how politeness should be defined, the ways in which it is realised in different cultural frameworks and the validity of a universal theory of politeness are of interest to a wide range of social science researchers, in particular pragmalinguists, sociolinguists, sociologists, social anthropologists and social psychologists. The significance of politeness for social anthropology, for example, derives from the fact that it lies at the junction between the study of certain forms of language usage such as address terms, honorifics, indirect speech acts, formulaic utterances, etc. and the study of processes of socialisation and consequent social behaviour.

The study of politeness focuses directly or indirectly on the presentation, maintenance and even adjustment of a concept of the "presentation of self" (cf. Goffman 1959) in the course of social interaction, on the historical growth of culturally specific patterns of behaviour, and on the distribution of status and power in social groups. Hence the primary goal of such study should be the investigation of how human beings successfully manage interpersonal relationships to achieve both individual and group goals. In the introduction to the collection of papers in which Brown and Levinson's article first appeared, the editor, Esther Goody, points out that

> [...] effective social living requires anticipation of the actions of others, calculation of short- and long-term costs and gains, and close attention to signals about the consequences of one's own behaviour. Such demands may have provided the stimulus which, together with language, led to the full development of the creative intelligence which leads us to designate our species *homo sapiens*. (1978: 1)

Seen from this angle, therefore, politeness can be interpreted as one of the constraints on human behaviour which help us to achieve "effective social living", and it is our intention with this volume of papers on linguistic politeness to deepen the research perspectives within this field by questioning more profoundly what polite linguistic behaviour actually is and what grounds there might be for claims of universality. At the same time we wish to broaden research perspectives by demonstrating the need for more interdisciplinary and cross-cultural approaches.

Politeness touches on issues that are crucial not only for the sociolinguist and social anthropologist but also in the life of every individual human being. It follows that the study of politeness phenomena should occupy a firm place on more social science and humanities research agendas than it does at present, and we shall therefore consider in this introductory chapter what the fundamental importance of a notion of politeness in linguistic and anthropological research might be. It is of course true that, in dealing with politeness, we are dealing with a facet of linguistic performance, so it is perhaps understandable that it might be considered by theoretical linguists to be of very little direct relevance to their own pursuits. Nevertheless, it is still surprising that little if any attention has been paid to the subject in the sociolinguistic literature. During this introductory chapter we shall argue that linguistic politeness is crucially a social phenomenon. In addition we shall argue that, understood properly, it might constitute an important key to the understanding of a number of sociolinguistic problems.

We shall highlight some of the main points in what is probably the most influential publication on politeness as revealed in language usage, viz. Brown and Levinson (1978 [1987]) and discuss some of the notions that underlie their investigation, viz. rationality, Goffman's concept of "face", the concept of imposition and the related notions of status and power. The chapters in Part 1 of the present volume deal critically with some of the major theoretical issues in linguistic politeness and ways in which it is socially and historically constituted. The chapters in Parts 2 and 3 are devoted to some empirical issues in politeness research and to the intercultural problems in defining and investigating politeness phenomena.

As the chapter by Held shows, European linguists in the first half of the twentieth century were certainly aware that forms of linguistic behaviour that we may now wish to label "polite", even though they did not always use exactly that label themselves, have a place in the study of language. We shall argue in this introduction that a distinction needs to be made between first-order and second-order politeness. We take first-order politeness to correspond to the various ways in which polite behaviour is perceived and talked about by members of socio-cultural groups. It encompasses, in other words, commonsense notions of politeness. Second-order politeness, on the other hand, is a theoretical construct, a term within a theory of social behaviour and language usage. Many of the linguists that Held considers deal with politeness on the first-order level. As she shows, however, problems begin to occur as soon as the term is used as if it were a second-order concept in a model of language usage.[1]

It was a virtual side remark by Paul Grice in his influential paper "Logic and conversation" (1975) that gave rise to the study of linguistic politeness within the framework of Anglo-American pragmatics and the ensuing attempts to develop second-order politeness concepts. In effect Grice proposed that other maxims than those he had suggested for the Co-operative Principle, which might be "aesthetic, social, or moral in character" (1975: 49), might also need to be developed in order to account fully for pragmatic meaning, e.g., a politeness maxim "be polite". Grice's paper had been circulating among linguists and philosophers in a pre-publication manuscript form since he first delivered it in 1967, so the suggestions he made had certainly had enough time to take root and give rise to such early work on politeness as that by Lakoff (1973, 1979), Leech (1983), Fraser and Nolen (1981), etc.

Hence it is not surprising that the most influential paper on linguistic politeness to appear in America and Britain before Brown and Levinson's work, Robin Lakoff (1973), suggests that Grice's maxims should be reformulated as pragmatic rules according to which utterances could be classified as well-formed or non-well-formed. In particular Lakoff maintained that it should be possible to judge the form of an utterance to be polite or not, although, as Fraser (1990) points out, she does not explicitly say what she understands politeness to be.

Indeed, one of the oddest things about politeness research is that the term "politeness" itself is either not explicitly defined at all or else taken to be a consequence of rational social goals such as maximising the benefit to self and other, minimising the face-threatening nature of a social act, displaying adequate proficiency in the accepted standards of social etiquette, avoiding conflict, making sure that the social interaction runs smoothly, etc. Linguistic politeness is then taken to be the various forms of language structure and usage which allow the members of a socio-cultural group to achieve these goals. If claims to universality are to have any substance at all in this context, we shall need to ask what fundamental principles of human social organisation underlie the goals themselves and how they are transformed into culturally determined patterns of behaviour. In the chapters by Watts and Werkhofer such problems as these are addressed. The pursuit of universals will necessarily involve us in second-order concepts, whereas the investigation into politeness in individual cultural frameworks will almost inevitably involve first-order concepts. As long as we attempt to keep the two levels of analysis apart, there is no reason why we should not search for universal principles and certainly no reason for lamenting that linguistic politeness can only be seen in terms of cul-tural relativity. On the contrary, we consider it to be of fundamental importance to investigate the relationships between the two.

Fraser (1990) posits four main ways of viewing politeness in the literature, the "social-norm" view, the "conversational-maxim" view (of which Lakoff's work is an example), the "face-saving" view and the "conversational-contract" view. The social-norm view posits that there are standards of behaviour in any society and in any age according to which the speaker is deemed to have spoken politely or not. Fraser maintains that these are normally associated with particular speech styles in which "a higher degree of formality implies greater politeness" (1990: 221), and assumes that there are few if any adherents of this approach to be found in the literature. However, the social-norm view of politeness corresponds to the kind of politeness that has been termed "discernment (*wakimae*)" by Hill et al. (1985), Ide (1989) and by Ide et al. in the present volume.

However, this way of conceptualising politeness should not be shrugged off so lightly. As we have seen, in examining linguistic politeness we are dealing with a lay first-order concept which has been elevated to the status of a second order concept within the framework of some more or less adequate theory of language usage. This being so, it is crucially important to state in what ways the two concepts differ, and this, as we have also seen, is rarely if ever done. Unless the theoretical second order concept is clearly defined and given some other name, we shall constantly vacillate between the way in which politeness is understood as a commonsense term that we all use and think we understand in everyday social interaction and a more technical notion that can only have a value within an overall theory of social interaction. Both Watts and Janney and Arndt attempt to make this distinction in their contributions.

More importantly, however, the social-order view of politeness assumes the setting of social standards and implies that social sanctions will be applied if these standards are not met. The Japanese term "wakimae" refers to the use of the standard in a formal setting. Processes of language standardisation, and here we mean the setting of stylistically appropriate as well as grammatical, lexical and phonological standards, crucially involves the exercise of power, very often institutionalised through language academies, societies for the propagation of "correct language", prescriptive grammars and dictionaries, and educational systems. A speaker for whom politeness directly or indirectly implies social stigmatisation and exclusion from the institutional acquisition of status and thereby the ability to exercise power over others is not likely to think of it in positive terms. The study of politeness as a set of behaviour patterns preprogrammed as social norms by those possessing power takes us, as it should do, straight into considerations of the wider social functions of politeness and obliges us to consider whether some other term might not be more appropriate for model-theoretic conceptualisations of politeness.

Lakoff's work (Lakoff 1973) was the first to consider politeness from the conversational-maxim point of view. In a later paper (1979: 64) she gives two rules of pragmatic competence:

1. Be clear.
2. Be polite.

Fraser (1990) considers the first of these rules to cover essentially the maxims of Grice's Co-operative Principle. The second rule is composed of 3 sub-rules:

1. Don't impose.
2. Give options.
3. Make *A* feel good.

One of the problems that confront us is that three notions of politeness are involved here, Formal/Impersonal Politeness in the case of sub-rule 1, Non-formal Politeness for sub-rule 2 and Intimate Politeness for sub-rule 3. We are never really told explicitly how these three levels of politeness are to be understood, nor – once again – what politeness itself is. Fraser (1990) also makes the pertinent point that since all three are addressee-oriented, we need to know how the addressee goes about discovering from the social context precisely what level of politeness is involved in any one case. However, it is evident from Lakoff's conceptualisation of the pragmatic rule "Be polite" that the speaker is confronted with a choice and that s/he needs to carry out a certain amount of cognitive work to reach the correct assumptions on the basis of which the appropriate utterance may be produced.

Despite Lakoff's early insistence that we are dealing with pragmatic rules, it is clear that politeness involves more than just pragmatic well-formedness, whatever that might be. In studying politeness, we are automatically studying social interaction and the appropriacy of certain modes of behaviour in accordance with socio-cultural conventions. If, as Goody suggests, interlocutors must calculate "short- and long-term costs and gains" and must pay close attention to "signals about the consequences of [their] own behaviour," then sets of pragmatic rules will not help us greatly in fathoming the nature of politeness. We must attribute to the speaker who produces a polite utterance a certain amount of cognitive work, and in investigating the kind of work involved we automatically enter the study of social psychology.

The second scholar working within the conversational-maxim paradigm is Leech (1983). Once again, however, politeness is never explicitly defined, but it is located among what Leech calls Interpersonal Rhetoric, i.e., the speaker's goals rather than her/his illocutionary goals. Leech enlarges the Gricean Co-operative Principle on a grand scale, adding to it a Politeness Principle and an Irony Principle. Like Grice he divides the Politeness Principle into a number of maxims (Tact Maxim, Generosity Maxim, Approbation Maxim, Modesty Maxim, Agreement Maxim and Sympathy Maxim) and goes on to suggest, along the lines of Halliday's scales of delicacy, that each maxim operates along a range of different scales (the Cost-Benefit Scale, the Optionality Scale, the Indirectness Scale, the Authority Scale and the Social Distance Scale).

Essentially the complex interplay of maxims and scales gives rise to very fine shadings of degrees of politeness all attuned to achieving the maximum benefit for speaker and hearer at the minimum cost, the ultimate goal being "comity". Leech identifies four types of politeness which relate to the goal of "establishing and maintaining comity" (1983: 104), Competitive Politeness, Convivial Politeness, Collaborative Politeness and Conflictive Politeness. Nowhere, however, do we learn how the speaker makes a choice between the kinds of language to be used in keeping with the type and degree of politeness chosen. The model is far too theoretical to apply to actual language usage and too abstract to account for either the commonsense notion of politeness nor some notion which fits into a general theory of social interaction. What arises from this approach is an implied classification of speech act types as polite or non-polite. In particular, indirect speech acts will appear in most circumstances to warrant the label "polite" whereas direct speech acts will only be polite under certain very restricted circumstances. What is interesting in Leech's approach is that politeness is not seen to have anything to do with pragmatic inferencing processes, but rather with the attainment of social goals. At this point we once again enter the realm of social norms.

The face-saving view of politeness derives from Brown and Levinson (1978), and it would be no exaggeration to say that it has been most influential in providing a paradigm for linguistic politeness which goes beyond a mere extension of the Gricean maxims. Its fundamental advantage over other approaches to the subject lies in the fact that it takes as its starting point Goffman's notion of face, interprets polite behaviour as being basic to the maintenance of face wants and links it in a significant way with the Gricean maxims without needing to extend these in any way. What Brown and Levinson call "bald on-record strategies" might involve simply following the maxims, whereas politeness strategies would involve violating the maxims in specific ways. It also discusses data from a range of languages other than English in order to underpin claims for the universality of politeness in language usage.

Basic to their universal conceptualisation of politeness is the rational model person, who is able to choose the appropriate way in which s/he should deviate from the Gricean maxims in the effort to maintain the mutual maintenance of face for both her/himself and the addressee in the most efficient way possible. The model person has both a "public self-image" which s/he wishes to project to other group members (Goffman 1967: 4) and a need to act without being impeded in any way by other members (Brown and Levinson 1978: 67). Goffman's notion is thus extended as "positive face", which is essentially the individual's public self-image, and "negative face", which is the desire for freedom of action to project this image. Hence, if the rational model person were to perform entirely in accordance with Grice's Cooperative Principle, s/he would very quickly threaten the addressee's face (either positive or negative), perhaps, in doing so, her/his own as well.

There are two problems with this basic paradigm, however. First, as Fraser (1990) points out, a direct injunction such as "Close the window" would represent for Brown and Levinson an imposition for the addressee, hence a face-threatening act. On the other hand, it would abide by the maxims of the CP. Our model person thus has the choice of going bald on-record or in some way minimising the FTA, i.e., s/he has a choice from a wide variety of politeness strategies.

However, while "Would you please close the window?" reaches a level of indirectness which minimises the FTA, another utterance such as "Do you think I could possibly prevail upon you to close the window?", which one would expect to minimise it still further, begins to have the opposite effect. There are situations in which this utterance can be processed to yield a number of inferences beyond the original imposition of closing the window, all of which would represent FTAs in their own right. The point at which "polite" utterances fade off again into additional FTAs cannot be determined by any set of rules for language usage. It is not only culture-dependent but also context-dependent within the same culture. Similarly there is a wide range of social contexts in which the direct injunction to close the window would not be interpretable as a bald on-record FTA. Would we have to state that there are social contexts in which abiding by the maxims of the CP is simply neither polite nor impolite, or, if we retain the concept of rational choice, could we not maintain that there are other factors than language usage which prevent the act from being an FTA and that, since the model person, knowing this, has chosen the direct injunction, s/he is being polite? Furthermore, what exactly is understood by the term "imposition"?

To be sure, Brown and Levinson attempt to deal with this kind of problem by suggesting that rational speakers may also assess the strength, or, as they put it, "weightiness", of an FTA so that they can act accordingly. They suggest the following formula:

$$Wx = D(S,H) + P(H,S) + Rx$$

W represents the "weightiness" of x, the FTA, which will determine the degree to which the speaker will choose an appropriate politeness strategy. W is computed by adding three values on a scale from 1 to n, D(S,H), the social distance between the speaker and the hearer, which they further qualify as "the degree of familiarity and solidarity they share", P(H,S), the relative power of the speaker with respect to the hearer, i.e., the degree to which the speaker is able to impose her/his will on the hearer, and Rx, the degree to which, according to some absolute ranking of impositions within the culture concerned, the social act x lies within the speaker's right to perform and is welcomed by the hearer.

Surely, however, the degree to which a social act is considered to be an imposition, i.e., Rx, depends crucially on P and D. So in order for the model person to be able to assess the value for R, s/he has to be able to calculate values for D and P first. No indication is given as to how this might be done. Similarly, knowledge of the value for P may rely crucially on knowing the value of D. On the other hand, it may not. The interlocutors may share a very high degree of familiarity and solidarity, in which case a Weberian notion of power such as that which Brown and Levinson use would lead us to believe that the P value will be low. But if one links the notion of power to that of status, as Brown and Levinson also do, then it can be shown that in a dynamic model of discourse interlocutors with a low D score are constantly struggling to invest themselves with more status from which it becomes easier to exercise power. Such power will not be of the institutionalised variety, but it will nevertheless be present (cf. Watts 1991).

Second, the fundamental notion of face, on which the Brown and Levinson model stands or falls, must be questioned more thoroughly. The term "face" is taken from the metaphorical expression "to lose face". There is no equivalent expression in English like "to gain face" or "to enhance face", although we can say "to save face". Face, as a way of referring to a personal self-image, is thus closely linked to status or prestige and as such it can imply competition and corresponding degrees of prestige. It is also significant that in Western European cultures the metaphor makes use of a part of the human anatomy which is closely linked to the primary senses of seeing and hearing and the faculty of speech, which is perceived by the addressee and which "hides" or "masks" the actual thought processes of the individual.

Perhaps it is as well to remind readers that English also possesses the metaphorical expression "to put on a good face". In a less competitive individualised form of social structure, however, status or prestige may either be far less significant[2] or may be conferred on the individual through the position s/he occupies in the social group. This is not to say that individuals, in whatever culture they have been so-cialised into, do not perceive of themselves in certain ways and wish to be thought of by others in certain ways. We merely wish to suggest that there is a danger of generalising a metaphor which implies the need to maintain status (cf. "to lose face"), the need to struggle for status and thereby power (cf. "to save face") and the need to pretend that what one says or does really does reflect what one thinks whilst knowing that this is not the case (cf. "to put on a good face") to other forms of socio-cultural organisation.[3] Such a conceptualisation of face as the basis for a universal theory of politeness runs a very real danger of ethnocentricity.

In addition, it is not clear whether Goffman's original notion of face can be extended in the way Brown and Levinson extend it to cover freedom of action and freedom from imposition, i.e., negative face. Brown and Levinson exemplify "the want of every competent adult member that his [sic!] action be unimpeded by others" as the maintenance of possessions, territories, personal preserves, etc., the right to act, freedom from interruption, etc. But how is negative face to be understood in a culture in which the possessions of individuals are at one and the same time the possessions of the community, or in which the individual's right to act depends crucially on the consent of the community? Both freedom from interruption and freedom from imposition are likewise very relative concepts indeed. Not only does it depend upon every individual's perception of the situation, but it varies widely from culture to culture. Brown and Levinson also dis-cuss the possibility that a concept of negative face may override that of positive face, such that the interpretation of the latter crucially de-pends on the former. This may indeed be a logical move, but if it turns out to account for patterns of social behaviour in a wider selection of cultures than at present, then the original notion of face becomes somewhat vacuous.

Deriving concepts of politeness from concepts such as face and face threatening act, however, has the great advantage of compelling us to take a greater account of social anthropology and social psychol-ogy than has hitherto been the case. Whether it will ever be possible to suggest a universal notion of politeness which can be used to assess how politeness is revealed in language usage must remain an open question. We happen to believe that it is not only possible, but also desirable. Linguistic politeness involves crossing many disciplinary borders and automatically involves us in interdisciplinary research. So it is comforting to feel that certain well-defined types of linguistic structure can be accounted for in accordance with certain well-defined pragmatic rules as polite. One's job as a researcher into linguistic politeness appears so much easier if these borders do not have to be crossed.

Unfortunately, however, we are nowhere near having reached that point, and the primary aim of the present volume is to display what kinds of empirical work can be carried out on the basis of the range of theories discussed whilst at the same time revealing the very real problems of definition and universality. Politeness, despite the eagerness with which empirical researchers have used existing theories, remains elusive. It is important for both social anthropological and linguistic research to get to grips with the notion of politeness more seriously and thoroughly, since we believe that it is tied up with the most basic principles of human, socio-cultural organisation involving conceptualisations of appropriate individual behaviour, in particular linguistic behaviour, the structuring of interpersonal relationships within social groups and, above all, the nature and distribution of power.

In his contribution, Ehlich argues that perceptions of politeness arise in any culture or group with respect to the interpersonal relations and social conventions agreed upon among the group members at the point in time that the interaction takes place. Politeness is thus a dynamic concept, always open to adaptation and change in any group, in any age, and, indeed, at any moment of time. It is not a socio-anthropological given which can simply be applied to the analysis of social interaction, but actually arises out of that interaction. It is thus not surprising that lay concepts in different languages do not show a one-to-one correspondence, as Ide et al. point out in their contribution, or even that there are languages in which no translation equivalent for the English "polite" exists at all. Igbo, for example, can only approach it through a notion of "good behaviour" (Greg Nwoye, personal communication).

This latter point brings us to a fourth alternative approach to the study of politeness which Fraser (1990) calls the conversational-contract view. He suggests that

> We can begin with the recognition that upon entering into a given conversation, each party brings an understanding of some initial set of rights and obligations that will determine, at least for the preliminary stages, what the participants can expect from the other(s). During the

course of time, or because of a change in the context, there is always
the possibility for a renegotiation of the conversational contract: the
two parties may readjust just what rights and what obligations they
hold towards each other. (1990: 232)

Conversational partners, in other words, enter a conversational
contract which is primarily determined by factors prior to the interaction but is also affected not only by the perceived goals of the conversational partners themselves with respect to the interaction but also by
shifts in relationships, distribution of power, goals and intentions of
the conversational partners, etc. during the course of the interaction.

Politeness for Fraser incurs "operating within the then-current
terms and conditions of the CC [Conversational Contract]".
Essentially, then, Fraser's understanding of politeness is very similar
to the notion of politic behaviour suggested by Watts in his contribution to this volume. Fraser suggests the following:

Politeness, on this view, is not a sometime thing. Rational participants are aware that they are to act within the negotiated constraints
and generally do so. When they do not, however, they are then perceived as being impolite or rude. Politeness is a state that one expects
to exist in every conversation; participants note not that someone is
being polite – this is the norm – but rather that the speaker is violating the CC. (1990: 233)

The chief advantage of the conversational-contract view of politeness is that it can account for the dynamic, changing nature of the concept, in both a historical sense and in the sense of ongoing interaction.
In addition, it helps to explain why not all cultures have a term that is
exactly equivalent to the English "politeness", although the members
of those cultures would certainly perceive their social actions to be
adequately labelled as such in English. Nor can we assume that the
terms that are in use refer to the same phenomena. There is a draw-
back, however. If we perceive when someone is being impolite rather
than polite, why is it that we can and do quite frequently refer to a person's social actions explicitly as polite? Surely, in these circumstances, we have still not come to terms with the fact that the lay notion of politeness is distinct from a second-order, model-theoretical
notion.

The chapters in the present volume have been arranged in order to present the reader in the first part with some of the theoretical problems that still remain, in the second part, to illustrate some of the empirical work that has been carried out on Western cultures, and in the third part to present politeness phenomena in non-Western cultures.

Part one, "The Theory and History of Linguistic Politeness", begins with a contribution by Richard Janney and Horst Arndt, in which they make a distinction between tact and social politeness. Tact is understood by the authors to define forms of social behaviour in which *ego* shows consideration for the concerns of *alter*. In a sense, then, it approaches the idea that conversational partners will abide by some form of conversational contract, as suggested by Fraser. Social politeness or "wakimae", however, is a little more than this and it echoes the marked adherence to forms of social etiquette that Fraser discusses as the social-norm view of politeness. Watts, however, goes a little further than Janney and Arndt. Although he sees a distinction between marked and unmarked forms of behaviour, thus essentially following the conversational-contract view, politeness is seen, perhaps a little idiosyncratically, as marked social behaviour which masks the real intentions of *ego*, some of which may not be altogether altruistic. In this sense, politeness may be perceived negatively. Watts also suggests in chapter 2 that, although it is not wrong to posit that what has often gone under the name of politeness may be a socio-cultural universal, we need to dig a little deeper and move into the realm of social anthropology to find its roots. We may also need to use a different term from "politeness", and he suggests "politic behaviour". Both these contributions tackle the second-order conceptualisation of politeness.

The chapter by Konrad Ehlich deals both with the question of terminology and with that of the historicity of politeness, thus focusing on both first-order and second-order levels. The two things are closely linked in that the terms that are commonly in use in any culture will reflect the social conditions under which "polite" forms of behaviour arose. The conceptualisations of an appropriate notion of politeness, however, will develop historically out of the conditions in which it arose and also those social conditions under which it undergoes change. Ehlich illustrates this by examining the socio-historical roots of polite forms of behaviour in the Middle East and tracing politeness through the late Middle Ages and the renaissance period to the present day. Ehlich's chapter is followed by one by Roger Sell in which historical considerations of politeness are combined with ways in which literary texts are read at the time of their publication and are interpreted in succeeding generations. The focus here is thus on a first-order notion of politeness. One interesting aspect of Sell's approach is that texts themselves can be seen to conform or not conform to the dictates of politeness expectations at the time of their publication, which Sell calls the "politeness *of* the text". During the reading process they may also be interpreted in accordance with a parameter of politeness, in which case the reader will react to the "politeness *in* the text".

In chapter 5 Gudrun Held offers a critical review of some of the politeness research that has been carried out within the field of linguistics during this century. She shows that there has been a significant rupture between earlier, continental European approaches and the American/British paradigm, which she takes to be most clearly instantiated in Brown and Levinson (1978). She presents three ways of conceptualising politeness, which she calls the "indirectness" frame, the "conflict resolution and social order" frame and the "politeness as social ritual" frame. Her broad view of research trends displays what we might call the "paradigm effect", in which the benefits that accrue from the rigour of the approach sometimes lead to the exclusion of other interesting phenomena lying outside the frame itself.

Chapter 6 contains a very valuable contribution by Konrad Werkhofer, in which he challenges the notion of universality, although he approaches the question from a different angle from Watts. Werkhofer locates the individualist, cognitivist and rationalist bias in Brown and Levinson's study of politeness, which is a feature of much of the criticism in the literature, but he also goes much further and shows that the rational model person would need to run through two distinct stages in generating an utterance. S/he would need to generate the utterance's literal meaning and then find ways of mitigating it in order not to run the danger of face-threatening. He then shows how the Brown and Levinson model has great difficulties in treating politeness as a social phenomenon, which it clearly is. The work of the German sociologist Georg Simmel offers Werkhofer a way of linking the study of politeness to the analysis of money as a personal and social good.

Part two, "Empirical Studies in Politeness", contains three chapters, all approaching politeness on the first-order level. The first of these by Annelise Knapp-Potthoff, chapter 7, presents empirical research carried out with advanced non-native speakers of English to investigate how politeness (or the lack of it) by native speakers is perceived in telephonic interaction and then conveyed to a third person. The non-native subjects (who are all of German mother tongue) are carrying out the interactional role of mediator in transmitting the information through what Knapp-Potthoff calls "mediating discourse". Both this chapter and chapter 8, in which Judith Stalpers investigates how business interactions between French and Dutch speakers are negotiated, are examples of the kind of cross-cultural investigation that needs to be carried out on politeness phenomena. Perceptions of politeness are likely to differ across cultures, sometimes quite alarmingly, and it is of crucial practical significance that we should know how to predict the kinds of communication breakdown that are likely to arise from such conflicting perceptions.

Chapter 9 presents an empirical investigation by Sabine Walper and Renate Valtin of the way in which children develop a concept of the "white lie". The investigation is based on Brown and Levinson's notion of face threatening and it begins with the hypothesis that as children develop a concept of *alter* in contradistinction to *ego*, they also develop the need to assess what acts will be threatening to their own and *alter's* face. The hypothesis is tested on a number of Berlin schoolchildren of different ages. The statistical evidence points very strongly towards a correlation between the development of a notion of face and the consequent polite avoidance of telling the naked truth in what we may call the "white lie".

Part three consists of four chapters on politeness in a non-Western cultural setting. The first of these, chapter 10 by Shoshana Blum-Kulka, is an investigation of how Israelis evaluate polite behaviour. She shows how metapragmatic conceptions of what constitutes politeness in fact differ in Israeli society. While there are particular types of social setting in which certain types of behaviour would be classified as polite and thus appropriate, there are certainly others in which politeness is viewed negatively. Blum-Kulka's contribution once again highlights the obvious need to differentiate between lay commonsense perceptions of politeness and a second-order notion, which must form part of a theory of language usage. It is at least very clear that we ignore lay interpretations of politeness at our own peril.

Chapter 11 by Sachiko Ide, Beverly Hill, Yukiko Carnes, Tsunao Ogino and Akiko Kawasaki, and chapter 12 by Florian Coulmas both deal with the concept of politeness in Japanese society. We have placed them together in order to present two perspectives on the subject, one from an overwhelmingly "Japanese" point of view, the other from a "non-Japanese" point of view. Ide et al. report on empirical research carried out on Japanese and American subjects to test their reactions to interactional situations containing verbal behaviours in six kinds of speech act, viz. rejection, request, compliance, protest, invitation and apology. Examining the concept of first-order politeness in relation to other concepts describing the nature of human behaviour, they demonstrate that the corresponding terms 'polite' and *teineina* are conceptually quite different. The result of this empirical study warns us against assuming the equivalence of the key term 'polite'.

Coulmas' contribution in chapter 12 presents a view of politeness within Japanese society which is based on several years of very close observation. His perspective is thus that of a cultural "outgrouper". He perceives the complexity of Japanese honorifics to be a question of linguistic etiquette which many Japanese find difficult to acquire. One might wonder how this honorific system of linguistic etiquette would function as the index of social status and power distribution. The question must remain open, however, and the purpose of juxtaposing these two contributions is precisely to generate further questions of general interest within the framework of linguistic politeness.

The final contribution to the volume in chapter 13 is by Manfred Kummer. His description of an honorific language from several perspectives, verbal and non-verbal, gives us some understanding of how and why Thai people exercise politeness behaviour according to the principle of benevolent modesty stressed by Buddhism and a hierarchical structure of society. It is salutary to be reminded of the fact that we all too often forget that many languages in the world other than Japanese also have elaborate systems of honorifics at greater and lesser levels of grammaticalisation. These deserve more attention in future.

The volume thus ends in an open-ended way. It is not our purpose to solve the problems of linguistic politeness, but rather to highlight the many problems which exist and which need to be addressed from the comparative, cross-cultural perspective, from the empirical perspective, from the historical perspective and from the theoretical perspective. And indeed there are in all probability several other perspectives which we have not been able to consider here. We have indicated during this introductory chapter that the study of politeness, whatever we take it to be, should not be something peripheral in linguistics and social anthropology. We have attempted to show, on the contrary, that a proper understanding of it as an all pervasive feature of human social interaction makes it a central concern in both disciplines, as well as a topic of great interest to social and developmental psychologists, literary scholars and social historians. In an age in which interdisciplinary enquiry is becoming more than ever necessary, the simple question of why we all find politeness to be of such importance becomes one of compelling depth and complexity, as we hope the reader will discover.

Notes

1. Work on address terms could thus be considered primarily work on first-order politeness, e.g., Brown and Gilman (1961), Brown and Ford (1964) and Braun (1988), which contains a very extensive bibliography of over 1100 references to the topic. Cf. also remarks by Ide (1988) in her introduction to the special issue of *Multilingua* 7(4) on politeness.
2. This appears to be the case in Igbo society, which has the reputation of being fairly egalitarian. The interests of the group are placed above those of the individual, so that it might also be possible to suggest a concept of "public face" (cf. Nwoye foithcoming). Cf. also Matsumoto (1988).
3. In an interesting article on the Hamar of Ethiopia Streckei (forthcoming) argues that, if we are to retain a notion of face, then we must evaluate its significance in other cultures. Strecker considers face to be a body-based metaphor for social organisation and suggests that other body-based metaphors might be just as significant in a proper intercultural analysis of politeness phenomena.

Part 1: The Theory and History of Linguistic Politeness

1. Intracultural tact versus intercultural tact

Richard W. Janney and Horst Arndt

1. Introduction

The modification of verbal and nonverbal behaviour to avoid conflicts is an important communicative activity in all cultures. The inevitability of misunderstandings in conversation (Blum-Kulka and Weizman 1988) compels people to express themselves tactfully if they wish to maintain a positive frame of communication with their partners. In an atmosphere of empathy and respect partners are able to view misunderstandings as temporary breakdowns in communication rather than having to interpret them as threats to face (Arndt and Janney 1985a, 1985b). Thus, in any culture, being tactful is an important means of maintaining the sense of cooperation and supportiveness necessary for successful interaction.

In this chapter we will argue that many problems of intercultural communication arise from the difficulty of finding appropriate ways to signal feelings and attitudes to foreign partners (Arndt and Janney 1984). We will claim that even relatively simple misunderstandings are sometimes difficult to regulate in intercultural situations because the techniques and strategies of tact for resolving them are not fully shared by the partners. Being interculturally tactful, we will claim, is a complicated skill that involves much more than simply translating politeness formulas from one language into another.

The chapter is divided into four sections; in the following section we explain what we mean by the term "tact", distinguishing this from standard notions of social politeness used in studies of conversational openings, turn-taking sequences, and other recurring conversational routines. In the subsequent section we discuss some of the biological and psychological roots of tact, pointing out that while conflicts are triggered similarly in all higher animals by innate feelings of aggression, attraction, involvement, etc., tact is a uniquely human, noninstinctive, culturally acquired solution to the problem of conflict avoidance. We then discuss the cultural bases of tact, suggesting how cultural and situational assumptions about tact influence people's ways of avoiding conflicts. And in the final section we explain some important differences between conflict avoidance strategies in intracultural and intercultural situations.

2. Social politeness versus tact

A few years ago we discussed some shortcomings of current notions of politeness, pointing out the need for more cooperation in developing a systematic approach to investigating this important aspect of communication (Arndt and Janney 1985b). A main problem, we suggested, is the lack of agreement among investigators about how politeness should be defined as a subject of study. As long as politeness is defined as (linguistically, logically, or conventionally) "appropriate behaviour", we argued, little in the way of an adequate approach to the subject is likely to emerge. Our suggestion at that time was to lower the level of idealisation, leave the analysis of rules of politeness (and other logical constructs) to philosophers, and begin paying more systematic attention to how people actually express their feelings to each other in everyday conversation (Arndt and Janney 1987b). In short, we advocated a shift from a logical approach to a socio-psychological approach.

From a socio-psychological point of view, politeness is not a static logical concept, but a dynamic interpersonal activity that can be observed, described, and explained in functional interactional terms. Within a given culture, almost any normal adult can be polite in impolite ways, or be impolite in polite ways. The former is politeness from a social point of view, and the latter is politeness from an interpersonal point of view (Arndt and Janney 1985a, 1985b, 1987b). Both types of politeness – social and interpersonal – are culturally acquired, and are interrelated in speech; but they are quite different, and it is important for investigators of politeness to distinguish between them. To avoid confusion in the following discussion, we will refer to the former as "social politeness" and to the latter as "tact" (see Figure 1, p. 24).

2.1 *Social politeness*

Social politeness is rooted in people's need for smoothly organised interaction with other members of their group. As members of groups, people must behave in more or less predictable ways in order to achieve social coordination and sustain communication. One of their main means of doing this is to follow conventions of social politeness (Bennett 1976: 177; Griffin and Mehan 1981: 199). Various terms have been invented in recent years for such conventions: e.g., "conversational routines" (Coulmas 1981), "politeness formulas" (Ferguson 1976), "compliment formulas" (Manes and Wolfson 1981), "politeness conventions" (Lewis 1969; Schiffer 1972), "formulaic expressions" (Tannen and Oeztek 1981), and so on.

The function of social politeness is mainly to provide a framework of standardised strategies for getting gracefully into, and back out of, recurring social situations such as: initiating conversation (e.g., greeting people, introducing oneself and others, responding to greetings and introductions, introducing topics), maintaining conversation (e.g., interrupting, holding the floor, changing topics, requesting repetition or clarification, giving or taking conversational turns, checking for or signaling attention/comprehension), terminating conversation (e.g., ending topics, ending conversations, bidding farewell), and so on. Tact is quite another phenomenon, with different functions in human interaction.

2.2 *Tact*

Tact is rooted in people's need to maintain face, in their fear of losing it, and in their reluctance to deprive others of it (Goffman 1967). As partners in social interaction, people are more or less dependent on each other to cooperate in maintaining the fragile balance of respect and consideration necessary for the preservation of face (Brown and Levinson 1978). One of their main means of doing this, and avoiding conflicts, is to be tactful (Arndt and Janney 1987b). Being tactful is not simply a matter of behaving in a socially "correct" way – i.e., following rules of social usage; rather, it is a matter of behaving in an interpersonally supportive way (Arndt and Janney 1985a, 1985b). It involves empathising with others, and not saying or doing things that threaten them, offend them, or injure their feelings.

Being tactful in one's own culture requires subtle modifications of verbal and nonverbal activities. To avoid threatening each other, most Westerners constantly modulate verbal messages with nonverbal vocal and kinesic messages to signal awareness of each other's feelings: e.g., becoming more indirect when talking about uncomfortable topics, using a rising intonation to turn commands into requests, ma-

	SOCIAL POLITENESS	TACT
FOCUS	*the group*: socially appropriate communicative forms, norms, routines, rituals, etc.	*the partner*: interpersonally supportive communicative techniques, styles, and strategies
FRAME	*interactional*: people's need for efficient, uncomplicated interaction with other members of their group	*interpersonal*: people's need to preserve face and maintain positive relationships with their partners
FUNCTION	*regulative*: facilitates the coordinated exchange of routine conversational roles and responsibilities.	*conciliative*: helps avoid threats to face, and facilitates the peaceful negotiation of interpersonal affairs

Figure 1. Social politeness versus tact

king criticisms in a pleasant tone of voice, smiling at each other, gazing toward each other, and so on (Arndt, Janney and Pesch 1984; Arndt and Janney 1983, 1987b).

The difference between tact and social politeness is that whereas the function of social politeness is essentially to coordinate social interaction – to regulate the mechanical exchange of roles and activities – the function of tact is quite different: namely, to preserve face and regulate interpersonal relationships. Metaphorically, we might say that social politeness is somewhat like a system of social traffic rules, while tact is more a matter of interpersonal driving styles and strategies. In fact, it is probably not social politeness that enables people to avoid most everyday interpersonal conflicts, but tact.

3. The psychological bases of tact

The difficulty with tact, from an intercultural point of view, is that it depends on multimodal communicative skills that are learned through social interaction (Lock 1978, 1980). Like other socially learned skills, these tend to be relatively culture-bound and are sometimes misinterpreted by members of other cultures. Nevertheless, not all causes of misunderstanding between people from different cultures can be traced to specific cultural differences (Sussman and Rosenfeld 1982). Biologists and psychologists point out universal characteristics of human interaction that make conflicts nearly unavoidable (Arndt and Janney 1979, 1980).

Although notions of tact vary from culture to culture, the impulse either so seek confrontations or to avoid them is rooted in human biology (Arndt and Janney 1987a). From an evolutionary point of view, tact seems to be a uniquely human adaptive response to certain innate, universal, biologically preprogrammed conflicts that arise whenever members of the same species interact. In both human and animal interaction, three issues require continuous renegotiation: (1) the issue of which partner is stronger, more assertive, or more dominant; (2) the issue of the partners' feelings of attraction or repulsion toward each other (Conte and Plutchik 1981; Daly, Lancee and Polivy 1983; Eibl-Eibesfeldt 1984); (3) the issue of the intensity of these feelings (Arndt and Janney 1979, 1983, 1984). Tact enables people to avoid, or at least to partially regulate, conflicts that arise during the negotiation of these three issues.

From a neurological point of view, feelings of assertiveness, affiliation, and involvement appear to be produced largely automatically in the brain (Arndt and Janney 1986). Neuroanatomical studies indicate that such feelings are triggered by similar subcortical regions in the brains of animals and humans alike (MacLean 1973). Feelings of assertiveness and emotional involvement, for example, are triggered by the human brain core, whose structure and functions are analogous in some respects to those of the reptilian brain core. Feelings of attraction and repulsion, on the other hand, are triggered by the limbic system, which humans share anatomically with the other mammals. Complex multimodal displays of emotion are coordinated by the neocortex, the brain's so-called "thinking cap", which is highly developed not only in humans, but in apes and other primates as well (Arndt and Janney and Schaffranek 1986; Arndt and Janney 1987a). Thus, it seems that human and animal emotions have similar neurological roots, and are to some extent manifested outwardly by similar physical activities (Eibl-Eibesfeldt 1984).

3.1 *Emotive communication versus emotional communication*

Research on physical displays of emotion during the past few decades has perpetuated the misconception that the communication of feelings among humans is little more than a somewhat more complicated version of what goes on between animals (Ekman 1965a, 1965b, 1972; Ekman and Friesen 1969; Izard 1972; Scheflen 1973; Scherer 1980). This view was originally expressed by Darwin (1872) in the nineteenth century, and has changed little since it was first formulated. The basic idea is that emotions are automatically signaled by visible and audible muscular actions produced by the autonomous nervous system. Because the autonomous nervous system is the same for all people in all cultures, proponents of the Darwinian hypothesis claim, displays of emotion must be relatively universal across cultures (Ekman and Friesen 1967; Ekman 1973).

Despite its common sense appeal, this view has been strongly criticised by many anthropologists and interactionalists (Arndt and Janney, and Pesch 1984), who argue that although it may be true that people are physiologically restricted to producing certain types of affective displays (e.g., signals of assertiveness/unassertiveness, like/dislike, involvement/uninvolvement, etc.), how they actually use and interpret these in different cultures is quite another matter. People's actual use of affective displays as communicative devices is often strategic. That is, signs of emotion are not always simply outward manifestations of internal states; often they are produced intentionally in order to project a particular definition of the situation and influence others' behaviour (Kraut and Johnston 1979: 1551).

For this reason, many investigators have begun to call for a more adequate account of emotion and for a more differentiated approach to studying the communication of emotion generally (Buck 1984). Following Plutchik and Kellerman (1980: 3), we may define an emotion as a relatively transitory affective state with partly uncontrollable psychobiological components, and partly controllable expressive components (Plutchik and Kellerman 1980: 3). On the basis of this definition, we may further distinguish between two interrelated, but different, communicative phenomena (see Figure 2, p. 28):

(1) *emotional communication*, in which affective displays are simply spontaneous, unplanned physical externalisations of internal affective states; and

(2) *emotive communication*, in which affective displays are produced consciously and used strategically in a wide variety of social situations to influence others' perceptions and interpretations of conversational events (Stankiewicz 1964: 240; Scherer 1979: 524; Couper-Kuhlen 1986: 174).

Whenever the possibility exists to use affective signals in this second sense – strategically, for purposes of emotive communication – there are cultural and social conventions regulating how this is done. Tact, as a highly developed form of emotive communication, is thus probably not pan-cultural, but in fact highly sensitive to cultural modifications and inhibitions. In a culture that restrains emotive displays – or, conversely, in one that encourages them – ways of being tactful are bound to be affected (Bolinger 1982: 530).

To summarise what we have said up to this point, on the one hand, people share many of the biological prerequisites for feelings of dominance/submission, like/dislike, and involvement/uninvolvement with animals. These feelings, and conflicts arising out of them, may be viewed as universal in a biological, evolutionary sense. They play an important role in all interpersonal relationships, and require more or less constant negotiation between partners. On the other hand, however, the expression of feelings varies considerably between animals and people, and among people, between members of different cultures. Whereas animals are limited to more or less spontaneous, instinctive emotional displays, people produce highly sophisticated, conventionalised, noninstinctive forms of emotive expression as well. By interacting in different social situations, they learn to use emotive signals strategically to avoid conflicts. They learn to be tactful.

3.2 Tact and face needs

As we suggested earlier, a fundamental preoccupation of people around the earth is maintaining or protecting face. Face, according to interactionalists, is the positive public self-image that every individual wishes to claim for himself (Goffman 1967). The desire to maintain face, and the fear of losing it, are universals transcending all cultural, ethnic, social, sexual, economic, geographical, and historical boun-

	EMOTIONAL COMMUNICATION	EMOTIVE COMMUNICATION
ACTIVITY	*instinctive*: the spontaneous, unplanned, physical externalisation of internal affective states	*learned*: the conscious use of affective displays for communicative purposes
FOCUS	*the individual*: people's need to adapt physiologically to powerful internal psychic stimuli	*projected 'others'*: others' projected feelings, perceptions, and interpretations in the situation
FRAME	*psychobiological*: people's need to adapt physiologically to powerful internal psychic stimuli	*sociopsychological*: people's need to adapt behaviourally to others in order to avoid interpersonal conflicts
FUNCTION	*cathartic*: releases emotional tension and helps maintain psychic balance	*strategic*: signals affective information in order to influence others' behaviour

Figure 2. Emotional communication versus emotive communication

daries. Threats to face, whether intended, accidental, or only imagined, are the basis of most interpersonal conflicts. They arise when people feel that their right to a positive self-image is being ignored or called into question by others. A conventional way of avoiding threats to face in all cultures is to be tactful (Arndt and Janney 1985a).

Tact is directed toward two basic face-needs: (1) the need to feel unimpeded, free, or self-determining within an inviolable, internal, personal preserve, and (2) the need to feel accepted, appreciated, or respected by at least some others (Brown and Levinson 1978: 63ff). We may call the former the need for personal face, and the latter the need for interpersonal face (Arndt and Janney 1985b). From an interactional point of view, these needs are antithetical to some extent: personal autonomy can sometimes be maintained only at the cost of giving up a certain amount of interpersonal acceptance; and conversely, interpersonal acceptance can sometimes be maintained only at the cost of reduced personal autonomy. Thus, personal and interpersonal face-needs often conflict, both within and between people, making it necessary for members of all cultures to develop complicated face-saving strategies.

Misunderstandings are nascent in almost any situation. Regardless of how carefully people try to avoid conflicts, every request, suggestion, evaluation, command, criticism, or difference of opinion of any kind can be interpreted as an implicit threat to face (Bradac, Bowers and Courtright 1979, 1980). In many cultures this situation is handled by becoming less self-assertive (e.g., becoming verbally less explicit, prosodically less emphatic, and kinesically less direct) and by signalling acceptance of the partner (e.g., wording negative messages in positive ways, using a pleasant tone of voice, smiling, etc.). While low assertiveness and high acceptance may be relatively valid across cultures as conflict avoidance techniques, it is doubtful, as we said, whether techniques and strategies for signalling these feelings in different cultures are universal.

The problem that this raises for investigators of intercultural communication is illustrated by the literature on Anglo-American tact. Various maxims have been proposed over the years for being tactful: "don't impose", "give options", "be friendly" (Lakoff 1974), "assume your partner is dominant", "don't go on record" (Leech 1977), "be supportive" (Arndt and Janney 1985b), and so on. Such maxims are little more than common-sense platitudes. Although it is possible to go beyond these and construct rules of tactfulness for Anglo-American speech, as Grice (1975), Searle (1975), Leech (1977), and others have done, the resulting frameworks tend to be highly culture-bound, and their usefulness in reducing intercultural misunderstanding is questionable. The reason for this is that people from different cultures often have not only different ideas about what counts as language, but also different ideas about what count as imposing, options, friendliness, dominance, supportiveness, and other key concepts. In some instances they may even have different ideas about what counts as logic. Given this situation, it seems unrealistic to assume that logical rule systems of tactfulness can be translated from one culture into another without losing much of their validity.

4. The cultural bases of tact

It is often noted that people from different cultures have not only different languages, but also different emotive styles and strategies of interacting. The latter are functionally related to the former, making both what and how things are expressed important features of communication in all cultures. Many problems of intercultural misunderstanding, we said, arise from the difficulty of finding tactful ways to communicate feelings and attitudes. This is because emotive communication, like cognitive communication, is guided by various assumptions that people accept unquestioningly as a natural consequence of growing up in a particular group (Moore and Carling 1982; Arndt and Janney 1984).

4.1 *Cultural assumptions*

All people in a culture who wish to be regarded as normal must eventually learn to make roughly similar types of inferences about their experiences. The penalty for not doing this is social exclusion, being labeled abnormal, retarded, defective, or deviant (Sarles 1977: 136). Thus, growing up to become a normal member of a culture is largely a matter of learning how to perceive, think, and behave as others in the culture do. By interacting with other members of the culture in different situations throughout their lives, people acquire broad frameworks of common knowledge, experience, expectations, and beliefs that enable them to be tactful (Moore and Carling 1982). Stored in the mind in the form of global assumptions, these frameworks consist of standard presuppositions about what the culture normatively defines as "reality", or "the way things are" in the world (Helt 1982).

Such frameworks are absolutely essential to tactful communication, because without them, as Mead (1934) points out, people cannot think about their own projected behaviour from the perspective of the "generalised other" and imagine how it might be interpreted or what its consequences might be. Among the many prerequisites for being tactful in one's own culture are roughly convergent assumptions about:

(1) basic human needs, drives, feelings, motives, intentions, etc., and how these may be inferred from behaviour in different situations;

(b) positive and negative social groups and their members, and how levels of intimacy and distance may be signaled in different situations;

(c) the basic dynamics of interpersonal relationships in the culture, and how levels of power and affiliation may be signaled in different situations; and above all,

(d) verbal, vocal, and kinesic communication in the culture, and about how signals in the different modes can be used to avoid conflicts in different situations (Arndt and Janney 1978b).

Once such assumptions are formed, they remain relatively stable and their influence on social interaction becomes almost automatic (Griffen and Mehan 1981: 199). Events that contradict them do not change them, but tend rather to be interpreted as incorrect, ununderstandable, or abnormal. For this reason, we may say that cultural assumptions are the more or less nonnegotiable basis of human tact (Arndt and Janney 1987b: 58ff). The problem when people from different cultures interact is that important parts of this nonnegotiable basis are sometimes missing. At these points their behaviour does not make sense, and communication temporarily breaks down. When this happens, both the disruption caused in the conversation and the conflicts that may develop between the partners depend on the type of behaviour that is perceived as incorrect, ununderstandable, or abnormal.

Breakdowns in propositional communication often have little lasting effect on conversation because they can usually be attributed to faulty linguistic knowledge, interference, or some other relatively unintentional, unthreatening cause – e.g., as when a tourist in Greece, wishing to say "good morning" *(kalimera)* to a fisherman, smiles and exclaims *"kalamares!"* ('squid'). Propositional misunderstandings of this type, while perhaps leading to perplexed shrugs or laughter, are not normally perceived as threats to face in the sense explained earlier, or as grounds for suspicion (O'Connor and Arnold 1972: 2; Wilkins 1974: 45; Gutknecht and Mackiewicz 1977: 108).

Breakdowns in emotive communication, on the other hand, can lead to serious intercultural misunderstandings, because instead of being attributed to faulty knowledge, they often tend to be attributed to incorrect attitudes, ununderstandable motives, or abnormal feelings (Garfinkel 1967) – e.g., as when an English woman in Japan is shocked when her housekeeper smiles and explains that she could not come to work because her husband died yesterday. For the Japanese woman the smile may be a tactful means of avoiding confronting her employer too unpleasantly with her own sorrow; for the English woman it may seem inhuman. The misunderstanding, in any case, is probably less a matter of divergent human values than of divergent cultural assumptions about the tactful uses of smiling in the situation.

4.2 *Situational assumptions*

The importance of situational assumptions in tactful communication has been demonstrated repeatedly by interactional psychologists and ethnomethodologists. Referred to variously as "definitions of the situation" (Goffman 1959: 13), "background expectancies" (Garfinkel 1967: 499), "anticipatory schemata" (Atkinson and Allen 1983: 459), or "frames of reference" (Mathiot 1983: 10), situational assumptions are working hypotheses that people adopt on a moment to moment basis to orient themselves in the ongoing conversation (White and Carlston 1983). They notice certain things about the partner and the situation in which they are conversing that remind them of previous experiences; they tentatively conclude that the present situation has various similarities with previous ones; and they take this (hypothetical) state of affairs for granted in interpreting the partner and planning their own actions (Goffman 1963; Arndt and Janney 1979).

Due to their embeddedness in cultural experiences, situational assumptions are indirectly related to, and derived from, cultural assumptions. Unlike cultural assumptions, however, they must not be fully shared in order for people to communicate. In fact, the attempt to share them is one of the main tasks of normal intracultural conversation. Generally, the more convergent people's situational assumptions are in a given instance, the more they feel that they understand each other; and the more divergent their situational assumptions are, the less they feel that they understand each other. Conflicts arise when people repeatedly fail to achieve some type of convergence.

Questions such as the following play an important role in being tactful: What kind of partner am I dealing with? What kind of person does the partner think I am? Are we equal or unequal? Do we like each other or not? Is the partner a member of a group with which I identify myself? What is the partner's role in the group? What do we have in common? How does the partner view our social relationship? What are the partner's motives? How does the partner expect me to talk ? What strategies have worked in the past with partners like this? Answers to questions like these more or less automatically lead people to adopt communicative strategies that are tailored to the situation as they see it. They also influence people's interpretations of their partner's behaviour.

Unlike cultural assumptions, situational assumptions are extremely unstable. They can exist only as long as events confirm them. If they are contradicted – that is, if the partner behaves in some way that seems odd, does not fit, or is plainly contrary in the hypothesised context – they begin immediately to break down. When this happens people typically react in one of three ways:

(1) if the contradiction is not important, or if it is no obstacle to fulfilling their momentary needs, they often simply ignore it – as when a hungry diner ignores an unexpectedly unfriendly waiter in a restaurant;

(2) if the contradiction poses an immediate problem that must be resolved before conversation can continue, or before momentary ends can be reached, people feel compelled to negotiate some type of agreement with their partners about whose assumptions about the situation will be honored – as when the diner asks the waiter to stop being so unfriendly;

(3) if the contradiction can neither be ignored nor negotiated, people have little choice but to break off contact – as when the diner decides to go to a more friendly restaurant.

The fact that situational assumptions can be negotiated in normal intracultural situations is very important, for it gives people a means of avoiding conflicts, or of regulating them before they become too serious. This is one of the main functions of tact: to project a certain definition of the situation for the partner's benefit in order to avoid an escalation of misunderstandings that could force people to break off contact. In this sense, tact is impression management, a means of modifying situational assumptions that enables people to avoid unnecessary confrontations and maintain effective communication (Patterson 1983: 111 ff.). In all cultures people learn techniques that help them

converse without getting into interpersonal difficulties. Saying "yes"
verbally and implying "no" nonverbally, for example, is a standard
tactful means of avoiding hurting partners' feelings in Western cultures. Stating commands ("come here") in the form of requests ("have
you got a minute") or suggestions ("maybe you ought to look at this")
is a tactful way of avoiding power struggles, and so on.

5. Tact as strategic conflict avoidance

To summarise the main points up to now, we have suggested that
although tact is a uniquely human form of conflict avoidance, the
conflicts that tact helps us to avoid are not uniquely human. They are
triggered by innate, biologically preprogrammed feelings of aggression, attraction, involvement, etc. in all animals above the level of
reptiles (Arndt and Janney 1986). Because conflicts disrupt group activities that are important for survival, all species have ways of regulating them. There is an important difference, however, between the
way animals deal with conflicts and the way humans do this: whereas
conflicts among animals are generally regulated by fighting or fleeing,
among humans they tend to be avoided in advance by complicated,
noninstinctive, culturally acquired techniques of tactfulness.

The function of tact, from a sociobiological point of view, is thus
strategic conflict avoidance (Leech 1977). Strategic conflict avoidance,
in contrast to fighting or fleeing, presupposes an ability to imagine
projected behaviour and predict its emotional consequences. This ability is highly developed in humans due to their enlarged neocortex,
with its specialised sequential (left hemisphere) and holistic (right
hemisphere) reasoning capacities (Arndt, Janney and Schaffranek
1986). Thus, although humans and animals share many of the same
prerequisites for starting conflicts, humans have a decided advantage
in foreseeing and avoiding them.

This advantage cannot be fully explained biologically, for it develops out of an individual's lifetime of experiences with others in a
group. Being tactful requires a highly developed ability to empathise
with others in the group and predict how they will respond in different
situations. This ability is culturally acquired and presupposes a vast
supporting framework of shared global assumptions about human nature, social relationships, interpersonal relationships, and communica-

tive behaviour. The culture-bound nature of much of this knowledge, we said, is one reason why people from different cultures often misinterpret each other's emotive signals.

5.1 *Intracultural tact*

In normal intracultural conversation people more or less automatically edit their verbal and nonverbal output so as to project a certain definition of the situation for the partner's benefit (Sarles 1977: 32). The important feature of being tactful in their own culture is not what they communicate, but how they communicate: i.e., their verbal, vocal, and kinesic styles and strategies in the situation (Arndt and Janney 1987b). Modifications of verbal directness and intensity, variations of intonation and tone of voice, changing facial expressions, shifting glances, and other activities provide a running commentary on what is said literally (Bolinger 1977: 4).

These activities, which are no less interpretable in the culture than the words and sentences of the language, are indispensable for a full understanding of the partner. People depend on these for information about each other's feelings, needs, motives, and intentions, and for a great deal of information about their momentary interpersonal relationship – which is signaled by, and changes continuously in response to, subtle shifts of assertiveness, friendliness, intimacy, attentiveness, etc. as they speak.

People use such signals strategically to influence each other's behaviour. Elsewhere we have explained in detail how this is done among Anglo-Americans (Arndt and Janney 1985b). The basic idea of Anglo-American tact is to minimise threats to the partner's personal face (i.e., the need to feel self-determining) while maximising support of his or her interpersonal face (i.e., the need to feel accepted). This is done mainly by varying levels of directness, modifying signals of positive and negative affect, and shifting the intensity of signals in different modes (Arndt and Janney 1987b).

Among Anglo-Americans, messages most requiring tact are those with positive or negative implications for the partner (Berger 1979). The general rule is that positive messages must be sufficiently emphasised, and negative messages must be sufficiently de-emphasised (Bradac, Bowers and Courtright 1980). If this does not happen – that is, if positive messages do not seem positive enough, or if negative messages seem too negative – conflicts often arise (Berger and Calabrese 1979). In the former case, a too weakly positive message may be interpreted as insincere, ironic, or sarcastic: i.e., as "damning by faint praise". In the latter case, a too strongly negative message may be interpreted as aggressive, unfriendly, or hostile.

For this reason, when communicating positive messages (e.g., when agreeing, thanking, making compliments, congratulating, etc.), Anglo-Americans tend to try to amplify the positive effect by acting more assertive, affiliative, and involved than usual in all modes. Verbally they are direct, explicit, and emphatic; vocally they use a falling intonation, a positive tone of voice, and heavy stress; and kinesically they often gaze fully at the partner and smile broadly. When communicating negative messages, on the other hand (e.g., when disagreeing, criticising, refusing, etc.), Anglo-Americans tend to try to soften the negative effect by acting more unassertive and uninvolved than usual (reducing the partner's loss of personal face), and by remaining as affiliative as possible in the situation (maintaining the partner's interpersonal face). Verbally they are indirect, inexplicit, and unemphatic; vocally they use a rising or a falling-rising intonation, and tend to avoid unusual stress; and kinesically they may avoid eye-contact, or may only glance briefly at the partner and smile (Arndt and Janney 1987b).

With the proper concepts, it is possible to develop models of the verbal and nonverbal techniques used in a particular culture when being tactful (Arndt, Janney and Pesch 1984; Arndt and Janney 1985a, 1985b). As we have shown elsewhere, such models can be unified into relatively complex multimodal frameworks of communicative choices and constraints, and can be complemented by systematic interpretive frameworks, yielding a sort of interactional grammar of emotive communication in the culture (Arndt and Janney 1979, 1981a, 1981b, 1983, 1987b). Yet, with respect to reducing intercultural misunderstanding, or improving interpersonal communication between people from different cultures, it remains questionable whether such frameworks alone are enough.

5.2 *Intercultural tact*

Throughout the chapter we have emphasised the importance of shared cultural assumptions in people's ability to predict each other's reactions, imagine potential conflicts, and avoid these by being tactful. Tact, we said, is a fully normal aspect of everyday intracultural com-

munication. Yet, the apparent ease with which people regulate interpersonal affairs in their own cultures is deceptive. In fact, the knowledge required to do this is no less complex than the knowledge required to speak the language. In many intercultural situations the
problems of the partners are completely different, and there is little
point in assuming that solutions to these problems lie in, or can be
derived from, culture-bound notions of appropriate behaviour.

A case in point would be Anglo-American tact, as we have just described it. Assuming that Anglo-Americans judge the sincerity of
positive messages by their assertiveness and involvement – on the basis of culturally acquired expectations about degrees of directness and
intensity necessary for communicative events to be considered
"assertive" and "involved" in their culture – we can imagine that under
normal circumstances a sincerely well-meaning Anglo-American will
automatically perform the activities necessary to get a positive message
across. In situations where this person feels that there is a possibility
of not being properly understood – as in a conversation with someone
from another culture – we can further imagine that he or she may emphasise verbal and nonverbal activities more than usual to avoid confusion (the equivalent of speaking words more slowly and clearly).
The result might be a sort of exaggerated version of a normal Anglo-
American positive message, e.g.,

> `HEY! That's a `TERRIFIC idea! `REALLY!
> (full gaze) (broad smile) (shoulder slap)

The type of reaction that such a display of Anglo-American enthusiasm might evoke in a foreign partner is fully unpredictable. As we said
earlier, if the partner comes from a culture where emotive displays are
encouraged – e.g., Italy – there may be no problem interpreting the
verbal, vocal, and kinesic intensity of the utterance.

On the other hand, if the partner comes from a culture where emotive displays are normally restrained – e.g., Japan – the intensity and
the kinesic intimacy of this communicative event might well be exceed-
ingly uncomfortable (Bolinger 1982: 530). At a recent workshop on
cross-cultural problems in international aviation, a Japanese language
instructor commented, "When speaking their own language, Japanese
people use almost no body language, facial indications or expressions,
very little intonation or stress, and no eye contact. [...] Most Japanese
people are intimidated by the tone or loudness of a person's voice, by
movements, and by close contact. In most conversations, Japanese

people keep a one-meter distance. They do not touch each other very often. [...] When they are speaking English it is impossible to change their personality completely" (Nojiri 1987). In view of such great differences, we are forced to wonder to what extent many basic techniques of Anglo-American tact are perceived and accurately interpreted by people from non-Western cultures.

As we said, cultural differences in communicative styles and strategies are embedded in, and supported by, unquestioned cultural assumptions that are difficult to change. Such assumptions are relatively nonnegotiable: behaviour that contradicts them simply tends to be interpreted as abnormal. For this reason, people from different cultures often remain something of a mystery to each other, especially at the emotive level, where differences in cultural assumptions may make it difficult to predict each other's reactions. These differences may be relatively small, as when people from Western cultures interact (e.g., Anglo-Americans and Germans), or relatively great, as when Westerners interact with people from Far Eastern cultures (e.g., Frenchmen and Vietnamese). Regardless of the degree of cultural divergence, however, the result is always some type of unpredictability – and unpredictability is threatening among strangers (Berger 1979). Ultimately, it may well be that tact in the intracultural sense is simply impossible in many intercultural situations.

5.2.1 Positive frames of communication

When people cannot rely on shared cultural knowledge in attempting to regulate their relationships, they usually try to find some other type of assumptive framework as a temporary replacement. This is not quite as difficult as the preceding discussion might suggest, because intercultural communication never takes place between idealised "members of culture" in vacuo (e.g., "Italians", "Poles", "Russians", "Americans"), but always between real people in real situations (e.g., a German dentist and his Turkish patient, a French businessman and his Spanish client, an American diplomat and his Russian counterpart). Generally, some aspect of the situation common to both partners is adopted as a frame of reference. This ad-hoc frame of reference, which is roughly prescribed by the partner's immediate interests, activities, or goals, temporarily replaces their respective cultures as the nonnegotiable basis of communication. For purposes of sustaining conversation, the partners tacitly agree to become members of a common, transcendent positive-reference group.

The function of positive-reference groups in intercultural communication is not to make the partners more understandable, but to make their behaviour more predictable. Within a positive-reference group frame, communication tends to be restricted to the interests that momentarily bind the partners in conversation. Thus, the dentist and his patient talk about teeth, the businessman and his client talk about business, and the diplomat and his colleague talk about international politics. Within these restricted areas, the partners' social and interpersonal roles are relatively well defined, and their behaviour is more or less prescribed by the frame.

An important secondary function of positive-reference groups in intercultural communication is to create a sense of affiliation between the partners. The fact that the partners share common interests in the situation is presumed in advance. Actually, it is their main reason for temporarily defining each other as members of the same group. The assumption of affiliation reduces the danger of threats to interpersonal face; the partners implicitly accept each other. This, plus the assumption that they are communicating in good faith, enables the partners to view each other's ununderstandable or inappropriate behaviour – e.g., unexpected directness, excessive loudness, too little smiling, too much eye-contact, unusual formality, uninterpretable vocal or kinesic gestures – as accidental rather than intentional. Within a positive-reference group frame, odd or disturbing emotive signals can be attributed to cultural differences, or to momentary personal problems, and must not be interpreted as interpersonal threats (Arndt and Janney 1984). Many kinds of behaviour that might offend or disturb people in their own cultures may thus be ignored or forgiven. Within such a frame, as long as the partners restrict communication to matters of common interest and refrain from overt aggression or hostility, there is relatively little danger of conflict.

5.2.2 Negative frames of communication

The danger of conflict increases, however, when people abandon subjects of obvious common interest and begin discussing matters unrelated to their immediate reasons for speaking (e.g., when the dentist and his patient begin discussing racial relations, the businessman and his client begin discussing politics, or the two diplomats begin discussing their religious beliefs). While this, of course, may lead to the discovery of new common interests, it can also lead to misunderstandings. Misunderstandings are fully normal in intracultural conversation, and they are usually easily resolved with simple techniques of tact that are taken for granted by members of the culture. In intercultural situations, however, misunderstandings are often more difficult to regulate, because the techniques of tact for resolving them are not fully shared by the partners. Simple misunderstandings can thus have important interpersonal consequences among foreigners. When people feel that they share neither common cultural assumptions nor common interests with their partners, they begin to feel uncomfortable (Berger and Calabrese 1975; Berger 1979). They become suspicious and begin to view their partners as members of a negative-reference group.

The function of negative-reference groups in intercultural communication is to make ununderstandable or inappropriate behaviour interpretable by defining one's partner as enemy. Within a negative-reference group frame, communication tends to either gravitate toward issues that separate the partners, or to break down altogether. The fact that the partners do not share common interests is often presumed in advance, as is also the fact that they do not accept each other and are not communicating in good faith. Such assumptions lead the partners to view each other's odd or unexpected behaviour as intentional rather than accidental, and to view much fully normal tactful behaviour as devious or dishonest rather than sincere. Within a negative-reference group frame, signals of self-assertiveness, nonaffiliation, and involvement tend to be overrated, while signals of deference, affiliation, and uninvolvement tend to be discounted or ignored. As long as partners restrict communication to the issues that divide them, there is little chance of avoiding conflict.

5.3 *Implications*

From the preceding it should be clear that being interculturally tactful requires somewhat different strategies than being tactful in one's own culture. In many intercultural situations notions of intracultural tact may simply be too complex to be useful in avoiding misunderstandings, and too ununderstandable for the partner. Subtle cross-modal techniques meant to reduce face losses, or to compensate for them in various ways, may in fact have quite unintended effects. Verbal and nonverbal emotive signals may be so minimally different that they are not noticed by the partner, or they may be so intense from the beginning that the partner is overloaded and cannot distinguish between them.

Given this situation, is it possible to be interculturally tactful? As we said, the answer to this question might ultimately be that people cannot always be interculturally tactful in the usual intracultural sense. On the other hand, they can avoid conflicts. This is done by managing impressions at the situational assumptive level, where the partner needs to know what sort of person he or she is dealing with. Here are a few guidelines for avoiding conflicts in intercultural situations.

(1) Try to maintain a positive-reference group frame of communication with the partner: seek topics of obvious common interest in the situation, try to avoid topics that are unrelated to your immediate reasons for conversing, and refrain from displays of self-assertiveness, positive/negative affect, or involvement that would be considered especially restrained or especially emphatic in your own culture.

(2) If misunderstandings or disagreements develop, try to avoid getting into a negative frame of communication with the partner: reaffirm your common concerns or interests in the situation, do not press the misunderstood issue, drop the subject if possible, and repeat (1).

(3) If misunderstandings threaten to develop into conflicts, abandon the attempt to maintain common territory with the partner and concentrate on avoiding aggression or hostility: stop all signs of assertiveness and positive/negative affect, be direct, and signal acceptance of the partner's right to have his or her opinion.

(4) If this fails, break off contact.

Finally, recognising that there are sometimes barriers to interpersonal understanding in intercultural situations, and realising that these are often cultural rather than personal barriers, can be helpful in interacting with foreigners. Above all, it can save us from compounding the problem by using strategies of tact from our own culture that may simply confuse our partners and breed uncertainty. As stated at the beginning of the chapter, the study of intercultural communication requires a special approach; there are no adequate intracultural solutions to problems of intercultural misunderstanding.

2. Linguistic politeness and politic verbal behaviour: Reconsidering claims for universality

Richard J. Watts

1. Introduction

My aim in this chapter is fourfold. Firstly, I should like to reopen the question of defining the term "linguistic politeness". I shall argue that research in pragmalinguistics and sociolinguistics over the past fifteen years has offered us definitions which do not always correspond with native English speakers' perceptions of the term "politeness", which is often evaluated negatively. I contend that negative evaluations within the framework of British-English culture can be traced back to eighteenth-century definitions and the social application of the term throughout at least the eighteenth and nineteenth centuries. The various realisations of linguistic politeness in language usage which have been discussed in the literature may more profitably be viewed as forms of a more general type of linguistic behaviour geared towards maintaining the equilibrium of interpersonal relationships within the social group, which I have elsewhere termed "politic verbal behaviour" (Watts 1989b).

Secondly, I should like to raise the problem of claiming universality for the diverse linguistic and non-linguistic phenomena to which scholars have attached the label "linguistic politeness". I shall present two approaches to the study of universals analogous to two approaches within theoretical linguistics, the typological approach and the underlying-principles approach.

Thirdly, in considering universality, I should like to review one of the phenomena to which both approaches have been applied, viz., terms of address, and some of the problems involved. Finally, I should like to demonstrate what my preferred approach to universals of language usage, viz., the underlying-principles approach, entails when locating and interpreting politeness phenomena which function as socially marked forms of politic verbal behaviour, by commenting briefly on five strips of verbal interaction.

The chapter is not, in the strictest sense, an overview of linguistic politeness research. The most comprehensive overview to date is the introduction to the new edition of Brown and Levinson's seminal article which was published as a book in 1987 and bears the revised title *Politeness: Some universals in language usage*, and there is little sense in repeating what they say here. A number of important issues within the field of politeness research still need to be tackled, however, not the least of these being the fundamental principle that linguistic politeness is a universal of language usage.

The negative side of politeness: linguistic politeness as a mask

Sell (1991: 208) discusses ways in which literary texts within a British socio-cultural framework may be considered polite. He suggests that in the Augustan age politeness "embraced intellectual enlightenment and civilization." A person in possession of these attributes in eighteenth-century Britain had access to the educated classes of society, which were virtually synonymous with the ruling elite. As Sell points out, politeness was inextricably linked to social class and socio-political power, so much so that those who did not cultivate politeness in their own individual styles of language usage were open to social stigmatisation and political persecution.

Smith (1984) gives us ample evidence of how non-conformity to the socially dominant style, which was essentially one of politeness, on the part of radicals and other political opponents of the establishment led, at least until the end of the Napoleonic Wars, to accusations of treason, to censorship, and to imprisonment. Throughout the fiction of the Victorian age there are also numerous reflections of the attitude that it was socially desirable to cultivate politeness. Politeness was a sign of good breeding and high social status, but it did not necessarily correlate with consideration for, and deference towards, other individuals.

If we scratch the surface of polite behaviour in the eighteenth century, we frequently encounter not only "inconsideration and irreligion" but also "positive selfishness, malevolence, evil" (Sell 1991: 210). In these circumstances:

> [...] polite manners would connote, not a refinement in feeling, but only the most sinister refinement in lying [...] (Sell 1991: 210)

Sell concludes the first stage of his argument as follows:

> [...] probably the best thing most people would say about politeness is that it is a social lubricant less nocuous than alcohol, probably useful, like free alcohol, for the *corps diplomatique*. Or, still more likely, that it is a velvet glove within which to hide one or another kind of iron fist [...] (1991: 211)

On the other hand, he is also quick to point out that we generally consider the term today in a much more favourable light, and he quotes *The English Theophrastus: or the manners of the age* (1702) as offering an early-eighteenth-century definition of the term which appears to link up with notions of conflict avoidance, appropriate verbal behaviour and avoidance or minimisation of face threatening, which, as we shall see, lie at the heart of most modem definitions:

> Politeness may be defined a dextrous management of our Words and Actions whereby men (sic!) make other people have a better Opinion of us and themselves. (1991: 108)

The definition in the *Theophrastus* reveals that politeness is a form of social behaviour encompassing both linguistic and non-linguistic activity; that it is a skill which, if acquired, is to be used in a rational, premeditated fashion to achieve very specific aims; that its principal aim is the enhancement of *ego's* self-esteem and his/her public status in the eyes of *alter* with a supplementary aim of enhancing *alter's* self-esteem (presumably, however, in the hope that it will indirectly be of use to *ego);* that it demands a subtle interpretation of the social context in which it is to be used.[1]

Let us compare the 1702 definition of politeness with a selection of those offered in the pragmalinguistic/sociolinguistic literature of the past fifteen years. Lakoff (1975: 64) interprets politeness as those forms of behaviour which have been "developed in societies in order to reduce friction in personal interaction." Whereas the 1702 definition referred specifically to English society (in all probability the educated classes of English society), Lakoff's definition indirectly claims universality. In doing so, however, the fundamentally egocentric aims of politeness, its subtle, premeditated application and the distinct possibility that it will be the verbal velvet glove to conceal the iron fist, are lost.

Leech (1983: 104) defines politeness as those forms of behaviour which are aimed at the establishment and maintenance of comity, i.e., the ability of participants in a socio-communicative interaction to engage in interaction in an atmosphere of relative harmony. The maxims which he suggests as part of a Politeness Principle to supplement Grice's Cooperative Principle, viz., Tact, Generosity, Approbation, Modesty, etc., may derive from an essentially British attitude towards politeness such as is evident in the 1702 definition. What is lacking, however, is, as in the case of Lakoff's definition, the basically egocentric nature of politeness behaviour. In addition, as Brown and Levinson (1987: 4) point out, if we need to posit new maxims every time we wish to explain how it is that interaction has nevertheless been carried out in an atmosphere of relative harmony, i.e., to account for the premeditated subtlety implied by the 1702 definition, we will simply end up with an infinite number of maxims, and the theory of politeness becomes vacuous.

Fraser and Nolen (1981: 96) suggest that politeness is the result of a conversational contract entered into by the participants in an effort to maintain socio-communicative verbal interaction conflict-free. Politeness is then nothing but a set of constraints on verbal behaviour. As in the case of Leech's theory, it is unclear how many constraints we will have to posit, since the nature of verbal interaction varies considerably with respect to the social setting, the participants, the goals of the interaction, the overall style of language to be employed, etc. (cf. Hymes 1972). Once again the basically egocentric nature of politeness is lost in this type of definition and the term becomes vacuous. The extent to which it can be emptied of virtually all content can be shown by a recent definition given by Braun (1988) in her work on terms of address, to which I return later, to the effect that politeness is evident wherever linguistic or non-linguistic behaviour is considered socially adequate. Braun's definition is derived directly from Fraser and Nolen's.

Brown and Levinson (1987), while not taking politeness to result from a set of pragmatic principles but rather from a more underlying need to minimise the imposition on the addressee arising from a verbal act and the consequent possibility of committing a face-threatening act, nevertheless understand it to refer to forms of behaviour which allow communication to take place between potentially aggressive partners (Brown and Levinson 1987: 1). Of all the modern definitions offered, at least we have a recognition by Brown and Levinson that the communicative partners might be potentially aggressive, i.e., that politeness could indeed be used as the velvet glove to soften the blow.

Inasmuch as they all agree that, whereas on the surface politeness may appear to fulfil altruistic goals, it is nevertheless a mask to conceal *ego*'s true frame of mind, these modern definitions of the term do not differ from the eighteenth-century definition. There is a clear difference, however, in the ends to which polite behaviour is put. For modern scholars the mask functions to avoid conflict, to tone down potential aggression, and to ensure that the interaction will be accomplished smoothly. For the cultivators of polite manners and good breeding in eighteenth-century England, the mask served a more important function, viz., to enhance their own social standing and signal their membership in an elitist social class. This could easily entail, and indeed often did entail (cf. Smith 1984), the conscious exclusion of would-be members or the outright persecution of out-groupers who opposed their claims to socio-political hegemony.[2]

This crucial difference with regard to the ends to which politeness could be put in the modern and the eighteenth century interpretations of the term gives rise to the following five important points:

(1) If within the modern framework linguistic politeness is claimed to be a universal of language usage, we must then conclude that all speech communities have linguistic ways and means at their disposal of masking less altruistic ends, i.e., of avoiding conflict and maintaining in a state of equilibrium the perceived fabric of interpersonal relationships. If within the early-eighteenth-century framework the same claim of universality is made, we are forced to the conclusion that all speech communities have at their disposal linguistic ways and means of enhancing *ego*'s social standing, of signalling membership in a social elite, and stigmatising and/or, if need be, persecuting non-members. Indeed, such linguistic ways and means may exist, but only on condition that the socio-cultural structure of the speech community ratifies them. Of the two conclusions arising from the claim of universality, the latter would be the more difficult to uphold. On the other hand, if the former can be upheld, we are forced to consider whether we are dealing in both cases with the same phenomenon of politeness.

(2) Conflict avoidance and maintaining the fabric of interpersonal relationships among the participants in a verbal interaction may indeed involve the use of many of the linguistic forms associated with the eighteenth-century concept of politeness. However, it is also true that the fabric of interpersonal relationships can equally well involve

several other types of linguistic behaviour not normally covered by the term "politeness", e.g., directly expressed orders, warnings, threats, etc., teasing, insulting, making statements that are open to interpretation as bald, on-record face threats, etc.[3] Put differently, all language usage may be interpreted in terms of whether or not the perceived fabric of interpersonal relationships is maintained. Conflict might be sought in certain types of social activity, e.g., political debates, discussion of controversial issues, quarrelling over personal rights and possessions, verbal duelling of various types, etc. The nature of the relationships engendered by the social activity may be opponential and antagonistic. Accordingly speech-event types will be required which give expression to confrontation and competition rather than collaboration and co-operation. Thus socially appropriate language usage can easily entail the very opposite of linguistic politeness. Here again we need a term which will cover the full range of linguistic behaviour which is deemed to be socially and culturally appropriate in any given social activity, and I shall argue that "politeness" will not do.

(3) In the eighteenth-century sense of the term, linguistic politeness is subject to changes in the overall structure of society through time. If the social constraints on politeness change, i.e., the features of that in-group which qualifies as the social elite of the age, so too will the forms of linguistic politeness. In this sense, rules of linguistic politeness are always regulative and ephemeral. They do not help to constitute the social group, but regulate membership to it and appropriate behaviour within it. Indeed, if the linguistic conditions for membership change radically such that cultivated gentility, polished manners, elegance, refinement, and neoclassical good taste are no longer desirable attributes for the aspiring in-group member, much of the validity for the term "politeness" will evaporate.

(4) The canon of politeness in the eighteenth century included ritualised forms of verbal behaviour which are commonly interpreted as forms of linguistic politeness in modern theories, e.g., appropriate ways of carrying out certain types of speech act such as thanking, complimenting, apologising, etc., appropriate speech events for initiating and closing an interaction (e.g., greeting, taking leave, closing a topic, etc.), terms of address and appropriate ways of displaying deference towards the addressee, etc. But the eighteenth-century canon included a much wider variety of features, e.g., the appropriate choice of lexemes (i.e., those which were taken as evidence for a neoclassical education and an awareness of good taste and current fashion), so-

cially acceptable topics for conversation, the appropriate relationship between talk and silence, between speaking and listening, socially appropriate ways of taking and relinquishing the floor, the avoidance of taboo topics, taboo lexemes, etc., the optimal length and structuring of turns at talk. All of these elements played a far greater role in helping the speaker to project "mental cultivation and polished manners, elegant refinement and neoclassical good taste" and "making other people have a better Opinion" of her/himself than ritualised verbal expressions, honorifics, and terms of address. Since all these elements formed part of a canon of politeness, we have a further reason for seeking another term which is more relevant to the discussion of the modern concept of linguistic politeness.

(5) Modern research on linguistic politeness phenomena has been carried out within a Western European/North American cultural framework which reaches back to the eighteenth-century paradigm at least with respect to its realisations and its masking function, although not with respect to its ends. Hence it has rightly been criticised for having a strong ethnocentric bias (cf. Ide 1989; Matsumoto 1989). However, we have seen that the eighteenth century paradigm was even more culture-specific in that it referred to the educated classes of society in England. Although it may have shared many features with similar behavioural codes in other European countries, we cannot be at all certain that an English native speaker today understands "politeness" in exactly the same way as the German native speaker understands "Höflichkeit" or the French native speaker "politesse". To give one small example, covert forms of linguistic politeness (I shall continue to use the term for the time being) include terms of address. These can be interpreted as linguistic forms which are not used in all cultures to mask *ego*'s real intentions and to enhance her/his social standing. Free terms of address, e.g., T (title) and TLN (title + last name), may be simply mandatory in accordance with certain specific features of the social activity such as social distance and dominance amongst the participants, the formality of the activity, etc., yet there is a surprising amount of variation even within Western European cultures. In Swiss German speech communities, for example, it is mandatory for a patient to address a medical doctor on consulting her/him as "Frau/Herr Doktor", but not as "Frau/Herr Doktor X" and for the doctor to return TLN (e.g., "Frau/Herr X") or T (e.g., "Herr Professor") to the patient. This is a case of socially adequate behaviour, but with none of the implications of the English eighteenth-

century politeness paradigm. Should we thus call these forms "polite"? In British culture, however, the patient may choose between T ("doctor"), TLN ("Doctor X"), the weaker form of TLN ("Ms/Mr X") or none at all. All four variants are socially adequate, but the choice of T or the stronger form of TLN might well be interpreted as a deliberate show of deference on the part of the patient. The choice of address term in British English culture is functionally significant from a social point of view, and the choice of T or TLN ("Doctor X") comes closer to the eighteenth-century politeness paradigm.

My conclusion from points (1)–(5) above is that we need to review our terminology and to introduce a more comprehensive notion from which politeness may be derived. The concept that I propose is that of "politic behaviour".

Linguistic politeness and politic verbal behaviour

If we take any strip of socio-communicative verbal interaction in any speech community within any culture, it is our job as ethnographers to discover what it is that allows that interaction to run smoothly such that socially significant meaning is engendered by and through it and what that meaning might be. It is also our job to locate points at which the pattern of meanings that we have constructed and from which we develop a set of expectations breaks down (cf. Agar 1986). Those points will be crucial for our understanding of how membership is defined in various social groups within the culture under scrutiny and how interpersonal relationships are negotiated, since they will present the interpretative model we are constructing with problems.

Let us now assume that the unmarked form of interaction, i.e., one without apparent breakdowns, is one in which balance is maintained in the structure of interdependent social relationships. In Watts (1989c) I have called the behaviour that one observes in these circumstances "politic behaviour" and defined it as "socio-culturally determined behaviour directed towards the goal of establishing and/or maintaining in a state of equilibrium the personal relationships between the individuals of a social group, whether open or closed, during the ongoing process of interaction" (p. 5). Such behaviour may of course be verbal or nonverbal. I have also suggested that the notion of "politic verbal behaviour" may be accounted for with Sperber and Wilson's theory of relevance, since it is behaviour which is aimed at ensuring that relevant contributions are made to the ongoing verbal interaction in the sense that Sperber and Wilson (1986) understand the term "relevant contribution". I shall not, however, elaborate on the interconnections here (see Watts 1989c).

The type of politic behaviour revealed by the verbal interaction must be assessed in accordance with the following five factors:

(1) the type of social activity in which the participants to the interaction are engaged (e.g., setting, communicative ends, institutionalised social relationships between the participants, degree of ratified membership in a social group, the open or closed character of the interpersonal network developed through the interaction, etc.);

(2) the speech events engaged in within that activity;

(3) the degree to which the participants share a common set of cultural expectations with respect to the social activity and the speech events making up part of that activity;

(4) the degree to which the participants share a common set of assumptions with respect to the information state (cf. Schiffrin 1987; Watts 1989a) within which the strip of interaction is developed;

(5) the social distance and dominance relationships in force between the participants prior to the interaction.

Two forms of marked behaviour may now be posited, one leading to communicative breakdowns and the other to an enhancement of *ego*'s standing with respect to *alter*, i.e., to "making other people have a better Opinion" of oneself. The first type of behaviour is "nonpolitic", the second, I contend, "polite". Thus what counts as polite behaviour depends entirely on those features of the interaction which are socio-culturally marked by the speech community as being more than merely politic. It is the ethnographer's job to define in accordance with at least the constraints listed under 1–5 above what counts as politic behaviour (if one so wishes, socially appropriate behaviour) and to identify and interpret stretches of interaction which include either breakdowns or enhancements.

Under this interpretation many of the strategies of positive and negative politeness suggested by Brown and Levinson will be explicable as socio-culturally determined politic behaviour. Similarly, the use of terms of address, honorifics, ritualised expressions and speech events, indirect speech acts, etc., all of which have been considered as examples of linguistic politeness, will only be interpretable as polite

forms if they go beyond their normal usage as socio-culturally constrained forms of politic behaviour, as I shall later show in the case of
terms of address. The honorific forms which are so ubiquitous in
Japanese and other Asian languages (cf. Koshal 1987) are lexicalised
and grammaticalised to such a high degree precisely because their use
depends crucially on *ego*'s perception of the total set of features in the
social activity which are relevant to the speech events of that activity,
as well as to the set of referents encoded in the speech events. As
Matsumoto (1989) points out, "[...] no utterance in Japanese can be
neutral with respect to the social context."

Hill et al. (1986) use the Japanese term *wakimae*, roughly translated as "discernment", to refer to "the almost automatic observation of
socially-agreed-upon rules" which apply to both verbal and non-verbal
behaviour into which Japanese children are socialised. Where no
choice between the use or non-use of honorifics exists for the
Japanese native speaker, it would be more adequate to consider such
grammaticalised forms as realisations of politic behaviour. Failure to
use them appropriately will clearly lead to breakdowns in the interaction, i.e., non-politic behaviour, which are in themselves meaningful.
In a situation in which form A is replaced by a higher form B when
form A would be adequate politic behaviour, we may well be justified
in considering form B a polite form, since the strategy of "volition"
has taken precedence over that of discernment. Thus, using Hill et
al.'s terminology, I will suggest that wherever volition supersedes
discernment in the choice of specific linguistic forms such as
honorifics, terms of address, ritualised expressions, etc., we are
dealing with politeness phenomena.

Linguistic universals and universals of language usage

Now that the scope of linguistic politeness has been narrowed down
by the introduction of a concept of "politic behaviour", let us consider
whether there is any warrant to claiming universality for it. Within the
field of theoretical linguistics two approaches have been made to the
question of linguistic universals. The first of these can be seen in
Greenberg (1963) and the second is contained in the whole of
Chomsky's work and that of the generative linguists who have
adopted and developed Chomsky's views.

The Greenbergian approach consists in comparing and contrasting linguistic systems in an effort to discover what types of linguistic structure are in evidence in the world's languages and what types of structure we may expect to see in language L given a certain configuration of structures which have already been ascertained. There is thus a tendency to consider the surface manifestations of a subset of languages, at whatever level of linguistic description one is seeking universals, although efforts have been made within the generative framework to establish common patterns at the level of deep structure (cf. Bach and Harms 1968). From the evidence gleaned through cross-linguistic investigations of this kind it is possible to set up linguistic typologies.[4] I shall henceforth refer to this approach as the typological approach.

The Chomskyan approach need not be considered as irreconcilable with the typological approach, although many disciples of Chomsky have claimed this to be so. Chomsky considers his form of generative linguistics to be an ongoing research project with the ultimate aim of reconstructing a Universal Grammar from which the grammar of all human languages may be derived. The universal principles he posits are, he maintains, ultimately biological and, although they are not open to observation, are empirically testable by pushing grammaticality as far as it will go and by entering the domain of non-grammaticality. The significant point about Chomskyan universals is that they are expressed as a bounded modular set of abstract principles which interact in a number of predictable ways to give core grammars, from which the languages of the world may be derived by means of setting linguistic parameters in various ways. The child's job is to discover from the input of linguistic data, on the basis of her/his innate Universal Grammar, to what core grammar the language s/he is acquiring belongs and what its parametric settings are. Hence, for Chomsky and his followers, linguistic universals are innate. This approach to linguistic universals I will henceforth label the underlying-principles approach.

In the light of these two approaches to universals in linguistic theory, let us now return to the question of what sort of universality might be meant in talking of "universals of language usage". We ought first, however, to consider what is meant by the term "language usage".

One way of interpreting it would be as the counterpart to Chomsky's notion of competence, i.e., as linguistic performance or the use of the individual's language capacity. This runs into difficulties as soon as we consider universal neuro-psychological constraints on performance. Chomsky (1963) and Chomsky and Miller (1963a) have gone into such problems in great detail, concluding that the investigation of performance constraints does not warrant a change in the generative paradigm of searching for the universals underlying competence. A great deal of psycholinguistic research has been carried out on language processing and monitoring (cf., for example, Fromkin 1973; Garrett, Bever and Fodor 1966; Prideaux 1984) which has also been of direct and indirect relevance to conversation analysis. Universals posited by this type of research have not been corroborated and are somewhat speculative. Some can even be shown to be the construct of a particular set of attitudes towards conversation into which we have doubtless been socialised, e.g., Jaffe and Feldstein's one-speaker-at-a-time principle (Jaffe and Feldstein 1970), which they maintain is a linguistic (sic!) universal.

We could interpret "language usage" to mean language in use or language used, which is not the same as equating it with performance. Whereas performance entails the performer so that the search for universals involves us in psycholinguistic research, language in use would seem to refer to the structure of language in a corpus of data and variations in that structure. Its study would thus belong to the domain of pragmatics and sociolinguistics. One universal here has a direct bearing on the validity of Chomsky's notion of competence, viz., that of a variable competence. The native speaker is believed to acquire a linguistic ability which enables her/him to make fine adjustments to linguistic structure in accordance with features of the social environment and the ongoing social activity (cf. Labov 1968, 1969b). This, however, is somewhat different from Chomsky's original notion of competence as an innate set of highly abstract principles from which the child must select the grammar of her/his language.

A further interpretation of language usage, and the one I believe to be Brown and Levinson's, is the use to which speakers, members of a socio-culturally defined group, put language, i.e., the symbolic value that both linguistic structures and also types of act carried out through language have in the culture concerned. The kind of competence with which we would be concerned here is thus communicative competence (cf. Hymes 1972a; Gumperz 1982).

Hence, if we return to the two approaches to linguistic universals and apply them analogously to this conception of language usage, the typological approach would consist in setting up typologies of the symbolic values that linguistic structures and speech acts have cross-culturally and making descriptive statements about similarities and differences. However, in politeness research this has often consisted of making the assumption that certain types of act are universal, e.g., thanking, complimenting, excusing, praising, etc., and of setting up typologies, which turn out to be little more than taxonomies, of the linguistic means by which native speakers may realise these cross-culturally. It has yet to be shown that such act types are universal.

The Chomskyan approach would aim to posit underlying principles of a more abstract nature, the parametric setting of which would result in subsets of symbolic values associated with interpersonal interaction patterns. The question as to whether such universals are innate is clearly an empirical one and does not lie within the domain of linguistics, but rather that of anthropology. Language usage can then be seen as one way in which such values can be encoded.

To show that this is Brown and Levinson's interpretation of universals of language usage, I shall now concentrate on the remarks that they make in their introduction to the new edition of their seminal monograph (Brown and Levinson 1987: 45–47) on the possibility of setting up a theory of a universal "symbolism of exchange". Following Malinowksi (1923) they suggest that the interpersonal rituals involving the exchange of goods (whether concrete or abstract) are founded in the familial, or kinship, domain. The more sacred, i.e., symbolically charged, the goods are, the more elaborate these rituals will be, and the most sacred thing that can be exchanged is "the social person". Moreover, the elaborateness of the ritual will also depend on the relationships of dominance and social distance between the receiver and the giver (cf. point 5 in the previous section), such that what Brown and Levinson call "intimate stuff" (their example being cooked food in Tamil society) may only be exchanged where dominance and/or social distance are minimal. Dominance is an asymmetric relationship, such that the person with higher social status may give "intimate stuff" (e.g., the cooked food) whereas the person with lower social status must respond by giving "non-intimate stuff" (e.g., services). On the other hand, social distance is a symmetric relationship such that both partners to the interpersonal interaction are expected to exchange "intimate stuff" when the distance is minimal but "non-intimate stuff" when it is great. In exchanging certain types of goods, dominance will take precedence over social distance, whereas for other types of goods the reverse will be the case. The balance between the two may be somewhat delicate in certain cultures.

If we now assume that in exchanging social persons, i.e., in engaging in social interaction, which in a very large number of cases will involve engaging in speech events, the individual is concerned with the projection of self, then there will be a potentially endless number of ways in which the sacred nature of the social person can be symbolised, one of the most obvious being either in the forms of language used in speech events or in the ways in which those speech events are negotiated (cf. points 1 and 2 of the previous section). A wide variety of extralinguistic acts (which may involve the use of language for their negotiation) will also be symbolically significant. I shall hypothesise that interpersonal relationships within the family in all cultures are governed (a) by what is considered to be "intimate stuff" and (b) by the ways in which exchange of "intimate stuff" is correlated with dominance and social distance. Forms of language and ways in which language is used to carry out certain types of act and to establish and consolidate perceived interpersonal relationships, i.e., forms of politic behaviour, reveal both the "intimate stuff" and the dominance/social distance settings.

I should now like to suggest that, if it can be shown that certain types of linguistic form exist in all languages and across all cultures to symbolise the sacred nature of the social person, then we are involved in setting up typological universals of language usage. The linguistic forms themselves may be grammaticalised or lexicalised as honorifics, bound forms of address (e.g., within the pronominal and verbal systems), etc., or formulaic forms (e.g., free forms of address such as kinship terms, titles, names, terms of endearment, etc.), and set structures to carry out specific types of ritualised speech act such as thanking, greeting, etc. Such structures have often been said to reveal politeness, and inasmuch as they are across-the-board phenomena, we are justified in considering the linguistic realisation of politeness as one type of universal within language usage. However, I shall argue that in accordance with the definition of politic behaviour given in the previous section, they do not in themselves constitute politeness. Used inappropriately or with the deliberate intent to disrupt the structure of interpersonal relationships, they are interpretable as realisations of non-politic behaviour.

If, on the other hand, it can be shown that the structure of verbal interaction is equivalent to negotiating ways in which the sacred nature of each individual social person can be projected whilst preserving the coherence and equilibrium of the social group, then the search for universals of language usage will lie at a deeper level and will consist in determining the underlying nature of "intimate stuff" and its interaction with notions of social distance and dominance in the culture being investigated. Such universals are more akin to Chomskyan linguistic universals than those of Greenberg, although any discussion of abstract sets of principles and constraints and any suggestion that such principles are innate must be avoided at this point.

Brown and Levinson's way of considering politeness is more compatible with the underlying-principles approach to universals of language usage than the typological approach. Their notion of "face", derived from the work of Erving Goffman, is clearly equivalent to the sacred nature of the social person, and although some of the linguistic means for carrying out strategies of positive and negative politeness are grammaticalised and/or formulaic, the great majority are techniques for carrying out potentially face-threatening acts indirectly (e.g., by minimising and maximising the explicit meaning of what is said), expressing solidarity with the hearer, bolstering up the latter's positive face when carrying out an act which threatens her/his negative face, etc. The linguistic means for negotiating the interaction along these lines are very varied even within one speech community. Across a wide selection of speech communities variability becomes even greater. Techniques of minimisation, maximisation, indirectness, solidarity display, etc., may appear to be similar, but even if we could show a high degree of cross-cultural agreement, the search for universals must surely take us to underlying, non-linguistic principles.

For this reason the notion of "politic behaviour" has been suggested to account for the insight that all verbal interaction involves the negotiation of the coherence and equilibrium of the social group, within which the sacred nature of the social person can be projected. When politic behaviour is governed more by social distance and dominance than by the exchange of "intimate stuff", grammaticalised honorifics and address forms, formulaic expressions, ritualised and semi-ritualised indirect speech acts, conventionalised means of face-threat minimisation and the maximisation of the addressee's positive face, solidarity display, etc., will be explicit in language usage. However, only when such structures represent the attempt by *ego*, for whatever reason, to enhance her/his social standing with respect to *alter* may they more profitably be called realisations of politeness. Hence politic behaviour, which is culturally determined and is "generated" from underlying universal principles, is transformed into polite behaviour under certain marked social conditions. It is an empirical question whether and/or where the one becomes the other in the speech community under investigation.

It follows from this discussion of the nature of the universals of language usage involved in the phenomenon of politeness that two lines of research may be followed, and have been followed, one concerned with the explicit linguistic encoding of social distance and dominance relationships in the negotiation of exchanging "intimate stuff" (most notably of the social person) in ritualised expressions and honorific forms, and the other concerned with ways in which the linguistic system may be used to symbolise the underlying changing nature of that exchange. The first approach, the typological approach, resembles research of the Greenbergian type whereas the second, the underlying-principles approach, entails the search for deeper underlying principles of socio-cultural organisation and is thus somewhat akin to the Chomskyan programme. I should stress, however, that neither approach excludes the other and a great deal of cross-fertilisation has been in evidence over the past twenty years.

Terms of address as realisations of politic behaviour and politeness

Previous to the work of Robin Lakoff the study of politeness in relation to language was largely the domain of those concerned with terms of address (cf. Braun 1988) and honorifics. Significantly, the former area of investigation has also appealed to psychologists (cf. Wundt 1922; Silverberg 1940), sociologists (cf. Kiddle 1953), and anthropologists (cf. Law 1948). Interest in the latter has been stimulated by more intensive study of those languages in which status and distance markers are encoded grammatically (e.g., Jain 1969 for Hindi; Harada 1976 and Ide 1982 for Japanese; Koshal 1987 for Ladakhi).

Braun (1988) documents extensively the continuity of interest in linguistic forms of address across a wide variety of languages, an interest which was stimulated by the realisation that forms of address are correlated highly with the parameters of dominance and social distance in all speech communities in which they form part of the linguistic system. They can thus be investigated cross-culturally as typological universals, and Braun's work is a good example of the wealth of important data which can be provided in doing so.

She reviews work by Brown and Gilman (1960) and Brown and Ford (1964), who focussed attention on the sociological parameters essential to the notion of politeness in address terms, although the term "politeness" was hardly referred to explicitly. Stress was placed in these early sociolinguistic studies of address forms on the distinction between T (*tu*) and V (*vous*) forms in pronominal systems as markers of the interdependence between power, distance, and dominance. However, the complexity of the interplay of relationships which will give rise to a T or a V form in any one given language was not fully investigated across a wide range of languages (cf. Braun 1988: ch.1).

Brown and Levinson (1987: 45) point out that both bound pronominal terms of address and free forms (e.g., titles, names, terms of endearment, etc.) are linguistic realisations of "intimate" and "non-intimate stuff" which depend crucially on underlying configurations of social distance and dominance. Those forms, bound or free, which are considered non-intimate are then classified as polite, politeness thus being the means by which the socio-cultural constraints on the exchange of social persons, or face, in interpersonal interaction can be signalled.

There are a number of problems with this assumption, however. All too often forms of address are simply equated with politeness (cf. Braun 1988; Braun and Schubert 1986) without any attempt being made to explain why. In other words, the research remains purely typological. For example, Braun merely suggests that politeness is a form of socially adequate behaviour (1988: 50), basing her argument on Fraser and Nolen's concept of a conversational contract constraining the behaviour of the participants in a verbal interaction. If both (or all) the participants abide by the rules of that contract, they are said to be acting "politely". Violation of the rules results in impolite behaviour (Fraser and Nolen 1981: 96). However, the crucial questions (What are the terms of that contract? How are they linked to the exchange of "intimate stuff" under conditions of social distance and dominance? and: How do members of a social group know when the contract has been broken?) remain unanswered. Instead of focusing on such underlying principles, Braun directs her attention to the assessment of which linguistic features make the linguistic forms themselves polite. A taxonomy of linguistic forms such as that set up by Altmann and Riska (1966) is felt to be a more valuable starting point for the encoding of politeness through address forms.

Without denying the validity of setting up linguistic taxonomies of forms of address, honorifics, and formulaic expressions as ways of encoding politeness, I would nevertheless suggest that investigations of language usage, in the sense that I have defined the term in the previous section, irrevocably lead the linguist into interdisciplinary research involving anthropologists, sociologists and sociolinguists. Braun herself mentions the difficulties in setting up the kind of rules that Brown and Gilman and Brown and Ford propose when we try to apply them cross-culturally, viz., that T forms, first names, terms of endearment and certain kinship terms are used to express "intimacy, juniority, low social status, or inferiority" whereas V forms and titles are used to express "distance, seniority, high social status, or superiority" (Braun 1988: 35). The tendency to vary sociolectally from intimate to non-intimate forms is, as she points out, by no means universal:

> Firstly, there are group-specific variants which do not fit into a gradation of intimate and distant, low and high status (e.g., the Finnish dialectal V *hän*, Tigrinya regional use of a V_2 variant), and secondly, this tendency is dependent on the stage of development in the respective address system. (1988: 36)

The apparent anomalies may be resolved if we are prepared to question the typological assumption that non-intimate forms encode politeness, presumably by virtue of showing deference, respect, etc., while intimate forms are not marked for encoding politeness. It is more profitable to consider both forms of language usage as realisations of politic behaviour and then to investigate the interplay of factors suggested in the third section of this chapter which give rise to them.

Let us postulate that in social interaction the display of deference and/or respect for the addressee is a verbal exchange of non-intimate stuff. In other words the addresser explicitly honours the sacred nature of the addressee's social person, or positive and/or negative face, when the parameters of social distance and dominance in the social activity are so set as to require this explicit verbal display.

If we take this to be a sociolinguistic rule, then there will be certain cultures in which it is constitutive, i.e., in which appropriate behaviour, verbal or non-verbal, is defined by the rule itself. As I noted in the third section, Hill et al. (1986) and Ide (1989) use the Japanese term *wakimae* to refer to the nature of this type of constitutive rule, and they translate it into English as "discernment". It should therefore come as no surprise that the complex honorific system of Japanese can be taken as grammaticalised and/or lexicalised (see also Matsumoto 1989), and that Japanese children acquire the system in the process of (a) acquiring their mother tongue and (b) being socialised into Japanese culture. In other cultures, however, the rule will be less constitutive and more regulative, i.e., participants in verbal interaction must decide how they wish to treat their own and their addressee's social person in order to judge the appropriateness of the explicit verbal display. Hill et al. (1986) and Ide (1989) suggest the term "volition" to refer to the nature of the rule.

Free terms of address in British English

Let us for the moment take Braun seriously when she suggests that politeness is nothing more or less than socially appropriate behaviour. This being so, the appropriate verbal exchange of intimate and non-intimate stuff will always be interpretable as polite behaviour. Two reasons can now be suggested for terms of address which do not appear to abide by the rules set up by Brown and Gilman and Brown and Ford. Either there exist certain settings of the social distance and dominance parameters resulting in clashes which can be resolved by the marked exchange of intimate stuff or non-intimate stuff, or participants in the verbal interaction have the freedom to reset the parameters as they deem fit. In this latter case we are confronted with Hill and Ide's volition culture. But in both cases it is necessary to study in detail the underlying socio-cultural factors to determine what constitutes polite behaviour.

What I have suggested, however, is that socially appropriate behaviour is in fact politic behaviour and not polite behaviour, and that terms of address are realisations of politic behaviour. The conditions under which certain terms of address are more appropriate than others need to be discerned just as much in a socio-cultural setting like the one from which I will take my examples (British English) as in socio-cultural settings like those in Japan, Ladakh, Korea, and other Asian countries. An incorrect assessment of the relevant socio-cultural factors, whether deliberate or not, can lead to interpretations of non-politic behaviour, i.e., to the wrong handling of intimate stuff and the violation of *alter*'s social person (or face). A correct assessment of the relevant socio-cultural factors and a deliberately over-politic, or enhanced, use of address terms, once again whether deliberate or not, can lead to interpretations of politeness.

Five examples may serve to illustrate the need for interpretation of an ethnographic type in order to get below the surface to the underlying principles. The examples are taken from a British English framework, since it is easier for me to judge what is going on. The social activity is a local radio phone-in programme in the North of England (BBC Radio Manchester) in which listeners may phone in and put questions on a specific topic to the programme moderator and an expert, who has been invited to participate. In so-called "open-line" programmes the moderator invites topics for discussion without the presence of an expert.

The setting is a radio studio in which the moderator and expert hear the incoming caller and are able to communicate with her/him by telephone. In (1) and (2) the participants are the moderator, the expert, and the caller (who are active) and a radio audience of a few hundred thousand (who are passive). The moderator CW has invited a former famous snooker and billiard player JC to talk about the sport(s), his experiences and to answer callers' questions. Prior to (1), JC has made a humorous remark about grandmothers enjoying the game and knowing the rules. Extracts (3) and (4) are taken from an open-line phone-in, in which only the moderator D is present in the studio. Listeners are invited to call and suggest topics for discussion. In (3) Mrs George is the first caller of the programme, Mr Severn in (4) the second. Extract (5) is taken from a phone-in in which the moderator M, a woman, is accompanied in the studio by an expert on questions about health and social security, A. Mrs W is their first caller. All occurrences of address terms are in bold type:

(1) 1 CW: E from Mosstown is our next caller. Good morning **E**.[5]
     2 E: Good morning **J**.
     3 JC: Good morning **dear**.⌈
     4 E: I had to- I had to laugh when you
     5   said about the grandmas with their knitting saying "Oh
     6   he- he's potted a red. He's :er(0.8): colour." I might
     7   tell you a lot of the old grandmas know the count. They

8   know how many th-there is for a red and for a black
9   and a blue etce⌈tera, and (0.9) a lot of the old grandmas
10 CW: ⌊I should think they do. My Mum does.
11   are waiting for the snooker to come on.

(2)   1 CW: Our next caller is M from Prestwich. Good morning **M**.
     2 M: Good morning **me dear**.
     3 CW: "My dear" [laugh⌈ing] How very nice of you to say that!
     4 J: ⌊Good morning **M** [laughing].
     5 CW: What would you like to ask?

(3)   1 D: Welcome **Mrs George**.
     2 G: Hello **Mr Hatch**.
     3 D: How do you do **madam**. Don't be formal. Dick's the name.
     4 G: Yes I know, and I prefer Richard.
     5 D: Oh. Right.Well you c– ⌈[laughing] you call me Richard.
     6 G: ⌊[laughter]
     7 G: I think when you've got a nice name like Richard, why they
     8   call you Dick I'll never know.
     9 D: Well d'you know, privately I entirely agree with you,
    10   but when you've been called Dick as long as I have because
    11   your family started it, there's no point in arguing really.
    12 G: No. Quite.
    13 D: However, you carry on.

(4)   1 D: Now I think we've got Mr Severn on. Have we?
     2 S: Good morning **Richard**.
     3 D: Hello **sir**.
          1.1
     4 S: :erm(0.8): I'd like to talk about :er(1.0): a progra/
     5   :er(0.9): an article on *Newsnight* last night.

(5)   1 M: ...and we've got on the line Mrs W. Hello **Mrs W**.
     2 W: Good afternoon.
     3 M: Would you like to put your query⌈ to A?
     4 W: ⌊Yes I would. :er(0.8): I'll
     5   make it as brief as possible.
     6 M: That's all right **me love**.

In (1) the caller is referred to by her first name, E, when the moderator, CW, informs the wider radio audience who the next caller is. In addition, he addresses her as E. She does not answer his greeting, which in any other circumstances may be interpreted as a face-threatening act. However, E is an elderly lady, possibly a little hard of hearing and in all probability believes that she is being addressed by the expert, to whom she wishes to put a question. She addresses him by his first name and is addressed in turn by a term of endearment. How are we to interpret this strip of interaction? The free term of address that we might reasonably expect is TLN (title [Mr, Mrs, or Ms] and surname). We appear to be confronted with a breakdown in the coherent pattern of address terms in English. After all, the occasion is public, the medium is non-visual, and we can assume that E has never previously met either CW or JC. Social distance is therefore great. How are we to resolve the breakdown, given the fact that the participants themselves display no signs of loss of face? On the contrary, they appear to be behaving appropriately, i.e., to be displaying politic behaviour.

With respect to the dominance parameter, explicit social status does not seem to play a role. None of the participants is ranked institutionally higher than any of the others (to the best of their knowledge, that is). Hence we must assume that the participants perceive themselves to be equals. CW certainly has the power to allow E to participate in the programme and, as a resource person, JC is also in a more powerful position. However, power need not always be equated with social status. The only perception of higher social status which might conceivably play a role in this strip of interaction is that JC is a well-known public figure.

The apparent breakdown can be resolved by reference to the five factors given in the third section, according to which verbal behaviour can be considered politic. The programme is aimed at creating an in-group identity for moderator, expert and callers at least for the duration of the programme. The purpose of the social activity is to allow listeners to participate actively in the programme and thereby to identify with their local radio station. Any caller accepted for the programme must therefore be prepared to act as a member of the perceived in-group, i.e., to act as if there were no social distance between the members. The feeling for membership is increased by the fact that the moderator varies his language to suit the incoming callers. In the case of a programme on snooker and billiards this is in fact quite easy. Even if the callers signal their social-class membership linguistically as middle class, interest in snooker and billiards shows a realignment to a traditionally working class sport. Evidence for this is provided a little later in the programme when JC suggests that prior to snooker's sudden popularity on television "if you were anything of a player, it was a sign of a misspent youth."

Hence, given a situation in which neither social dominance nor social distance are significant, the exchange of verbal intimate stuff in the form of first names and terms of endearment is appropriate behaviour and is therefore politic. This does not of course mean that it is not open to any of the participants to use terms of address which display deference and respect. To do so, however, would be to engage in over-politic, i.e., overtly polite, verbal behaviour. Rules controlling address terms in English are subject to a complex interplay of socio-cultural constraints (cf. 1–5 in the third section) such that native speakers need to exercise their powers of discernment in order to choose the socially appropriate term of address as much as Japanese native speakers need to be able to discern the features of the social context which will motivate the correct choice of honorific forms. Hill et al. and Ide are thus correct in suggesting that politeness in this type of culture is determined by strategies of volition. I would, however, suggest that the same is true of verbal politeness in Japanese, given the definition of politeness offered earlier. More importantly, the decision as to what makes a particular term of address polite is not made by equating forms displaying deference, etc., with politeness, but by taking an underlying principles approach to universals of language usage and investigating how terms of address contribute to politic verbal behaviour.

Extract (2) is an interesting example of how the participants' shared cultural expectations with respect to both the social activity and the speech events that make up that activity, as well as to their shared assumptions concerning the information state may be manipulated to create humour. FN (first name) address and terms of endearment have been accepted by the participants as politic behaviour, but up to this point in the interaction only CW and J have made use of the privilege. M is the first caller to address the moderator with a term of endearment – *me dear*. CW promptly refers to the term by producing the exclamation *How nice of you to say that!*, which appears to represent a breach in our expectations within this strip of verbal interaction. The anomaly of the exclamation can be resolved by interpreting it as deliberate over-politic, hence polite, verbal behaviour. In addition, CW prefaces the exclamation with laughter in order to forestall any interpretation of the utterance as self-enhancement or *alter*-enhancement. Note that J also overlaps CW's ironically intended polite verbal behaviour with laughter and a return to the politic strategy of FN address.

Extracts (3) and (4) are further examples of a moderator manipulating the socially appropriate terms of address for humorous effect, although his behaviour in (4) creates a temporary communicative breakdown. The two extracts should be considered together, since the pattern of verbal behaviour established through the interaction between the moderator and the first caller is carried over to the greeting sequence between the moderator and the second caller, Mr Severn.

Disregarding the parameter of social dominance, as we did for extracts (1) and (2), we are left with the observation that perceived social distance is the parameter which governs the exchange of non-intimate stuff in the form of TLN address terms. The verbal behaviour displayed by both D and G in lines 1–2 is in keeping with those features of the social context which have been discerned as appropriate, hence politic, for the social activity. In line 3, however, the moderator enhances the term of address to *madam*, thus transforming it into a clear indicator of polite rather than merely politic verbal behaviour whilst at the same time encouraging her to disregard the social distance parameter and address him informally – *Don't be formal. Dick's the name.*

How is this strip of interaction to be interpreted? The two parts of his turn at line 3, the reciprocated greeting and the admonishment not to be formal, contradict each other, such that the enhancement of *ego*'s standing in the eyes of *alter* can hardly be achieved through the polite term *madam*. There is, however, a wider audience of radio listeners to consider. What type of "opinion" (using the term used in the 1702 definition) would he like that audience to form of him?

While radio phone-in programmes clearly serve the purpose of imparting information to the audience in response to questions from individual callers, they also have the function of entertaining that audience. In open-line phone-ins this function takes precedence over the imparting of information. Part of the moderator's reputation is the extent to which she/he entertains and amuses her/his audience, and the effect is often achieved at the expense of individual callers. Hence, the address term *madam* is polite in that it is uttered with an ulterior motive in mind, albeit not with respect to the caller herself. This is an excellent example of the masking function of politeness, or even of what Sell calls the "velvet glove to hide the iron fist". G interprets the moderator's move in precisely this way but is quick to react with her evaluation *I prefer Richard*. Moderator and caller resolve the breakdown with laughter and then go on to negotiate each other's reasons for preferring the full name *Richard* to the nickname *Dick* before moving on to the topic which the caller wishes to raise.

In extract (4) the second caller tries to capitalise (a) on the invitation to use FN terms of address and (b) on the previously negotiated form *Richard*. His assumption, a reasonable one in the circumstances, is that this style of address in the greeting sequence is part of the appropriate, hence politic, verbal behaviour for the social activity in question. The moderator, however, uses the same tactic as in (3). He reverts to an over-politic, hence polite, term of address – *sir*. Let us assume that Mr Severn has heard the strip of interaction between D and G and that he has interpreted the greeting sequence, as we have here, as the creation of humour for the benefit of the wider audience but at the expense of the caller her/himself. Confirmation of these assumptions is provided by the significant inter-turn silence of 1.1 seconds before he begins to introduce his topic, by the filled pause at the beginning of his turn and by the evident difficulty he experiences in structuring the turn. He displays clear signs of confusion, arising perhaps from the face-threatening nature of D's switch to a polite term of address. Significantly, the ensuing interaction between caller and moderator is characterised by tension and opposition.

Taken together, extracts (3) and (4) are good examples of terms of address used deliberately to enhance *ego*'s standing in the eyes of the addressees, i.e., as polite verbal behaviour used in its masking function. In both extracts the moderator made use of the strategy of volition rather than discernment, but the resultant interaction was not in each case conflict-free. In (3) the caller herself was responsible for the re-establishment of harmonious interpersonal relationships, whereas in (4) neither the moderator nor the caller were able to reinstate an atmosphere of harmony in the strip of interaction ensuing from the greeting sequence. Apparently, the establishment of the appropriate type of politic verbal behaviour for local radio phone-ins is largely dependent on the use of address terms in the reciprocal greeting at the beginning of each new section of the overall social activity.

A similar situation is in evidence in (5), in which the first caller is addressed by TLN (*Hello Mrs W*). The caller, however, does not include an address term in her greeting, thereby opening up a possible interpretation of non-politic verbal behaviour. The brusque, although socially appropriate way of inviting the caller to put her question to the expert may be evidence that this is how the moderator has interpreted

Mrs W. But when the latter, clearly confused, intervenes, pauses and then apparently indulges in apologetic behaviour – *I'll make it as brief as possible* – M simply reinterprets the situation as one in which the caller, who is in need of help and advice, is insecure, nervous, and possibly a little embarrassed at having to air her problems in as public a social activity as a radio phone-in programme. The choice of a term of endearment, interpretable as the exchange of intimate stuff, signals a narrowing of social distance and dominance and is an indicator of solidarity towards the caller.

In this way, Mrs W is given verbal confirmation that she is an accepted member of a perceived in-group for the duration of the programme. The exchange of verbal intimate stuff thus represents politic behaviour in establishing the requisite form of interpersonal relationship for the purposes of the activity. However, the moderator has to make use of her powers of discernment rather than volition to arrive at the correct inferences.

Conclusion

We may conclude from this brief analysis of address terms used in local radio phone-in programmes that within the framework of British English culture they may reveal either politic or polite verbal behaviour. The exchange of address terms can be considered as the exchange of verbal intimate or non-intimate stuff, but the correct choice of one over another depends on how the participants to the interaction interpret the social distance and dominance relations valid for the stretch of social activity in which they are engaged and the types of speech event they produce.

Part of the speaker's communicative competence will be an ability to interpret the complex of features in the social event which determine one term of address in preference to another. It is thus reasonable to suggest that this aspect of communicative competence into which individuals have been socialised is in fact discernment and that it is just as operative in British English (and other Western European and North American cultures) as it is in Japanese. As we have seen, it is less automatic than the grammaticalised and lexicalised forms of politic behaviour in evidence in the Japanese system of honorifics. In fact it requires ongoing interpretation of the verbal interaction and the fabric of interpersonal relationships created or maintained and strengthened through it.

Nevertheless it can be argued that the values set in accordance with a number of social anthropological parameters such as social dominance, social status, power, and social distance both inside and outside the dominant kinship structure will determine when the exchange of verbal intimate and non-intimate stuff, i.e., the exchange of social persons (or the mutual respect of face), represents politic verbal behaviour.

The claim of universality is, I maintain, only valid at this level. To put it another way, we might begin by asking ourselves what discernment consists of for the culture under investigation. Answering the question entails the application of a universal-principles approach to universality in the attempt to explain how it is that speakers are able to interpret features of the social activity in order to engage in socially appropriate verbal interaction, or politic verbal behaviour.

The definition of linguistic politeness offered in this chapter sees it as a marked extension or enhancement of politic verbal behaviour, as a conscious choice of linguistic forms which, in accordance with the dictates of the time and fashion, are conventionally understood to be an attempt on the part of *ego* to enhance her/his standing with respect to *alter* – for whatever reason. It is thus not deviant behaviour; it is not in other words non-politic. However, it is certainly marked, and its functions may easily be non-altruistic and clearly egocentric. In this understanding of the term I hesitate to suggest that linguistic politeness is a universal of language usage, unless it can be shown typologically that every culture makes use of volitional strategies of marked *ego*-centric politic behaviour. Perhaps the burden of proof lies on those working within a typological paradigm.

Notes

1. This is interpretable from the noun phrase *a dextrous management*.
2. Smith's examples of victimisation range from Thomas Paine through John Horn Tooke and others to William Cobbett.
3. Cf. Brown and Levinson (1978, 1987) for definitions of these terms.
4. Cf., for example, the work of Hansjakob Seiler in the "Kölner Universalien-projekt".
5. Full names will not be given in extracts (1), (2) and (5).

3. On the historicity of politeness*

Konrad Ehlich

> 'Hat doch Takt seine genaue historische Stunde.'
> Adorno (1944: section 16)

1. Politeness as a universal concept

There are few social phenomena of significance that have the mark of their own historicity so indelibly etched into the terms used to refer to them as – in various languages – politeness. In German, e.g., the term *Höflichkeit*, which refers to the locus of its genesis, the *Hof* ('court'), is a living reminder of the conditions which gave rise to it. Indeed, the German word can hardly be uttered without invoking those conditions. The term 'court' itself also has a clear historical foundation.

There is a second term, taken from the Latin, that was used alongside *Höflichkeit*, viz. *urbanitas* ('urbanity'). The particular *urbs* ('city') that it referred to was Rome, which was the unique image of and pattern for the city in the Western world. It is not, as in later times, the court with its way of life and its social demands which determines the image of politeness in this case, but the big city, its way of life and its social demands. Carrying out politeness in a humanistic framework evokes such historical connections, and they, in turn, call up the image of the city.

To repeat my point, it is seldom that words display such a direct mark of the circumstances surrounding that which they denote. They are seldom so saturated with historical experience, and we only need to lift off the lid of the self-evident to find that mark.

But even such historical clarity cannot counterbalance the present-day verdicts of historical forgetfulness. Discourse on politeness exalts politeness to the level of a *philosophia practica perennis*. It assumes the permanence and timelessness of a *conduite de l' homme*, which today is usually given the label "universal". In the process and practice

* The author expresses his deep gratitude to Richard J. Watts for his translation of the original German text of this chapter. The texts from German sources have also been translated by Richard J. Watts: they have not been taken from "official" English versions.

of this type of labelling the historical quality of that very label is also suppressed.

Of course, the process of forgetting and making others forget profits from the very varied etymological transparency of words, the ease with which the traces that their genesis has endowed them with can be wiped out. And among the European languages there are, of course, also those whose widely used expressions for the phenomenon of politeness do not allow us to recognise precisely this historical dimension. Unfortunately, the English language is one of these, i.e., that very language which is at present most widely used in scientific discourse. It is true that by way of French it possesses the terms *courteous*, *courtesy* and *courtliness*, in which the connection with *court* is as obvious as it is, e.g., in German. But the common term for the German *Höflichkeit* and the French *courtoisie* is *politeness*, which is derived from very different sources. Thus in English clues towards taking up historical connections are not present in everyday language usage.

2. Politeness: phenomena, expressions and conceptualisations

At this point we hit upon a complex problem, one of those which has received very little attention in modern linguistics, viz. the relationship between expressions, "meanings" and the states of affairs denoted by them, in particular in their respective historical dimensions. A progressive shift of focus away from this area of study and, as a consequence, its virtual elimination, marked the beginning of the modern science of language (Saussure's shift from diachrony to synchrony). Thus, although the etymological transparency of certain languages points towards historical connections, others are not amenable to this approach. However, we should not let this prevent us from following up etymological clues. On the other hand, for my present purpose, it is wise to consider first which aspects of this area of research are immediately relevant here.

If we take this approach, the following aspects can be distinguished:

(a) There are various types of *term* in use in important European languages for the phenomenon of politeness.

(b) Some of these terms contain transparent clues concerning the historical *constitutive* constraints for the phenomenon of politeness.

(c) Other terms from which it is not possible to derive such clues are due to other aspects of the phenomenon of politeness and implicitly refer to them.

(d) It is relatively easy to reconstruct the terms referring to the phenomenon of politeness and in this way to set up semantic units for each case.

(e) The phenomenon of politeness does not exist, as it were, "in and of itself", independent of its network of semantic connections. The terms themselves are part of, an expression of, stabilising factors of co-occurring *concepts of politeness*.

(f) Concepts of politeness should not be made automatically coterminous with the phenomenon of politeness. At the same time, however, it should be pointed out that politeness is not independent of such concepts. It is not a natural entity, but one which has evolved historically, or, to be more precise, one that has been *constructed historically*. Concepts of politeness are thus an integral part of politeness itself, of its history, its evolution, its development and its historical implementation.

(g) The *conceptualisations* of politeness developed in scientific research should be distinguished from the *phenomenon* of politeness and *concepts* of politeness that exist in a society. Scientific conceptualisations make use of everyday expressions to define politeness, and they very often do so in a completely unquestioning, matter-of-fact way, in other words – unscientifically. In many cases the relationship between these conceptualisations and the phenomenon that they examine remains unexplained.

(h) The conceptualisations of science are at one and the same time an integral part of the social debate about and the social appropriation of the phenomenon of politeness. Thus, they are in themselves subject to that same historicity which is characteristic of politeness – and which in general they seek to eliminate. In turn this state of affairs is itself worthy of analytic interest.

The aspects referred to thus far are linguistic and intellectual, and they concern expressions, concepts and conceptualisations. Quite clearly, we are confronted with a very complex picture, which, on the one hand, is determined by the problematic and scarcely penetrable relationship between words and concepts and between both of these and the entities they are meant to represent. On the other hand, an additional complexity arises from the fact that the phenomenon itself is social. Nor are the concepts and conceptualisations located beyond this social sphere. They are not meta-concepts, not those independent instances accessible to and fostering reflection, a reflection that would allow a detached analytical examination of the phenomenon itself. Rather, they are themselves part of that selfsame historical and social process, a specific sub-section of which they are required to understand and/or investigate.

This constellation of factors is characteristic for the hermeneutic process: that which could be and ought to be the *explicans* is at one and the same time the *explicandum*, but is only revealed through the progressive process of understanding the *explicandum*. The constellation is made even more complex by the object of study itself. The phenomenon of politeness has been assumed to be, as it were, self-evident. Understanding it has not been thought to be problematic, and the object of study is taken to be generally accessible. But it would be obviously and openly naive to accept this point of view. In addition, we cannot simply decide on what constitutes the phenomenon of politeness. On the contrary, the language-bound nature of the concept is revealed by our understanding of what is to be evaluated as polite. This set of problems can be seen both within individual speech communities and in the contrastive analysis of expressions, concepts and the phenomenon itself across speech communities.

We cannot simply escape from "language-boundedness". It is itself a constraint on our identifying the object of study. So the need for a hermeneutic approach, the unavoidable surrender to the movement of the "hermeneutic spiral", is merely strengthened by the social nature of the object of study, and overcoming the hermeneutic dilemma is only possible if we give ourselves up to it. It can only be researched from within, not from some seemingly external position.

For the phenomenon of politeness two aspects in particular are relevant. Two things are understood as "polite" in the actions of the interactants: (1) the specific status of socially developed regularities of action; (2) going beyond that which is socially required within the framework of these regularities.

In effect both (1) and (2) can only be recognised through a comparative approach. An action only appears polite when it fulfils a specific constitutive status of social intercourse in comparison with other groups (1). In the case of the individual, on the other hand, an action appears polite when it displays something in addition to or beyond what is agreed upon as "normal behaviour". In this case the actor retains as an option the possibility of "it could be done differently." Thus the polite form of the activity is positively marked – and also marks the person who carries it out positively.

In what follows I shall attempt to thematise a sub-section from the overall spectrum, which (a) contains some critical points in the history of the phenomenon. At the same time, in doing so, I shall (b) illustrate the historicity of politeness. (The aspect of individual marking mentioned under (2) above will not be dealt with in detail in this chapter.) The analysis will consider more general concepts in the concrete form in which they appear in social interaction. In particular it will be linguistic phenomena of politeness that I will focus on (section 4). Before doing so, I will discuss some more general aspects of politeness (section 3). In sections 5–8 four case studies will illustrate the rise of politeness and the conditions under which it occurs; the development of explicit concepts of politeness is examined; and the progress towards a transformation into a conceptualisation of politeness will be described with the example of the development of politeness in German. Finally, some consequences for present-day politeness conceptualisations will be drawn (section 9).

3. Politeness: general determinations

To begin with, we need to examine the term "polite" in a little more detail. What does it mean when human "behaviour" can be, and indeed is, characterised as "polite"? Qualifying an activity as "polite" entails carrying out a particular type of qualification, and we need to ask how we might achieve a closer analysis of that qualification.

We begin by distinguishing between action in general and a specific individual action. Let us first take the latter and call an individual action by an actor A the F of A (F_A). In order for F to qualify as polite, it is not enough simply to summarise certain qualities of the action F. In particular such a summary cannot simply be carried out by the actor A. It is rather the case that the qualification "polite" is only applied if an agreed upon standard S is invoked. Those criteria that are used in the qualification are contained in the standard. Thus "politeness" is not a given, but is related to a standard that lies outside it. Alongside the standardisation of politeness there is a second way in which the qualification is relative. As I have pointed out, the qualification cannot simply be carried out by A her/himself. (It is obvious that the actor may anticipate possible qualifications, but anticipation itself does not constitute the qualification.) Qualifications are carried out by a third party who possesses the necessary evaluative competence. S/he may be the actor B with respect to whom the action is carried out, but s/he may also be beyond the activity frame within which F_A takes place. Let us call this third actor C. It is then s/he who applies the action F to the standard S. In other words, C carries out a *judgement* by applying the standard S in order to decide on the politeness of F_A.

Attributing the predicate "polite" to an action F_A by an actor A is thus the result of a judgement on the part of a third person C, who applies a standard S. It is only by virtue of deriving from and being carried out within this dual relativity that the politeness of an action can be determined. Politeness is not a feature inherent to the action, but is connected with an interactional relationship which is itself transmediated by a standard. The judgement thus occurs *post actionem*. The connection enters into the planning and carrying out of the action as something anticipated.

Hence politeness displays a structure which is characterised by a dual transmission. It is (a) derived *post actionem* as the result of a process of judgement, and this in turn (b) takes account of a standard lying beyond the action itself. By virtue of its dual transmission politeness is certainly not a simple, straightforward feature of actions. In order to be able to qualify politeness as such, we need to know what constitutes the standard S, the constitutive process being social. At the same time we need to know what constitutes the evaluative competence, and this can be achieved by the individual who passes judgement participating in that social process. In working out an anticipation the actor A takes account of these relationships when s/he structures her/his interactional activity.

Politeness as the predication of a prior action, since it is a qualification of the action F_A, is thus revealed as something which concerns the modality of that action. The actor's choice of options sets the polite variety alongside the non-polite and the impolite. The modal character of politeness would not exist if A did not in principle possess a set of options. Hence non-optional politeness is not possible.

At this point we need to guard against a misunderstanding which might arise (cf. in Jhering II [1883: 362] on the confusion between motive and purpose). The determinations just developed cannot be substantiated in any empiricist sense. We are rather dealing with the actor's choice between alternative actions, and this choice is established by principle. The alternative actions themselves may be restricted by social conditions, but this does not prevent basic optionality from being a condition of "polite" activity. So we are not dealing with an individual alternative, but with a thoroughly social one. The "polite actor" is none other than the complex combination of, on the one hand, attribution and, on the other hand, anticipation. In this sense politeness in itself reveals its own social transmission.

The essential basis for making a judgement is a comparison, in which S is applied to the concrete action F_A. For this purpose it is not enough to have merely set up the standard; we have to assume that the third party C has some experience in applying it. Politeness turns out to be a form of reflexive activity. Both the evaluator and the actor have already emerged from the simple naivety of their activity, from the self-evident "it-is-as-it-is" of that activity. By virtue of this reflexivity it is highly improbable, basically even impossible, to identify polite activity as naive, i.e., as the kind of activity that is over and done with in the here and now.

The characterisation developed so far emerges in the course of history, and in its development it realises itself as what it is. Thus the standard S is not simply "there" – which holds equally true for "politeness" as a whole. This entails that the "early" phases of the development towards politeness (both in a historical and in a systematic sense) do not directly display the difference with regard to the elementary, univocal type of action which implies confidence in itself. In the first instance, reflexivity is immediately inherent in linguistic practice. This stage of reflexivity should be distinguished from a second one, which makes reflexivity accessible to itself. Finally, the possibility emerges of summing up and systematising the results of the second step.

The existence of these three stages of reflexivity seems to offer a possibility of direct comparison with the distinction of expressions, concepts and conceptualisations of politeness. However, this does not imply a direct equation or identification of the two roles. The moves from stage one and stage two to stage three are of a highly complex nature, such that a detailed determination of the relationship should be undertaken. Indeed, we already find with the first stage that expressions for politeness have a tendency to emerge only at the end of the process and are not previously at the actors' disposal.

With regard to the latter concept one could, from a methodological point of view, follow the invitation simply to apply the everyday terminology in order to find out what the role is that politeness plays for "the group" that developed it. What is said in the book title *History of the vocabulary of politeness* (Hans P. Krings 1961) is not yet in itself a sound indicator of the phenomenon of politeness.

On the contrary, we find a systematic change between the first series "expressions/ concepts/ conceptualisations" and the three phases of reflexivity – which are often reluctant and delayed with regard to what happens in the first series; but this is none other than an ordinary phenomenon, since the latter are very often systematically and factually delayed when compared to the processes of development in the first series.

The essential content of the educational history represented by the English term for politeness, i.e., "that which is polished", or by the Dutch term, i.e., "that which is planed" (or worked on, *beschaafdheid*), is developing this kind of reflexivity. The individual actor must go through this educational history before being able to act politely. In doing so, s/he has learnt to recognise the third party C as the limit placed on her/his natural activity, although C withdraws behind what is realised by her/his judgement, viz., the standard S. In S the third party, who might also be the second actor B at whom the activity is directed or whom it concerns, is generalised. The standard is the generalised "other", which in C's evaluation is only instantiated as the limit placed on A carrying out the action F_A – up to the point at which A must anticipate this limit in planning her/his activity. Overstepping the limit, however, would incur sanctions, and it is these sanctions which form the background for the standard S. Thus polite activity is an activity that recognises the socially constructed limit as being relevant to the activity itself. In and of itself it does not exist.

In what we have seen with respect to an individual polite action, its societal nature is at the same time always the obvious reason for it to be defined as polite. S is present in A's plans to carry out an action through the anticipation of judgement, and for this reason the standard, by virtue of the fact that it forms the precondition for the polite social activity, is constituted socially from a series of such activities. The individual polite action is always social precisely because of the necessary role played by the social standard in realising it. Hence we can recognise polite activity as social activity. The latter determines that the extent of the individual activity is limited by its necessary reference to the socially developed standard, just as, in experiencing this limit, it in turn leads to an elementary reflexivity in which an element of freedom is realised.

As the analysis of the individual polite action has shown, it is always social, i.e., one which cannot be understood without its broader context. The dialectic between the individual and the general is also present in determining the individual.

Just as reference to the standard is absolutely necessary for qualifying the individual action as polite, so too is it necessary for attempting to attribute politeness in cross-group comparisons. However, whereas in relation to individual actions by individual actors the standard is developed by the group itself and reproduced when politeness is attributed, the attempt to find a standard beyond those groups can become caught up all too easily in two different traps: in ethnocentricity or in apparent universality. Both may occur together – and this is more often than not likely to be the case, viz., when an ethnocentric or historically specific standard is raised to the status of a universal.

4. Politeness and language

Present-day ideas of politeness often consider a close relationship between politeness and language as something obvious; on the other hand, however, this close relationship needs further consideration. The relationship between language and politeness has only been developed as central to both in recent research (in particular Leech 1983; Brown and Levinson 1978). Leech in particular sees in politeness an essential dimension of that area of language with which linguistic pragmatics should deal.

Held (1990) has reconstructed in detail how older linguistic literature reveals a number of ways in which the question of politeness can be tackled. Within stylistics in particular politeness is thematised from a specific philosophical, subjective-idealistic point of view ("Lebensphilosophie"). Leo Spitzer (1922, 1928), Bally (1909, 1913) and Lerch (1933) represent this theoretical approach. In Spitzer's work the concept of politeness is seen entirely in connection with his analysis of the phenomena of *parole*. For him the concept of politeness still remains firmly anchored in the hierarchical structure of society (Held

1990: 13). It is appropriate to this individualistic orientation and to the reference to *parole* that Held (1990: 13) is able to speak of "luxuriantly commented individual observations." Eugen Lerch adopted the concept of consideration for one's conversational partner and identified politeness with the display of respect through the expression of "modesty, distance and self-possession" (Held 1990: 13). He posits a "syntax of respect" (Held 1990: 13) in which he deals with something that is still a central aspect of politeness-oriented linguistic analysis today, viz. "modality". Other, more sociological (Havers 1931) or psychological approaches (as far as Kainz 1941) thematise the relationship between politeness and language in the light of their basic theoretical positions (Held 1990: section 3.2 and section 3.3).

As a rule, all these approaches towards the thematisation of politeness take as their starting point certain linguistic phenomena for which the prior concepts of politeness adduced from each individual case to the next are taken to provide an explanatory framework wherever the limits set by the canonical theory of linguistics do not envisage explanatory or even analytical possibilities for obvious sub-domains of language. In other words, pragmatics, understood as the additional application of this concept with respect to a previously defined core linguistics, only ends terminologically in a feeling of dissatisfaction. Like a shadow, this feeling accompanies the recurrent attempt to exclude certain linguistic phenomena from the range of linguistic objects. Nevertheless, the relationship between politeness and language from standpoints such as these emerges as an analytical problem from a concept of politeness which gave rise to the need to consider language. It is all too clear that conceptualisations of politeness depend on concepts of politeness – most of them to a high degree "culture-dependent", hence ethnocentric – which are the expression of historically realised forms of politeness, as has been shown above (section 2). (It is therefore not surprising that a large amount of this literature in Europe has been produced by the Romance-speaking cultures, which are felt to be particularly "polite", and in turn by scholars who were active either in situations of language contrast or against such a background, e.g., Spitzer or Lerch [cf. Held 1990: section 4.1].) In particular Albert Dauzat (1912), who explicitly uses his normative propagation of politeness in the battle against the *influence facheuse* ('annoying influence') of slang on *langue,* shows how intensively such research can serve the purpose of retaining existing social subcultures and their politeness standards (Held 1990: 19).

Linguistic pragmatics did away with the stigma of marginality which was associated with the study of the linguistic realisations of politeness – at least insofar as this stigma is not applied to pragmatics itself. The more recent, systematic research into politeness mentioned at the outset of this section makes this particularly clear, and it does so by demanding clear sets of principles and systematicity. Yet these demands simultaneously perpetuate the previous history of the discipline and the generally uncontested claim that certain linguistic realisations are the expression of politeness. The connection itself does not arouse much attention and arouses none at all in the sense of a historically trained awareness of problems.

This situation is difficult to cope with. It, too, reveals a practical and theoretical hermeneutic problem. "Pre-judices" are at the same time a necessary starting point from which one can begin to revise them, and it is only by going through this process that the object of research can be properly identified.

We are therefore forced to take as our point of departure the present state of affairs in lay conceptualisations of politeness and the way in which these have been transferred to the definition of the relationship between language and politeness. At least this means that some aspects of politeness have something to do with language. It is generally agreed that this is the case for such subsystems of language as address forms and methods of "modalisation" in all their various linguistic dimensions. It is also true for parts of the lexicon and – perhaps – for some of the phenomena that have been introduced by way of the standard interpretation of Grice's work into the framework of pragmatics as "communicative principles" (cf. Grice 1975).

An area like that of the modal verbs, which may be understood as a core area for methods of modalisation, shows how direct an effect an ethnocentric bias can have. In the European languages, most of which are closely related, modal verb systems are historically among the most recent developments. We can see this quite clearly from the fact that even in so narrow an area as that of the Germanic languages and in languages that are close neighbours like English, Dutch and German considerable differences can be noted in the relevant subsystems. Since the linguistic forms used to construct these systems are largely the same, this fact is all the more surprising. Use of the inherently multifunctional elements of the modal verb systems for the purpose of realising politeness begins in each individual case within the set of elements that are functionally differentiated (and need to be differentiated analytically). The structure of the linguistic and communicative picture which emerges from such a constellation does not leave us much room to expect initial transparency. If we look at other linguistic systems, we find even in Greek, which is comparatively poor in modal verbs, a whole morphological system, that of the optative, which allows the speaker to express part of the functional area which is expressed by modal verbs in English, Dutch and German. But if we then consider, e.g., Ancient Hebrew, i.e., a non-Indo-European language, we find that a morphological differentiation equivalent to the optative is missing, as is a well-developed modal verb system. Much of what is contained in the Greek linguistic system, on the one hand, and in the linguistic systems of English, Dutch and German, on the other, is lumped together in an undifferentiated way in one form, the so-called "prefix conjugation".

It would be relatively easy to show for other linguistic subsystems what this example illustrates. If we are to focus on the obvious part that politeness plays in language usage, we will therefore need to redirect our attention to a few frequently cited candidates for the expression of the relationship between linguistic and other activity in order to find a starting point. In order to do this, I shall focus in particular on the linguistic procedures of address in the examples to follow. It is in this area that various attempts at systematisation have been made (cf., for example, Kohz 1985, and the extensive bibliography by Braun, Kohz and Schubert 1986). I do not intend to deal with this systematisation here, but will merely thematise the characteristic aspect of it, which will allow us to trace the features of a notion of politeness.

5. Example 1: Politeness in the Ancient Orient

5.1 *The Near East as a socio-historical area*

Let us now try, with a few examples which are well documented historically and which can be considered reasonably clear, to follow up the question of how politeness arose and developed. One suitable area to consider is the world of the Near East. It offers an exceptionally good field of observation for social phenomena and is characterised above all by the following features:

(a) We have at our disposal a cultural documentation of social developments and processes in written form that reaches back over five thousand years.
(b) This documentation is enriched by an astonishing abundance of other, particularly archaeological data.
(c) If we consider the whole area, conditions of life for the inhabitants developed in comparatively similar ways.
(d) The feature mentioned under (c) provides the necessary prerequisite for a systematic, comparative and socio-historical analysis which can examine the specific features of individual influences in comparatively favourable conditions.
(e) Within the general developmental framework mentioned under (c) similar large-scale changes have occurred over the last four thousand years, which enable us to recognise and describe lines of socio-historical development.

For my present purposes I shall not consider the "modern" development of the area, i.e., the period of European colonisation, decolonisation and national independence with the accelerated integration of the region into the world market, nor shall I consider the medieval and post-medieval formation of "states". I shall concentrate on the Ancient Near East, and I shall only consider more recent periods of history inasfar as they reveal socio-economic and socio-historical developments which can be used structurally in illustrating certain lines of development in the Ancient Orient. In particular this will be appropriate for the continuity of nomadic forms of existence as well as the transition to agrarian forms.

The following process is characteristic of the region. Alongside the two types of existence mentioned above a third may also be considered characteristic, viz. the formation of larger agglomerations which are particularly noticeable in places where increased and intensified production was possible combining agriculture and livestock. To begin with, such places were to be found in the large river valley areas (Nile, Euphrates, Tigris). In the course of time, however, urban settlements could be found in other locations, these being made possible by more advanced technologies in both forms of production.

5.2 *Structures of address forms in Ancient Israel*

The agrarian and nomadic forms of existence display a variety of combinations and transitional forms. With respect to linguistic activity they also show characteristic differences. Forms of technology in agrarian cultures are associated with an almost explosive increase of knowledge – at least relative to that period of history. This generated the need for knowledge to be saved and transferred, and this need was dealt with by means of specific new text types, e.g., that of the "proverb", in which elementary regularities providing the important prerequisites for the success of production are fixed and transmitted. For the nomadic form of existence (with its small livestock) other text types are fundamental, e.g., itinerary-like lists which indicated the position of central water-holes, even those in more remote regions, to which the nomads could go in cases of extreme drought. This type of knowledge must have been passed on from generation to generation.

Thus in the context of factors such as these text structures achieved a considerable complexity. If we compare these with the linguistic forms of everyday communication, e.g., forms of address, we are confronted with what at first sight seems a totally different picture. The well-known Old Testament scholar and orientalist Köhler, e.g., has the following to say:

> Generally address is completely formless, a simple "thou", at most accompanied by the addressee's name or an expression which refers to the addressee in accordance with his social or kinship status. [...] It is most important to bear in mind that all the members and classes of a people refer to one another as "thou". This gave life an equitable, democratic, conciliatory nature. (1922: 37–38)

The passage "in accordance with his social or kinship status" in the first part of the quotation from Köhler needs to be characterised more precisely. For nomadic and simple agrarian conditions it does not hold good in this form. In his article Köhler deals with the relevant passages from his corpus, as it were, ahistorically. On the contrary, the use of kinship terms frequently occurs, as we would expect for the social structure of large families (cf. Lande 1949: 20ff.). This type of address form is vertically reciprocal (ʔabi 'my father', for example, *Gen.* 22, 7; 48, 18; *beni* 'my son' [*Gen.* 22, 7f.; 27, 1. 8. 18. 20f.; *Gen.* 27, 13, where it is uttered by a mother to her son]; *bitti* 'my daughter', *Judg.* 11, 35). It is also horizontal (ʔaxi 'my brother' *Gen.* 33, 8 and passim ʔaxotenu 'our sister' *Gen.* 24, 60).

This kinship terminology opens up the first opportunity for expanding the system of address terms – in effect it is the only opportunity that elementary nomadic smallholding conditions will allow. In the case of encounters with non-members of the extended family (the *mišpaxa*) the problematic nature of encounters with strangers can be reduced by temporarily accepting them into the *mišpaxa* by means of address. Thus Jacob uses the expression 'my brothers' (*ʔaxay*) (*Gen.* 29, 4) with the shepherds he meets, although they are totally unknown to him and he to them. However, the situation of possible conflict, which arises through any encounter with those who are territorial strangers, is neutralised and made safer. Jacob draws upon a *mišpaxa* relationship and thereby makes it clear that he has no intention of threatening them.

This expansion of the system of address terms beyond the *mišpaxa* can hardly be counted as a specific form of "politeness". We are dealing here with more elementary rules to deal with problematic contact, rules which concern life and death. Such encounters are exceptional. In general the assignment of territory to wandering nomadic smallholders is unproblematic. Where such encounters are problematic, recourse is made to a quarrel, which, in extreme cases, can involve the need to look for new territory (cf. *Gen.* 26, 19–22). However, claiming kinship terminology later offers one possible basis for the development of "polite" address terms.

We now know that characterisations which can be derived from ancient Israelite documents can be found again and again throughout the Middle East, and they can be found wherever conditions are similarly structured, i.e., wherever nomadic conditions prevail in later periods, conditions that are structurally parallel. Thus as Østrup (1929) writes:

[It] is clear that the usual form of address is the second person singular; regardless of differences in rank and age in Arabic the universal form of address is Thou. In its unpretentiousness, which has lasted through the ages, we recognise the expression of that democratic tendency which has been typical of the character of the Arabic people since earliest times. Primitive living conditions in the desert did not leave much room for social or material differences to be felt to any extent [...] For this reason Arabic is not so rich in complex address terms as other oriental languages. (1929: 20)

If we leave aside that characteristic expression *Volkscharakter* ('character of the [Arabic] people') as a notion that was typical for the sociological and ethnological literature of the thirties in Europe, we come across a striking parallel between this description and Köhler's characterisation above of the ancient Israelite situation; at the same time the general societal character of this system of address is made clear.

It is now interesting to see how this picture undergoes differentiation, which has to do with constellations that concern the edges of the basic primary family units. In particular those human beings who have been forcibly integrated into these basic units and "dehumanised" by being classified as "objects" rather than "subjects" play a role here. In other words, an elementary master-slave relationship finds its way into the language of address. This relationship, characterised by the terms *cäbäd* 'slave' and *ʔadon* 'master, lord', represents the most refined pair used as a "candidate" for a "polite" form of address. The "other" receives the qualification *ʔadoni* 'my lord'. The different ways in which this form of address is used "have their common counterpart in the deprecating reference to oneself as a slave" (Köhler 1922: 39).

Alongside this type of self-reference which invokes the master-slave relationship where it is not present we have another area, viz. meetings with strangers. This situation represents an elementary peripheral aspect of life, particularly in nomadic conditions. A characteristic example is the meeting between the three men and Abraham sitting at the entry to his tent *(Gen.* 18). Abraham addresses them as *ʔadonai* 'my lords' and continues, "Would that I had found mercy in your eyes that you do not pass by your slave" (similarly in *Gen.* 19, 19). I shall not discuss the differences between the form of address in the singular and that in the plural here (on this point cf. the commentaries on *Gen.* 18f.). This application of the terminology "slave" vs. "master" proves to be an important and highly productive point of departure for the development of "polite" forms of address.

As soon as more complex social relationships are created, this characterisation can be used in a number of different ways. The development can be seen in the immediate pre-kingdom period of Ancient Israel, e.g., when a woman in a somewhat precarious situation in the temple dares to contradict the priest (Hannah to Eli, "No, my lord [*ʔadoni*] " 1. *Sam.* 1, 15f.; cf. verse 26). From the same period the *Book of Ruth (2,* 13) contains a similar reference in the way in which Ruth addresses Boas, "Let me find favour in thy sight, my Lord; for that thou hast comforted me, and for that thou hast spoken friendly unto thine handmaiden, though I be not like unto one of thine handmaidens." Similar occurrences can be found frequently in the stories of Elia and Elisa (cf. 1. *Kings* 18, 7; 2. *Kings* 4, 16; 6, 5). (Clearly we are not referring here to cases in which someone uses the expression ʔ*adon* with the "personal suffix" -*i* ('my') when he addresses his real master. The examples given under b. by Köhler [1922: 40] belong to this form of address.)

The actual modification of this system and the consequent development of address terms that can more narrowly be called "polite" occur with the establishment of a kingdom in Ancient Israel. This process, which was contested over a relatively long period of time (cf. 1. *Sam.* 8, but also as early as Jotam's fable, *Judg.* 9), resulted in a fundamental transformation of social relationships. It also led to a situation in which parallel structures existed alongside one another for centuries, gradually wearing one another down. The development of a kingdom, a military structure and a modification of the legal system led to the establishment of special social groups in the immediate environment of the king. It is in these groups that we find the bearers of a new address structure, the expression 'My lord King' (1. *Sam.* 24, 9), which combines the term 'my lord' to refer to the king (1. *Sam.* 22, 12) with the term 'King' (*hammäläk*) (e.g., 1. *Sam.* 22, 20). In this way the master–slave relationship is transferred in the form of a socially established generalisation to the internal structure of Israelite society. The subjects surrounding the king see themselves as his slaves (cf. the references given in Köhler 1922: 43f.). This new structure even overlays that of the *mišpaxa,* e.g., when Absalom (2. *Sam.* 15, 7f.) characterises himself as "slave" with respect to his father David; "I pray thee, let me go and pay my vow, which I have vowed unto the Lord, in Hebron. For thy servant vowed a vow while I abode at Geshur in Syria."

The structure of "politeness" (in the sense of "courtesy") in address terms is thus already centred on the very development of a court. The social differentiation which has as one of its consequences the fact that a court comes into being, gives rise to "polite", i.e., "courteous", forms of address.

It is then extended to the point at which a general, abstract form takes the place of the simple address term 'my lord' (ʔ*adoni*) the address term in which the expression for lord ʔ*adon* is now put into the plural is combined with the corresponding "personal suffixes". In this way the form ʔ*adonai* is produced. According to Köhler it should be understood as an abstraction, meaning 'my lordship'. This is how Elia addresses King Ahab's "master of the court" (1. *Kings* 18, 3) (ʔ*ašär* *cal-habbayit,* 'he who is over the house') (verse 8), "[...] go, tell thy Lord (*ladonä(i)ka*), Behold, Elijah is here." (Cf. verse 14.)

This form *ʔadonai* (which, it should be pointed out, is most widespread in a religious context as a way of addressing God) also penetrates the stylistic register of reporting (Köhler 1922: 42), thus giving evidence of the significance and widespread use of the expression. Its use in the Joseph story, which presupposes, as is well known, conditions under the Egyptian Pharaohs, is almost a classical occurrence.

Hence a complex picture emerges for Ancient Israel, which allows us to trace various phases of social development in the system of address terms. The development of polite forms takes place at the social periphery of the fundamental early forms of social organisation, the *mišpaxa.* The master–slave relationship, which is still an exterior aspect of this form of organisation, constitutes the basis for the standard (cf. section 3 above) of what was later to become politeness. In the development of the kingdom the basis for the societal generalisation of this relationship is to be found (although it remained problematic) and hence one condition for the possible application of corresponding terms of address in social interaction.

Because of the failure to carry through this form of social organisation, the recurrent problems to which it gave rise and the constant conflict between "royal" and "pre-royal" conditions – a conflict which was to determine the course of Ancient Israelite history – the system of address terms did not become stabilised in Ancient Israelite society. The short extract from the conversation between Absalom and David (2. *Sam.*, 15, 7f.) clearly shows the fluctuation between the expressions 'your slave' and 'I'. We frequently find the same kind of fluctuation in one and the same speech by individual speakers (Köhler 1922: 44).

Thus the result of historical development – which also implies that we are likely to achieve similar results in a synchronic investigation of politeness – is a diffuse picture in which very different address strategies can be used alongside with and in contrast to one another. However, this apparent diffusion can be shown to have definite causes. It is the expression of that situation of social conflict to which it owes its existence.

The historicity of politeness thus becomes evident when we examine Ancient Israelite developments. At the same time considering socio-historical development clearly reveals the structure of a politeness *system* in the process of change. The oldest form, the form 'thou', which is bound to the structure of the *mišpaxa,* continues to be the basis for address terms. The development of a standard for what we might specifically call "politeness" is not yet present in this system. Equality is the basis of relationships between individual *mišpaxa* members; wherever inequality exists, in the relationship between male and female members, there is no need to find a social solution to it in specific politeness forms. The master-slave relationship provides the basis for the gradual development of that standard, which, as soon as it is generalised or in the process of being generalised in social structure, serves as the foundation on which "polite" forms can be developed, and this goes as far as creating linguistic expressions as abstract forms of expressing politeness.

5.3 *Nomadic Arabia; Ancient Egypt*

It would be interesting to carry the analysis further to see how these relationships are carried over to the relationship to God in Ancient Israelite society, but this lies outside the scope of the present chapter. Instead I should like to close this section by mentioning two parallels. I have already touched on the similarity with developments in Arabic above. In this case the final phase, as we might now expect from historical developments, was never accomplished in the same way as it was in Ancient Israelite society. Østrup (1929: 21) writes that "Arabic, on the other hand, never experienced the breakthrough of language usage so characteristic and general in Hebrew that 'my lord' (ʔ *adoni*) even substitutes for the pronoun of address." The same might be said for the added expression 'your slave'. On this point Østrup (1929: 21) mentions that "the free Arab in the desert was never anyone's slave, and his descendants, even those living in towns, have retained the memory of that fact in their language usage."

Wherever we see apparent exceptions to this general characterisation, they can be traced back to Turkish influences:

> In polite address we often hear *ja sidi,* 'my lord', or *efendim,* 'my lord', a loan word from Turkish, which, particularly in Egypt, is used when employees address their employers. This appears to be a leftover from a not too distant past in which the ruling class on the Nile was Turkish-speaking. (1929: 20f.)

For the added expression in which the speaker characterises himself as knave or slave we can also say that "a flowery means of expression in Turkish [...] developed [...] It is certain [...] that **Turks** today still love flowery circumlocutions for the first person singular expressions some of which such as [...] 'the dust of your feet' inevitably recall for us an old Oriental style. The vassals of the Assyrian Grand Kings refer to themselves as 'the dust under your feet' in letters to the king" (1929: 21). In general Østrup speculates that this language usage is related "to the Ancient Assyrian period [...] through various Persian links," just as in general "the Turks [...] in everything related to etiquette and forms of politeness [...are] dependent on older models, Byzantine or Persian" (Østrup 1929: 21).

I shall not enter a discussion of Assyrian-Babylonian conditions here (cf. in summary Salonen 1967 and 1957-1971 on greetings; Renger 1972-75 and, for Assyrian, Garelli 1972-75 on the court-state). On the other hand, I should like to make a second reference to Ancient Egyptian conditions, since with Hermann Grapow's (1960, 2nd. ed.) important work we have at our disposal a copious special monograph on the question of "how the Ancient Egyptians addressed one another, how they greeted and spoke to one another." The relationships shown there allow us to recognise very similar conditions to those that I have analysed with regard to Ancient Israelite society, without being in possession of such a clear data basis for socio-historically early forms. It should be pointed out, however, that the picture differs from these conditions particularly after the terminology of polite address terms related to the court became established. In characterisations for the king such as 'that great one there' social distance is increased. The shift from 'thou'-deixis (in Ancient Egyptian this is realised by stressing the corresponding suffix, Grapow 1960: 15) enters the set of descriptive terms: 'his majesty'. Finally 'thou'-deixis is completely replaced by 'one' (Grapow 1960: 20, 115, 198). Table 1 (p. 91) provides a summary of Ancient Egyptian address terms.

6. Example 2: Aspects of the development of politeness in Ancient Greece and Rome

Address terms and greeting formulae are clearly only one subset of linguistic procedures and forms of activity that can be functionalised for the purpose of expressing politeness. It would be worthwhile to

Table 1. *Ancient Egyptian address terms, following Grapow (1960)*

Addressee		Self
A1	thou ↓↑→ (14ff; 79) -- (suffix) (15ff; 52ff) you ↓↑→ (14ff; 52ff)	I ↓↑→ (179ff) we ↓↑→ (180ff)
A2	*name* ↓↑→ (16ff; 25; 34)	*name* ↓↑→ (185)
B	father (31 etc.) my father (14; 31 etc.) my brother ↓ (54/ 195) my sister → (35)	 thy brother there (184) thy son there (184)
C	my friend ↓ (16ff; 33f; 36; 54) my *NP* ↓ (appellative noun, re- lative phrase qualifying the ad- dressee etc.) (52ff)	
D	*title* (16ff; 31)	*title* (185)
E1	my lord ↑ (16ff; 60ff) (in isolation since EA) duke my lord ↑ (41f)	the servant of *x* ↑ (47; EA)
E2	maid-servant → (35)	 the servant there ↑ (182ff; 196) + 3rd person the great one there ↓ (183; 196)
E3	thy person ↑ (39; 47 (EA))	
F	thy majesty ↑ (39f; 196)	my majesty ↓ (182; 184f) + 1st person
G1	one ↑ (20; 198f; 115)	
G2	*passive construction* ↑ (196; 198f)	*passive construction* ↓ (199)

↓	from high to low	*NP* = noun phrase
↑	from low to high	*x* = name, NP
→	equal	EA = the El Amarna period
(as far as indicated in Grapow)		(1377–50 B.C.)

The figures in brackets refer to the page numbers in Grapow.

look more closely at other areas of social activity in Ancient Israel and Ancient Egypt, e.g., rules governing the right to speak, social contact, the expression of respect and the expression of disregard such as scorn, etc.

It would be particularly interesting from the point of view of politeness to take a closer look at the large area of ancient oriental "wisdom" (Hebrew *xokma*) and the Egyptian equivalent *maat* (which may in many ways have served as a model [cf. Assmann 1990]). If one were to carry out this research, the results would have to be evaluated within the context of social development which gave rise to them. It would, however, exceed the limits that I have set myself for the present contribution. Instead I shall look briefly at greeting and address formulae in Ancient Greece. For this purpose I shall refer to Zilliacus (1949, 1953, 1964 and 1983). In this context it is remarkable how simple the system remained for a very long period of time. It is not until very late in Greek antiquity that "politeness attributes" are assigned to individuals, a custom which is quite distinct from the rigid *epitheta ornantia* that were in use in early periods (cf. Zilliacus 1964: column 40). This even goes so far that as late as Herodotus "it is noticeable that one cannot even find titles in address terms between the King of the Persians and his courtiers" (Zilliacus 1964: column 474). Here too the introduction of kingship and emperorship and, in particular, the development of a bureaucratic apparatus tend towards a considerable differentiation in terms of address, which is advanced in mutual contact with Latin and allows politeness to be expressed.

We note a further development of this trend in particular in the late Roman and Byzantine era:

> About the beginning of the fourth century a clear demarcation in the use of A[ddress] terms can be distinguished. The constant increase in bureaucratic tendencies in public life, which led to the distribution of civil servants and dignitaries into specific social ranks, makes itself felt. (Zilliacus 1964: column 481)

In this late period we also find the first roots of a *pluralis reverentiae* – as a reaction against the *pluralis majestatis* (Zilliacus 1964: column 490). In the letters of the Hellenic kings the latter is still largely "isolated" (ibid.). In the era of Ptolemy even the king himself is "regularly addressed with the 'thou' form" in petitions (Zilliacus 1964: column 491). The colloquial plural 'you' form can be traced back to the "indeterminate sociative plural" (ibid.) rather than to the reverential plural of court circles. A similar situation can be sketched out for Latin: "Even in Rome the 'you' developed from the sociative epistolary plural; the official politeness use is secondary" (Zilliacus 1964: column 492).

It is not until the imperial era that the use of the expression *ave* can be noted, and it stems "possibly […] from the Punic", i.e., from an oriental context (Zilliacus 1983: columns 1217f.). The situation for the expression 'lord' *(kyrie)* in address terms is quite similar: "No references for Kyrie as a polite form of address in Greek can be found before the first century A.D." (Zilliacus 1964: column 494).

Hence in the Latin and Greek situation for a long period of time there is little in the way of address terms that would justify making use of the category "politeness" at all. Within the culture of Ancient Greece it is difficult to make out any development towards politeness either in characteristic language usage or even in relation to a relevant social standard. On the contrary, social "togetherness", at least in the system of address terms, is neutral with respect to such developments. It is only when a strong social internal differentiation develops beyond situations in which men of equal rank came together (e.g., *andres Athenaioi,* 'men of Athens'), i.e., in despotic relationships of one form or another, that we see address terms which give rise to the expression of politeness. This development owes more to intercultural contact with the East than to genuine linguistic developments in Latin and Greek. It is from here that the light of politeness for the Greco-Latin world is turned on, displaying the full extent of intercultural borrowing and investment.

7. Example 3: From the Middle Ages to the early modern period, or: programmes and propaganda

The social relationships that we have dealt with so far show very clearly how forms of politeness gradually evolve in specific social conditions. These processes can be best exemplified in the development of terms of address. Social differentiation gives rise to the need to have forms of communication differentiated and in particular to unfold forms of contact as a means of expressing it. In most cases the process goes hand in hand with corresponding social transitions; wherever they are developed parallel to one another, politeness can also be transferred in an intercultural context.

Thus, if forms of politeness are also developed in these historical processes with varying degrees of intensity, there are still no explicit verbalisations to show the relationship. The world of Ancient Israel has no "equivalent" term for "politeness", not even one which might be roughly or approximately equivalent. The first real signs of an equivalent can be seen in the Latin terminology referring to 'townliness', *urbanitas* (cf. p. 71 above).

The feudal world of the Middle Ages does not display an unbroken tradition from Greek and Latin antiquity with respect to politeness. Social breaks and upheavals through the course of several centuries have a disruptive effect on its further development. However, in the high Middle Ages a notion of politeness in the narrower sense of the term does crystallise, and simultaneously a terminology is developed, i.e., a concept of politeness, by means of which and in which the members of the court can communicate with one another about the forms of their social actions. In his famous monograph *Über den Prozess der Zivilisation* (*On the Process of Civilisation*) Norbert Elias (1936/1969) has given us a detailed reconstruction of how 'courtoisie'/'courtesy'/'cortezia'/'hövescheit'/'hüfscheit' developed, and how they were then replaced by the concept of "civilitas" (1: 76ff.).

By means of the concept of "politeness = courtesy" "the secular upper classes in the Middle Ages, or at least some of the leading groups within those upper classes, find a way of expressing their self-confidence, i.e., that which distinguishes them according to their own feelings" (1936/1969, 1: 79). The various expressions mentioned above "point, very directly and far more revealingly than later expressions for the same function, towards a specific social location. They say, 'This is the way to behave at court.' Through such expressions it is in the first instance the circles of courtly knights surrounding the great feudal lords who designate [...] what distinguishes them according to their feelings, the specific commands and prohibitions that were first developed at the great feudal courts and then spread into somewhat wider social classes" (ibid.). Hence it is precisely at this point that we can take up the historical connection that I referred to at the beginning of this chapter.

The translation into French of Egidio Colonna's *De regimine principum* already introduces the notion of *courtoisie* (cf. Kremos 1955: 12). In a series of glosses the linguistic transformation of this type of propaganda is revealed. *Courtoisie* presents itself as a suitable means of substituting older, positively occupied social concepts or amalgamating them. Alongside the *urbanus* ('the urban man') we have the *facecus* (=*facetus*) ('the refined, pleasant man', even 'the witty man') and also the *frugalis* ('the frugal man'), who was the sober, thoughtful courtier (Kremos 1955: 12). The process of subsuming all these concepts under *courtoisie* is one aspect of the propagandistic development of a politeness concept which is built up around the basic knightly virtues of loyalty and mutual trust (cf. Dupin 1931).

While the development of *courtoisie* in the Middle Ages spread very little in a vertical direction, a fundamental upheaval took place at the beginning of the Renaissance period. Elias maintains the following:

> During the sixteenth century the use of the term *courtoisie* in the upper classes of society slowly recedes, whereas that of *civilité* becomes more frequent and then finally gains the upper hand in the seventeenth century, at least in France. (1936/1969, 1: 95f.)

In turn this concept, which in the last instance owes its propagation significantly to Erasmus, is replaced two hundred years later in the process of physiocratic reforms by "civilisation" (Elias 1936/1969, 1: 60). In contrast to a mere reference to "the state of *moeurs* or cultivation" or to "manners, social tact, [...] the consideration that one person owes to another, and [...] several related concepts" (Elias 1936/1969, 1: 60), civilised society, which is put into opposition with barbarity, is confronted with new duties, and in the social enforcement and fulfilment of these duties its protagonists take it not only as their mission but also as the justification of their special position, i.e., of their social existence.

In contrast to the development of "polite" forms in the Ancient Orient it is above all noticeable that such a development is essentially supported by a corresponding literature. Both the medieval notion of politeness and the concepts of *civilitas* and *civilisation* have their propagandists, who help to construct specific text types each of which culminates in an extraordinarily large number of examples in relation to the possibilities for text production. They represent a whole literature of their own, to which not only Erasmus' widely read *De civilitate morum puerilium* belongs but also the *Book of the Courtier* by Castiglione, which was a formative influence for a whole epoch. Politeness is embedded in a discourse concerned with its justification and propagation and those who carry out the discourse are at one and the same time exponents of what they wish to convey to their readers.

The propagandists of politeness can be seen as a mirror of sweeping processes of social transformation. The series of concepts set up in Elias' lists is characterised by the process of social changes. The programmes themselves reflect these changes from a position close to the centre of social structure or what constitutes a, or the, motor of social change. Thus it is not by chance that in Northern Europe a renaissance humanist, Erasmus, contributed in a fundamentally significant way to the realisation of a programme for a new type of politeness, which in particular was related to the needs of the developing urban culture of the Rhine valley. (Erasmus' activities concerned precisely this area from Basle to Rotterdam.) The replacement of *courtoisie* by *civilité* during the sixteenth century and then with astonishing success in the seventeenth is the expression of a process of adaptation, but it is at the same time also the expression of the gradual formation of new social relationships. At the beginning of this process urban culture is only a transitional element in the movement towards the establishment of the late feudal court, which can be distinguished from the late medieval court by processes of centralisation and of overcoming the narrow boundaries of localism. Prototypically this transformational process is realised by France, which for decades, even centuries, becomes the locus for developing the programmes and methods of propagation of those forms of politeness that were topical at any one point in time. Even in England Lord Chesterfield, who published the two volumes of his *Letters to his son,* which was intended as an educational tract, was oriented towards French models. Zaehle (1933: 141) maintains that "his real teachers [...] were the French, who, he was convinced, could not be equalled in the realm of polite manners. Again and again he recommends that his son should imitate them. He praises the Abbé de Bellegarde's *Reflexion sur ce qui peut plaire ou déplaire* as an extremely useful and usable book and appears in various ways to be not unaffected by it." German processes, which were generally rather late in developing in the seventeenth and early eighteenth centuries, were influenced in large part by the French example.

We find the first detailed reconstruction of German developments in Manfred Beetz's (1990) monograph *Frühmoderne Höflichkeit (Early modern politeness*), which is based on copious source studies of "the art of complimenting". The principal areas in which, to use Beetz's term, "social-ethical" authors wrote and were read are characteristically those which were socially most highly developed, i.e., the Protestant areas of Germany:

> If we review the most important politeness theoreticians of the seventeenth and early eighteenth centuries, we discover in Moscherosch, [...] Harsdörfer, [...] Weise, Thomasius, Riemer [...] only Protestants. (Beetz 1990: 79)

In terms of regions it was Wettinian Saxony, in particular the university cities of Leipzig and Jena, the Electorate of Brandenburg with its university city of Halle (since the time of its foundation in 1694) and, among the free imperial cities, Hamburg, which were the centres of the "art of complimenting" (Beetz 1990: 83ff.). Catholic Germany was largely oriented to the translation of works from the Romance-speaking areas of Europe, in particular from the most highly developed centres of culture in Italy and Spain. Thus we find translations of Castiglione's *Courtier*, Guazzo's *De civili conversatione*, Giovanni della Casa's *Galateus* and Antonio de Guevara's *Court school* (Beetz 1990: 105).

The seventeenth and early eighteenth centuries reveal themselves as the golden age of the compliment: in 1598 the expression 'compliment' occurs for the first time in a German text (Beetz 1990: 109). A genus-specific typology develops for compliments, and "complimenting" becomes virtually the focal point of politeness discourse.

We can determine quite precisely what the social status and social function of this discourse were. The model was the court. Hence we read in J. G. Neukirch's (1726) *Politisch-moralische Maxime in der Conversation mit hohen und niederen Personen beiderlei Geschlechts, auf Universitäten, auf Reisen, bei Hofe, im Vaterland und überall wohl zu leben und wohl zu reden* ('*Moral political maxims in conversation with high and low persons of both sexes for living and speaking well at universities, on journeys, at court, in the mother country and everywhere*') (quoted from Beetz 1990: 226) that "politeness, modesty and everything pertaining to galantry are equally enthroned at court." The social goal is, according to Beetz, to cooperate "together in securing social and political peace."

Taking rules for politeness to heart is equivalent to recognising the social system which is reflected in and supported by these rules. In the Baroque period we might add the adoration of a social hierarchy willed by God. Authors on polite manners reveal open ideological intentions in demanding of their readers that they identify with the political creed of absolutism. De Caillières demands that one should "let one's love of the existing order of things be recognised from one's social behaviour" (Beetz 1990: 186).

In detail the effects of this can be seen in a complex process of maintaining an equilibrium with respect to the social core area and in carefully balancing out how to determine and achieve the necessary social distance towards those who are higher and those who are lower in the social hierarchy. Christian Thomasius, one of the principal propagandists of an advanced politeness culture and without doubt one of the most interesting personalities in Germany in the second half of the seventeenth century, explicitly reveals these "directives for behaviour in three possible status constellations" (Beetz 1990: 236):

- In the face of those higher in the social hierarchy one should not show oneself to be either servile or clumsily confidential.
- In the face of social equals one should show neither a serious, monk-like distance nor a ridiculous fraternising proximity.
- In the face of those lower in the social hierarchy one should be neither arrogant nor display "untimely familiarity".

Programmes for politeness and the way in which they were propagated in accordance with the relevant social processes show politeness to be a concept which occupies a central place in forming ideas in the modern age. Ideological "modernisation" processes are carried out largely by way of changes in politeness. The various transformations of feudalism into late feudalism are expressed in the development and gradual transformation of politeness for the sphere of social or, more precisely, political interaction. In its most highly developed form, i.e., at the absolutist French court, politeness discourse is at one and the same time the expression and the consequence of an increasing social powerlessness in central sections of the nobility. For these sections carrying out the rituals of courtly politeness offered a subsidiary area of social activity which corresponded less and less to real political or economic power. In this way a dichotomy of social activity arose for those social groups which did not directly exercise power, but rather paid with their own loss of power for the privilege of being close to it. For these groups politeness became an important means of moving in a social contradiction. Politeness took on the quality of a surrogate for other forms of social activity, which, from the point of view of changing absolutist conditions, no longer had a place in the social structure. This dichotomy was only experienced and thematised in its full force by those representatives who did not even have access to the surrogate activities of politeness within the sphere of court power. Loci for an opposition to power became institutionalised, in particular the salon, although it was only possible for the latter to develop by playing an active part in the further transformation of politeness (cf. Beetz 1990: 247f.). At the same time it was essential that politeness, whilst maintaining its function for the organisation of social intercourse, was on the point of moving into a new era in which the bourgeois middle classes were to supersede the court.

8. Example 4: The appropriation of politeness by the bourgeoisie in Germany

Whereas the transformations of medieval forms of politeness into modern humanistic and baroque forms took place principally by way of diffuse shifts – corresponding to the de facto "modernisation" character of the transformation from feudal to absolutist political structures – the process by which the bourgeoisie appropriated politeness was of a much stronger revolutionary character. Politeness is included among the ideological goals of the bourgeoisie and is first put to use to invest the bourgeoisie with greater social significance, so that their growing economic prosperity and significance in the overall social structure could be appropriately stressed. The final goal of this process, however, was to effect a wholesale shift in social relations in order to ensure that bourgeois forms of social intercourse were the hegemonic ones in society.

In this process the protagonists of the English bourgeoisie played a central role (cf. in particular Zaehle 1933: section V, 139ff.), and in this case too the Germans were late to adapt to what was happening, i.e., the ideological spread of politeness began via the translation of such journals as *The Tatler*, *The Spectator* or *The Guardian*. German journals imitating these English models represented the second step in the process.

The confrontation with forms and concepts of politeness that had been developed and propagated for a period of over two hundred years follows two paths. On the one hand, the results of this development were challenged polemically and, in particular, satirically. On the other hand, new concepts were spread as adaptations of politeness. It was central personalities on the German intellectual scene such as Gott-sched, Gellert and, above all, Lessing, who followed both paths. Critical discourse characterises lengthy periods of the eighteenth century from the thirties right up to the period immediately prior to the French Revolution. One year before the French Revolution Adolph Freiherr von Knigge's *Uber den Umgang mit Menschen (On human social intercourse)* was published. This has been referred to as "the sum of one person's life experience and at the same time of a way of life typical of the Age of the Enlightenment" (Fehn, Raabe and Ritterhoff 1977: 70). It was also a work that concluded the adaptation of politeness to the new social conditions in Germany in such a way that facilitated the transmission of politeness into the nineteenth century.

In addition to a new set of protagonists, a new set of concepts is developed for the new politeness. Above all, the "modernisation" of politeness takes on bourgeois forms in the shift to a bourgeois age in one or another significant way. Polemics against "gallant politeness" are carried on as polemics against its place of origin, France. On the contrary, the new form of politeness is taken to be specifically "German" – and this was, it should be noted, at a time when the expression was far from being transformed into its later national political meaning (cf., for example, on the process of "inventing the nation", Anderson 1988). On the other hand, an opposition is developed here which was to remain perennially problematic for the acceptance of "politeness" *(Höflichkeit)* in German. (This problem, tellingly formulated by Baccalaureus in Goethe's *Faust 2* (Act 2) as "In German you lie when you are polite," gave not only the title but also grounds for criticism to one of the most interesting recent conceptualisations of politeness in modern German scholarship, viz. Harald Weinrich's "Lügt man im Deutschen, wenn man höflich ist?" ["Do you lie in German when you are polite?"].)

The whole of the critical area which was to determine politeness in the period to follow was already covered by Gottsched. Zaehle (1933:

148) states the following:

> In *The sensible female rebukers* [...] Gottsched sets himself the job,
> carrying on from Thomasius' discourse on the appropriate form in
> which one should imitate the French in everyday life, of contributing
> towards the strengthening of national morals by sharply criticising
> "frenchified" morals and fashions. He makes fun of *politesse*, which,
> he maintains, is not natural to Germans. He makes fun of French and
> Italian daintiness, exaggerated turns of speech and complimenting in
> accordance with the fashion of gallantry. Good taste is just as frequent
> among the Germans as the French, who, among the peoples of
> Europe, have elbowed themselves quite indecently into positions of
> advantage with their *bon gout*.

In satirical sketches Gottsched caricatures the gallant cavalier "with
his delicately balanced manners, with his dainty steps and bows and
his artificially constructed compliments 'a so-called *galant homme* is a
person [...] who spends his time with festivities, with eating and
drinking, and, if need be, does some physical exercise to make himself popular with people who are watching' [*The sensible female
rebukers*, Part I, Stanza 10 [...]]" (Zaehle 1933: 149).

The ideal of the *Biedermann* ('honest man', a term which later received the sense of 'petty bourgeois') is opposed to the maxims for
behaviour which are related to court life, the *Biedermann* being
German whereas the courts are "un-German". The *Biedermann* is
characterised by "his wise house-keeping, the exemplary education of
his children, the loving and paternal attitude he takes towards the servants, his relaxed way of dealing with those lower on the social
scale." The *Biedermann* is someone "who honestly and openly seeks
his advantages in a lawful manner, who is concerned with increasing
the powers of his intellect and disposition in sensible intercourse with
learned and honest people" (ibid.). The content and form of linguistic
action are presented in a different light from that in which it had been
propagated for a period of a hundred and fifty years. Johann Georg
Hamann (1730–1788), a failed economist, "man of the world" and
finally supervisor in a packing department in Königsberg, the "Magus
of the North" (Friedrich Karl von Moser; cf. Winter 1984: 237), joins
in with these polemics and states, "a little ill-manneredness is still
more acceptable than empty, polite prattle" (Zaehle 1933: 148f.).

The new terminological frame for this concept of politeness is to be
found in the propagation of a new expression, the purpose of which is

to replace that of gallantry. Gottsched considers that the word 'gallant' is so misused that everything "that can be seen, heard, smelled, tasted, touched and felt must be called gallant, extremely gallant and completely gallant" [*The sensible female rebukers*, Part I, Stanza 10 [...]] (Zaehle 1933: 148). The new expression is *artig* ('well-behaved', 'civil'). *Artigkeit* 'civility', "which from now on [...] ousts gallantry more and more, can be taken virtually as the symbol of the new fashion of the age" (Zaehle 1933: 148f.).

Of course, even this concern with the content, form and purpose of politeness has its characteristic representatives of compromise, which could hardly have been otherwise if one considers general social and political conditions in Germany at the time. Those who were prepared to compromise considered, whilst bowing demonstratively in the direction of the court, the possibility of spreading the innovative power of the new concept of politeness more or less under the cloak of compatibility with the very thing with which it was in contrast. However, the conditions of bourgeois social activity had progressed too far to allow it to be simply generalised. Lessing's work represents the culmination of this confrontation.

Campe still recommends that social conflicts which also occur only too easily for the citizen's daily social activities in his/her dealings with the courts of small states should be solved by avoiding "wherever possible contact with courtly circles" (Zaehle 1933: 163), but otherwise by stoically enjoying his/her practical bourgeois superiority in refraining from open conflict. However, Lessing (1729–1781), the most important German author at the beginning of the classical period of German literature and at the same time a victim of these historically delayed small state structures of late political absolutism, typical for Germany in the middle of the eighteenth century, articulates unavoidable conflict openly and becomes openly polemical against politeness, transforming his polemics systematically in various types of text. For him, very much more strongly than was the case for Gottsched, politeness becomes "Frenchness". Setting up a German national culture is dependent on the prior criticism of French imports, and this is no less the case for the theory of aesthetics in which Shakespeare is contrasted with French "alexandrinism". But it would be wrong to interpret the opposition to "Frenchness", as it were, in the conceptual terms of the nineteenth or even the twentieth century. When Lessing criticises the courtly, the depraved, the humorous French, he is criticising just as much "a concept of life whose country of origin [...] is

France, but which has now become merely the primary indicator of the sphere of the court: the courtly concept of civilisation [...], the criticism of politeness is aimed [...] in the first instance at the social sphere in which life is carried out in accordance with a concept of civilisation characterised by notions of the court, courtliness and the courteous, and which exercised a strong influence on Europe from the court of Louis XIV. Lessing deliberately dissociates himself from this concept, attacks it as immoral and thus shows himself as being a representative of an anti-court bourgeoisie of the eighteenth century which, after a period in which it accepted the principles of this form of behaviour, now sees it as put-on and non-bourgeois" (Claus 1983: 25). Madeleine Claus has submitted this critical process to a careful analysis and has worked out in exemplary clarity how, at the centre of Lessing's criticism, we find the nobility orienting itself towards the French pattern and "in particular the German bourgeois who does not realise that his behaviour is not reconcilable with bourgeois ethics" (Claus 1983: 26).

Argument and dispute take the place of empty complimenting:

> Even if the tiuth were not divined by any single dispute, truth has nevertheless profited from all of them. Dispute has nourished the spirit of examination, it has kept prejudice and prestige in a constant state of unsettlement; in brief, it has prevented painted untruth from occupying truth's legitimate place. (Lessing VI, 407)

While in the person of the Prussian King Frederick II a French-oriented ruler of the German intelligentsia prolonging French court culture in the critical work of Voltaire in the Age of the Enlightenment in his tract *De la littérature allemande* assesses the lack of "civilisedness" in that literature, Lessing's critical work brings us to a turning point at which the courtly concept of politeness snapped for the Germans.

The best-seller *Ober den Umgang mit Menschen* (*On human social intercourse*) by Baron von Knigge, which was translated within a very short space of time into Danish, Dutch and even English (Fehn, Raabe, Ritterhoff 1971), no longer has as its protagonist the "courtier", but rather "the person". This person is the bourgeois-citizen who is aware of his specific, though limited possibilities for social activity in the bourgeois universe and realises his ends in such a way that those of other citizens are also realisable. Von Knigge writes:

However, in this work I have not intended to teach the art of misusing
people for one's own ends, of ruling over everyone at will and setting
everyone in motion for one's own personal desires. [...] The honest
man cannot make everything of all men, nor does he wish to do so;
and the man of firm principles does not allow others to make everything of himself. But each upright and wise person wishes and is able
to make better people at least do him justice; to make no one despise
him; to create peace from outside; [...] to create enjoyment from social
intercourse with all classes of people; to have others not misuse him
or lead him by the nose. And if he acts patiently, consistently, nobly,
carefully and in an upright manner, he can create for himself general
respect, can in the end even carry through almost any *good* thing if he
has studied people and does not let himself be put off by any difficulty. (Knigge 1788: II, 336)

In his main work Knigge (although, like Lessing, he despaired at
the real facts of social relationships) succeeded in emancipating politeness far enough from its connections with the court to achieve the
bourgeois transformation of forms of polite activity which appeared
sufficient in social relationships in Germany for the period to follow.

In terms of form Knigge is indebted to the propagandists of complimenting, but in terms of what he says he replaces them. On the
other hand, Lessing, in his critical, even polemical discourse, created a
transition to a thematisation of politeness which no longer simply
propagated its new forms and set itself against the old forms, but also
took the first steps towards a type of *conceptualisation*: politeness is
seen in its social frame and can then be put into perspective through
this perception.

In this way the example of politeness displays the beginnings of a
form of discourse which was to embrace the historicisation of all
forms of thought half a century later and which could only be ousted
with difficulty in the second half of the nineteenth century. The bourgeois appropriation of politeness reaches its completion in von
Jhering's great work entitled *Zweck im Recht*, an explicit theory of
politeness in the context of "human" aims (cf. Werkhofer's contribution to this volume), which was developed, however, in connection
with the "historical compromise" between the nobility and the bourgeoisie that was characteristic for the "Second Empire" in Germany.

Conceptualisations and the polemical oppositions they display in
the late eighteenth century, on which we have so far focused in repre-

senting the development of politeness in this epoch, should not lead us into forgetting that this dispute was more than the lonely pursuit of a small class of intellectuals. On the contrary, unless they were concerned with their own unique problems, they carried out the argument with a view to the social changes that are only abstractly conveyed by the term 'bourgeois'. It becomes immediately obvious which actors occupied the middle stage with respect to the new forms of social intercourse if we focus on which leading actor played the role of the man of court, viz. a clearly protagonistic bourgeois figure, the merchant. At the very beginning of the transition this is articulated with absolute clarity, e.g., when C. Weise puts it in the following way as early as 1696:

> The person with the greatest intelligence, the gieatest power and the
> greatest cleverness to earn money should clearly be placed before all
> others. (p. 522, quoted in Beetz 1990: 276)

In addition, this new leading figure does not even have to be distinguished from the intellectual propagandist of the post-gallant era of politeness. The "free writer" who, in contrast to the official and thus secure "poeta laureatus" of the baroque age, tries to support himself by means of his writings by carrying his books "to market" or, more precisely, to the Leipzig Fair or who has them carried there by the bookseller shows clearly that the protagonist, the propagandist and the profiteer of the "new politeness" can very easily come together in the one person.

9. The historicity of the present

I have tried to trace the historicity of politeness by means of four examples. However, they are no more than examples. A fully developed history of politeness would serve to strip them of their mantle of exemplification and to determine their precise position in the system.

But even as examples they are enough to show that "politeness", in opposition to an obviously popular conception of it and its reflection in the most recent conceptualisations offered in the social science and linguistic literature, is not only a historical phenomenon which belongs to the twists and turns of history and is just as sufficient for those twists and turns as history itself, but that the recognition of its historicity is an almost inalienable condition for understanding it.

The general conditions for politeness (cf. section 3) were illustrated by means of the ancient oriental developments of address terms (section 5). These conditions are the *boundary* and the *standard* necessary for politeness to crystallise, without which politeness can have no place. The standard takes a long time to develop historically. The social differentiation within a social structure that develops in the kingdom and what forms around it offers the opportunity for such a historical development.

The question of the standard has to be tackled to explain the politeness forms of the medieval and post-medieval worlds. Whereas the world of antiquity only feels the need to develop forms that can be characterised as "polite" by developing an explicitly social construction of that which surrounds central power and already discovers this standard *in potentia* by orienting towards this central power, the standard is set in the Middle Ages as a way of assigning membership to a social group and thereby of creating a new, internal social boundary. In both cases, however, these relationships maintained a simultaneous continuity in the formation of basic political structures. Polite (courtly) activity characterised the court and only the court, and this was explicitly understood.

Courtly (polite) activity became the object of programmes to be propagated. Concepts of politeness were developed and circulated. These concepts changed in the course of the transformation of feudalism into late feudalism and absolutism. Politeness as a concept and politeness as an *ensemble* of forms of activity took on new functions in the historical process (cf. sections 6 and 7).

Even the transformation of absolutist into a bourgeois society, as the German example shows (section 8), drew on the culture of politeness already developed in that completely new, polemically propagated forms and standards of activity took the place of courtly forms and standards at the same time as the significance of current views was recognised for bourgeois social intercourse. The tendency towards universalisation grew concurrently. The principal reason for this lay in the citizen's perception of her/himself as "the ultimate model person". In a theory of law this new standard was given an explicit formulation only to step finally into the background and, in the commonness of everyday practice and the triviality of books on good manners, to receive that banal form of propagation and realisation that still today guarantees an apparently generalised politeness – at least as it is imagined to be.

My examples from the history of politeness are presented as illustrations of the historicity of politeness. They are not therefore restricted to a conceptualisation of history as merely the past. The historicity of politeness continues into the present and in the present. This raises the question as to what the validity of present-day conceptualisations of politeness might be. We can add to this a second question on the social needs that these conceptualisations satisfy. For example, what does "face" (Brown and Levinson 1978) mean for a fully developed bourgeois society, and what does its universalisation mean, since this appears characteristic for present-day scholarly studies on politeness the world over, even though contrasting social anthropological data in ethnographic literature might yield other results (cf. Strecker forthcoming)? Tendencies towards universalisation themselves have a history and a time, viz. at points when the self-evident generalisation of singular forms of life no longer holds. The question of universality is a specifically modern question that only emerges on the horizon when societies are made insecure by the anthropologists' revelation of a multitude of human forms of life.

At the same time it is a question that is a consequence of the social circumstances in which various formations of politeness are present in petrified form – like the amalgamated concepts that correspond to these formations. The French bourgeois philosopher Henri Bergson was surely one of the first to formulate the need for a politeness that has been lifted out of historicity. He saw a way of doing this in conceptualising *a politesse du coeur* that would promise to allow for *une définition générale de la politesse* (Kremos 1955: 17). Twentieth century thinking about politeness operates within this horizon – and it forces us to eliminate from our consciousness precisely that historicity to which it owes its existence.

New thinking about politeness is required (cf. Watts and Werkhofer in this volume). The historicity of politeness is one of those characteristics which cannot be eliminated by way of abstraction. It deserves its historical locus in a conceptualisation of politeness which is reflexive in nature with respect to history and to action theory. This locus might turn out to be a starting point for a development of politeness in the sense of the social actors' self-enlightenment in relation to their social activity, and it might itself contribute to that self-enlightenment.

4. Literary texts and diachronic aspects of politeness

Roger D. Sell

1.

A period's own notions of politeness are connected with its sense of human nature in general. But even in periods whose overall tone we may think of as one of lofty idealism, there have been cynics; and there was much human behaviour to which the cynics could point in illustration of the baseness of man. Similarly, even in periods of apparently widespread disillusionment, there have been those in whose breasts hope sprang eternal; and there were at least some shining exemplars of human nobility. Many periods probably seem neither mainly the one way nor mainly the other. In which case the disagreement about human nature, and therefore about politeness, was even more pronounced.

As in all philosophy, so in moral philosophy, the disagreements can often be traced through what are competing, though sometimes only implicit, definitions of central terms. What, for instance, did "prudence" mean in eighteenth-century England? Did it mean a narrow calculation of personal advantage, associated if necessary with hypocritical dissimulation? Or did it mean a wise foresight, a conscientious husbandry of God's vineyard? Well obviously, Sister Western, in Fielding's *Tom Jones*, lives up – or rather, down – to the first of these definitions, accommodating the virtue in question to her own innate pride, guile and suspiciousness. For Squire Allworthy, in the same novel, on the other hand, the second definition would ring much more true, even though this does not prevent the good-hearted gentleman from making several sorry misjudgements of his fellow mortals. In Sophia, again, Fielding conceptualises a prudence that is a kind of tertium quid, "wise as serpents, and harmless as doves" (*Matthew* 10: 16).

Sometimes, what literary writers show us is that a term associated with a high view of man in one age, in subsequent ages is taken up by people who have a decidedly lower, or at least different, view. So the term itself narrows in reference – perhaps inconspicuously at first – and can even become ironised, in which case the disputants rally each other in terms of a binarism of old-fashioned/new-fangled. This is certainly the case with a number of words whose more lofty meanings have at some stage been close to that of "politeness". "Gentle", "courtier", "chivalry", for instance, did not, by the seventeenth century, entail everything they had implied for Chaucer or the translator of Castiglione. The middle-class was buying etiquette books in order to teach themselves a gentlemanliness which, obviously not their birthright, and far from an autotelic moral good, would be a means to the realisation of social ambition. Those denominated courtier in *Hamlet* ranged from the sententiously foolish, to the popinjay, to the timeserver. And the chivalrous don, in an English translation well nigh simultaneous with the Spanish original, was quaintly tilting at his windmills. In our own day, I suppose, we most often hear "chivalrous" on the lips of feminists, a smearword connoting antediluvian patriarchal subterfuge.

"Politeness" too, in English-language cultures at least, has for three centuries been involved in similar processes. In the eighteenth century it could have, like "prudence", both loftier and baser connotations, but since then the loftier connotations have faded a good deal, so that the term has sometimes been ironised like "chivalry", and its baser connotations have largely come to dominate, at least in what people think about it consciously (cf. Sell 1991).

At the zenith of its lofty meaning, politeness was the quintessentially Augustan aspiration, involving a view of man as both source and beneficiary of the blessings of civilisation and intellectual enlightenment. Philosophically underpinned by Shaftesburian benevolism, ameliorism, and moral sensibility, it was associated with the metropolitan aristocracy and opposed to rural life and cultural provinciality. It meant a high degree of mental cultivation and elegant refinement, polished manners and neo-classical good taste. Such qualities were said to be their own reward, and they were epitomised in a polite conversation that was well-informed and pleasurable – easy, free, natural, pliant, open-ended, humorous. They were also reflected in what was called polite literature. The politeness of literary texts *was* these qualities.

Used by students of English literature, the term politeness is still almost invariably applied to eighteenth-century writers, and with something pretty close to this lofty meaning. Even in the eighteenth century, however, "breeding", "manners", and "politeness" could already carry more cynical connotations, connotations which clearly bore some relation to the way people were actually behaving. Clearly, too, the more unedifying operations of politeness were not confined to intercourse between individuals. Politeness was also part of the larger ideological apparatus by which the aristocratic elite of the metropolis for so long marginalised the Tories and maintained the Whig supremacy.

Nineteenth-century novelists offer countless glimpses of the continued interweaving of politeness with issues of class and power, politeness now regularly being perceived as a mask or a means, and associated with callous selfishness. In Jane Austen's *Emma*, Knightley's dislike of Frank Churchill's facility in writing "a fine flourishing letter, full of professions and falsehoods" (Chapter 18: Austen 1816: 148–149) is not to be explained simply by his jealousy of a rival for Emma's love. It also really is a matter of the kind of man Churchill is, human kind still being partly defined here in terms of the urbane/rustic binarism. Churchill, it may be remembered, at one point says that he returned to town merely to have his hair cut, and he remains that kind of man even when it turns out that his trip had other purposes. Indeed, he is placed as one who allowed that deception – and deceptions far more grievous – to gain ground in the first place, thereby showing his sheer failure of consideration for the woman he professes to love. Again, in Dickens' *Little Dorrit* William Dorrit, painfully unsure of his own class status after all his years in the Marshalsea debtors' prison, pays Mrs. General – though such low pecuniary arrangements can never be mentioned by their real name – to Augustanise his daughter, and the instructress's understanding of her commission leads her to chastise even the slightest sign of that New Testament sentiment which in fact makes Amy such a good child. Dickens's ventriloquistic dramatisation of outdated and misguided propriety is in a spirit of exuberant ridicule:

"If Miss Amy Dorrit will direct her own attention to, and will accept of my poor assistance in, the formation of a surface, Mr. Dorrit will have no further cause of anxiety. May I take this opportunity of remarking, as an instance in point, that it is scarcely delicate to look at vagrants with the attention which I have seen bestowed upon them by a very dear young friend of mine? They should not be looked at. Nothing disagreeable should ever be looked at. Apart from such a habit standing in the way of that graceful equanimity of surface which is so expressive of good breeding, it hardly seems compatible with refine-

ment of mind. A truly refined mind will seem to be ignorant of anything that is not perfectly proper, placid, and pleasant." (Book II,
Chapter 5: Dickens 1857: 530)

Since the time of Dickens, much has happened to undermine the
prestige of the high Augustan ideal still further. The industrial and urban society which upset the old balance between town and country has
itself given way to post-industrialism and the global village. Two
world wars have not served to heighten people's sense of the magnifi-
cence of human accomplishment. The associated processes of social
levelling, or the advances of democracy, real and apparent, have made
Shaftesbury and his illustrious contemporaries simply difficult to remember, and those who do remember, those who admire and perhaps
themselves exemplify wide cultivation and polite manners springing
from an underlying moral decency, have long since lost any ideological dominance. Any suggestion that something called politeness might
arouse as much excitement as it still did in the breasts of William
Dorrit or of Mr. Knightley's more skittish neighbours in Highbury
would be widely greeted with mere incredulity, and the idea that it
could have deep roots in the fully cultivated human mind would be still
more alien. Now, many people probably think of politeness as little
more than a social lubricant less nocuous than alcohol, or as a velvet
glove within which to hide one or another kind of iron fist. The main
exception, as I say, would be literary scholars specialising in the
eighteenth century.

Anthropological linguists therefore seem a good deal more up to
date. Brown and Levinson (1978, 1987), on the basis of empirical
work in three widely separated language cultures, have universalised
politeness across history and geography, and at the same time
narrowed it right down, as the linguistically realised strategies by
which human beings hold their own or grasp for more. Their work
thus forms an interesting pendant to Marx on the class struggle, Freud
on sex, Adler on power, analyses which have so signally contributed,
not always in ways their originators would have countenanced, to our
age's dominant cynicism.

Brown and Levinson posit a model person with two endowments: a
practical reason which enables him to work out what means can be
used to achieve any of his given ends; and face. Face has both a negative aspect, in the simple desire to be left alone and free to do as he
wants, and a positive aspect, in the desire that other people actually

approve of him and include him in their own circle. In the calculations of his practical reason, the model person also assumes that other people are endowed with positive and negative face as well, and that his own goals are more likely to be achieved by taking this into account. The politeness options arise when the model person wishes to do or say something which in some way threatens another person's face – to commit a "face-threatening act". At this point I myself am inclined to ask whether the politest thing would not be to refrain from such an act in the first place, and I should receive support from some of the eighteenth-century accounts of politeness; Fielding, for instance, concluded that *"Good-breeding,* ... or the *Art of pleasing in Conversation,* ... may be reduced to that concise, comprehensive rule in Scripture: *Do unto all men as you would they should do unto you"* (Fielding 1903: XIV 249–250). Such a course, however, might reduce the likelihood of the model person's own goals being realised, and for Brown and Levinson politeness only comes into play as he manoeuvres to increase that likelihood. In their account, then, the most polite strategy is to commit the face-threatening act, but in a way that is "off record", with its threateningness veiled in metaphor, irony, understatement, hints, and so on, so that the actual meaning is to some extent negotiable and the other person not openly forced to recognise it (e.g., "Damn, I'm out of cash, I forgot to go to the bank"). Less polite, though still polite to some extent, are two "on record" strategies involving redressive action: negative politeness and positive politeness, by which the model person, though now explicitly performing the face-threatening act, nevertheless pays deference, respectively, to the other person's negative and positive face (e.g., "Excuse me, but would you mind lending me five pounds?" and "Lend me a fiver, old boy?"). Lastly there is a bald on-record strategy, in which the act is performed with no polite redress at all (e.g., "Lend me five pounds").

2.

This, then, is what many people think today on the question of politeness. Yet even though it is a position now fortified by a solid body of scholarship, who knows where they will stand in ten years' time? Nothing will ever fix the reference of "politeness" to human behaviour once and for all. The varieties of human behaviour, and the meanings of the terms which are used to describe it, are for ever in transition.

My own work on politeness (Sell 1985a, 1985b, forthcoming a) is itself some proof of this last claim. On the one hand I believe that even in a period which had no explicit concept of politeness, politeness considerations would nevertheless be operative, and I accept, in a cynical modern way, that important aspects of politeness have to do with face, and that the distinction between negative and positive face is useful. Yet on the other hand I already differ from Brown and Levinson, in that I do not see politeness as a principle in isolation from others, and I do not see it as coming into operation only when people face-threateningly address each other, talk about other people, or make commands, requests, or enquiries. I see all interaction, and all language, as operating within politeness parameters. Politeness, one might say, or a sensitivity to politeness considerations, is mankind's patient, sleepless super-ego. This is not to say that I could parse all interaction according to some behavioural grammar, nor that I could closely and comprehensively map every new utterance in a discourse on an underlying interaction. I do believe, though, that politeness considerations are interwoven with everything we say and do.

There is, I have suggested, a pragmatic politeness spectrum in every cultural milieu, such that everything done and said will be experienced as either to some or other degree impolite, or as quite neutral as to politeness, or as to some or other degree polite. In this way of thinking, moreover, though not in the terminology I happen to have used, I seem to be very close to Watts (present volume). My behaviour experienced as polite is Watts's explicit politeness. It includes ritualised, formulaic behaviour, indirect speech strategies, conventionalised linguistic strategies for saving and maintaining face, address formulae, indirectness, the minimising of imposition, hedging, the conferral of in-group status, feigned modesty, and so on. This explicit politeness Watts sees as a conventionally interpretable and marked subset of "politic behaviour", and politic behaviour is "socioculturally determined behaviour directed towards the goal of establishing and/or maintaining in a state of equilibrium the personal relationships between the individuals of a social group [...] during the ongoing process of interaction." The behaviour which in my account is experienced as neutral as regards politeness is close to what Watts calls unmarked politic behaviour, while that experienced as impolite in my account is Watts's impolitic behaviour. One of the most important features of our accounts is that they both stress ongoing strategic considerations even in the spectrum's central reaches of behaviour not overtly polite.

Indeed, I have argued that politeness can begin further back than it does for Brown and Levinson: it can begin with the choice of act, which may not even be a matter of conscious deliberation. Like Fielding, I would see the performance or non-performance of a face-threatening act as already impolite or polite.

A further difference from Brown and Levinson is that on my view politeness can also start much later: I believe that it is perfectly possible to perform an act which is not in itself a face-threatening act in such a way that it is nevertheless experienced as impolite. Even to-day, that is, and despite the cynical things which both the man in the street and anthropological linguists might consciously think about it, I believe that politeness is experienced, not only as the velvet glove on the iron fist of isolated offensive acts, but also as an overall style of behaviour that is decidedly to be approved of. Ideologically speaking, it is as if politeness were no longer felt to be dangerous, and this may even allow a partial reversion to eighteenth-century norms. People now may actually be more pluralistic than Dickens and Jane Austen. Although not prepared to let somebody, or some class, gain sway over them by sheer cultivated behaviour; although under no illusion that they themselves, by maintaining or acquiring cultivated behaviour, can hold sway over others; and although therefore feeling, as I have already suggested, that politeness on the whole is really neither here nor there: perhaps they nevertheless react as if cultivated behaviour did have a value.

This harmless non-coerciveness of much polite behaviour today brings us to what I call the paradoxes of politeness, again something which does not receive much recognition in Brown and Levinson. I too shall not deal with this in detail; it is really a set of special problems for scholars whose aim is a close and comprehensive mapping of utterance on interaction. But certainly one such problem is that politeness is often experienced by the person who practises it as not achieving very much. Often politeness is just as much a matter of routine convention – ritualised and formulaic, even – as subject-verb concord, so that to omit it would be almost unthinkable, and to include it is not felt to bring any particular rewards: omission is perhaps the only way to provoke any reaction at all. Another paradox I have already mentioned: a not-impolite act can be experienced as impolitely executed. Again, a polite manner can be experienced as impolite. More generally, by adopting a polite strategy people do not always, in practice, achieve their goals; they sometimes achieve them by *im*polite means; and sometimes they achieve them not at all. True, in any situation the politeness spectrum has a pragmatic reality. But as far as the effects and pay-offs go, the question of where people choose to place themselves on it is very much a matter of calculated risk, a tight-rope walk between too much politeness and too little. An act performed by one person is received as impolite, whereas, performed under the same circumstances by a virtually identical person, the same act is received as polite. And so on. The more one thinks about it, the more one feels, as with interaction in general, that politeness does not work in predictable ways, and that those who handle it most skilfully are somehow uncanny. If they happen to be literary artists, this is presumably one aspect of – old-fashioned idea! – their genius.

3.

These, then, are my own general notions about politeness in March 1989, but it may be that I shall live long enough for them to change in some important respects. They are already somewhat different from those of certain other scholars, and part of what I have been doing here is to place them in an historical retrospect. But how, more particularly, do I apply them to the field of interaction between literary writers and their readers – to the politeness, not of Mrs. General or other characters within the mimetic world of literary texts, but of the literary texts themselves as they are experienced by readers?

According to Leech (1983: 104–105), politeness is largely irrelevant as an aspect of most written discourse. In my account, however, the politeness of literary texts is vital: it is the surest sign of their interactive dimension, and this was the reason why I became interested in it in the first place. Literariness, on my view, cannot be defined in terms of a single function or set of functions, or in terms of one or more intrinsic features. I embrace, rather, a definition of literature which is nominalistic and socio-cultural: a literary text is a text which is designated literary within a certain milieu. For me, the study of literature is therefore ultimately a kind of socio-cultural history, which proceeds by establishing relationships between aesthetic or other norms and particular phases of civilisation, and by tracing the interaction of individual writers with society at large. Even if literary authors themselves embrace formalist, structuralist, or post-structuralist theories which in one way or another deny the interactive dimensions of literary texts, the interaction still takes place, and the denial is one aspect of it (cf. Sell 1986, 1989). Through a discussion of their politeness I wished to underline this point.

It has seemed to me that I could achieve this relatively straightforward end by tracing politeness dimensions both in the choice of subject-matter and language, and in the helpfulness of presentation. In other words, my frame of reference again differs considerably from that of Leech (1983). Within his interpersonal rhetoric Leech does have a politeness principle, but it is separate from the cooperative principle, which for him consequently seems to have no politeness dimension at all. By contrast, the early work on politeness by Lakoff (1973) saw conversational rules of cooperative clarity as a subset of the first of her three politeness rules: I) Don't impose! II) Give options! III) Be friendly! My detection of politeness considerations at work in both selection and presentation is very much in this spirit.

A writer who maintained absolute *selectional* politeness would scrupulously observe all the taboos and conventions of social and moral decorum operative within the culture, never saying anything, and never using any words, which would be in the least face-threatening, whether positively or negatively. Selectional politeness thus embraces features both from the underlying interaction between writer and readers, where the choice of some types of subject matter constitutes a face-threatening act, and from the linguistic expression: some types of language, as Brown and Levinson show, mitigate such an act; but also, within a given social group various types of language are themselves offensive or inoffensive, quite irrespective of the interaction which they harness.

Again, a writer who maintained absolute *presentational* politeness would observe Grice's Cooperative Principle at all costs, so that readers would never be in the slightest doubt as to what was happening, what was meant, or why it was being said. Thanks to the advances of linguistic pragmaticists, psycholinguists, text-linguists, and discourse analysts, we now have at least five concepts which help to concretise cooperativeness: discourse deixis, salience markers, frames/scripts/scenarios/schemata, sectional boundaries, and communicative dynamism.

But then there are the paradoxes and the uncanniness of politeness, the interactive gambles. Absolute politeness, of either kind, will obviously not do. Obsequious over-selection would rule out much of the

pleasure of literary texts, much irony and satire, much gentle goading
of the reader by the writer. Dull over-presentation, again, would rule
out certain elements of surprise, suspense, or intellectual and moral
stimulus, generally leaving readers with too little work to do for themselves, and with that much less opportunity for real engagement with
the text.

In trying to illustrate all this, I have discussed Chaucer, partly
looking at isolated details, but also raising the question of whether it is
possible to talk about styles of politeness, to which I answer with a
carefully qualified affirmative.

Much more illustration from texts is needed, but so too is empirical
study of reader response. My suggestion has been that the politeness
dimension of literary texts is actually what we respond to first of all in
them, in a kind of interactive gut-reaction. Thus for F.R. Leavis certain rhythms immediately signalled a mixture of selectional affront and
presentational boringness:

> It is by a kind of incantation, a hypnotic effect figured in the endless
> pulsing of drums playing so large a part in Don Ramón's campaign,
> that Lawrence tries to generate conviction, and he produces boredom
> and a good deal of distaste. (Leavis 1955: 71)

> In the end we find ourselves protesting – protesting against the routine
> gesture, the heavy fall, of the verse, flinching from the foreseen thud
> that comes so inevitably, and, at last, irresistibly; for reading *Paradise
> Lost* is a matter of resisting, [...] and [...] we surrender at last to the
> inescapable monotony of the ritual. (Leavis 1936: 43)

And sometimes the offensiveness is enough to stop a reader reading
on, or to affect a critic's entire structure of elaborate evaluation. As in
other areas of life, we can suspect that gut feelings may precede and
determine rational argument.

The reason why the politeness of literary texts, probably more than
the politeness of any other type of language use, lends itself to
diachronic study is precisely that the responses of earlier readers have
come down to us. They take the form of literary criticism, book and
theater reviews, comments in letters, commonplace books and diaries,
and so on. These sources do have their limitations, needless to say.
They do not provide direct answers to many of the questions we
should like to ask. They tell us a lot less about the earlier responses to

some works than to others. And there can also be other factors which make the comments of one dead informant difficult to relate to those of another. Nevertheless, used with patience and discretion, they can provide material for empirical and diachronic reception studies which probably represent our best hope for some kind of history of politeness.

4.

How, then, should we try to locate detailed changes in politeness in a shortish period? Clearly, we should be under no illusion that we can read a literary text, focus on the politeness issues it raised, and then turn to the responses of earlier readers to see what was said about them. We ourselves are historical beings, tending to respond according to the criteria of our own reading community. It may well be that this community responds to some aspects of both *The Plumed Serpent* and *Paradise Lost* with much the same feelings of boredom, distaste, and protest as F.R. Leavis did. But equally well it may not, or it may now find one of these works offensive but not the other. The only way to arrive at anything like certainty is to study the earlier responses first, and as extensively as possible.

What once seemed outrageous is hardest to guess at when the texts in question have subsequently been canonised as great literature. It is, I realise, a cliché that all great original works shock and surprise, and it may not even be true: despite much intelligent speculation (for instance by Press 1958), we shall not be able to say that all great works have seemed equally offensive until we have looked at all the available evidence, and perhaps not even then. But many great works certainly have offended, only to become, with the passing of the years, more familiar and "expected".

In 1992, then, it is hardly possible to be shocked by the following lines:

> April is the cruellest month, breeding
> Lilacs out of the dead land, mixing
> Memory and desire, stirring
> Dull roots with spring rain.
> Winter kept us warm, covering
> Earth in forgetful snow, feeding

A little life with dried tubers.
Summer surprised us, coming over the Starnbergersee
With a shower of rain; we stopped in the colonnade,
And went on in sunlight, into the Hofgarten,
And drank coffee, and talked for an hour.
Bin gar keine Russin, stamm' aus Litauen, echt deutsch.
And when we were children, staying at the arch-duke's,
My cousin's, he took me out on a sled,
And I was frightened. He said, Marie,
Marie, hold on tight. And down we went.
In the mountains, there you feel free.
I read, much of the night, and go south in the winter.
What are the roots that clutch, what branches grow
Out of this stony rubbish? Son of man,
You cannot say, or guess, for you only know
A heap of broken images, where the sun beats,
And the dead tree gives no shelter, the cricket no relief,
And the dry stone no sound of water. ...
(Eliot 1969: 61)

As far as we can tell, Eliot's niche in the pantheon is now his for ever. We are just as likely to come to his poetry as to Wordsworth's or Shakespeare's. We are just as likely to hear it explained and extolled by a schoolteacher. We are just as likely to learn some of it by heart, including, perhaps, the passage just quoted. How could we, now, be surprised by something so much a part of the culture around us, and so deeply internalised? Eliot demanded the attention of our fathers and grandfathers by being outrageous. But he demands ours because he is a classic.

Classics seem polite. With Eliot now, impoliteness becomes an issue only when new writers desecrate *him*. We concede, perhaps, that for his time he was original, and we can probably even say how. But unless we possess an unusually energetic and well-informed historical imagination, we can no longer feel in our bones the affronting unsettlingness of such originality. We talk of it too exclusively in terms of qualities of mind, imagination, or ear. Its interactive social dynamics are nowadays different.

Yet before we have read many pages of the *Critical Heritage* volumes on Eliot (Grant 1982) we can feel ourselves beginning to re-live the original tensions. We begin to see the poem almost as if for the first time, and it is a straightforward and even rather plodding task to make an inventory of the features which aroused the strongest protest, together with flagrant examples of each.

Among the features raising considerations of selectional politeness, some were partly a matter of diction: the baffling and allegedly over-learned use of quotations and allusions, many of them involving foreign languages, and hardly illuminated by the cryptic end-notes; or the destabilising alternation from grand style to cockney slang. But the selection of subject-matter was even more upsetting, since many readers found much of what Eliot actually had to say and describe fundamentally unpleasant. The very first line inverted the usually joyful associations of spring (which were at least as old as the first line of *The Canterbury Tales);* the talk of the human mind or human life as a heap of broken images was hardly less depressing; and this was only the beginning. Not that some very grim things had not been said in earlier poetry. True, Arnold had had the decency to remove the distressing "Empedocles on Etna" from his collection of 1853, but Tennyson – still deeply venerated in 1922 – was in places very bleak, and even the poetry of Masefield or the Georgians – which we now oversimplify as all hearty seafaring or blithe pastoralism – had stretches of dour enough realism. Eliot, however, did seem to be raising miserableness to a new level, and to be miserable most of the time. There seemed to be so much sordid sterility and blank despair, and the effect was all the more shattering because of fleeting lyrical hints of love or beauty or fulfilment.

But the strain on presentational politeness was perhaps even greater. The basic problem was of coherence, a problem the end-notes were often felt to highlight rather than solve – "a poem that has to be explained in notes is not unlike a picture with 'This is a dog' inscribed underneath. Not, indeed, that Mr. Eliot's notes succeed in explaining anything, being as muddled as incomplete" (Lucas 1923). Not only did Eliot not translate the foreign quotations. He did not make it clear how they fitted in with anything else, or, indeed, how anything fitted. There was no overall story: the notes said one should see everything in the light of the Fisher King myth, but passages such as the pub scene, the rape of the river nymphs, or the coupling of the typist and the young man carbuncular seemed to dramatise what could be episodes in several separate narratives. There was no clear sense of who was speaking: the notes hinted that all the voices somehow belonged to Tiresias, yet Tiresias seemed a shadowy figure, and this still did not help one to move from, say, "April is the cruellest month" to "Bin gar keine Russin, stamm' aus Litauen, echt deutsch". There was no clear discursive line of philosophical argument: there were only snatches of thought and apparently random juxtapositions of images. And there was not even a consistency of verse-form or stylistic level. A more chaotic composition – though that was surely not the right noun! – was difficult to imagine.

In both selection and presentation *The Waste Land* had in some respects been anticipated by Pound's "Hugh Selwyn Mauberley" and by Eliot's own "Prufrock" and "Gerontion", but the responses of early readers show that Eliot was now raising the stakes in the interactive game of politeness far higher. What, then, made him think that people might go on reading? And why did they, actually? Of course we can never have full answers to either question. But by carefully relating the text of the poem to the early responses, and also to what Eliot himself did or said in other contexts, we can make intelligent guesses.

The poem's selectional offensiveness was mitigated, I suggest, in two main ways, one of which has to do with those hints of love, beauty, or fulfilment. As I have said, these partly worked as a foil which made the sordid sterility and blank despair seem even more distressing. Yet at the same time they could clearly be read in their own right, and the poet of

> – Yet when we came back, late, from the hyacinth garden,
> Your arms full, and your hair wet, I could not
> Speak, and my eyes failed, I was neither
> Living nor dead, and I knew nothing,
> Looking into the heart of the light, the silence. (Eliot 1969: 62)

could meet admirers of Dante or Rossetti half-way, and perhaps more than half-way. Indeed, an odd kind of *gestalt*-switch could occur, whereby all the sordidness and sterility became the foil to the intense moments of spiritual anguish, yearning, and dawning vision. The tendency of readers to process the text in this way was encouraged by some of the most well-known passages of English literary criticism from earlier periods – for instance, Keats on *King Lear*:

> [...] the excellence of every Art is in its intensity, capable of making
> all disagreeables evaporate, from their being in close relationship with
> Beauty and Truth [...] (Keats 1954: 52)

– , but Eliot's own earliest criticism, for instance the essay on Dante that concluded *The Sacred Wood,* was a still more immediate stimulus:

The contemplation of the horrid or sordid or disgusting, by an artist, is the necessary and negative aspect of the impulse toward the pursuit of beauty. (Eliot 1920: 169)

After the publication of *Ash Wednesday* and the news of Eliot's confirmation, such readings were well on their way to becoming orthodox. In 1947 Helen Gardner could write: "Most people would agree today, in the light of Mr. Eliot's later work, that the original critics of *The Waste Land* misread it, not recognising it as an *Inferno* which looked towards *a Purgatorio "* (Gardner 1947).

The other kind of selectional mitigation was for a different kind of reader, and "mitigation" is actually a misnomer. The point is that there were readers who positively acquiesced in the poem's offensiveness of theme because it seemed to them, not misplaced, but profoundly clairvoyant. These were readers for whom the First World War had brought an end to civilisation and hope, for whom the present was a ghastly charade of shadows, a barren wilderness, for whom modern technology and society represented a betrayal of mankind's ancient sources of strength. Or perhaps they were readers who finally saw things in this way as they began to contemplate *The Waste Land.* Once again, the reading strategy was reinforced by things quite external to the text of the particular poem. Eliot's own early criticism often seemed to take the sordid and the disgusting as the basic fact of modern life. Soon "The Hollow Men" seemed to be further elaborating the hopeless meaninglessness of the age, and by 1931 Edmund Wilson was persuasively seeing Eliot's "poetry of drouth" as the mirror of post-war society. In 1932 the following widely influential gloss was offered by F.R. Leavis:

In considering our present plight we have … to take account of the incessant rapid change that chaiacterises the Machine Age. The result is breach of continuity and the uprooting of life. This last metaphor has a peculiar aptness, for what we are witnessing today is the final uprooting of the immemorial ways of life, of life deeply rooted in the soil. (Leavis 1932: 71)

Such readings seemed to harmonise, furthermore, with accounts of modern life to be found in other contemporary writers such as Lawrence and Huxley.

As for the poem's presentational impoliteness, even the most cursory examination of the text revealed one feature which sharply qualified the impression of overall incoherence. Locally, *The Waste Land* had a perspicuousness of sometimes almost unbearable intensity, and this alone was presumably enough to keep some readers reading.

> A rat crept softly through the vegetation
> Dragging its slimy belly on the bank
> While I was fishing in the dull canal
> On a winter evening round behind the gashouse. (Eliot 1969: 67)

About this and numerous other phrases, lines, passages there was, quite simply, nothing unclear. On the contrary, there was much that was not only clear but strangely fascinating.

This somewhat paradoxical state of affairs did not pass without comment, but for some readers the local clarity has never wholly redeemed the overall confusion. In 1960, Graham Hough still described the poem as being basically in the Imagist tradition, which is capable only of brilliant lyrics and short-term effects (Hough 1960). Early champions of Eliot such as Pound, I. A. Richards, Conrad Aiken, Leavis, and Cleanth Brooks, however, certainly were able to provide various rationalisations, partly suggested, as we should by now expect, by Eliot's own criticism. Three in particular offered especially powerful reading strategies.

One argument was that Eliot had chosen the only form capable of capturing the nature of modern life. This was anticipated by Eliot's immensely influential essay on the Metaphysical poets, published a year before *The Waste Land:*

> We can only say that it appears likely that poets in our civilisation, as it exists at present, must be *difficult*. Our civilisation comprehends great variety and complexity, and this variety and complexity, playing upon a refined sensibility, must pioduce various and complex results. The poet must become moie and more comprehensive, more allusive, more indirect, in order to force, to dislocate if necessary, language into his meaning. (Eliot 1951: 289)

In 1943, Yvor Winters was to attack this argument as an example of the fallacy of imitative form: "Eliot, in dealing with debased and stupid material, felt himself obliged to seek his form in this matter: the result is confusion and journalistic reproduction of detail" (Winters 1959: 70). Yet many other readers came to feel that it was profoundly appropriate to its theme that the poem should be "a heap of broken images", "fragments ... shored against my ruins", and the abrupt transitions from one thing to the next were further justified as a collage technique like that sometimes used, for similar reasons, in the visual arts in the Modernist period.

A second rationalisation developed the implications of that "refined sensibility" of the poet on which contemporary civilisation "plays". Here again the essay on the Metaphysical poets was seminal, in effect giving a new lease of life to Coleridge's account of poetic imagination as manifested in a reconciliation of opposite and discordant qualities:

> When a poet's mind is perfectly equipped for its work, it is constantly amalgamating disparate experience; the ordinary man's experience is chaotic, irregular, fragmentary. The latter falls in love, or reads Spinoza, and these two experiences have nothing to do with each other, or with the noise of the typewriter or the smell of cooking; in the mind of the poet these experiences are always forming new wholes. (Eliot 1951: 287)

This and similar formulations were of crucial importance to the development of American New Criticism, with its eloquent attempts to demonstrate new unities underlying the ironies, ambiguities, paradoxes, tensions, and apparent discords of literary texts. So it was hardly surprising that the method came to be applied, by Cleanth Brooks, to Eliot himself. Brooks finds that from the poem's multi-layered ironies and incongruous juxtapositions there emerges a sense of the oneness of experience and the unity of all periods. Interestingly enough, Brooks's concluding sentence nicely rebuts protests over presentational incoherence and selectional unpleasantness in the same breath: A "statement of beliefs emerges *through* confusion and cynicism – not in spite of them" (Brooks 1939: 172).

Thirdly, there was the argument that to look for a narrative or discursive thread in a poem is at once too simple and too sophisticated a procedure. One of the precedents in Eliot's own criticism was from *The Use of Poetry and the Use of Criticism* (1933) and ran as follows:

> The chief use of the "meaning" of a poem, in the ordinary sense, may be ... to satisfy one habit of the reader, to keep his mind diverted and

quiet, while the poem does its work upon him: much as the imaginary burglar is always provided with a bit of nice meat for the house-dog. This is a normal situation of which I approve. But the minds of all poets do not work that way; some of them, assuming that there are other minds like their own, become impatient of this "meaning" which seems superfluous, and perceive possibilities of intensity through its elimination. (Eliot 1933: 151-152)

This line of argument was of course thoroughly concordant with the contemporary dogmas of psychoanalysis and Surrealism, but Eliot more characteristically saw the "possibilities of intensity" in terms of "The Music of Poetry" – this was the title of a lecture on the subject in 1942 (Eliot 1957). This music could originate, before words, in a rhythm; and the reader did not need to understand the words in order to appreciate it. As early as 1926, I. A. Richards had expatiated on the complex psychological organisation of *The Waste Land's* "music of ideas" (Richards 1926), and many subsequent commentators have dwelt on subtle interweavings of mood and tone. In time, the poem's five parts came to be compared with the movements of a Beethoven string quartet, an interpretative strategy further encouraged by "The Music of Poetry" and in the structure and title of *Four Quartets*.

To recapitulate, then: Actively encouraged by Eliot himself, there grew up around *The Waste Land* a body of commentary which served to soften the poem's offensiveness. Its selectional impoliteness came to be weighed against a perceived desire for spiritual wholeness, or against an acclaimed honesty about the modern condition. And its presentational impoliteness came to be read as a formal equivalent to its modern themes, as the expression of a refined and ultimately unifying sensibility, and as the expression of deeper, non-cerebral modes of knowing and being. With both kinds of politeness, the discussion revealed some sense of Eliot's gamble – of the socially interactive tension between different aspects of the text: between the images of sordidness and futility and the images of love and thirst; and between an overall incoherence and the local intensities.

All literary texts, I have argued, to some extent challenge existing norms of politeness if only in order to win attention and be interesting. But one aspect of the revolution in literary taste associated with *The Waste Land is* certainly that it challenged them to an unusual degree. The compensations for, and re-interpretations of, that challenge needed an unusual degree of reinforcement, both in the text of the poem itself and in the debate surrounding it.

5.

I see no reason to suppose that changes in the politeness of literary texts, as I have described it, are essentially different from changes in the politeness associated with other kinds of human activity. I believe that a society's conventions of politeness, in all spheres of interaction, are sometimes more honoured in the breach than the observance. For one reason or another, somebody starts to do something unexpected, or to omit to do something expected. And if persuasive rationalisations, reinterpretations, and compensations are found, the breach is accommodated, so contributing to a revised sense of the polite.

In the case of *The Waste Land* the assimilation of the impolitenesses was certainly facilitated by two further factors which would operate in other spheres of behaviour as well. What was at issue here was not so much the detailed nature of particular breaches, as of the credentials of their perpetrator and the context of the perpetration.

In the first place, we do not react so violently to impoliteness if we think its perpetrator did not "really mean it", as we say. The impoliteness of a madman, a drunk, an absent-minded professor, a person in a great hurry, counsel for the prosecution, a very close friend or loved-one, is simply not very offensive. And the fact is that Eliot's early poetry, once again as the result of his own criticism, was felt to be not wholly expressive of him as a man: true poetry, it was said, was impersonal. Only in the past twenty years or so have we come to realise what a travesty of Eliot's work this is. Of course I am not suggesting that Eliot started the red herring as a conscious strategy of compensation for impoliteness – my guess is that he wanted to shield his unhappy private life from the prying public, that he in genuine modesty believed that his own feelings were too small for poetry, and that he in any case really did think poetry should be impersonal. My point here is only that, persuaded by "Tradition and the Individual Talent" and other early essays by Eliot, the first readers were conditioned to defuse the expressivity of *The Waste Land,* and that, had they not done so, they would have found it far more offensive affectively. In the climate of ideas within which they read it, the poem simply could not seem full-bloodedly rude. Slightly to modify Eliot's famous dictum, the assumption on which they read was that the more perfect the artist, the more entirely separate in him will be the man who offends and the mind which creates.

But secondly, even if readers did begin to think that Eliot "really meant" his impoliteness, they could also come to feel that they had no right to be offended. This is always the way if the perpetrator of impoliteness has appropriate kinds of social prestige and public image, as Eliot, from very early on, certainly did have. He was held in considerable esteem as the editor of *Criterion*. Through his job with Faber and Faber he became the most important arbiter and Maecenas of contemporary poetry. He was for ever throwing out, with a more-than-Johnsonian authority of tone, hints for a new literary history according to his own criteria. And increasingly, and publicly, he associated himself with forces of ideological reaction, deliberately cultivating an old-fogey persona to boot. Thanks to the stories that circulated about him he rapidly became a kind of living legend – Virginia Woolf wrote to her brother-in-law: "Come to dinner. Eliot will be there in a four-piece suit" (quoted in Gordon 1977: 83-84).

The deflection of other people's outraged protests by a facade of propriety worked its way from the life back into the literary texts. In everyday life, he sometimes far exceeded usual norms in the conferral of negative face. On one occasion in 1923, for instance, he positively shocked Richard Aldington by raising his hat to a sentry outside Malborough house. This gesture, symptomatic to his biographer of residual American ignorance of British customs (Ackroyd 1985: 166), suggests, underneath the bowler hat and dark suit, an Eliot close to the Prufrock who has "seen the eternal Footman hold my coat, and snicker". Throughout Eliot's poetry, there is in fact a long sequence of characters, personae, or voices caught in the throes of almost masochistic humility – from the social insecurity and inferiority complex of Prufrock to the self-abasement before God in *Four Quartets*. The politeness dramatised within Eliot's poetry, in other words, like the politeness Eliot cultivated in life, is sometimes completely at odds with the politeness *of* that poetry, which was decidedly aggressive towards its readers. The politeness in the poetry often belonged to an age long since past, and was a main aspect of the reassurance he offered.

Not that either was more real or more true, of course. And Eliot's deferential offensiveness or offensive deference is a riddle more exceptional in degree than in kind, supporting lofty and more cynical accounts of politeness in equal measure. This is one reason why I have tried to combine loftiness and cynicism in a concept of politeness altogether larger than that now fashionable. My main argument, however, has been that by studying the politeness portrayed *in*, and the politeness expressed *by*, literary texts we come to see that human behaviour and the meanings of moral terms are for ever in flux. If, as William Blake and others have argued, history moves through opposites, Brown and Levinson's account of politeness may one day be replaced by one that is more entirely benevolist than even I could accept – at present.

5. Politeness in linguistic research

Gudrun Held

1. Introduction

Linguistic research into politeness is closely associated with the names of Lakoff (1973, 1975, 1977), Leech (1977, 1980, 1983), and Brown and Levinson (1978, 1987). These writers have attempted to approach the definitionally fuzzy and empirically difficult area of politeness with pragmatic means, to derive a number of basic theoretical notions, and to find evidence of politeness in linguistic forms. The common basis of their work, the so-called Grice–Goffman paradigm, indicates one way of coming to grips with the phenomenon of verbal politeness which, because of the variety of forms in which it has been taken up and applied to a large number of formal and functional areas of language (cf. Brown and Levinson 1987: 1–54), represents what I shall call the classical approach in explaining polite interactional modalities.

These models have certainly done great service in revealing and abstracting out the multi-level relationship of tension, so typical for politeness, between universality and specificity on the one hand and strict conventions and situation-specific variation on the other. Yet in the process the broad scope of polite behaviour has also undergone a certain reduction to rational, goal-directed behaviour strategies in which the component of respect is almost exclusively anchored in indirectness.

In line with the development of linguistic pragmatics the focal point of this research has been Anglo-Saxon, the result being that the English language is not only the primary object of research and source of data for linguistic politeness but is also responsible, in its function as a metalanguage, for terminological concepts that are often hard to translate into other languages.[1] In the eighties the privileged position of English has been somewhat undermined by German linguists. Alongside the critical reception of Anglo-American pragmatics[2] it is primarily peculiarities in the structure of German, such as particles, whose complex functions as illocutionary modifiers have provided the impetus for the theoretical discussion of politeness and given rise to the concerted and continuous research in this particular problem area (cf. Bublitz 1978; Franck 1980; Lange 1984; Werlen 1984; Weinrich 1984; Zimmermann 1984, 1985).

On the other hand, the Romance languages lag far behind this development. Regardless of the cultural and historical pride of place that they can claim with respect to politeness in Europe and the Western world and that led to the first ever linguistic remarks on the phenomenon (cf., for example, Dauzat 1912; Bally 1913; Spitzer 1922; Brunot 1922; Beinhauer 1930), pragmatic interest in questions of politeness has only recently begun to emerge in a halting, sporadic fashion – a development which even the appeal by Duranti (1974) entitled "Cortesia e rispetto: un aspetto poco studiato della competenza linguistica" has not been able to influence.[3]

2. First results of politeness research

These general remarks on the state of the art in politeness research show that the awareness of a problem area and the method of dealing with it are decisively influenced by the historical development of scientific enquiry, foci of interest, and paradigmatic approaches. In the present chapter my aim will be to examine this question more closely in relation to the link between politeness and language. I shall not be concerned with giving a critical résumé of the pioneer work by Leech or Brown and Levinson, but rather with giving a rough survey of the history of the approach, spanning the 20th century, which will attempt to bring together the most important theoretical and methodological approaches to the theme of politeness and language and to show certain heuristic developments and contrasts. It is my belief that these can be grouped taxonomically in accordance with a number of basic points.

In order to understand this taxonomy, however, it is necessary to give the following brief sketch of some aspects of the complex research situation, which starts from the basic assumption that politeness can be defined and identified as an inventory of everyday modes of behaviour in avoiding or smoothing out conflict (cf. Zimmermann 1985: 71).

2.1 *The paradigmatic framework of politeness research*

The fact that politeness represents a social norm that can be observed empirically in language and reliably analyzed by means of language has long made it an important object of study in linguistics. The results show that questions of politeness – except for system-oriented paradigms such as structuralism and transformational grammar – have been tackled in every linguistic field of enquiry. Incentives towards studying the problem reach as far back as the German Romantic movement and were taken up by the school of idealism to bolster theories about the relationship between psychological feeling, national character, and verbal creativity (Spitzer 1922; Beinhauer 1930; Lerch 1933).[4]

Politeness was also used in the so-called French school, in the form of early reflections on language and society, in order to explain the social conditioning of linguistic systems (Bally 1913, 1927; Brunot 1922). Later it played a role in the controversy over language functions from Bühler (1930) through Kainz (1941–1965) to Halliday (1973). Finally, with the movement towards pragmatics, it became a central theme. From this point on, because of its connection with the acting and speaking subject, politeness has been of interest as an intentional, goal-oriented, situation-specific selection of linguistic strategies between *ego* and *alter*.

Within the framework of pragmatics, where language is considered in terms of action, it is primarily speech-act theory which has succeeded in accounting for the linguistic aspects of the phenomenon of politeness. This has been achieved on the one hand through the concept of indirectness (Searle 1975; Lakoff 1973; Leech 1980, 1983), and on the other hand through the connection with generalised, but situationally definable, speech-act types (Walters 1981).

In addition, the interpretative paradigm of ethnomethodology and conversation analysis has introduced a number of aspects that are decisive for the interactive character of politeness – such as the primacy of the hearer, forms of sequential organisation, and ritual order. From this perspective it can be deduced in first approximations that conflict-free relations and positive cooperation – in contrast to the normative point of view – can also be carried out or attained by means of redundancy and explicitness (Edmondson 1981; Owen 1983; Blum-Kulka 1987).

Finally, and not least in importance, in the ethnographic framework politeness is evidence for the culture-specific realisations of action and expression routines (Coulmas 1981a, b). Not surprisingly this has been used contrastively for the prescriptive didactic aims of language learning – thus closing the circle by returning to traditional concepts.

2.2   *The relationship between politeness and linguistic form*

The object of research within which politeness is explained and de-fined is extremely heterogeneous. Alongside theoretical treatises on politeness which see it as the totality of interpersonal forms of behaviour on all linguistic levels it has been focused upon in the investigation of specific areas of linguistic structure which express the speaker's attitudes and are thus not explicable by semantic, but rather by pragmatic means. Lexical units with interpersonal and discursive functions play an important role here, e.g., signals of cohesion, con-versational words, connectives, gambits, etc., as well as so-called illocutionary indicators with mostly weakening functions such as particles, modality markers, hedges, epistemological qualifiers, etc., and also some indicators on a morphological or syntactic level.[5] Despite their different linguistic nature, these phenomena can be con-sidered characteristic of the spoken code. Nevertheless, we are often left with the impression that they form a marked sub-paradigm within the linguistic system, a sub-paradigm whose component parts divide up the continuum of politeness in different ways.

A further area of politeness research has been opened up by linguistic work on speech acts. While speech-act theory restricted the utterances to simple sentence units, the German *Sprechhandlungs-theorie* and later on interaction theory extended the perspective to longer sequences such as turns at talk. These complex acts can be characterised with respect to their function for the interaction in toto and according to whether they imply cost or benefit for the inter-actants. They can be split into two contrasting groups, which Goffman (1971) calls "remedial interchanges" vs. "supportive interchanges". The term "supportive acts" refers to behaviour patterns that respect *alter's* social personality by paying her/him the necessary attention. They create a good interpersonal relationship and guarantee a felicitous process of communication by means of the due ratification of social expectations. In this positive function, supportive acts have become conventionalised in different ways in individual cultures, thereby forming the basic components of a general code of politeness. However, due to a high degree of routinisation, they play a subordinate role in linguistic theory (cf. Held 1988a). The pragmatic understanding of politeness rests exclusively on the second group, the so-called "remedial acts". This has led Lavandera (1989: 1201) to see the "main weakness" and consequent one-sidedness of such rational explanatory models of interaction in their orientation toward a "tyranny of conflict". Indeed, verbal signals of politeness are primarily derived from acts which, because of their inherent potential for conflict, Brown and Levinson (1978) have defined as "face threatening acts", referring here to utterances whose illocutionary force in the sense of social norms needs to be weakened, diverted, or strategically "reworked" in accordance with the situation. The main area of research within this understanding of politeness are requests, which are certainly the easiest to understand semantically but rather help to create a one-sided picture of politeness.

Taken all in all, however, the interest in speech as complex action encourages us to pay attention to the context, to the situation which, with the perspective of the interpretative paradigm, has begun to shift from objective generalisation to an evaluation of the subjective point of view. Researchers realise that linguistic indicators are not in themselves polite, but that the interplay of all the linguistic and situational factors generates a polite effect in the hearer, which needs to be interpreted as such by her/him (Fraser and Nolen 1981; Sager 1981).

2.3 *The methodological coverage of politeness*

Most work on language and politeness, traditional and pragmatic, illustrates theoretical statements with intuited situations (cf., for example, Lakoff, Leech, also Arndt and Janney 1985, this volume) or looks for appropriate examples deductively in more or less authentic text corpora (e.g., Stati 1982). However, with the increasing pragmaticisation of linguistics, empirical methods have now been given priority. In the process, speech-act theory, which has been criticised for its isolated, constructed examples (Streeck 1983), has nevertheless shown a tendency towards quantitative methods, i.e., attempts are made to correlate utterance types with certain situational parameters on the basis of frequency of occurrence (Walters 1981).

The interpretative paradigm has caused a new "mentality" with researchers from conversation analysis, viz. the investigation of speaking *in actu (cf.* Schulze 1985). Although I believe that a pure ethnomethodological approach can contribute little towards defining verbal politeness, the main focus *of* empirical methods is beginning to move in a qualitative direction: together with the criteria of speech-act theory this seems to guarantee the greatest success in researching politeness.

3. Taxonomic perspective of politeness as an object in linguistics

Against the background *of* this rough assessment of the state of linguistic politeness research[6] a number of different concepts of the phenomenon itself can be discerned, which seem to correspond to certain paradigmatic approaches. Taken together from a taxonomic point of view, they will reveal different formal and functional aspects of this "fuzzy" object of research, which is onomasiologically so difficult to define.

3.1 *Understanding politeness from a causal-deterministic viewpoint*

The causal-deterministic way of looking at politeness is dominated by the idea that social norms are bound to effect the relevant linguistic system from the outside and thus to leave behind traces in its lexicon and grammar. The traces themselves can then be described by the linguist as a marked inventory of forms. Hence a one-way cause-and-effect system is thought to exist, the conventions of which are produced by the speaker through an unproblematic form of behaviourism and explained by the linguist in a causal-deterministic way. This traditional point of view is to be found in pre-pragmatic linguistics (cf. Held in press), although it is also in evidence in several works in which politeness conventions are dealt with either as part of the grammar[7] or onomasiologically by means *of* hermeneutic methods (cf., for example, Elwert 1984; Weinrich 1986).

With certain provisos, the way in which the "cause", i.e., politeness, is observed or understood to begin with is not only responsible for the scientific angle from which the area of research is entered. It also effects the formal identification with the object of study and further linguistic analysis of it. As in the pre-scientific literature on manners and social comportment, politeness is understood as a common-sense, unproblematic concept (cf. Valtl 1986: 39) which consists of means of showing deference and respect to *alter* and which is consciously used by *ego* to achieve her/his aims. The following factors are important and they reflect the transmitted value judgements of a hierarchically ordered society, establishing rights and privileges which are still valid today (cf. Krumrey 1984):

Status conscious behaviour, which is essentially realised in the respect paid to *alter's* social rank. An essential feature of this type of politeness is the so-called "master-servant dialectic" (Raible 1987: 151), i.e., the continuous balancing act of *alter* exaltation and *ego* de-basement by the deliberate use of compliments and humility strategies ("servility hyperboles", Kainz 1969: 22), an act that finally shifts from being a social to a communicative duty.

Moral comportment and (bourgeois) decency which shows a concern for general human dignity and the maintenance of one's personal sphere. This type of politeness implies protecting the partner from unpleasant intrusion, respecting taboos and negative topics as well as reducing or avoiding territorial encroachment.

Both a) and b) are still important in determining the functional range of politeness (cf. the dichotomy "positive" vs. "negative politeness" in Brown and Levinson 1978), and they are the basis for many behavioural conventions and petrified formulae which still define verbal politeness today. Viewed diachronically, another value of the aspect of formality has been added. Distanced formality and ceremo-nial elaboration characterise politeness as a "social lubricant" (Watts, present volume), which transforms the egoistic goals of the individual into a hedonistic game with *simulatio*. In the French *grand siècle* this form of behaviour was carried to excess.

Early linguistic research was concerned with using both basic normative aspects of politeness to exemplify two different ways of thinking:

(1) Politeness is taken to be a "social modality" (Gabelentz 1969: 474), which is assigned an objective value and determines the language system of the relevant society from the outside as a superordinate norm. It should thus be studied linguistically as a fact of *langue*, i.e., the grammar.

This interpretation is suggested mainly by the representatives of the French School, whose linguists insist more or less explicitly on external influences (Gabelentz, Brunot), more concretely on a "linguistique externe" (Saussure, Bally), or – in psychologising fashion – on "ethical secondary functions" (Kainz). They investigate the relationship between social norms and language, or they demonstrate the effects on different linguistic levels, above all in the lexicon and in morpho-syntax (cf., for example, Dauzat 1912: 161f.). The behavioural inventory which they set up in this way is generally interpreted as the objective proof of the habit-forming and the cementation of cognitive structures – *pensée* 'thought', *Geist* 'mind' or *Leben* 'life' being some of the key terms in this pre-pragmatic understanding of politeness. These cognitive structures are a collective possession, but are differentiated by national characteristics and give rise to a certain typological idealisation.

(2) However, other first steps consist in separating polite modes of behaviour from this objectively secure base as being a "psychological modality" (Gabelentz 1969: 472). By means of the observation and "intuitive" interpretation of text extracts individual modes of expression are focused upon, which are associated with the inner feelings of the individual against the background of collective categories (Spitzer 1922).

In the first instance, German idealism is responsible for this promotion of politeness to the level of *parole* and thereby to active everyday dialogues determined by particular psychological states of mind. Individual utterances given the label "polite" are certainly seen as non-repeatable creative acts, but they are always the individual crystallisation of the collective style, i.e., of the *Umgangssprache* 'colloquial language' of a people, whose typical attitudes they reflect. From this point of view, the individual does not act pragmatically and intentionally but to a certain extent like a marionette. S/he is the unique and creative representative of a language community whose values and norms are anchored in the quasi-magical term *Wesen* or *Wesensart* 'being' or 'type of being' (cf. Spitzer 1922; Beinhauer 1930; Lerch 1933).

It is precisely in the discussion of the phenomenon of politeness that pre-pragmatic linguistics clearly reveals its tendency to make a deterministic link between the essential character of a nation and its language. The collective norms of a community, it is thought, can be found both in the language system as a social product and in the individual speaker's utterances. However, the speaker is not only a reflection of the cultural framework within which s/he is embedded, but also a subjectively creative individual. In the ways in which politeness was understood during the first half of the twentieth century the recognition of these creative moments within politeness behaviour was still attached first and foremost to the causes, amongst which psychological manifestations of a general state of human existence were counted, but not situational variables. The main result of the traditional approach to politeness phenomena, viz. an awareness of the deterministic relationship between content functions of showing respect and linguistic conventions, has remained important for later – pragmatic – approaches.

3.2 *The indirectness approach to politeness*

The indirectness approach is the central point of interest in pragmatic, speech-act theoretic discussions of politeness in language. Although they start from different theoretical and methodological premises, the three classical approaches by Leech, Lakoff, and Brown and Levinson are precisely those which have shifted the identification of indirectness with politeness into the centre of the discussion on the basis of their interpretation of Searle (1975) and Grice (1975).

I believe that the success and subsequent influence of these approaches are not only to be seen in the ability to define indirectness in its interactive function, but are also based on the fact that the traditional idea of respect and tact is given its most plausible shape through theories of indirectness. By virtue of the fact that indirect verbal behaviour is ideally suited for mitigating conflict situations, modifying necessary attacks on the addressee's personal sphere and thereby insuring the mutual protection of face, the concern with indirectness combines the traditional and the pragmatic views of politeness.

The starting point for these approaches is to be found in Grice's cooperative conversational maxims (Grice 1975), which are consciously violated at countless moments in everyday interaction in favour of deliberate vagueness, a heightening of the "etcetera assumption" (Garfinkel 1967: 18) and associated context-dependent implicatures. The fact that interactants have no difficulty in decoding discrepancies such as these between sense and force can be ascribed to superordinate rules of behaviour already familiar to them. Such rules of behaviour put social well-being, a harmonious communicative relationship, and a conflict-free pursuit of goals before the efficient transfer of information. The novelty in the pragmatic view of indirectness is its functional range: in contrast to the behaviouristic stress on form in the traditional display of respect, the various aspects in the functional flexibility of the indirectness approach are the result of an individual process of selection made by the speaker on the basis of the subjective evaluation of her/his relationship to *alter*, the situational variables and the consequent extent of her/his actions in relation to the shared balance between cost and benefit (Leech).

Thus indirectness represents for pragmatics the decisive move towards describing politeness in the field of tension between a conventional framework and spontaneous language usage, i.e., between constitutive, regulative, and individual mechanisms, and is thus a plausible basis for model-theoretic abstraction. By postulating an inverse proportion between indirectness and conflict potential (cf. Leech's formal and substantive explanation of the optionality scale [1983: 123f] and Brown and Levinson's four types of indirectness [1987: 60]), it becomes easier to operationalise politeness: it can be graded between a negative and a positive pole, and, seen in this way, it is a product of the utterance and the situation, which can be derived from a reduction in the level of conflict and the degree of success in communication.

However, beyond the deference aspect expressed in traditional instructions on good manners, the identification of politeness with indirectness has deeper biological and psychological roots that need to be shown more clearly, roots that spring, as a consequence, from communication theory.

Starting from the realisation that "distancing is the prerequisite for any dialogical behaviour" (Eibl-Eibesfeldt 1978: 336), ambiguity, often rejected by semantics, or the vagueness of linguistic symbolism, can be considered as the basic rule of interaction (cf. Garfinkel 1967: 18ff.; Wittgenstein 1967: 335ff.; Schaff 1974: 231 ff.). In addition, it also provides the opportunity for an adequate management of inherent advantages. Together with conflict situations and actions, increased vagueness, i.e., the indirect utterance, thus becomes a conscious strategy, which makes concessions to *alter*'s normative expectations and thereby achieves egocentric goals.[8] Within the spectrum from conventional forms (and formulae) to situation-specific hints, the politeness of indirectness is therefore founded on the following points, which lead researchers (cf. Holly 1979: 26f.; Müller 1980; Heeschen 1980; Franck 1984) back to basic features of interaction such as the mutual assumption of unspoken common knowledge, contextual binding and an increased dependence on the partner's cooperation:

- Indirectness lowers the obligations of both partners in interaction and thus relieves them of direct responsibility. For the speaker this means that s/he may take over the "waiting" position and has the freedom to indulge in further conversational turns; for the hearer it means freedom of decision, the free opportunity of making a counter move, and a chance to continue according to her/his personal preferences.
- By appearing to put all the cards in the addressee's hand, indirectness gives rise to continuity with a greater readiness on the part of the hearer to cooperate, encourages the hearer's willingness to accept and produces conflict-free agreement.
- Because of its prophylactic flexibility, which enables both partners to adjust, to retract, or to adapt gradually to communicative developments at any time, indirectness is an explanatory "technique for maintaining face" ("Technik der Imagepflege" – Ehrich and Saile 1972: 286). Face-threatening, embarrassing mistakes and possible sanctions are thereby avoided.

With the central role of negative politeness and of the benefit scale oriented to *alter*, Brown and Levinson and Leech have put indirectness into the centre of pragmatic politeness models with the result that a crass overestimation of Grice's approach emerges. Even if the latter cannot be maintained in an extension and revision of speech-act theoretical understanding, on the basis of its teleological plausibility research has long been greatly influenced by it (Bublitz 1980; Werlen 1983, 1984; Zimmermann 1979; etc.).

Because of the almost exclusive application of these theoretical ideas to the speech act of request a specific line of thought has been established within the interpretation of indirectness, a line of thought which tackles politeness quantitatively by measuring the frequency of relationships between utterance conventions typical for request acts and certain situational parameters which are derived from the P, D, and R factors postulated by Brown and Levinson.[9] For these empirical investigations, centred on the studies in Walters (1981), politeness is essentially the product of the perception of certain forms of indirectness in certain situational constellations. The latter relate to general sociolinguistic variables such as age, sex, social class, and institutional contexts, but also to factors such as first- and second-language acquisition, and are interesting from an applied social science point of view.

But the question as to which situational variables determine particular performance data *qua* indirectness conventions has not even been adequately answered for request and command situations. As Hill et al. (1986) have shown with comparative data from Japanese and American English, it is not only "discernment" (from the Japanese *wakimae* – "the almost automatic observation of socially-agreed-upon rules", 1986: 148) which plays a role here, but also, especially within the European cultural framework, "volition" ("the aspect which allows the speaker a considerably more active choice", 1986: 148). Nevertheless, by means of such quantitative analyses as these, based as they are on speech-act theoretical premises, the first steps have been taken on the road to operationalising verbal politeness as a socio-pragmatic function.

It is thus evident that the indirectness approach, despite its one-sidedness, occupies a central position in accounting for politeness, since, apart from the ease with which it can be understood, it has provided definite formal and situational results.

3.3 *Understanding politeness as a supportive relationship*

The stimulus towards overcoming the primary correlation between politeness and indirectness is already contained in Goffman's antithetical concept of "face" and the interactional rituals associated with it. However, caught up in the rational interpretation of *alter*'s claims for weakening the basic illocutionary functions, it has been pushed into the background. Widening the perspective methodologically from the single speech act through the structurally more complex speech event to the interactive sequence and new interpretations of the normative speech framework have made it clear in a number of different ways that the minimisation of conflict potential is not necessarily the same as linguistic minimisation *qua* indirectness. Researchers have become aware that the same function can also be carried out by other forms of behaviour of a substantive, structural, and dialogical nature.

Without reducing the intended aim of creating a benefit for *alter*, attention has been directed to other situationally determined needs than the simple maintenance of "positive politeness" and the general claim for respect. Such needs are clarity, explanation, and justification, the need to persuade, etc., which all function in the sense of polite attention and have more significance at certain moments for *ego* and *alter* than veiled or weakened illocutions. Hence politeness has been extended from extenuating consideration for one's partner to a general hearer-oriented type of utterance ("recipient design", Sacks et al. 1974: 727), which may include a variety of behaviour types. It is only important that they should correspond with the needs of the partner with respect to the situation and encourage a positive interactional relationship. As we already know, this enhances the speaker's aims in any case.[10]

A more open perspective of this kind leads politeness into the area of Goffman's concept of "face-work", which is termed "relational work" (*Beziehungsarbeit*) and "image work" (*Imagearbeit*) in German pragmatics (Holly 1979; Sucharowski 1982; Adamzik 1984) and, in contrast to normative politeness, "politic behaviour" by Watts (present volume).

Politeness is thus no longer the property of an utterance limited to the sentence unit, but of a structural combination, a complex action or sequence of actions. It is obvious that this broader understanding of politeness is revealed by the methods of discourse and conversation analysis and that the "concept indicators" (Schulze 1985: 75) are no longer merely individual signals on different linguistic levels, but rather complex combinations of various means which are only partly linguistic.

If we take as our point of departure the concept of "recipient design", in order to sum up this broader perspective of politeness, which can be characterised in general as "supportive" or "conciliatory", a number of approaches can be identified. Although it is possible to lump them together, they are far from representing a theoretically and methodologically homogeneous group as is the case with indirectness models.

3.3.1 Understanding politeness as maintaining equilibrium

In this section I shall deal with all those pragmatic approaches which look at polite behaviour from the point of view of the antithetical structure of mutual wants represented by Goffman's "face" concept as balancing the opposing strategies of "positive politeness" and "negative politeness" in accordance with the situation. Following this type of approach, forms of indirectness or avoidance behaviour can be combined or permuted by considering *alter*'s desires regarding any kind of benefit.

The discussion of politeness as a continual balance between face-saving and face-maintaining is carried out on two levels, which are frequently, although not always profitably, mixed, viz. on the functional level and on the formal one. In this way, supportive acts like complimenting and flattering are discussed as approach strategies.[11] Primarily, however, attention is focused on formal procedures which, because they contrast with "minimisation" strategies, I have elsewhere (Held 1989) termed "maximisation" strategies. On the one hand, these operate on the affect level by increasing emotional participation for both partners; on the other hand, they strengthen informative cooperation by encouraging redundancy and explicitness (cf. Müller 1979, 1980). However, a number of questions have hardly been put systematically (cf. Held 1989); e.g., how are these strategies to be connected to politeness? in what contextual and situational distributions do they occur? what is the relationship between them and conflict produced in a face-threatening act?

In looking for typical forms of politeness, linguistic research is only concerned with setting up the dichotomy between minimisation and maximisation. Hence House and Kasper (1981: 166) divide their "politeness markers" into "downgraders" and "upgraders." Brown and Levinson (1987: 146ff.) mention "strengtheners" and "emphasisers" alongside "weakeners." In both cases, however, form and function are mixed to a certain extent. This leads to the role of maximisation in supportive acts, in which intensification has become conventional, being hardly distinguished from the role maximisation plays in situations of potential conflict and face-threatening acts as a method of weakening the illocution. Schulze (1985: 222ff., 1986) has made the first attempt to unite this formal antithesis functionally with his concept of "strategic indeterminacy" (*strategische Unbestimmheit*), which is carried equally by forms of "underdeterminacy" and those of "overdeterminacy."

3.3.2 The anticipatory understanding of politeness

This way of looking at politeness, introduced by Zimmermann (1984, 1985), leaves enough room to conceive of politeness both functionally and structurally in far broader terms than the indirectness approach.

Zimmermann reaches politeness by way of the classical analysis of indirect speech acts, but in order to explain them, he has recourse to a psychological model which combines aspects of the theory of symbolic interaction with the concept of real fear. In this way the "institution of politeness" in itself is linked to an "irrational, neurotic" form of fear, the "fear of disharmony in relationships, of the charge of wrong behaviour, of unjustified claims for self-realisation, a fear that the other person might 'bite back'" (1978: 607).[12] Guidelines for behaviour and the responsibility for evaluating it are thus polarised on *alter,* who is basically felt to be the sanctioning judge and whose perspective as such is taken over in assessing any kind of action. In order to counter this negative function it is necessary to conceive of acting as the anticipation of potential reactions by *alter, i.e.,* to "be ahead" of one's partner in the truest sense of the term and thus prophylactically to ward off conflicts.[13]

However, Zimmermann does not merely identify the concept of the "anticipation of possible recipient reactions" with indirectness behaviour, with respect to which he talks of *Auslassungshandlungen* 'acts of omission' (1984: 140). He also sees the concept as being one of the characteristics of text generation, with the result that his approach involves both an extension from the single speech act to the level of structure and discourse and also an extension of politeness phenomena to "selected actions" *(Auswahlhandlungen), i.e.,* situationally adequate selections, and "subsidiary actions" *(subsidiäre Handlungen)* (1984: 140).

With "subsidiary actions" Zimmermann seems to be hinting explicitly for the first time in linguistics at a factor which, from a moral, ethical point of view, has long played a decisive role for politeness, viz. grounding or justification. According to Scott and Lyman (1968) and Keller (1984), this helps responsible social actors to explain behaviour which is considered inappropriate in the case of transgressive acts (in Brown and Levinson's sense, face-threatening acts!) and by stating plausible reasons to bridge the gap between action and expectation verbally. In such cases social psychology talks of "accounts" and defines these as procedures of a social order, which are always "placed in accordance with the positions of the interactants, but are standardised within a culture, so that certain forms have become stabilised terminologically and are routinely expected whenever the activity goes beyond the framework of expectations" (Scott and Lyman 1976: 74).

Looked at in this way, giving an appropriate reason for carrying out acts of conflict fulfils a similarly polite function as the illocutionary mitigation of the utterance itself. By including under the heading of "subsidiary actions" additional modes of behaviour that have the function of accompanying a dominant action and supporting its illocution, the linguistic understanding of politeness is extended in a natural way to include the whole complex of actions, which is to be interpreted as a chain of illocutions (cf. the discussion in Rosengren 1984).

By means of everyday conversations Edmondson (1981) investigates what the different functions are that exist between the internal structures of a turn and what influence with respect to preventive actions results from them for the recipient. Without explicitly talking about politeness, he nevertheless offers a major contribution to our understanding of its linguistic realisation, which concerns not only single indicators, but also complex action structures. According to Edmondson (1981: 122–129) such supportive moves can have the following functions when aimed at the needs of *alter*:

- anticipating the (expected) questions by partners concerning the "why" of the performed (transgressive) action (grounders);
- preventive answers to expected questions concerning the "how" of adequate reactions and/or a possible course of action (expanders);
- prophylactic defence against possible criticisms by one's partner, the neutralisation of her/his social fears, and the timely weakening of negative consequences (disarmers).

By considering structural "extras" the linguistic understanding of politeness has turned away from single, marked, grammatical conventions to a total impression dependent on the situation, i.e., to a pragmatic mechanism in which a complex chain of formulated illocutions is involved. In this mechanism the focus, the face-threatening act, may be represented directly, but it can also be completely substituted by subsidiary actions. This allows us to look at the "off-record" concept, i.e., total indirectness, in a new functional light. Edmondson's discourse analytic investigation also demonstrates the aspect of negotiation, i.e., of working out the subsequent discourse with complex turns up to the point at which both parties finally agree.[14] This is a stimulus to interpreting politeness as an evolutionary, interactive concept which is dependent on reactions by and/or the understanding of the co-interactant.

3.3.3 Understanding politeness from an emotive point of view

In their article entitled "Politeness revisited" Arndt and Janney (1985) call upon linguistics to take another critical look at the earlier treatment of verbal politeness, which in their opinion has been primarily norm-oriented. They then suggest an alternative way of approaching the uniquely interpersonal phenomenon of politeness. Their basic idea is that it should be explained within the "emotive dimensions of speech" (1985: 286) and its forms of expression should no longer be looked for only on a verbal, but rather on a prosodic and kinesic level.

As evidence for their hypotheses Arndt and Janney go back to a biological, psychological framework (cf. also Janney and Arndt, present volume) and work out three parameters which are involved in the fundamentally "multimodal" (1985: 281) transmission of politeness in dyadic interaction and which leave behind traces on all levels of representation: confidence, positive-negative affect, and involvement (1985: 287–292). Using this type of model, Arndt and Janney refute the indirectness approach and make various affective verbal and non-verbal minimisation or maximisation procedures indicative of politeness in accordance with positive or negative feelings. These indicators are systematically summarised in tabular form (1985: 297f.).

As the definition of emotive communication shows – it is made explicit in Janney and Arndt (present volume, n.b. in contrast to emotional communication!) as a form of interaction "in which affective displays are produced consciously and used strategically in a wide variety of social situations to influence others" (p. 27) – this way of understanding politeness must also be interpreted as rational. Indeed, the authors latch onto Goffman's "face" concept and like classical works on politeness take conflict avoidance as their point of orientation. However, what is different is the methodological opening towards a greater variety of forms and functions which lie within the scope of interpersonal supportiveness and differ from conventional social politeness by giving precedence to the spontaneous subjective and situation-dependent moment.

3.4 Understanding politeness as prepatterned speech

In its strict orientation to form this type of approach to politeness has always represented the opposite side of the coin to functional and strategic considerations. It is a well-known fact, and one that has often led to negative experiences when conversing abroad in a foreign language, that politeness has something crucially to do with language-specific forms and formulae. For this reason it has always enjoyed a great deal of attention in linguistics. The idiomatic aspect, which sets up a close relationship between politeness and linguistic routinisation and automatisation, has also become the object of attention in pragmatics. Patterns of behaviour and phraseological elements are seen as important components of communicative competence. At the same time they give access to culture- and language-specific expressions of politeness and are thus of central interest to anthropology and ethnography – in contrast to the universalistic discussion of action theory.

It would be going too far to sift through this heterogeneous research field looking for politeness formulae and conventionalised habits. Instead, I shall briefly discuss two principal points of departure which are responsible for very different conceptions of politeness within this form-oriented framework and highlight very different objects of observation and description, viz. the anthropological, ethnological concept of "ritual" on the one hand, and the concept of "routine" in its common-sense understanding on the other.

3.4.1 *Politeness and ritual*

The concept of ritual is more or less present in most analyses of politeness (cf. Brown and Levinson 1987: 43f.), but only a few studies focus on the question (cf. Hartmann 1973; Werlen 1984). Politeness is not only connected with constantly recurring linguistic formulae but in particular with recurrent behaviour patterns, which regulate social interaction and gain their function and significance from the specific constellations for which they are obligatory. As a consequence, the concept of ritual is applied to a variety of structural and thematic factors – e.g., in the dichotomous division of basic strategies of politeness into approach rituals and avoidance rituals (Werlen 1983), in accordance with speech-act theoretic criteria in greeting, thanking, and excusing rituals (Hartmann 1973; Owen 1983) or from the perspective of conversation analysis in opening and closing rituals (Werlen 1984).

However, looking through the literature, one is struck by the fact that in connection with politeness a very superficial concept of ritual is used (cf. Hartmann 1973: 139; Valtl 1986: 48f). Primarily this can be traced back to Goffman's influence. In explaining his social psychological theory of "face" as a "sacred thing" (Goffman 1967: 32), Goffman encouraged the comparison with religious rituals and hence sought to grasp the "little ceremonies of everyday life" heuristically. It is only when one has a closer look at the anthropological literature (Gluckman 1962; Callan 1970; Leach 1976) that one realises why politeness can be seen as ritual beyond the Goffman paradigm and what problems this poses for linguistics:

- According to Callan (1970: 80f.) ritual represents in a biological sense a kind of regulation, control, and integration, which is transferred from the power conflicts of aggressive behaviour in the animal world to social relationships of sovereignty and territoriality.
- Rituals are fundamentally useful for the "symbolic mastering of situations" (Hartmann 1973: 139). As such they encompass "intersubjectively valid elements acceptable within groups and whole societies, elements which represent something 'else' in their function as a total activity" (1973: 139).
- On the basis of the ceremonial nature of representation, rituals also become formally fixed as action patterns valid as entities which have been completely separated from the original signification of the individual parts and thus fulfil nothing but expressive pragmatic functions.
- The value of rituals lies in the regulation of social encounters, in the function of adaptation and accommodation by the individual to her/his community of reference and in overcoming the complexity of real factual situations by reducing them to habitual partial structures which are constitutive in helping the social actor to reconstruct and to project.

These points show that the anthropological understanding of ritual displays a number of points of contact with politeness, but must be considered with a great deal of skepticism as an exclusive explanatory framework. As the pragmatic models have clearly shown, politeness is more than a greeting ritual or a presentation ceremony, i.e., only a small part of it may be equated with a basic set of conventional forms that recur stereotypically. The sense and meaning of politeness forms neither lurk in the dark, nor do they have a purely ceremonial value. In contrast to ritual, politeness is characterised to a far greater extent by subjective variation, which may break through preconceived barriers without violating the norms and exceeding the bounds of sense. I am thus of the opinion that it is precisely the practical aim of politeness, its use as a well-calculated strategy adapted to the situation, that stands in opposition to the concept of ritual, bound as the latter is to irrationality.

3.4.2 *Politeness and routine*

Another, mainly traditionally oriented area of research connects politeness with formal routine, i.e., it is located in phraseological-lexical units, which are still looked at in accordance with onomasiological criteria (cf., for example, Roche 1965; Elwert 1984; Weinrich 1986) or are discussed in a rudimentary way in relation to their pragmatic function (cf. Gülich and Henke 1979; Clark and French 1981; Pierini 1983).[15]

Analogous to the previous section I confine myself here to the theoretical discussion concerning the usefulness of the concept of routine for the linguistic analysis of politeness. This was initiated in the ethnological work by Ferguson (1976) and has as its central representative Coulmas (1981a, 1981b), whose main arguments will be summarised briefly.

By combining the hypothesis of verbal stereotypes with the ethnographic method followed by Hymes, Coulmas reaches a new pragmatic definition of routine formulae and thereby of verbal routine in general. In doing so, his ideas form a link to the theory of ritual and the controversies connected with it (cf. also Coulmas 1979). Coulmas' point of departure is formal categories, i.e., he defines routine formulae as "function specific expressions with literal (sic!) meaning for the realisation of recurrent conversational moves" (1981a: 69), which guarantee the ability to anticipate social events and thus increase the cooperation between the interactants. By reflecting on the discourse distribution of situations in which they could be applied (1981a) and on the central problem of ethnographic thought, viz. intercultural and historical variation, and by citing exemplary categories from the traditional codex of politeness as evidence, Coulmas reaches a completely new version of the concept of conversational routine. He makes a basic differentiation between action routines and expression routines, i.e., he distinguishes "strategies and patterns of occurrence" from "verbal stereotypes" (1981a: 124), whereby what one does routinely should be considered as theoretically and thus linguistically different from what one says routinely.[16]

As we have seen, the tension between ritual and routine is the major component with which the linguistics of politeness has always had to deal. Even in these somewhat form-oriented approaches what is expressed is the dialectic between universality and individuality, between passive politeness (social politeness) and the active, situation and goal specific "treatment" of *alter* (social tact).[17] However, they provide an impetus for the discussion of culture-specific realisations of polite behaviour (Coulmas 1979b) and of typological perspectives (Altmann and Riska 1966) and are the only ones which indicate useful ways of studying the historical dimension of verbal politeness (Coulmas 1981a: 159–173; Neuendorff 1987; Held 1988). In the centre of this research are also questions concerning an application to language acquisition, language didactics, and intercultural communication (Coulmas 1977, 1979a). It is noticeable that the relation to sociological ways of looking at politeness is particularly strong: hence observed linguistic forms can be combined with the classical concept of "standard of behaviour" (Krumrey 1984) just as easily as with the theory of "culturemes" (Oksaar 1981, 1988), which has scarcely been adequately reviewed as yet. The only thing that is important is that verbal indicators should not be looked at in isolation but as part of a complex behavioural process which can nevertheless be empirically described via language usage.

4. Concluding remarks

This review of the various approaches to the study of verbal politeness in the light of the development of linguistics has clearly shown that, in its omnipresent ambivalence between universal and culture-specific aspects, between conventional social realisations and those spontaneously produced in accordance with the situation, the surface of this extensive subject has barely been scratched. It has been impossible to discuss every aspect thoroughly. Several questions have not been solved but rather brought to a head. From this point of view the linguistic concern with politeness is a task for the future, not a thing of the past.

Notes

1. For example, the central concept of "face" is rendered in German, alongside the literal translation as *Gesicht,* as *Image* 'image', *Selbstbild* 'self-picture', or *Fremdbild* 'strange picture', etc. "Face work" yields *Beziehungsarbeit* 'relational work' in Sager (1981), *Imagearbeit* in Holly (1979), or *Partnerarbeit* 'partner work' in Müller (1979). Concepts such as "positive" and "negative politeness" also give rise to heterogeneous translations. With respect to these terms research in the German-speaking area needs to reach an agreement as to whether *Zuwendung* 'support' and *Vermeidung* 'avoidance' are appropriate terms (Werlen 1984; Valtl 1986: 59-60).

2. Above all I am referring here to the so-called *Sprechhandlungstheorie, a* German version of speech-act theory with some extensions, whose most important representatives, Wunderlich, Ehlich, and Rehbein, are at the same time severe critics of American pragmatics.

3. Recent remarks on politeness behaviour in the Romance languages can be found for French in the work of, for example, Roulet (1980, 1981), Kerbrat-Orecchioni (1987), Raible (1987), Held (1988a); for Italian in Benincà et al. (1977), Stati (1982, 1983); and for Spanish in Haverkate (1987).

4. Cf. Held (forthcoming).

5. For reasons of space I will not give more detailed bibliographical references. But cf. the list of titles in Held (1988b).

6. It would have been necessary to take into consideration the definitions of politeness among the points mentioned for an assessment. This has, however, alieady been convincingly done by Arndt and Janney (1985: 281-285). (Cf. also these authors' contribution in this volume.)

7. This field covers above all research on address-forms which still takes pride of place in the linguistic study of politeness. Cf. the commented bibliography by Biaun, Kohz, and Schubert (1986) for a view of the general state of research in this area.

8. Cf. in addition the principle cited in Heeschen (1980: 261) of *do ut des,* which, with certain reservations, is generally valid for indirectness.

9. These investigations and the data used make it clear that factor R, (rank), defined by Brown and Levinson as "imposition", i.e., the weight of an action, is on a completely different level from the social, outwardly imposed variables P (power) and D (distance). R cannot be objectified and should certainly be more closely defined and measured as a product of subjective evaluation.

10. In this connection, the problem of relevance for politeness must be approached in a new way (cf. Watts 1989; Jucker 1988). According to Fraser and

Nolen (1981: 97), what is relevant is what coriesponds to the "conversational contract."

11. Only in the most recent linguistic developments has the compliment, as a theoretically defined speech-act type, been recognised as having central signif-icance and thus forming a clearly delimited area of research within politeness linguistics. Cf. in addition Wolfson and Manes (1980, 1981); Kerbrat-Orecchioni (1987), Keil (in press) and, from the point of view of conversation analysis, the exemplary investigation by Pomerantz (1978).

12. Literal translation of the German metaphorical expression *zurück-beissen*.

13. In German *zuvorkommen* 'come before; anticipate' is a metaphor which indi-cates polite behaviour. Its literal sense, lost in common use, is indeed that of anticipating *alter's* wants and claims.

14. Research on the interactive understanding of politeness is extremely heteroge-neous and has not yet gone beyond the initial phase. It covers mainly the in-vestigation of necessary sequential pairs or series in the case of apologising, of requests, of expressing thanks, of compliments, in which conversation ana-lytical questions influenced by Sacks are combined with ritual aspects (cf. Owen 1983; Lange 1984; Weiser 1975; Clark and Schunk 1980; Held 1988a; Wolfson and Manes 1980; Pomerantz 1978). The concept of "preference or-ganisation" is a promising approach for an interactive view (Levinson 1983: 332f; Atkinson and Heritage 1984: 53-165), which, however, has not as yet been applied systematically. Interactive appioaches have also been taken into consideration in the sporadic investigations of specific conversational types, such as shop conversations (Roulet 1981; Schulze 1985), ordering in a restau-rant (Ehlich .and Rehbein 1972), talk shows (Holly 1979). The results from family discourse may be awaited with interest (cf. Watts 1991; Blum-Kulka 1990).

15. Although one has the impression with respect to some living languages that this lexical area has been sufficiently investigated linguistically, nevertheless, it has not been possible to find systematic investigations such as that by Kremos (1955) for requesting and thanking formulae, so that even in the tradi-tional area of politeness formulae there remains much work to be done.

16. In Held (1988), on the basis of thanking routines, it could be shown that this differentiation from the linguistic operationalisation of politeness is ex-tremely fiuitful. Thus from the diachronic point of view it was found that thanking, although it is an action routine, does not – as might be mistakenly believed – imply an expression routine.

17. This differentiation is presented contrastively in the contribution by Janney and Arndt in this volume.

6. Traditional and modern views: the social constitution and the power of politeness

Konrad T. Werkhofer

This venture needs a cautious introduction. In their essay on politeness phenomena Brown and Levinson (1978: 63) present, "tongue in cheek, a Model Person", a "cardboard figure" to be played with. While ascribing a whole cognitive machinery to that model person – taking an approach that might appear to have psychological and sociological pretensions – what they are in fact concerned with in the bulk of their paper is something quite different. Their essay is an attempt to reconstruct systematically – no tongue in cheek this time – the rationality that underlies polite talk, and their model of the speaker, rather than reflecting what might actually be going on within any real speaker's mind, is a means to that end, an idealisation or device brought into play in order to, hopefully, solve a problem in linguistic pragmatics, and not in the psychology or sociology of language.

But polite language use has of course to do with real persons, and Brown and Levinson's model might be and has in fact been understood as explaining how they go about this task. In this chapter, then, I shall, in spite of Brown and Levinson's warnings to the contrary, take what they say about their model person literally, wondering how s/he will behave, what s/he can do and what not. That may at times look like rough play, like tearing the puppet apart and looking into its head, trying to find out what kind of mechanism may be driving it. Only later shall I begin to collect the pieces together again, putting them, or at least some of them, back together. I shall, in other words, critically reconstruct Brown and Levinson's model with regard to its psychological and sociological implications.

While thus apparently centring around that essay, however, what I shall be aiming at in the end is not just a review article. Working towards an alternative account, I shall outline and defend a framework that, hopefully, will both justify my complaints and integrate what, in spite of their weaknesses, is still to be learned from traditional and modern views – and from Brown and Levinson's essay – thus still drawing on what I have criticised before.

1. Two difficulties

The act or behaviour of being polite is performed by an individual agent and yet it is, at the same time, an intrinsically social act, social, that is, in the dual sense of being socially constituted and of feeding back into the process of structuring social interaction. It is in this latter sense that we may speak of the power of politeness, the power of a symbolic medium that, being used and shaped in acts of individual speakers, also represents social standards of how to behave or of what kind of conduct is considered "just and right". Politeness thus mediates between the individual and the social, motivating and structuring courses of action as well as being instrumental in performing them.

Among the symbolic devices that serve such functions linguistic ones have been considered as being particularly interesting or important; hence the fact that analyses of politeness have mainly started from linguistic points of view might seem to follow only naturally. Thus, while by no means being the only one to be taken into account here, the linguistic medium has been treated as if it were, and, rather than dealing with linguistic aspects needing to be complemented by other, equally important ones, these other aspects have been reduced to the point where politeness research could be established within the confines of what is coming to be accepted as linguistics proper.

These linguistic approaches have difficulties, however, the first of which being that they have been divided into "traditional" and "modern" branches (Werkhofer 1985, 1986b).

The modern view of politeness is essentially individualistic. Starting from Gricean notions it subscribes to a model of the speaker as a rational agent who is, during the initial phase of generating an utterance at least, unconstrained by social considerations and thus free to choose egocentric, asocial and aggressive intentions. Anticipating that what s/he is just about to say would – if expressed literally or "directly" – be heard as threatening the addressee's face, s/he will modify the utterance, using politeness as a means or strategy of mitigating such face-threatening connotations. The polite utterance is then a compromise between saying as much as possible of what the speaker had actually been intending, on the one hand, and avoiding the risk of a social conflict, on the other.

As seen from a traditional point of view, by contrast, politeness is governed by social forces, not by individual ones. Here polite forms of speech express respect or deference in accordance with given social dimensions, especially with the relative social status of speaker and addressee, sometimes taking into account bystanders, and with the social relations between these parties. Adopting a behaviouristic methodology these social dimensions are dealt with in quantitative terms, as vaguely defined "independent" sociological variables, and, thus, as entities that are taken to somehow determine the polite meanings of the linguistic forms under consideration. The mechanisms of determination themselves, however, namely the purportedly "causal" relationships between these variables, on the one hand, and polite meanings, on the other, are treated as being predictable on the basis of these "independent" variables and, in this sense only, as being "explained". Rather than being attributed to the individual speaker, then, the process of individually producing an utterance is given no theoretical status whatsoever in the traditional approach.

That these views are diametrically opposed to each other in accounting for politeness either in terms of individual or of social motivations may be obvious, and it may also be obvious that the modern view is more complex in virtually taking both kinds of forces into account. We might be led to conclude, then, that either (a) the modern view is superior to its traditional counterpart, thus presumably also being adequate, or that (b) both views should be combined in order to account for both individual and social aspects, but, unfortunately, such conclusions would be premature.

The reasons are, in a nutshell, that the modern view is biased towards a one-sided individualism, a bias that is not only due to the role ascribed to the speaker's initial face-threatening intention, but to other individualistic premises. As not all of them are openly declared, the difficulties arising from such individualism and from the corresponding neglect of social dimensions tend to be overlooked or grossly underestimated by the adherents of this view. For example, all versions of this view either neglect social realities completely or, adopting a remarkably simplistic, traditional approach, reduce them to only a small set of vaguely defined dimensions which are then relegated to a secondary status, thus again emphasising individualism. As a consequence, the traditional view, in spite of its deficiencies, still has something to offer: it still represents what any general concept of politeness must account for, namely the centrality of normative aspects, of respect, social identity and social order.

Thus, being biased as they are in one way or another, both traditional and modern approaches to politeness confront us with the dilemma that, while neither of them can completely be rejected, neither of them is also fully acceptable. And even impressive efforts to combine elements of both views – I refer to Brown and Levinson (1978, 1987) here – could not really overcome this dilemma.

As if these difficulties were not enough, we have to face still other, equally serious ones: both views imply a static universalism, dealing with the phenomena of politeness as if they were to be accounted for in terms of a relatively small set of identical concepts or principles across cultures and as if they were essentially synchronic, timeless entities. Both approaches do not enable us, then, to explore processes of change and the differences between societies and social groups that may ensue from them. To explore such processes and differences would of course be desirable: going beyond the crude dualisms of "independent" vs. "dependent" and of social vs. individual factors, we might then begin to understand how politeness is actually constituted and used not only in terms of purportedly universal principles, but in both universal and specific terms, thus finally taking into account social realities, be they traditional or modern ones. Working towards these ends, I shall take three steps in this chapter:

The first will be a critical reconstruction of the modern view and, in particular, of Brown and Levinson's voluminous essay (1978). Unrevised and updated only by way of adding a new preface (1987), it is a classic that even now, more than ten years after its first publication and in spite of the numerous criticisms that have in the meantime been advanced, is still accepted by many more than any other single source as a frame of reference for much of politeness research – if only in the sense that every new effort is still compared with it. This outstanding status is due to the fact that these authors bring together and discuss, in a rich, scholarly collection, the heterogeneous elements of this view, that they include traditional elements, and that, in so doing, they construct a provokingly ambitious, complex theoretical system.

Nevertheless, and in agreement with at least some of Brown and Levinson's own conclusions (to be found in the preface to their reissued essay, 1987), I shall argue that their model needs to be revised. Due to a Gricean, cognitive approach, it embeds elements of a socially oriented, traditional approach into a version of the individualistic modern view, thus systematically playing down the importance of the social aspects it seeks to integrate. This first section, then, will lead to the conclusion that a different framework is indeed called for.

Perhaps surprisingly, the second step will be a short excursion into theories of money and of economic exchange. The more general analogy between language and money is of course by no means a new one (see, for example, Parsons 1963/1980; Coulmas 1990) and the analogy between politeness and money is not new either. Playing an important role in the modern view (Werkhofer 1986a; Blickle 1986a, b), it has been stated most radically in Clark and Schunk's (1980) interpretation of Brown and Levinson's model – radically insofar as these authors treat politeness as if it were indeed a kind of money, used by a polite speaker who is portrayed here as economic man. Brown and Levinson's approach might appear to be less economics-oriented, but once we know what to look for, the family resemblance to economic man is visible enough.

If reconsidered in the light of a broader framework, however, this economic approach turns out to be naive, not because politeness and money would not be comparable – which, as this comparison will show, they are at least in one regard – but because even money and monetary exchange, as media that are typically thought of as allowing for a maximum of individual freedom, are socially and historically constituted, thus not being explainable in terms of individual intent or interest alone. In developed market economies, however, money may become a social force itself, a force that, like politeness, playing the role of an active, "powerful" medium, will feed back into the processes that had once given rise to it.

The third and final section will draw conclusions, summarising analogies as well as differences between politeness and money. A framework of politeness as a socially and historically constituted, powerful symbolic medium can then be outlined, a framework that will take into account both individual and social forces, thus reconciling what is to be learned from traditional and modern views and – in spite of what may appear to be a rather critical treatment in this next section – from Brown and Levinson (1978/1987), too.

2. Rethinking the modern view

The modern view of politeness draws mainly on two sets of ideas: the first set, Grice's reflections on "conversational implicature" (Grice 1967/1975), formulate the distinction between "what is in fact meant" or understood as being implied or "indirectly" conveyed by an utterance, on the one hand, and what is explicitly or literally said, on the other.[1] A second source is Goffman's metaphorical notion of "face" (Goffman 1955/1972). By way of a first approximation the notion of politeness that has been synthesised on this basis can be outlined as follows.

The distinction between what is meant and what is said takes the form here of assuming that the polite utterance reveals the speaker's true intentions only indirectly. There is, to begin with, the message the speaker originally intends to convey; it would, if it were uttered as intended, to a larger or lesser degree, threaten the addressee's face.[2] Realising this state of affairs, the speaker will then feel compelled to modify or transform what s/he is just planning to say, but has not yet uttered in such a way that what will in fact be said in the end will, in addition to the first, intended meaning, now carry a second one that will hopefully avoid the threat to the addressee's face or compensate for it, thus achieving two ends at the same time: that of expressing the speaker's intentions as much as possible, on the one hand, and that of doing so indirectly enough not to run the risk of a social conflict, on the other. Politeness is then a kind of indirectness.

That both Grice's and Goffman's ideas have in a way been used here may be obvious, and the authors of this view have repeatedly confirmed that they have. But is the synthesis they have achieved a successful one? Grice's and Goffman's conceptions differ considerably both from each other and from the modern view, so constructing a politeness theory on this basis will turn out to be a problematic, inherently contradictory venture.[3]

2.1 *Gricean origins*

Perhaps the most important source of the modern view are Grice's William James Lectures and, in particular, the first published part of them (Grice 1975). Grice explicitly mentions a maxim "Be polite", but this remark should not be mistaken as indicating that his reflections would have anything to do with politeness. Quite on the contrary, politeness is only an example here – and a significant one – of what Grice is not at all concerned with. His conversational maxims are "specially connected [...] with the particular purposes that talk (and so, talk exchange) is adapted to serve and is primarily employed to serve," and he is stating them "as if this purpose were a maximally effective exchange of information." And, though conceding that "this specification is, of course, too narrow" (Grice 1975: 47), Grice leaves no doubt about what his approach in fact is and that simply adding a politeness maxim would not be in line with it.

But is this not just what the authors of the modern view are setting out to do? Beginning with Robin Lakoff (1973) – who literally repeats Grice's politeness maxim, presenting it not as an example of what can hardly be dealt with in Gricean terms, but as, hopefully, adding to his approach – they all start from the two premises that "Grice's theory of conversational implicature and the framework of maxims that give rise to such implicature is essentially correct" (Brown and Levinson 1987: 3) and that, at the same time, it can be combined with premises of a quite different, socially oriented kind, thus giving rise to a theory of politeness. What this theory is meant to explain, however, is the opposite of what Grice had been aiming at: while his speaker, without literally expressing them, seeks to convey and in fact successfully does convey his true intentions, the polite speaker of the modern view will tend more or less to hide and obscure them, if necessary to the point at which they are no longer understandable.

True, the authors of the modern view are not completely unaware of that discrepancy; they do in some sense realise that Gricean cooperativeness and what they see as politeness may be at odds with each other. Leech, for example, notes that "Grice himself, and others who have invoked the CP [that is, the conversational postulates, K.T.W.] have understandably reflected the logician's traditional concern with truth, and hence with propositional meaning" whereas he, in working towards a theory of politeness, is "more interested in a broader, socially and psychologically oriented application of pragmatic principles" (1983: 80). And Brown and Levinson (1987: 5) note that the Gricean postulates are "'unmarked' or socially neutral (indeed asocial)" and that they are "of quite different status from that of politeness principles." But if this is so, how, then, can the theory of politeness start from the presumption that "Grice's theory of conversational implicature and the framework that gives rise to such notions is essentially correct"?

The authors of the modern view deal with Gricean and politeness theory as if the discrepancy were not a theoretical one, but were simply one of different subsystems within the speaker's mind. And thus Gricean maxims and politeness principles appear as nicely co-existing and complementing each other within the confines of the same cognitive system, so that what before had been an incompatibility of theoretical approaches appears now as being just a psychological conflict.

But are politeness principles, as Brown and Levinson (1987: 5) suggest, in fact to be understood as being "principled reasons for deviation" from the rational efficiency the Gricean approach assumes? Are they, in other words, just a special case that can be subsumed under other, more fundamental, ultimately Gricean principles of communication? As seen from the modern point of view, this might indeed seem to be what they are. Starting from a Gricean position as regards the speaker's intentions, this view at the same time includes social factors. Due to the greater importance ascribed to the Gricean element, however, these social elements and, as I shall show, the whole aspect of politeness, appear to be of lesser, in fact secondary importance, less important, that is, than "true", and that means here "referential", communication. Thus that and how Gricean elements are built into and adapted to this construction make it a difficult, inherently contradictory one.

Goffman's face metaphor contributes to these difficulties, too: Though to some degree socially oriented – more so at least than the Gricean approach – this notion abstracts from macro-sociological dimensions. And being selectively received, it only partially serves the function it is meant to serve here, that is, it does not really compensate for the asocial nature of the Gricean model. I shall come back to these complaints.

2.2   *The politely "indirect request" as a paradigm case*

However, let us examine the modern concept more carefully. Perhaps the best way of doing so is, as I have argued elsewhere (Werkhofer 1985), the paradigmatic example of this approach, namely the politely "indirect request". As in much of the post-Gricean debate on indirectness phenomena, the indirect request has achieved this status in the sense that some versions of the modern concept deal with it exclusively (Leech 1977, 1980; Clark and Schunk 1980) and that others which do not (Brown and Levinson 1978/1987) argue as if the analytical scheme that has been proposed as applying to politely indirect requests[4] could be generalised to all other kinds of polite utterances as well. Imagine that the speaker says:

(1) Can you pass me the salt?

and that this utterance is both meant and heard not as the question that it would be if taken "literally", but as a request. The modem view then assumes (1) to be an – if only moderately – polite version of an imperative or command like:

(2) Pass me the salt!

While being identical to *(2)* in "illocutionary force", (1) is seen here as polite because and insofar as it avoids the threat to the addressee's face that would be implied by a command like (2).

2.3 *Relativity to "context"*

A first premise that enters into this type of interpretation has to do with the relativity with respect to what is usually referred to – in a notoriously vague terminology – as the "context" of the utterance. Note that the interpretation of (1) as a polite version of (2) has recourse only to the utterance itself, thus ignoring such relativity.

Leech (1983) proposes circumventing the relativity problem by explicitly distinguishing "relative" from "absolute" politeness, where "relative" stands for "perceived as being related 'to some norm of behaviour which, for a particular setting' is regarded as typical in 'a particular culture or language community'." "Absolute" politeness would then be free of such relativity. It might be objected that this kind of relativity is an essential characteristic of politeness (cf., for example, Silverstein 1976: 31 and passim), but Leech postulates that "general pragmatics may reasonably confine its attention to politeness in the absolute sense" (1983: 84) – thus demonstrating that he, indeed like all other authors of the modem view, wishes to confine himself to the properly linguistic pragmatics of politeness.

2.4 *A production model*

However, leaving language philosophical stones unturned, I shall proceed as if the interpretation of (1) as a polite version of (2) were in principle correct. The mechanism of how, according to the modern view, this type of politely indirect utterance would have to be generated can then be accounted for in terms of a production model, a model that, though only rephrasing Brown and Levinson's model[5] and spelling out what I take to be implicit there, differs in two respects:

– I shall firstly consider the "face-threatening act" as being part of the model. Remember that Brown and Levinson's summarised argument (1978: 65) begins, from left to right, with the "estimation of risk of face loss", thus presupposing that the "face-threatening act" is already "there", having been brought into play before. According to the logic of this approach this act can only be an act or intention of the speaker; it can thus be seen as in fact being part of what is described here.

– I shall secondly, again as I understand it to be implied by their model, consider the steps of firstly generating the face-threatening act and secondly choosing one or more strategies as being part of the sequential procedure of generating a polite utterance, a procedure that can then be represented by a directed graph or by the following linearly organised information processing model:

Stage 1: Generating the intended message: The speaker begins by generating (as the impolite version of the paradigm case here, the politely indirect request) a command. The output of this first stage, however, namely the "speech-act" (Brown and Levinson's "face-threatening act") that has thus far been generated remains tacit.

Stage 2: Estimating the risk of threatening face: Anticipating that the command s/he has generated would threaten the addressee's face, s/he now evaluates it in terms of the amount of threat that would be implied. This is where the sociological variables "power" (P, for the power the addressee has over the speaker), "distance" (D, for the social distance between speaker and addressee), and "rank" (R, for the imposition the intended message would entail for the addressee) come in.[6] Each of these variables is scaled, that is, represented as a numerical value on a continuous scale, and taken together – the authors propose to aggregate scale values by simply adding them up, but allow for more complex algorithms – they quantify the threat against the addressee's face. This numerical value – Brown and Levinson's "weightiness" – is the output of stage 2 and the input to stage 3.

Stage 3: Choosing and applying a strategy: The initially generated imperative will now be transformed into a request that is appropriately indirect and, in this sense, polite. The degree of transformation is determined by mapping the weightiness value onto a hierarchy of super-strategies, a hierarchy which, like the scale of weightiness values, is unidimensional. The operating principle is that the higher a given weightiness value is, the higher will be the position of the super-strategy that is employed.7 Three pairs of weightiness values and corresponding super-strategies may suffice here to indicate the general logic of this mechanism:

– Minimal value: A minimal value of expected threat leads to a minimal transformation. Thus a low weightiness value will leave the imperative essentially intact; it can now be produced as it has been generated, without any further modification (Brown and Levinson's super-strategy "Bald on record").

– Maximal value: For a high weightiness value the position of the applied strategy in the hierarchy of all strategies will also have to be high, that is the intended message will be mitigated to the point where still recognising the speaker's initial intention becomes very hard or even impossible (Brown and Levinson's "Off record").

– Intermediate values: This is the case for which the model has been constructed in the first place. A value between the two extremes of minimal and maximal weightiness will lead to a transformation that, while rendering the utterance sufficiently polite, leaves the initial intention intact so that its meaning can still be inferred; this transformed version will now be uttered. (Brown and Levinson further distinguish "positive" from "negative politeness", postulating in their original essay that "positive politeness" occupies a higher position in the hierarchy of super-strategies than "negative politeness" – an assumption they later concede is probably unwarranted (see Brown and Gilman 1989: 164ff.).

2.5 *A first approximation: A hybrid model or "internal dialogue"*

The first thing to be noted is that this model combines two quite different kinds of entities. There are, on the one hand, "intentions", "acts" or "strategies" that can clearly be identified as having to do with what the speaker thinks or does. And there are, on the other hand, notions that have to do more with the addressee, as, for example, the addressee's face or the anticipated reaction of the addressee – which is not explicit here, but how, if not in terms of some anticipated reaction of the addressee, would the speaker be able to think about the threat to her/his face?

Starting from a Gricean approach to the speaker's intentions and combining it with a notion of "face", this model presupposes a specific relationship between *ego* and *alter*, namely an antagonistic one. This antagonism takes the form of a dialogue, but of a strange kind of dialogue that only takes place within the speaker's mind: s/he generates, as a first turn, what s/he actually intends to say. This move remains tacit so that the next move is not the addressee's answer to the first one, but is the speaker's anticipation of what the threat to her or his face would probably mean to the addressee. The polite utterance is then the third move or the speaker's second turn in this fictive dialogue. While thus assuming that a dialogue goes on within the speaker's mind, what is not explained here is the case where the face-threatening event has in fact happened and where the speaker only then, in a subsequent utterance, has to compensate or to "make good" for it. This does not seem to be explained by the model.

2.6 *Individualism I*

By marked contrast to these apparently "dialogic" or "socially oriented" features, however, this model is an individualistic one in at least four respects:

(a) It is a cognitivistic or mentalistic one in that it describes what is going on as taking place within the cognitive apparatus of the individual speaker.

(b) The whole procedure is triggered by the speaker's initial act or intention.

(c) The sequential structure of the procedure is a linear one, that is, the flow of information is in one direction only, from stage 1 to stage 2 to stage 3, and there is no feedback. Thus, while what happens during stage 1 will determine or constrain what can happen during later stages the reverse is not true. Due to its linear characteristic this model in no way allows later stages to feed back into earlier ones. This implies – by way of a corollary to and together with (b) – that the speaker's initial intention is unconstrained by whatever may come later, i.e., unconstrained by social considerations.

(d) The speaker's initial intention does not exploit the whole range of possible communicative intentions, but is confined to the limited subset of egocentric or face-threatening ones. This assumption is of course quite explicit in Brown and Levinson's essay; it only gains its full significance, however, in conjunction with premises (b) and (c), which are not so explicit.

Each of these characteristics can be criticised, not in the sense that what it assumes would be impossible or completely unrealistic, so that there would be no corresponding empirical evidence whatsoever; there may indeed be cases where the individual speaker strategically plans and generates a politely mitigated face-threatening act, thus more or less conforming to this model. But this is only a special case, and postulating that it must be the general one rules out whole classes of utterances and distinctions between different kinds of utterances, thus severely restricting the generality of this approach.

(a) Cognitivism: The model's cognitivism, or the "within-the-skin" assumption, has perhaps the most dramatic consequences. Though not stating this premise explicitly in their original essay, Brown and Levinson (1978) repeatedly allude to it marginally and in footnotes and asides. By contrast to their more recent preface (1987) they consequently stay true in the 1978 version to a cognitive approach, and they do so even with regard to aspects that might be thought of as not just being subjectively held by, stored or processed "within" the speaker, but as being social or "external" realities.

Consider, for example, the "sociological variables". The authors explain that "these are not sociologists' ratings of actual power, distance, etc., but only the actors' subjective assumptions of such ratings" (1978: 79ff). Later, however, commenting on empirical studies that seem to more or less support their claims (1987: 15ff), the authors can be understood as accepting the sociological variables as what we might have taken them to be in the first place, namely as representing social realities and, thus, external factors. But why should the speaker, the addressee and the bystanders (who are, by the way, hardly mentioned by Brown and Levinson anyhow) not realise that social realities can both be objectively given and subjectively held, and why should they not clearly distinguish these possibilities? Why should they not perceive the variables as dynamically interacting and conflicting with each other? And would we not consider the language user who does not distinguish between what is subjectively held and what is socially given a rather strange figure?

A line of retreat for the real cognitivist would be to argue that reducing social realities to cognitive representations and thus assuming only one set of factors, namely cognitive ones, this model is a parsimonious one, more parsimonious, that is, than any model that would

have recourse to different kinds of factors. This type of methodological or epistemological argument breaks down, however, as soon as the
model it favours can be shown to be too narrow to represent what it is
meant to represent – which, I hope I can show, is the case here.

A less abstract way of defending this model would be to claim that
during the process of generating an utterance the speaker must at least
once retrieve and apply her/his knowledge of the sociological variables
in question. But why only once, why not repeatedly? Why should we
assume that all the information employed by the speaker is simply
"stored"? Why should the speaker not, in order to adapt to a situation
that may already be novel as s/he enters it and that may develop and
change while s/he is planning and saying what s/he has to say,
constantly take in new information, thus proceeding in "real time",
drawing on whatever external data may be available to her/him?

As one consequence of this type of cognitivism the distinction
between the conventional, pre-patterned utterance and the non-conventional one is blurred[8] (cf. Ferguson 1976; Coulmas 1981). If each
and every utterance is generated by only one kind of mechanism, then
how this distinction can be upheld is in fact hard to see. Is there not a
difference between a socially and historically pre-patterned, highly
conventionalised utterance and an individually or even idiosyncratically generated one? And does conventionality not considerably effect
the meanings that can be conveyed? Are there not noticeable differences between utterances that are obviously conventional in form and
therefore, it would seem, more likely to transport conventional
meanings than utterances that, being unique in form, can be taken as
expressing unique meanings?

Or consider the notion of face. Brown and Levinson (1978: 67 and
295ff, fn. 11) refer to it not in terms of socially created, interpersonal
realities, but of wants of the model person, and, thus, of intrapersonal
ones. Again later, however, while commenting on a literature that
deals with face in terms of cultural dimensions, Brown and Levinson
(1987: 13ff) do not seem to object to that perspective either – although
it is opposed to the one they had emphasised before.[9] Again we may
want to ask why the model does not distinguish between both possibilities.

(b) The initial intention: This premise rules out all cases where the
production process is not triggered by an initial intention of the
speaker, but by some other act or factor. Take, for example, the situation where you meet someone you usually and habitually greet; under

such circumstances greeting may be a more or less automatic, conventionalised habit or routine that is best described not so much in terms of the speaker's intent, but of situational factors. This is of course not to say that, by contrast to what I have just argued with regard to the conventional vs. un-conventional distinction, situational factors would not be processed by the speaker's cognitive system. What I want to emphasise here is the distinction between quasi-automatic, well-established behaviour elicited by an external "stimulus", on the one hand, and the intentionally planned and generated act,[10] on the other. Interestingly, greetings (cf. Hartmann 1974) are not among the strategies listed by Brown and Levinson. Also not included are congratulations – comparable to greetings in that they can be seen as typically triggered by the calendar, as by a symbolic medium that regulates social life and is thus relatively independent of individual intent – thanking (Held in press) and apologising (Owen 1980; Lange 1984; Trosborg 1987; Vollmer and Olshtain in press).

(c) Linearity: The linearity premise rules out cyclical production processes. The speaker may create an utterance not linearly, but incrementally, beginning to talk before the utterance has been generated from beginning to end. Processing may then be of a "cyclical" or "parallel" type, that is the speaker may, while s/he is already speaking, go back to the planning stage, and s/he may do so repeatedly, thus continuing to make up and change his mind on what to say next, depending perhaps on changing impressions of how the situation at hand develops and on how well s/he feels s/he has been faring thus far. In order to allow for these modes of processing the linearity assumption must be given up.

Let me just mention here that linear models of the type "input – processing – still more processing..." are inadequate for many other types of information processing, too – an insight that has more or less become a commonplace among cognitive psychologists (cf. Neisser 1976). A cyclical or recursive model will of course cover linear cases – but not vice versa.[11]

(d) Threatening face: The assumption that the initial intention is a face-threatening one rules out the case of neutral or pro-social intent. For example, if James is extremely fond of telling a particular story, the speaker, being aware of that fact may, even though s/he is not really eager to hear that same story again, want to do James a favour by saying:

(3) James, would you mind telling me that story about ...?

Or, assuming that the addressee would be pleased to help her/him, the speaker may say:

(4) Can you help me?

even if s/he in fact does not really need or want help. Yet, applying the above model we would be misled to believe in both cases that her/his intentions are face-threatening ones.

2.7   *Individualism II: Politeness as money*

Clark and Schunk (1980; Schunk and Clark, unpublished) derive empirical predictions from the Brown and Levinson model. In order to be able to do so in a maximally straightforward way, they concentrate on what I have claimed is the paradigm case here, namely on the politely indirect request, and paraphrasing it in terms of an economic metaphor, they reformulate and slightly radicalise the model.

This theoretical move allows them to be more specific than Brown and Levinson are about the speaker's true intentions. What he is asking for are "goods" or "information", and he wants the addressee to provide them for him. For the addressee, on the other hand, compliance would mean investing time and effort, and would thus be costly. Anticipating this state of affairs, the speaker, in order to have a chance to succeed, will enter into a cost-benefit reasoning, estimating costs and trying to combine his/her request with the appropriate amount of politeness, as the price to be offered. Politeness thus becomes a kind of money – a term not used, but clearly implied by Clark and Schunk.[12]

Clark and Schunk present their study and Brown and Levinson (1987: 17) accept it as supporting their approach. This is not surprising, since, while Clark and Schunk's predictions do in fact follow only from their economic metaphor, not from Brown and Levinson's original "face-as-basic-wants" approach, both accounts are not as different as they might appear to be insofar as Brown and Levinson (1987) tend to associate the notions of cost-benefit with their approach – an association that is shared by other authors of the modern view. And is the individualistic, rationally planning, quantifying and calculating speaker of Brown and Levinson's original essay not a close enough relative of economic man?

One may want to see the empirical demonstration Clark and Schunk are aiming at as being a success, but it is only a partial one. Having constructed a hierarchy of six broad request-types that have "the same indirect meaning", but do, according to the authors, vary in politeness – as, for example, *Can you tell me where Jordan Hall is?* vs. *Shouldn't you tell me where Jordan Hall is?* – they ask their subjects to rate these requests on a seven-point scale (from "very polite" to "very impolite"). The ratings turn out to be more or less as predicted, but a significant variance remains unexplained (Clark and Schunk 1980: 119), indicating that the cost-benefit approach is only partially valid.

In a second series of experiments Schunk and Clark (unpublished; personal communication) prepare short, fictitious scenarios, thus offering their subjects an opportunity to produce the utterance the speaker in the scenario would probably produce. Under these some-what more realistic conditions the subjects do not produce the single-sentence type the authors had presented before; Schunk and Clark call what they get now an "extended request", by which they refer to requests that, rather than still conforming to the single-sentence type, typically consist of a sequence of sentences, including such diverse elements as openers or prefaces (*Excuse me, Sir...*), justifications (*I really need it*) and compensations (*I'll pay you back on Friday*).

Thus what the authors had been presenting in their first series of experiments as the politely indirect request may to some degree be an artifact, and we may presume that under more realistic conditions, as, for example, in social role play or in naturalistic observations, the typical request would turn out to be even more complex. For example, polite utterances may turn out typically to be developed over several turns, so that, rather than taking place only in the speaker's mind, an extended production process and a real dialogue can be shown to occur. Observations of this kind would of course still further discredit the linear, mentalistic, "within the head" approach.

Another result runs counter both to the cost-benefit approach and to Brown and Levinson's "rank of an imposition" variable: the weighti-ness of the imposition implied by an utterance does not seem to determine the degree of politeness that is employed. For example, when asking for a "costly" favour, these subjects do not consistently come up with a more polite format than in asking for a "cheap" one. This study casts some doubt both on the "rank of an imposition" variable and on the economic or cost-benefit approach as a whole, then – at least insofar as we consider the subject's performance in this half-realistic, role-play situation as an adequate test.

A clue as to what is probably wrong with the economic approach to politeness comes from Ervin-Tripp's naturalistic observations of children in Californian middle-class families. Some of them discover that politeness, rather than just being a means to the end of "getting what you want" or of "buying" favours from others, has to do with whether an utterance is considered as an acceptable or appropriate one at all in a given situation. If, for example, the child makes an attempt to intrude into an ongoing conversation between two adults, then what is required is to do so in an adequately polite manner, thus indicating that the speaker is aware of and respects the addressee as being already engaged in a conversation with somebody else. Here an utterance is polite, then, insofar as it signals that the speaker knows what would be just and right to say in a given situation, but whether compliance can then be achieved will, as it seems, depend on other, additional factors (Ervin-Tripp, personal communication. See also Ervin-Tripp 1982). Thus, rather than being just a "strategy", a means of "getting what you want" or a kind of money, politeness may have to do with what is considered just and right with regard to a particular social event or with the construction of social realities and with social order.

2.8 Scalability I

Another set of assumptions Clark and Schunk's (1980) first study might seem to be testing for has to do with scalability. Brown and Levinson assume, as you may recall, that the weightiness of a face-threatening act and the degree of politeness determined by it are unidimensionally scalable. Unfortunately, Clark and Schunk's study is not so much a critical test, but an attempt to demonstrate that adequate results can be produced. This is evident in the fact that, though in a way testing for it, these authors do not seriously consider any theoretically meaningful alternative – and the classical "null-hypothesis" is hardly ever theoretically meaningful. But the meaningful alternative of multidimensionality is not really considered here. The possibility that there may be more than one dimension involved is, as in Brown and Levinson's framework, not even explicitly stated, and the notion of unidimensionality is more or less smuggled in as if justifying it were not necessary. At the level of experimental manipulations the study does not leave much of a choice, either, as to what kind of reaction the subject may find adequate. All s/he is required – and is allowed – to do is judge in terms of the scale of politeness the experimenters provide, so that the rating turns out to be a kind of forced choice procedure. Thus whether polite requests are unidimensional or not and whether the explained variance here attests to unidimensionality can hardly be ascertained on the basis of these data.[13]

In a study that combines elements of Clark and Schunk's first and second series of experiments (Werkhofer 1984b), subjects have again been confronted not with pre-conceived sentences, but with scenarios that give an opportunity to play the role of the speaker, saying what s/he would say in the situation given. Instead of asking what the speaker would say in the situation given only once, as Schunk and Clark did ("Imagine that you are in this situation; what would you say?"), however, this procedure was repeated, so that, in addition to a first utterance, the subject would produce a second, "more polite" one. The procedure was again repeated, both for an even "more polite" one and for two "less polite" alternatives, yielding, in addition to the subject's first version, two more polite and two less polite ones and thus a five-point mini-scale of politeness.

The subjects (students and personnel of a German Institute of Psychology) were perfectly able and willing to do what we had instructed them to do, and yet some of them spontaneously gave comments like: "Well yes, one could say… (such and such) … but I don't really think that would be polite; it would be ridiculous (or: strange, stupid, overly deferential, etc.), and I wouldn't really use this."

Such willingness to comment freely on the experimental situation had been encouraged by a preceding semi-structured interview situation in which the subject was given ample opportunity to describe typical situations of being polite and to define politeness. Thus, being less rigidly instructed than in the Clark and Schunk study, these subjects clearly take the opportunity to distinguish between a mere repertoire of linguistic forms, on the one hand, and the forms they think they would in fact use, as being in a more serious sense than in Schunk and Clark's case appropriately polite ones. And their spontaneous remarks tell us that for some scenarios at least only one more or less narrowly circumscribed type of polite utterance is perceived as appropriate. We may conclude, then, that at least the subjects in this study view politeness as being relative "to some norm of behaviour which, for a particular setting" is regarded as typical in "a particular culture or language community" (Leech 1983: 84) and that, as soon as we are willing to take such relativity into account, the scalability assumption that had been introduced by the authors of the modern view and apparently been verified by Clark and Schunk is probably quite misleading.

The same study allowed us to test a second aspect of scalability. If the politeness of an utterance varied in one dimension only, and if, as Brown and Levinson suggest, "The more elaborate the request is, the more polite it is," then we may expect that "more polite" versions are longer then "less polite" ones (cf. Schönbach 1974). This hypothesis was partially confirmed, that is, utterances that according to the instructions would have to be "more polite" were indeed longer than the merely "polite" ones, with the exception that "less polite" utterances, by contrast, were not subject to the same set of rules, containing less of what Brown and Levinson and Clark and Schunk seem to presuppose to be a homogeneous set of devices.

"Less polite" utterances turned out to be of a different type altogether. In generating them, subjects did not just eliminate "polite" elements, using less of the same, but they now added elements of another, markedly "rude" sort, so that the less polite utterances were again longer. So the notion of a unidimensional, homogeneous scale of politeness did not seem to hold. Moreover, there were only very few "unmarked" versions, that is, the straightforward directive that might also have been expected, as the negative end of a politeness scale, hardly ever occurred. One may want to ask whether these data, being still only staged ones, can be replicated under naturalistic conditions. Such reservations notwithstanding, these results cast some doubt on the notion of "scales of politeness".

2.9 *"Sociological variables"*

The fact that Brown and Levinson include the sociological variables "power", "distance" and "rank" might be perceived as compensating for the individualism of their proposal. I shall argue, however, that it does not, and that, rather than attesting to the ultimately social nature of that approach, the notion of "sociological variables" is a conceptually vague, simplistic and traditional one.

In order to see why this is so remember how these variables have been built into the model I have described above. Being only "actor's assumptions" (Brown and Levinson 1978: 79ff) their values can only be assessed for a given face-threatening "act" or intention. Feeding into a relatively late stage of the production process and thus being relegated to a secondary status, they will have no effect whatsoever on what the speaker intends to say in the first place. The role of social realities is further relativised by reducing them to numerical values on only three dimensions and by finally aggregating these into only one weightiness value.

But not only is the social sphere represented in a simplified format; it is also conceived in remarkably vague terms: Brown and Levinson (1978: 85) suggest that "power", "distance" and "rank" should not be taken literally, but in some wider sense, thus subsuming other factors, among them some that, like "occupation", "ethnic identity" or "situational factors", might seem not to be covered by any of these concepts. But can P, D, and R cover all the social and situative eventualities Brown and Levinson want them to cover? Vaguely defined as they are and then widened to encompass an even broader range of meanings, the sociological variables are so fuzzy that quantifying them becomes a difficult, if not impossible, task indeed.

In the preface to the reissued essay, reflecting on the criticisms they had provoked, Brown and Levinson (1987: 16) concede "that there may be a residue of other factors which are not captured within the P, D, and R dimensions", that there may be doubts about the precision and falsifiability of their proposal, and that, due to the "rather complex reflexive reasoning that takes account of the implied presumptions about the addressee's beliefs" real precision in this area may not be achieved (Brown and Levinson 1987: 11). Their principal position, however, still is that "research seems to support our claim that three sociological factors are crucial in determining the level of politeness which a speaker (S) will use to an addressee (H)" (1987: 15), namely the variables P, D, and R.

This conclusion is not convincing, not only because of the empirical criticisms Brown and Levinson mention, but for more fundamental, methodological reasons. Although apparently integrated here into a modern view, the sociological variables approach is a rather dated, if not obsolete one. It echoes the traditional, behaviouristic methodology in the name of which, too, social realities used to be vaguely defined as parameters which were then dealt with as if they determined linguistic politeness (cf. Kendall 1981; for a more recent bibliography see Braun 1988). Being in fact aware of the enormous difficulties associated with such determinism in their original essay (Brown and Levinson 1978: 309, fn. 96), Brown and Levinson still have recourse to it[14] – perhaps, we may suspect, in order to concentrate on other, more linguistic and/or pragmatic issues. Much more could be said on the obsoleteness of the "sociological variables" approach. Being defined as static entities that determine polite meanings, these variables represent a narrow approach to social realities, an approach that neglects the dynamic aspects of social language use – aspects that may have no systematic status in the traditional view, but should be at the very heart of a modern one.

2.10 *The face metaphor*

I mentioned above that Goffman's notion of face has inherent limitations, has only selectively been received by the adherents of the modern view and that its theoretical integration into the framework that has been primarily inspired by Grice is poor.

Face is "the positive social value a person effectively claims for himself by the line others assume he has taken during a particular contact" (Goffman 1972: 319). In addition to being claimed by the individual and being granted by others, face may also be "confirmed by evidence conveyed through impersonal agencies in the situation. At such times the person's face clearly is something not lodged in or on his body, but rather something that is diffusely located in the flow of events [...]" (Goffman 1972: 320). Goffman thus clearly goes beyond the model of the self-contained, strategically planning and acting individual, the model to which the modern view subscribes. And, as another element that has been overlooked there, Goffman speaks, if only vaguely, of "the flow of events", indicating that the notion of face can be connected not only to a narrow, naively realistic notion of the "here-and-now", but to processes that may go on over longer stretches of time.

Goffman later briefly mentions the notion of "social order", but this notion plays only a minor role here: Goffman distinguishes "social order" in a wider sense from "ritual order". For social order in a wider sense, a kind of schoolboy model seems to be employed: if a person wishes to sustain a particular image of himself and trust his feelings to it, he must work hard for the credits that will buy this self-enhancement for him; should he try to obtain ends by improper means, by cheating or theft, he will be punished, disqualified from the race, or at least made to start all over again from the beginning. This is the imagery of a hard, dull game. (Goffman 1972: 344)

Ritual order, by contrast, does not conform to this model:

Whatever his position in society, the person insulates himself by blindnesses, half-truths, illusions and rationalisations. He makes an "adjustment" by convincing himself, with the tactful support of his intimate circle, that he is what he wants to be [...] And [...] if the person is willing to be subject to informal control – if he is willing to find out from hints and glances and tactful cues what his place is, and keep it – then there will be no objections to his furnishing this place at his own discretion, with all the comfort, elegance and nobility that his wit can muster for him. (Goffman 1972: 344).

Thus, connecting face only to social order in a narrow, "ritualistic" sense, Goffman locates it in a private sphere, as being supported by an intimate circle. This approach is at once interesting and simplistic. It is interesting, I think, insofar as social realities are seen here as being many, as being fragmented, unstable and not always "real" in a naive, pathetic sense. We are thus encouraged to go beyond the realism of Goffman's "schoolboy model" – and also, let me add, of the "sociological variables" approach.

The simplification here is that the private, "ritual" sphere is rigidly separated from the "hard, dull game" of social order in the wider sense. If the phenomena of face were in fact to be located only within the small world of micro-sociological phenomena, or in the even smaller one of an intimate circle, what could then still be understood would perhaps no longer be very interesting, and some aspects of face could no longer be understood at all. Official social positions, and that means positions that must be described in macro-sociological terms, will most probably correlate with specific face wants, but these would, according to Goffman, only have to do with the macro-social order from which he abstracts and would thus appear to have nothing whatsoever to do with face.

But, its difficulties being not only due to the neglect of macro-sociological dimensions, the face metaphor confronts us with yet another, related one: alluding to the realities of archaic, small-scale societies, terms like face and ritual are usually understood as being universally applicable to all kinds of societies. This implies, unfortunately, that they may not be very helpful in addressing any culturally or socially specific issues.

Receiving Goffman's face metaphor selectively, the authors of the modern view deliberately reinterpret it in unambiguously individualistic terms, abstracting not only from the dimension of ritual order, but from all kinds of social order and so, as I have argued at length above, they unduly favour individualistic, Gricean elements over the social ones taken from Goffman.

2.11 *Scalability II, or: Overgeneralising the model of polite indirectness*

Up to this point Brown and Levinson's model has been described as if it only referred to the paradigmatic case of the politely indirect request, but this is of course due to my attempt to critically reconstruct the architecture of this model. However, it is not only applied to the politely indirect request, and thus to the case where assuming that politeness mitigates or masks face-threatening intentions may be relatively plausible; the authors also claim that it can be generalised to virtually all other kinds or "super-strategies" of politeness. These super-strategies are then said to form a scale or hierarchy, thus presupposing that the set of phenomena to be dealt with is a homogeneous one and again assuming unidimensional scalability – this time not only at the level of polite indirectness, but of many other politeness phenomena as well. Thus an approach that is not even applicable to all politely indirect requests is generalised – or, I would contend, overgeneralised – to other cases where it does not apply at all.

Referring to critical comments (cf. Strecker 1988) Brown and Levinson (1987: 18) concede that "these authors have persuaded us that we may have been in error to set up the three super-strategies, positive politeness, negative politeness, and off record, as ranked unidimensionally". They still maintain, however, that "despite the various deviations from our expected hierarchy that have emerged from some of these experimental tests,[15] no one (to our knowledge) has come up with clear evidence of a counter-ranking" (Brown and Levinson 1987: 20).

But unidimensionality is among the key assumptions of the modern view. Only if all politeness devices carried one kind of function, namely that of compensating for face-threatening intentions, and if the degree of threat itself varied in just one dimension, would the mechanism of mitigating threat make sense. If, on the other hand, the super-strategies are not unidimensionally rankable, then the logic of this whole approach breaks down. If not by mapping the weightiness value on a unidimensional hierarchy of strategies, how else, then, should the mechanism of strategy selection operate? What remains to be asked is not whether any alternative ranking has been empirically demonstrated, but whether and how a model that has thus been falsified can still be revised or saved. We may ask, for example, what other dimensions are involved.[16] And can the strategies of politeness – as another premise of this same mechanism – still be assumed to form a coherent, homogeneous set at all?

Coupland, Grainger and Coupland (1988: 254ff.) offer an answer to this question – and it is a negative one:

> While positive politeness [...] is relevant to all aspects of a person's positive face, negative politeness [...] is specific to the FTA in hand. This is to say that [...] it is only negative politeness that is strictly to be seen as redressive of an act which threatens [face; K.T.W.] [...] positive and negative politeness emanate from different intentions and lack the functional "sameness".

Again, however, Brown and Levinson (1978: 106) are well aware of the problem and, we may conclude, of the fact that the constructive tour de force they offer is a difficult one:

> Unlike negative politeness, positive politeness is not necessarily re-dressive of the particular face want infringed by the FTA; [...] in positive politeness the sphere of redress is widened to the appreciation of alter's wants in general or to the similarity between ego's and alter's wants.

2.12 Conclusions

I have described the difficulties of the modern view as resulting, firstly, from the fact that cognitive, asocial notions borrowed from

Grice are juxtaposed to a reduced version of the face metaphor and to vaguely defined, deterministic sociological variables. Each of these sources being difficult in itself, they are combined here to the effect of rendering that view a difficult, indeed contradictory one.

Approaching referential meaning in terms of the speaker's intentions and in terms of conversational maxims that, in order for communication to be efficient, would have to be known to both speaker and addressee, Grice abstracts from the distinction between both parties. Starting from the premise that "Grice's theory [...] is essentially correct," Brown and Levinson reformulate this position by postulating that the intentions of the polite speaker must be face-threatening or antisocial ones. The fact that this assumption is no longer consistent with the Gricean framework can in itself hardly be criticised, but subscribing to a deliberately individualistic, in fact antisocial model of the speaker, the modern view introduces the remarkable premise that there must be, as a prerequisite for politeness to occur, a fundamental antagonism between the speaker's intentions, on the one hand, and social aspects, on the other.

What is borrowed from Goffman's notion of face cannot – for reasons that have to do both with the inherent limitations of Goffman's framework itself and with the fact that it has been received only incompletely – compensate for or bridge this antagonism. The fact that he abstracts from macro-sociological dimensions is reinterpreted in the modern view, so that instead of merely abstracting from macro-sociological dimensions, face is now no longer described in terms of what may go on, during a dynamically unfolding event, between different parties, but in terms of what is assumed to be represented within a single speaker's mind.

These asocial and anti-social connotations are further elaborated at more specific levels, in the production model I have shown to be implied in Brown and Levinson's construction. Like all other versions of the modern view, this model, taking the politely indirect request as a paradigm case, treats politeness as a kind of indirectness. The antagonism between the individual and the social is not only reflected by the premise that the intention of the speaker is a face-threatening one; the whole mechanism of generating an utterance is characterised in mentalistic, intentionalistic and linear terms. As it is triggered by an intention of the speaker, social factors can only come in later. Thus already relegated to a secondary status, their impact is further reduced by defining them vaguely and by representing them in terms of ultimately only one quantitative value. The strategies of politely mitigating the speaker's initial intention are then determined in two ways, firstly by this intention itself and, secondly, by social factors which, however, again depend on this same initial intent.

Being elaborated in terms of this model the face-threatening intention, by contrast to Brown and Levinson's original "face-as-wants" assumption, takes on a new quality. Later statements of the modern view explicitly endorse a cost-benefit approach, an interpretation that is accepted by Brown and Levinson and that can in fact – once we know what to look for – be shown to correspond to their original account insofar as there the polite strategist is endowed with both ego-centric motivations and with a strategically planning and calculating rationality, the kind of rationality that is typically ascribed to economic man.

As a consequence what can be represented here is only one extreme case of individually-generated, strategically-minded language use, a case that, however, is no longer compatible with the initial premise that "Grice's theory [...] is essentially correct"; rather than conforming to that theory, this type of language use, deviating as it were from communicative cooperation, would be of a different kind altogether. We thus have to face the situation that instead of one concept, "communication", there are now two, and that one of them, namely polite communication, is defined only negatively, as a way of avoiding or compensating for the undesirable consequences of "true" communication, or even of breaking communication entirely. What is lacking here, then, is an attempt to understand in what sense both types of communication can still be said to be communication at all.

The conclusion I suggest is that these difficulties arise from two dualisms that have been built into the modern view: there is, firstly, the dualism between communication (in a Gricean, cooperative sense) and polite communication or, as the modern view describes it, non-communication, and there is, secondly, the dualism between the individual and the social. This second dualism becomes most explicit in the antagonism between economic man and society. Turning to this notion in the next section I shall show that this antagonism is not a necessary premise and that it may itself be socially and historically constituted, thus probably not being universal. Hopefully, this excursion into economic theory will shed some light on orthodox economic man and on the one-sidedly individualistic relationships to others that have come to be associated with "him", exploring how else then – if not in dualistic terms – social relations can be described.

3. An excursion into money and market economy

> To treat money solely as a private durable good is undoubtedly useful, and therefore to that extent "true" [...] However, it gives us a view of the social consequences of variations in the purchasing power of money that is surely sufficiently misleading as to justify [...] the adjective "false". (Laidler and Rowe 1980)

Speaking of economic man, we may notice that, far from being the lifeless cardboard figure which Brown and Levinson introduce him as, "he" is alive and well not only in the thin air of academic disciplines, as, for example, in economy, in psychology – where "he" has been said to represent an "American ideal" (Sampson 1977) – or in language-philosophical and linguistic circles. Being also at home in non-academic life, it is better to take "him" seriously, as a myth or "metaphor we live by" and, thus, as standing for values and beliefs we may not be able to dismiss so easily.

The theories to which I shall refer in this chapter are opposed to or complement the orthodox notion of economic man and the values that have come to be associated with it in that they bring into focus – by marked contrast not only to the Anglo-Saxon mainstream of economic theory, but also to an orthodox materialist, Marxist position – the social and historical conditions and consequences of economic individualism, not in the sense of denying the role of the individual, but, quite on the contrary, in the sense of exploring this role more fully and from more than one side, including social, historical and cultural dimensions and thus also allowing us to deal with the different forms it may take. It is this common perspective that allows us to combine these theories, in spite of what may separate them in other respects, as together charting a neglected territory.

3.1 *Simmel's philosophy of money*

Georg Simmel's *Philosophy of Money* (1900) is a "grand theory"; treating money and monetary exchange in a broad sweep, it ranges from abstract, meta-theoretical and methodological reflections to empirical observations and from the prerequisites to the consequences of monetary exchange,[17] thus integrating perspectives that might be perceived as mutually excluding each other. One of these sets of apparently incompatible perspectives, the dualism of money either as a private good or as a public good, is an overarching theme of the book. While from the first point of view the utility maximising individual is the key to understanding money, it may also be regarded, from the second point of view, as "a social institution and quite meaningless if restricted to one individual" (Simmel 1907, cited by Laidler and Rowe 1980: 101).

It is this dualism between the individual and the social that makes the orthodox, commonsense notion of money comparable to the modern view of politeness. There, too, both kinds of aspects are thought of as being diametrically opposed to, and as in a sense mutually excluding, each other.

Taking money as just one out of a much larger set of possible examples – a set that would include, as from Simmel's perspective surprisingly similar institutions, the code of ethics, the legal system and, I would add here, the principles of politeness – Simmel shows that this kind of dualism is unwarranted and that the apparent opposites can be reconciled, not in the sense of proclaiming that, instead of social conflict there would now be social harmony, but in the sense of demonstrating how both individual and social elements enter into and are interrelated in economic transactions. He can thus be understood as outlining a very general, multifaceted or "dialectical" framework, a social history of money that should allow us to reconstruct how individual and social aspects are actually related at more specific, empirical levels – where both conflict and harmony may occur.

At a first, philosophical, or meta-theoretical level Simmel starts from an idealistic, Kantian position. This is an interesting parallel to Grice, whose maxims echo Kantian categories, too. Although sharing this common vantage point, however, both authors proceed in quite different directions. Whereas Grice – dealing with a medium that, perhaps ironically, might appear as typically inviting more socially oriented uses than money does – confines himself to an asocial cognitivism, Simmel avoids such one-sidedness. With recourse to Kantian, epistemological or cognitive categories only in the sense that he sees the subject as being endowed with the knowledge that is required in understanding the "value" of material objects, Simmel emphasises, by contrast to an empiricist, "tabula rasa" kind of approach, that what is meant by "value" cannot simply be "learned" or "associated", but must be understood in terms of the more abstract kind of knowledge of which the category of value is an example. And only insofar as this kind of understanding is available will the subject be able to assimilate and organise whatever experience with valuable objects she or he may happen to make.

At a second level Simmel integrates this philosophical approach with a sociological and practical one, showing that economic exchange can only be performed if and insofar as the value of objects is not only subjectively held, but also socially confirmed in acts of exchange. Thus the individual vs. social dualism is overcome here in two ways, the first being that, rather than focusing on cognitive categories alone, he sees cognitions as being connected to a symbolic medium, namely to money or monetary exchange. The second anti-dualistic move is that what Simmel refers to as "economic exchange" is not an encounter of autonomous, individual agents, but "a sociological phenomenon sui generis, an original form and function of social life." It is one of the "most primitive forms of human socialisation; not in the sense that 'society' already existed and brought about acts of exchange but, on the contrary, that exchange is one of the functions that create an inner bond between men – a society, in place of a mere collection of individuals" (Simmel, cited after Laidler and Rowe 1980: 98).

In such exchange subjectively-held as well as socially-granted values are relevant. They may eventually, but not necessarily converge; only if and insofar as they do, however, will the exchange be a purely economic one. Money will then be exchanged for goods, services or objects and its value will thus – if and insofar as it is accepted as in fact representing the value of these objects – be "objectified". The purest expression of objectified value is money. Simmel assumes that subjective assessments are, to some degree, typically affected by such objectification, and that, insofar as this is the case, individual and social aspects will not necessarily be opposed to each other.

These notions are complemented, thirdly, by historical and empirical ones. During early stages of economic development the value of money derives from the more or less direct comparison to material goods and thus merely facilitates transactions that could in principle be accomplished without using money, by a direct give-and-take of objects alone. More complex types of exchange become possible as the association with specific goods gradually loses its importance. Insofar as an economy is based more and more on money, this medium will be defined in increasingly abstract ways, as a generalised good that can be used to buy anything that is available.[18]

This process of abstraction not only affects the practical means or "behaviours" of performing exchange; it structures the fantasies and desires of the participants and thus the very process of motivating economic activity – a process of which the individual may often hardly be aware. Thus, rather than simply being driven by economic man's desire to maximise profit, economic exchange turns out here to be set in motion by forces that may and usually will themselves be socially generated ones.

The desire for particular goods or services may increasingly be replaced by the more abstract, generalised desire to get, regardless of any specific needs, money and, as an extreme possibility, the desire to accumulate money may become an end in itself. Thus being transformed into an increasingly abstract and efficient medium, money may acquire what we may call – introducing a term that is implied by, but does not occur in Simmel's treatment – a "power" of its own, which means that, no longer just serving the intentions of individual users, as in principle a means to whatever ends they may desire, the medium now is an end and an "active" force in itself. It may thus turn against those who once created it and who should be, but no longer are its masters. Simmel (1957: 95) refers to this kind of process as the "tragedy of culture".

Let me underline here that this notion of a powerful medium is not an empty metaphor. Only insofar as we accept money as in a sense being a relatively autonomous, active entity – rather than its only being put to use by rational economic man – will we be able to understand its role as a medium. And only this role as a medium will allow us to reconstruct, for example, in what sense economic systems may develop a dynamic of their own.

In spite of this active, powerful nature, though, money is by no means a completely autonomous entity. It requires a guarantee by other social institutions and thus by the community, "as to the acceptability of money for useful commodities in a stable ratio of exchange" (Laidler and Rowe 1980: 99). The growth of social institutions that serve such functions will promote the growth of a money based economy, and the availability of money will make the individual less dependent on the whims of particular other individuals. As a consequence there may be a trend "in the direction of making the individual more and more dependent upon the achievements of people but less and less dependent upon the personalities that lie behind them" and although, today, "[...] we are much more dependent on the whole society through the complexity of our needs on the one hand, and the specialisation of our abilities on the other, ... we are remarkably independent of every specific member of this society" (Simmel, cited after Laidler and Rowe 1980: 99).

That the individual directly depends on other individuals may be more characteristic of undeveloped than of developed economies[19] or such dependence may at least be much more direct in traditional societies than in modern ones. Insofar as transactions on the basis of interpersonal relations are increasingly replaced by mediated and impersonal ones, the modern individual might indeed appear to be set "free". But what kind of freedom is this, and what is the price to be paid for it?

Writing before the turn of the century and confronted with the decline of customs and values that were to a large degree still aristocratic ones,[20] Simmel tended towards a conservative pessimism. While willing to concede that a growing money-based economy might facilitate relationships over a physical, social or cultural distance, he tended to emphasise the numerous negative, unexpected, and undesirable side-effects these new opportunities would have. For example, replaced by new ways of relating to others and of assuring a social identity, behaviour patterns that once prevailed might either change qualitatively or disappear completely. And, based only on money, the new relationships and identities seemed likely to be relatively superficial, not very reliable and fragmented ones. Thus while in one sense being set free from interpersonal bondages, the modern individual might be related to society increasingly in terms of antagonism and alienation.

Evidently, then, the antagonistic relationship to society commonly ascribed to economic man appears here not as part of "man's nature", but as itself being a – probably unintended – effect of economic development.

As another, equally unintended side-effect of modern economy, distinctions between what is part of a social identity ("what you are") and what can be bought and sold ("what you have") may become diffuse to the point where what once had been considered an inalienable part of the person may later become an object of economic exchange. An obvious example here is the prostitute who "sells herself". Another is the land-owner who, if he sold his land, would give away something to which his identity is tied so closely that he may hardly be able to replace it by anything else money will buy. (Simmel refers to economic conditions here where the chances of buying something else and of building a new identity on these possessions are small.) Or take, as still another example, the value of labour. In a money-based economy labour can be bought and sold and doing so may come to be widely accepted to the point where the old maxim that whoever sells his/her work for money cannot be a true aristocrat or gentleman loses at least some of the rigour it once had.

Taken together, then, due to the growth of money-based economies values like honour, character, shame, and dignity that had once been held in high regard will more or less disappear and new ones will emerge, changing what Simmel calls "the style of life" (1989: 591ff). One of these new qualities is a type of rationality which Simmel calls the "calculating character of modern times" ("das rechnende Wesen der Neuzeit", 1989: 612ff) – a formulation that can be understood as critically referring to the planning and calculating rationality of economic man and, let me add, of the "modern" polite speaker, as to a markedly historical, modern achievement.

3.2 *Market economy*

In *The Great Transformation* (1944) Karl Polanyi – though apparently unaware of Simmel's as yet untranslated work – adds to and corrects it in two regards. Firstly, in order to overcome the difficulty that, occurring even in poorly developed economies, the fact that money is used at all hardly explains how economic, social and cultural change are brought about, Polanyi introduces the notion of "market economy", defined here as a self-regulating economic system that is unimpeded by any external, social or political forces. Being thus set free, the market will – this is Polanyi's central argument – tend to dominate all other social institutions, virtually undermining or destroying not only sub-systems, but the social system as a whole. And so the development of market economy, rather than being due to a quantitative increase of monetary exchange alone, can only be accounted for in terms of the autonomy of the economic system relative to virtually all other social systems. Being a recent, fairly modern achievement, this relative autonomy of market economic systems became fully visible, in the theoretical formulations to which Polanyi (1978: 157ff) refers at least, only around the end of the eighteenth century.

Before the advent of market economy – and this is the second point where Polanyi corrects Simmel – the relationship between economic and non-economic systems had been of an entirely different kind. Influenced by an ethnocentric thinking that was still common around the end of the nineteenth century, but since then has been rapidly falling into disrepute, Simmel saw primitive man not so much as a social being, as both being supported and constrained by social institutions, but – though in other regards emphasising the historicity of individualism – as driven by his immediate needs and desires, thus being motivated to engage individually in barter and to draw profit from it. Polanyi, by contrast, borrowing from social anthropological sources that had not yet been available to Simmel, argues that primitive exchange is typically organised in ways that more or less make it contribute to the self-maintenance of the social system as a whole.

Furthermore, the local markets that did exist in primitive society were usually quite small, hardly tended to grow and thus affected economic and social life only marginally. Polanyi shows that the rise of a modern market economy cannot be explained as simply resulting from a mere quantitative increase in barter or from an ever-increasing use of money, but from qualitative changes in foreign trade, that is, from kinds of trade that transcend geographical boundaries – in early stages often not in peaceful, economic, but in aggressive ways, in a joint venture of economic and non-economic, political and military forces.

Economic motivation can then be seen – summarising Polanyi's point (and drawing also on Sahlins [1965], who, starting from Polanyi's position, further elaborates it) – not as universal, but as occurring in at least two different forms. Whereas modern economies tend to be – insofar as they conform to Polanyi's definition of a market economy – relatively autonomous sub-systems, this does not seem to be the case with primitive exchange. Being embedded in and serving the purposes of an all-encompassing super-structure of kinship relations, the economic element is relatively unimportant there, being not nearly as differentiated or relatively autonomous as it might be under modern circumstances. Thus even where the economic element plays a role in primitive society – and these authors leave no doubt that it does

– it will typically not be driven by the egocentric, asocial motivation typically ascribed to economic man.

It is for these reasons that Simmel's still relatively micro-sociological account must be complemented by a more macro-sociological one and that, for the same reasons, the notion of the utility maximising individual or of "economic man", which, as Simmel had already tried to show, is a socially and historically relative one, must be revised, incorporating the additional, macro-sociological and historical dimensions that had until then been neglected.[21]

Thus, while correcting and complementing Simmel's approach in some regards, Polanyi does not discredit it as a whole. Both accounts can be seen as complementing each other and as converging towards a common perspective insofar as they run counter to the dualism between individual economic motivation and activity, on the one hand, and the social system, on the other, by showing that the exchange of money, though performed by individuals, is an intrinsically social medium, a medium that is affected by and in turn itself affects the motivations and the practices of the participants.

4. Conclusions and consequences

Returning to politeness, the third and final step to be made in this chapter will be that of exploring the analogy to money. In spite of the criticisms I have raised against the economic, cost-benefit approach to politeness, this analogy can indeed be drawn. In so doing I shall of course not go back to that one-sided approach, but to the social and historical one developed by Simmel and others,[22] trying to show in what sense it provides an alternative both to the individualism of the modern view and to the social determinism of the traditional one.

4.1 *Analogies*

While thus starting from an analogy to money I shall refrain from assuming it to hold at all levels, including the more specific ones of both media – where similarities in one regard would be outweighed by striking contrasts in others. The view I shall defend here is that of politeness as being analogous to money at least in one regard, namely at the level of the general approach Simmel demonstrates – or which I take him to demonstrate. This interpretation, extracting some elements and leaving out others, allows us to borrow from Simmel's work without thereby subscribing to it as a whole,[23] thus getting around some of the more problematic aspects of his construction. Let me identify, then, what I think would have to be the key elements of that interpretation:

(i)   Politeness, like money, is a socially constituted medium.

(ii) Again like money, it is a symbolic medium in the sense that its functions originally derive from an association to something else, namely to values.

(iii) Like money, too, politeness is historically constituted and reconstituted; its functions and the values it is associated with are essentially changeable ones.

(iv) During its history, the functions of politeness turn into a power of the medium in the sense that it may, rather than being only a means to the ends of the individual user, itself motivate and structure courses of action.

(v)   Correspondingly – and due to other forces, too – the chances of the user to master the medium completely (which would mean being able to use it according to his/her wishes) will be diminished.

These assumptions capture the still quite abstract outline of a socially and media oriented, "dialectical" approach. The fact that politeness is socially constituted does not imply here that individuals would not play a role, but that what happens between them cannot be accounted for in ultimately individualistic terms. Being a medium, politeness is seen here as "standing between" or "mediating" between individuals. It may do so because this medium, due to its social and historical constitution, carries certain functions that later, during the course of its history, turn into a power. The power of the medium can thus be seen as being due to the process of transforming or sediment-ing what had once been functions into a power of the medium itself.

Though socially constituted, politeness may then itself motivate and structure courses of action, feeding into social processes and, thus, into the very conditions of its own existence or maintenance. It is in this sense that politeness is seen as "standing between" or "mediating" between the individual and the social.

As the functions of politeness are changeable, one might want to presume that the individual user will be able to more or less employ the medium according to her/his wishes. But, due to the fact that these functions turn into a power of the medium – and due to other factors, as for example, brute force or social sanctions – the chances of the individual user to master it will correspondingly be diminished. Insofar as this is the case the role of the individual user will be a rather limited one. The reason is not that this role would in any way be irrelevant here, but – as we are concerned here with the agent only insofar as s/he is polite – the part s/he will be expected and allowed to play is written in again essentially social terms.[24]

4.2 *Social values*

As to the functions of politeness, the analogy to money, more precisely to Simmel's notion of "value", is a starting point. Later, however, this analogy will turn out to be only a partial one:

(i)   The social values from which politeness derives its functions are social order and social identity.

(iia) Social order and, as part of it, social identities are defined in terms of rights and duties.

(iib) Rights and duties vary with the relationship to *alter*.

(iic) Which kind of conduct is considered appropriate is relative to *ego*'s position in that relationship to *alter*.

The rights and duties that make up an identity are often thought of as being essentially reciprocal ones.[25] In this case – which is an ideal, relatively simple one – the rights of *ego* in that identity would correspond to the duties of *alter* and vice versa. Social identities and social order would then combine or even be reconciled – should the distribution of rights and duties be accepted as "fair" or "just"; note that nothing is being said here on whether they have to be equally distributed! – individual and social aspects. They could thus be seen as being claimed as well as granted – an aspect that, as you may remember, is part both of Goffman's description of "face" and of Simmel's analysis of the value of money. Also, social identities and social order would have the character of both structuring – thus in a sense making possible or facilitating – and of constraining behaviour. Let me underline here the dual, ambivalent character of politeness as facilitating and/or constraining behaviour. In the case of reciprocal, mutually accepted rights and duties at least politeness will not be perceived as being a repressive or constraining force but as being more or less helpful.

One may want to object, however, that this is all said only by way of a definition, as applying to a simplified, ideal case, and actual social behaviour is not very likely to be like that. For reciprocal rights and duties to be established and upheld, they would either have to be "negotiated" and/or agreed upon, or the definition of rights and duties would have to be brought about by other factors not identified here such as, for example, by brute force. But people may not, as a rule, agree on their respective rights and duties; they may not even be aware of the fact that they should. Or should they not?

Yet in spite of these objections, this ideal case is important in two senses: it allows us, firstly, to understand a pattern of presuppositions and expectations that can be thought of as underlying not necessarily actual behaviour, but the perceptions and evaluations we may have of it. Even where rights and duties have not really been negotiated and/or accepted, what is right and wrong may be assessed on the grounds of this presupposed, perhaps counter-factual pattern of reciprocal rights and duties. This pattern thus enables us to understand the moral and ethical connotations[26] of politeness – connotations that would seem to follow naturally from being associated with social order.

The same association with an ideal case also allows us to understand, secondly, that politeness – endowed as it is with a power of its own – may be perceived as being associated with accepted rights and duties even where these rights and duties have not been negotiated and/or accepted. This is the case in much of conventional behaviour, that is, whenever the "right" form is used and accepted "auto-matically", without a reflection on the part of the participants as to what its underlying functions might be.

According to this view, then, in order to be polite social acts and behaviours would have to be appropriate in the first place. This would imply that – by contrast to the modern view – the role of individually and strategically generating and modifying given behaviour patterns would have to be a secondary, derived one. It would follow that the room left for "investing" considerably more or less politeness than is required – as would be the case in flattery, mockery, sarcasm, irony, etc. – is limited and that, as soon as the polite agent goes beyond these limits, demeanour may no longer be perceived as polite, but as something else. Note that this point of view stresses the relativity of politeness and that therefore the notion of "scalability" would seem to be a misleading one.

4.3 *Persons*

Being thus defined in terms of rights and duties, the relationship of *ego* to *alter* may appear here as being a rather rigidly prescribed and static one. There are several factors that may render this prescription a less rigid one, the first of which is:

(i) A person usually has more than one social identity.

Someone may, for example, have the social identities of being a doctor and an employer and her or his position in each of these identities as well as the conduct that is expected from her or him will vary accordingly. For example, s/he may relate, in the identity of being a doctor, to either a patient or to a nurse. Insofar as the rights and duties of *ego* and *alter* vary between these identities, the behaviours that are considered "just and right" in each of them may vary, too.

An interesting consequence of this analysis arises if two or more of these identities are in play, each of them being defined in terms of rights and duties – if, for example, the nurse is both an employee and a patient:

(ii) The rights and duties that make up the different identities of a person may clash.

There is thus a source of intrapersonal conflict that has not necessarily to do with an antagonism between *ego* and *alter*. Note that whereas politeness might be – and is in the modern view – thought of as resulting from an essentially interpersonal conflict, this is not the only possibility here.

4.4 *Acquisition and usage*

On the one hand, then, due to the multiplicity of identities and due to the fact that the individual may, to some degree at least, be able to choose between them, the construction of social behaviour may become a confusingly complex and delicate enterprise. On the other hand, politeness is a socially and historically constituted, powerful medium, and the definition of social identities can be taken to imply that the individual may not at all be free to choose whatever course of action s/he may want to choose. Insofar as the medium is a powerful one, it will begin to motivate and structure courses of action and, correspondingly, the user will not be able to master the medium completely. If this is the case, the user will not be able to employ it according to her/his wishes. Moreover there are the coercive forces and sanctions that constrain social behaviour in particular settings; I have chosen to not consider them here for reasons of simplicity, but they are of course ubiquitous. We may then ask how, under such difficult, ambivalent and even contradictory conditions the user will ever be able to acquire the medium:

(i)   The process of learning or acquiring politeness is one of recon-
      structing, cognitively and/or practically, the medium.
(ii) The knowledge of the user will thus be a cognitive and practical
      one, too.

In order to be able to use the medium the user will have to recon-struct, practically and/or cognitively, how it has been constituted. Thus, instead of either simply being "learned" or trained or based only on other cognitive capacities of the individual, the process of acquiring and using politeness will have to be, to some degree at least, a practi-cal or tacit one.[27]

As the process of constituting the medium has been a social, inter-active and practical one, so the process of passing it on to other users will have to be social, interactive and practical, too. And only insofar as this is the case will the user be able to master the medium com-pletely.

But will the individual ever be able to accomplish this task? Due, firstly, to the number of the social identities that may be involved, due, secondly, to its power, and due, thirdly, to the complexities of the acquisition process, the task of mastering the medium may seem to be a virtually impossible one. How then should the individual acquire the ability to do so?

4.5   *Simplifying the medium*

A first way of using the medium in relatively simple ways is due to the largely practical nature of the medium. The individual may use it as the not so proficient user of a computer might use a "macro"-procedure, that is as a procedure that enables her or him to achieve ends by means of which s/he is only superficially aware, thus doing many things at the same time without having to care about the the details of what s/he is actually doing. Complex social realities could thus be managed by using relatively simple, but powerful means.

This type of use would be advantageous to the user insofar as s/he might use a macro-procedure economically, keeping in mind or in her or his "working memory" relatively little of what is actually going on. However, the same feature might also – and I shall argue that this is the more likely case at least where the medium of politeness is a full-fledged system – turn out to be quite disadvantageous in that, at the same time, incomplete mastery and/or knowledge of the system may induce the user to do things s/he is not completely aware of and would, if s/he were aware of them, probably not want to do. The power of politeness may thus, for example, lead the user to create or maintain realities s/he would not choose to create – if only s/he saw what those realities were like and if, as a further condition that is often not met, s/he were able to escape them.

Note that this latter condition would make the traditional account a relatively plausible one. Insofar as the individual is not enabled to master a given system of politeness – a likely outcome wherever that system is full-fledged – it will be very hard for the individual to creatively use or even reprogram the system according to her/his wishes. Or, even worse, s/he may not even be aware of the options that are available in using that system.

A second simplification derives from the fact that being polite is not the only way of creating or respecting social value. The creation and maintenance of social identities depends – as economic development does – on the growth of institutions that define and guarantee what can no longer be interpersonally negotiated.

Epilogue

The analogy to money has obviously not been exhausted here. One may want to speculate, for example, in what way the process of abstraction Simmel describes might affect politeness. Is it an abstract medium? Or is the social order with which it is associated in modern societies more abstract than in traditional ones? Much more could also be said on the role of institutions. And there are some obvious gaps in Simmel's account: very little has been said, for example, on political power. As this dimension may heavily affect social structure, it may be necessary, before we go on to speculate further, to close these gaps at least theoretically.

Notes

1. The modern view does of course not only draw on Grice, but on a growing literature that has been inspired by his lectures. As politeness theory does not seem to be feeding back to that literature, I shall not comment on it here.
2. The "want" to maintain face is often ascribed to the speaker as well as to the addressee. From the point of view of the production model that, I shall argue below, is implied in this view, however, this assumption has not really been integrated. See fn. 6 below.
3. Speech-act theory could be cited here as a third source here; it is an important one insofar as the modern approach is usually understood as applying to the single utterance or sentence, not to longer stretches of talk.
4. See, for example, Searle (1975/1979).
5. In what follows I shall refer to Brown and Levinson (1978, 1987), as a representative, and to Clark and Schunk (1980; see also Schunk and Clark, unpublished), as a radicalised interpretation of the modern view. Because my main concern here is the individualism of this view and the neglect of social aspects that goes with it – a feature which Lakoff's (1973), Ervin-Tripp's (1976) and Leech's (1977, 1983) accounts essentially share – I shall not comment on where these authors deviate from Brown and Levinson's statement. (But see the comment on Leech's "interpersonal rhetoric" in Brown and Levinson, 1987: 15, fn. 15.)
6. Cf. Brown and Levinson (1978: 81ff.). Here the fact that the indirect request – as politely rephrasing an imperative – is the paradigmatic case becomes evident. While an imperative or a request will under many circumstances be heard as entailing an imposition, other messages may not. Note also that speaking of an imposition, clearly implies that the threat is directed against the addressee. Any inappropriately phrased utterance might of course in principle be perceived as threatening the speaker's face, too, but I do not see how this model could account for this case. For further arguments against the asymmetrically individualistic, speaker-oriented nature of the model see what is said below under the headings "Individualism I" and "Individualism II".
7. This procedure is only defined for the case of mapping one weightiness value onto one and only one super-strategy. There is thus no unambiguous solution provided for the case where more than one strategy is employed – a case Brown and Levinson (1987: 143) obviously wish to include if they suggest that "the greater the number of compatible outputs the speaker uses the greater the politeness he may be presumed to intend".
8. Brown and Levinson (1978: 137ff) do mention the possibility of being "conventionally indirect", but they do not systematically distinguish conven-

tional, pre-fabricated utterances from individually generated ones.

9. We shall see below that Brown and Levinson (1987) also accept the cost-benefit approach, thus remaining ambivalent with regard to the notion of face as wants.

10. I am of course not arguing for a revival of behaviourism, but for a type of theory that avoids the pitfalls both of behaviourism and of cognitivism, so that both the highly learned, quasi-automatic reaction and the individually generated act can be accounted for.

11. The question of linear vs. cyclical processing is not new; it is discussed, for example, in Mead's (1934) treatise on the expression of affect, and there are precursors of this debate, for example, in eighteenth century ideas on how the actor is best enabled to express affect on stage (cf. Werkhofer 1988).

12. In real business negotiations the buyer will probably not begin by offering or even paying a price, but will rather leave that part to the seller. That these roles have been reversed here may be due to what I have characterised above as the cognitivism in Brown and Levinson's approach.

13. Partially redoing Clark and Schunk's first experiment Kemper and Thissen (1981) use Kruscal's non-metric scaling procedure. They prefer the unidimensional solution, but whether this is a critical test of the unidimensionality premise cannot really be judged from the data they present. For example, this study – as well as other, similar ones (see Clark and Schunk 1981; see also Blum-Kulka 1985/1987) – shows that the results of such scaling operations vary considerably as a function of precisely how the set of examples is composed and presented.

14. Perhaps the most severe of these difficulties is the fact that the data that are taken to support such determinism are usually only correlational, so that in order to find out whether variable A is determined by B or vice versa, whether both A and B are determined by a third variable C, or whether none of these causal relationships holds, other, independent data would be needed – a requirement that has hardly ever been observed in politeness research and is indeed, even with the advent of path-analysis, extremely difficult to observe.

15. They refer to Shoshana Blum-Kulka's (1985/1987) experimental demonstration that "(contrary to current theories of politeness) indirectness and politeness do not represent parallel dimensions" (Brown and Levinson 1987: 131).

16. As soon as more than one dimension is involved there may no longer be a unique solution of the scaling problem, and the rankings on any single dimension become more or less arbitrary. The set of points can then be rotated relative to the dimensions that are involved and coordinates can be assessed in various ways.

17. The first complete English translation having appeared only in 1978

Simmel's book has hardly been received in economic circles; Laidler and Rowe (1980) argue, however, that Simmel and the school of "Austrian economics" to which he belongs might considerably contribute to economic theory, providing solutions where other approaches have failed.

18. The modern gold standard is an example of the fact that, though becoming more "abstract", this association cannot be given up completely; it will understandably be particularly important in times of economic crisis.

19. Simmel is aware of the fact that money means of course something different to the poor than to the rich – a fact that relativises what is said here on developed economies for those who earn the fruit of such development.

20. For example, in contrast to France or Great Britain the ritual of duelling – originally an aristocratic custom, later one to be observed also by the bourgeois who had to defend the "honour" associated with a high public status – had still not yet become entirely obsolete in Germany (Frevert 1988; Elias 1989).

21. Arguing against Polanyi, Nash has claimed that the essential characteristic of peasant and primitive economies is not the absence of a motive of gain, but the existence of social organisations which directly channel economic choice, on the one hand, and a set of sanctions which operate to keep economic deviants in physical as well as moral jeopardy on the other (Nash 1961: 186). But why should the individual give way to such pressures? While the fact that such pressures are real enough in many societies cannot be denied, Nash's defense of economic individualism overlooks that the individual's psychological outfit and, thus, the motivation of the individual will typically not remain unaffected by the repressive system. For example, moral pressures would hardly be effective, unless we consider the individual's willingness to submit her- or himself to them.

22. For the sake of simplicity I shall refer to Simmel's theory of money and the corrections and additions by other authors I have mentioned above as together forming one source.

23. For a more complete discussion see Werkhofer (1989a).

24. In a similar vein, Shotter (1973, 1976) distinguishes between people as personalities and as "natural" agents – referring to the levels or units of analysis employed by the observer, not to a dualism between man and animal.

25. For a particularly clear, but harmonistic discussion of social identity see Goodenough (1965).

26. The importance of these dimensions can be illustrated both by Ervin-Tripp's observations on which I have briefly commented above and by an observation in my own study (Werkhofer 1984b). Having produced the polite utterance I had been asking for the subject gave a comment I had not been asking for:

"Well [...] and then he would have to do what I requested him to do!" – thus indicating that politeness can be seen as being connected to a dimension of obligation.

27. I have elsewhere (Werkhofer 1986b) tried to connect the type of approach proposed here to a model of social development.

Part 2: Empirical Studies in Politeness

7. Secondhand politeness

Annelie Knapp-Potthoff

1. Introduction

Politeness is generally conceived of as taking place between two or – with a recent extension of perspective (cf. Brown and Levinson 1987) – more people engaged in a communicative encounter. In many situations of intercultural contact, however, things are much more complicated, not only in view of the fact that misunderstandings may arise because of culturally diverging face wants and preferences for the use of certain politeness strategies over others in different cultures. Neither do complications arise only because interactants in intercultural contacts may experience difficulties in performing politeness with the limited means of their learner languages. Rather, at least two other factors seem to be involved:

1. In intercultural communication, more so than in other types of communication, face-threatening acts and their redress do not operate on the inter-individual level alone, but – by processes of attribution and stereotyping – tend to have consequences for higher levels of social organisation as well.
2. There are types of intercultural discourse in which the interactional structure itself seems to create problems in the communication of politeness. One such type of discourse is mediator discourse, i.e., that particular type of intercultural communication in which understanding is established with the help of a non-professional interpreter. In mediator discourse politeness cannot be communicated immediately, but only "secondhand". Furthermore, it is characterised by a particular participant framework (cf. Goffman 1981: 146), with the respective different participant statuses influencing the way politeness is dealt with.

This chapter focuses on how politeness is handled within this non-simple participant framework. Other important issues in the discussion of politeness, like the question of universality or the role of Power and Distance factors, will not constitute the main concern of this chapter.

2. The participant framework of mediator discourse

Let us start by briefly characterising the participant framework of mediator discourse. For reasons of relative simplicity, we will assume that there are three participants in this type of interaction, two of whom (those with the primary communicative intentions, who will be called primary interactants in the following text) have very similar statuses as participants. These statuses differ, however, from participant statuses in simple dyadic interactions. For example, the primary interactants' potential for managing turn-taking by themselves is severely limited. Moreover, they have the option of introducing a particular type of change of footing (Goffman 1981) at practically any time in the interaction by engaging in a "private" conversation with the mediator, consequently changing the other two participants' statuses. In private conversations between a primary interactant and a mediator, the latter's status is changed to that of a full-range participant and the other primary interactant's status to that of not even a bystander or over-hearer, but to someone who is only present, not "politely showing disinterest in who or what is accessible", as in the cases described by Goffman (1981: 132), but rather showing interest in who or what is *not* accessible to him. Incidentally, reducing a primary interactant's participant status in such a way can be regarded as a face-threatening act in itself. Thus, every action that the mediator or the other primary interactant takes in order not to exclude a primary interactant from communication this way is a matter of politeness specific to mediator discourse. I will discuss other types of such politeness later in this chapter.

A mediator's participant status is not only that of a bystander, but rather that of a "ratified participant" (Goffman 1981: 132), with tacitly assumed rights, responsibilities, and duties. A few of these may be briefly mentioned: the mediator is largely responsible for the organisa-tion of turn-taking; he/she has extended rights of interrupting (e.g., in order to limit turns of talk to a manageable size); the primary interac-tants cannot but trust in the mediators' making the greatest possible effort to convey their intended meanings; basically, he/she has to speak "for others", and not for himself/herself: mediating is a "speaking for others" activity (Knapp-Potthoff 1987).

3. The pilot study

Prior analyses of mediator discourse (Knapp-Potthoff and Knapp 1986, 1987) have indicated that there is a tendency to neglect the mediation of interactional meaning in favour of mediating transactional meaning. Furthermore, it turned out that there were certain linguistic elements that seemed particularly resistant to mediation. These observations led to the hypothesis that politeness which its addressee receives only secondhand (or rather: "second-mouth") might not be the same as that which its original producer had intended, and this for reasons of discourse structure.

The previous data on which these observations were based are limited in several respects, however. First of all, the possibility cannot be ruled out that the neglect of interactional meaning in mediation was only incidental, as the context-conditions were in no way controlled. Secondly, it might be argued that the loss of verbal interactional meaning in those data may have been compensated by non-verbal cues and a limited amount of immediate understanding taking place between the primary interactants, which the mediators have taken into account and relied on.

Therefore, the data of the present pilot study were recorded under more controlled conditions. It was decided to pre-structure the interactions to be recorded and to introduce systematic variations. An important element that was introduced into the interactions was the use of the telephone. In order to rule out any possibility of partial immediate understanding of the primary interlocutors – verbally or non-verbally – without the mediators' intervention, and the mediator relying on such unmediated additional communication taking place, it was decided that the primary interlocutors should be remote from each other in terms of place: the German speaker conversed over the phone with the mediator, who was located in the same room as the English speaker. By this arrangement, the mediator had to carry the whole burden of "transporting" meanings from the speaker of English to that of German and vice-versa. Supposing a similarity between talk on the telephone and other talk settings with the exception of opening and closing sequences (cf. Schegloff 1979), the influence of peculiarities of telephone conversations on these data can be considered relatively small. Certainly an additional element of artificiality is introduced, as there is no natural motivation for the speaker of English not to be answering the phone himself, but there is also a certain additional advantage: As speaking for others on the phone is a fairly common monolingual everyday activity (e.g., if someone cannot answer the phone himself/herself, because he or she is in the bathroom, busy with the baby, etc.; cf. Knapp-Potthoff 1987), this study may shed some light on problems of monolingual "speaking for others" activities, where politeness is conveyed secondhand as well.

Three different interactions over the phone were recorded and analysed. The situations were arranged in such a way as to allow a compromise between controlled elicitation on the one hand and relative naturalness of the task for the mediators on the other. Whereas the primary interactants were the same in all three interactions (the native speaker of German and the native speaker of English were both staff members of the University of Düsseldorf), the mediations were done by three different mediators. The mediators, three advanced university students of English, were not informed about the particular focus of the experiment (i.e., "politeness" being at issue), but were only aware of the fact that their management of a complex communicative situation was being studied. The primary interactants, however, were fully informed and even got detailed instructions. They were provided with scripts for the interaction, but were encouraged to add or change anything if they felt the interaction required it. The scripts were prepared on the basis of an authentic interaction which centred around the problem of interactant A asking interactant B to give back to the university library a book that A needed himself and which B had failed to return. Thus, inherent to the problem was a substantial threat to B's face. On the basis of this interaction, three different versions of A's part, which was to become the German speaker's part, were constructed.

The three versions are identical with respect to the nature of the problem, the objective amount of face threat, and the solution to the problem that was finally found. The three versions differ, however, in the following respects:

- In version 3, the German speaker's part is less polite than in the other two versions. This was accomplished by deleting most of the elements that could be considered the results of politeness strategies and by deliberately adding elements of rudeness. The resulting version 3 was unequivocally considered markedly less polite than the other versions by native speaker informants.

– The German speaker's part in versions 1 and 2 differs with respect
to the length of turns, particularly in the expository phase. Thus,
whereas in version 1 – after some introductory remarks – he politely exposes the nature of the problem and only afterwards, when
the mediator has mediated what the general nature of the problem
is, gives details about the book under discussion, the speaker of
German communicates both the general nature of the problem and
the details about the book in a single turn in version 2. The length
of turns was manipulated in order to get some insight into the effect
of length of turn on the processing of politeness phenomena.
– Versions 1 and 2 also differ with respect to the order of sentences
within turns.
– Moreover, the three versions differ slightly as a result of the interactants occasionally freeing themselves from the script.

4. Results

For the purposes of analysis it seemed useful to divide the verbal
material of each interaction into 4 sections:

Section A: the set of utterances produced by the German speaker,
directed at the mediator;

Section B: the set of utterances produced by the mediator, directed at
the English speaker;

Section C: the set of utterances produced by the English speaker,
directed at the mediator;

Section D: the set of utterances produced by the mediator, directed at
the German speaker.

One of the most obvious results of the study is the levelling of
politeness in the B-sections: the marked difference in politeness that
was purposefully introduced into the construction of the three A-
sections is not retrievable in the B-sections, i.e., the corresponding
mediated sections. In the more detailed analysis below it will be
demonstrated that this is the consequence of two processes at work in
conveying politeness secondhand: 1. politeness reduction in mediator
discourse, and 2. mediator-discourse-specific politeness. I will discuss these two processes in turn.

4.1 *Politeness reduction*

Let us start with some examples to clarify this point. All three interactions are full of cases where the mediated form of a text produced by a primary interactant does not reflect the verbal realisations of politeness inherent in the original formulation.

(1) Interaction 1:

G: *Ehm, tut mir leid, dass ich da drängen muss. Aber ich brauch's wirklich ganz dringend.*

M: He says it's urgent.

(2) Interaction 1:

G: *Ich wollt' eigentlich nur fragen, ob es möglich ist, dass Herr E. ein Buch aus der UB zurückgibt, das ich selbst ganz dringend brauche.*

M: He would like to ask you to bring it (i.e., the book, A.K-P.) back to the library.

(3) Interaction 2:

G: *Ich wollt' eigentlich nur fragen, ob es möglich is, dass Herr E. ein Buch aus der UB zurückgibt, das ich selbst ganz dringend brauche. (.) Eh, ich hatte das schon vor längerer Zeit vormerken lassen, aber das Buch is immer noch nich zurückgekommen, und zwar is das* (title and shelf-mark, A.K-P.), *und es tut mir wirklich leid, dass ich da drängeln muss, aber ich brauch's wirklich ganz dringend.*

M: Ja, eh (..) well, erm, he's asking for a book which he wanted to/ to take from the library (.) for a couple of weeks and now he's erm (.)/ and he's asking if you here in/ in the office and the title of the book is/ eh, wie war das noch mal?

It might be argued that the limitations of the mediators' learner language(s) are responsible for such reductions (cf., for example, the analyses by House and Kasper 1981 and Davies 1987). This is, however, hardly a satisfactory explanation for the fact that substantial reductions in politeness can be found in the D-sections as well, i.e., in those cases where the direction of mediation is into the mediators' native language.

(4) Interaction 1:

E: Oh dear, yes, my God, I really must apologise, hm, it looks as though I haven't returned it. I've got a reminder here.

M: *Hm, er/ er entschuldigt sich grade, er hat grad eine Mahnung entdeckt, wie mir scheint.*

(5) Interaction 3:

E: Well, that/ I'm afraid that's a bit difficult. Erm. Because the book isn't here, it's at home. And I'm in/ in a bit of a hurry. Erm, I wonder (.) if he could collect it (.) at my place.

M: *Äm, es is schwierig, denn er hat das Buch nicht hier, sondern zu Hause und hat im Moment keine Zeit, es zu holen (.) und ähm bittet Sie, ähm, vielleicht vorbeizukommen und zu holen.*

Even though the mediators may have problems in expressing politeness in English as their non-native language, it is fairly implausible that such problems should exist for comprehension.

In the following sections, I will argue that the observed reductions in politeness can be attributed to mediator-discourse-specific processes, because this type of discourse with its particular participant structure is characterised by a) limitations on the expressibility of politeness, and b) limitations on the clarifiability of politeness.

4.1.1 Limitations on the expressibility of politeness in mediator discourse

To begin with, it has to be taken into account that in non-professional interpreting mediated versions of texts are hardly ever literal translations of the original versions, but rather reformulations (see Knapp and Knapp-Potthoff 1985). Apart from the limited capacities of a mediator's memory, this is due to the participant structure of mediator discourse itself: a mediator is not an impersonal "translation machine" but a potentially fully-fledged participant. With respect to participant status, he or she is a "marginal person", always on the verge of speaking for himself/herself. Therefore it has to be made clear at any moment of the interaction who is responsible for the particular speech-acts performed, who can or has to meet their felicity conditions, i.e., who does the asking, apologising, greeting, etc. Thus, the descriptive use of performative verbs is characteristic of mediations: a mediator reports rather than translates the meanings produced by a primary interactant. We find a typical case in example 4: the English speaker's utterance *Oh dear, yes, my God, I really must apologise* is mediated as *Hm, er/ er entschuldigt sich grade* 'Hm, he/ he's apologising.' The reporting mode, however, raises severe problems for the use of politeness strategies: as Levinson (1983: 245, 255) has pointed out, modifications of performative verbs, for example adverbs, do not necessarily have the same meanings in performative and in descriptive usages. This seems to apply to equivalents across languages, too. So the mediator is quite right in not translating *I really must apologise* as *Er muss sich wirklich entschuldigen* 'He really must apologise' or as *Er entschuldigt sich wirklich* 'He's really apologising' or even as *Du liebe Güte, ja, mein Gott, er muss sich wirklich entschuldigen* 'Oh dear, yes, my God, he really must apologise'. But can the mediator's actual translation be called "adequate"? Clearly, by deleting hedges on illocutionary force, relevant nuances of meanings are lost in his version: nuances of politeness. The ensemble of modifications to the English speaker's apology communicates a lot that is related to the English and German speaker's face. The information that the speaker of English recognises the German speaker's needs as relevant (the exclamatory expressions), the information that the English speaker does not normally do things like this (exclamatory expressions as expressions of "shock" at his own negligence), and a certain indication of his non-responsibility for the fact that he is put into a position to apologise.

In order to achieve a more adequate mediation, the mediators might have used other devices to compensate for the non-usability of the politeness strategies employed by the primary interactants. A viable solution might have been to make descriptive meta-statements of the sort "He's apologising, and he seems to be very sorry, because he realises this is very important for you," etc. However, none of the mediators uses such a device of "descriptive politeness" in my data. I would like to suggest that this is mainly due to the fact that his/her task is an extremely complex one, and the possibilities of performing complicated sub-tasks, which involve higher-level processing and a complete reformulation, within the complex overall-task, are severely restricted.

Interestingly, the mediators do mediate politeness strategies – or at least attempt to do so – in cases where these strategies can be coped with on the propositional level and do not require macro-level processing. Take, for example, those instances where the German speaker tries to redress the English speaker's negative face by accepting his apology (cf. Brown and Levinson 1987: 67) in the two polite interactions 1 and 2:

(6) Interaction 1:

G: *Hmhm, ja (.) das is ja nich weiter schlimm, jetzt is die Frage nur: wie komm ich da dran?*

M: Hm, it doesn't matter very much. The thing/ (.) the problem is/ however
        still remains: How can he (laughing)/ how can he get the book?

(7) Interaction 2:

G: *Ach! Mmh, tja, die Frage is jetzt eh ... wie komm ich dran? Is ja sons nich*
        weiter schlimm.
M: Okay, erm, he/ he is not sure (.) erm (.) how he's getting the book now,
        because erm it's not that/ it's not a problem

The hypothesis that the mediators prefer lower-level processing is
further supported by the fact that in the examples above they retain the
respective order of sentences within turns.

What the data suggest, then, is that the realisations of different politeness strategies are not equally accessible to mediation, but rather
differ in degree of accessibility. This does not mean that the respective
meanings of those strategies that are difficult to access cannot be expressed by the mediator at all nor that they are untranslatable, but
rather that they are more unlikely to be mediated because of the
complexity of processing required for the mediation task. It may be the
case, however, that this effect can be counteracted by the primary
interactants structuring their texts to be mediated in particular ways.
For example, the realisation of otherwise badly accessible politeness
strategies may be supported by their occurrence within very short
turns of speech or by the primary interactant giving the mediator an
explicit order to mediate politeness. Further research is necessary to
determine the ways in which the primary interactants themselves can
influence the adequacy of mediation by the way they structure and
formulate their talk.

It will also be a task for further research to investigate whether a
continuum of politeness strategies with respect to their accessibility to
mediation can really be established. The reflections that follow are
meant to provide a basis for formulating hypotheses for such research,
referring to the list of strategies given by Brown and Levinson (1987).

Very low on a scale of accessibility may be a strategy which relies
on the use of in-group identity markers (Brown and Levinson's
strategy 4 for positive politeness). It seems fairly improbable that
primary interactants will use such a strategy at all in mediator
discourse, in view of the fact that the mediator will have to re-for-
mulate the utterance in a different language anyway. Extremely low
accessibility will also hold for those strategies that require a lot of
interactive cooperation on the part of the primary interactants within

the discourse, as the "seek agreement"-strategy by repetition of part or all of what the preceding speaker said, or Brown and Levinson's strategy 15 for negative politeness, the use of ellipsis. The scripts for the German speaker contained an example of an incomplete sentence (*Ja, tjaa, mmh, wenn er vielleicht trotzdem/*), but after the experiment he reported that he found this strategy hardly performable in the actual interaction, and so he did not attempt to use this strategy in versions 2 and 3.

Other candidates for low accessibility to mediation seem to be the following strategies of positive politeness: exaggeration (strategy 2), the use of the "vivid present" to intensify interest to a hearer (strategy 3), tags (strategy 6), the use of the inclusive "we" (strategy 12), and in the field of negative politeness some forms of conventional indirectness (strategy 1) and all sorts of hedges (strategy 2).

On the other hand, there seem to be politeness strategies with relatively high accessibility to mediation. In the field of positive politeness these are strategy 1 (notice, attend to hearer) or the raising of safe topics as a way to seek agreement (strategy 5). It is interesting to note, however, that the other way of seeking agreement that is mentioned by Brown and Levinson, i.e., repeating part or all of what the preceding speaker has said, is far less accessible to mediation.

Up to now I have not yet made explicit one very important cause for the difficulty of realising politeness strategies in mediator discourse: accessibility to mediation is not only influenced by the indeterminacy of the mediator's participant status, i.e., by the very fact that potentially he/she, too, may be the initiator of speech-acts, but also by the fact that communication between primary interactants within mediator discourse is an intrinsically distanced form of communication, which prevents all immediate cooperative activity that is inherent to some politeness strategies. An excellent example is the, I am tempted to say, impossibility of realising a strategy of repetition to seek agreement in mediator discourse.

4.1.2 Limitations on the clarifiability of politeness

I would like to suggest that a further reason for the reduction of politeness in the mediated versions is the low accessibility of politeness to clarification. As mentioned above, the complexity of the task of mediating a turn of speech often exceeds a mediator's processing capacities. In principle, he/she is entitled to limit the length of a primary interactant's speaking turn by interrupting, without this interruption generally being considered a face-threatening act of high ranking, if considered one at all. When processing problems arise, he/she can also ask for repetition, either in a general way "Could you please repeat that?", or in a specific way. With specific requests for repetition or clarification, however, problems arise. Whereas many requests for repetition or clarification of transactional meaning can be found in all three interactions (and in all the other data I have), there is virtually no example of a clarification request concerning politeness. In fact, it is difficult to conceive of a way in which such a request might be formulated. For the clarification of transactional meaning, however, there are conventionalised formats of request, which are indeed used by all three mediators in mediating the details of the book under discussion:

(8) Interaction 1:

M: *Könn' Se den Titel noch mal sagen?*

(9) Interaction 2:

M: *Könn' Se mal wiederholen? Vor allem Signatur? Und den Namen? – Und dann langsam die Signatur – und (.) Signatur? – Äh, könn' Sie die Zahl nochmal sagen? Fünfhundert? – War das achthundert und dann?*

(10) Interaction 3:

   Wie war das noch mal? Wie war/ – Nochmal bitte? – Nochmal.

Thus, if necessary, as was particularly the case in the German speaker's extremely long expository turn in interaction 2, the mediation of transactional meaning can be aided by very long clarification sequences, and information that was not grasped during the initial processing of a speaking-turn can be retrieved. Politeness, however, if not processed right away, is most likely to be lost for ever, because it does not seem accessible to clarification in discourse.

4.2 *Mediator-discourse-specific politeness*

Politeness in mediator discourse need not, however, only be dealt with in terms of politeness reduction. Rather, elements of added politeness, which seem to be specific to this type of discourse, can be observed in the B- and D-sections as compared to the A- and C-sections.

4.2.1 *Omission of rudeness*

Version 3 of the A-sections is characterised not only by a significantly smaller number of realisations of politeness strategies, but by the occurrence of many expressions that can be considered really rude. Examples are: *Mein Gott, das is doch/ kann doch nich wahr sein; Is doch unmöglich, geht doch gar nich, det is doch/ is doch bescheuert; Ja, ja, wie ich's gesagt habe.* Characteristically, the mediator completely neglects these elements in her mediations. This may be due to the same reasons as the non-mediation of certain politeness strategies by all three mediators. In this type of discourse, it would not have been appropriate either to give direct equivalents for these expressions of rudeness, and additional processing capacity would have been needed for macro-level processing with the result of the mediator saying something like "He seems to be very upset about it." Another plausible explanation is, however, that the mediator deliberately missed the critical elements in her mediation because of a desire to minimise face threat. Whatever her motives, the effect is an increase in politeness in the B-section of interaction 3 compared to the A-section. This effect contributes to the observed levelling of politeness in the three B-sections.

4.2.2 *Laughing*

All three A-sections contain one face-threatening act which is much higher in ranking than all the other ones. It is performed very similarly in all versions, with only little politeness added by the use of a strategy of impersonalising and a tag. The act refers to the German speaker's refusal to co-operate in the solution of the problem and to placing the whole responsibility for returning the book on the English speaker as the "guilty" one. It is realised as something like "Ich denke, normalerweise is doch so, dass derjenige, der 'n Fehler macht, auch selbst dafür gradesteht, oder?" In interaction 1 as well as in interaction 3 the mediators accompany their mediation of the respective turn by laughing. In interaction 2 the face-threatening act under discussion is also associated with laughing, although in this case it is not the mediator who laughs, but rather the German speaker, who – spontaneously and uninduced by the script – reacts by laughing when the mediator has mediated the English speaker's response *Really, I'm not sure about that.*

For the mediator in interaction 3 the example above is the only instance of laughing, whereas the mediator in interaction 1 laughs in four of his speaking-turns. All the contexts in which the mediator laughs are very similar insofar as they are associated with face-threatening acts of relatively high ranking:

1. when mediating the English speaker's utterance *I think it's a bit strange. I don't eh/ I can't imagine that I've still got it.*
2. within his mediation *The thing/ the problem is/ however still remains: How can he* (laughing) / *how can he get the book?*
3. (laughing) *He says that usually the one who makes the mistake is the one who* (laughing) (.) *has to eh well/ to eh well eh make it good, as it were.*
4. when mediating the English speaker's utterance *Well, really, I mean that G makes mistakes occasionally as well.* (In this case, the mediator had already laughed together with the English speaker at the time of termination of the latter's utterance.)

The co-occurrence of laughing with face-threatening acts of relatively high ranking suggests that laughing can be a very powerful device for minimising face threat, with particular advantages for use in mediator discourse. I do not wish to claim, of course, that laughing as a politeness strategy is restricted to such discourse, but rather that it is particularly suitable for this type of discourse and may to a certain degree compensate for the non-occurrence of other politeness strategies. Obviously, laughing is independent of linguistic material, and although there is certainly a lot of individual and probably culture-specific variation in the way laughing is performed, there is usually enough similarity in the performances to allow the identification as "laughing". As a consequence, by employing laughter as a politeness strategy, the mediator is freed from the burden of verbalising a politeness strategy in a particular language, but he/she can laugh "between languages", so to speak. As a further consequence, both primary interactants may feel addressed by the mediator's laughing at the same time – and be able to join in. As an additional advantage, the complicated constraints on turn-taking in mediator discourse are relieved for once. Thus, a certain immediacy of discourse is regained.

There is still another advantage of laughing as a practical politeness strategy for mediator discourse to be mentioned. By being void of linguistic material, laughing can serve many face wants at the same time: those of both the primary interactants and his/her own ones. To me it seems that in co-occurring with the extremely face-threatening act discussed above, the mediator's laughing has the effect of reducing face threat for all three participants: the threat to the English speaker of being considered wholly responsible or even "guilty", the face threat to the German speaker of being considered extremely rude and uncooperative, and the face threat to the mediator himself of being identified with such uncooperative behaviour. That his own face may be at stake here is suggested by the fact that in my data laughing is initiated by the mediators themselves in most of the cases and cannot be considered as attempts at mediating politeness strategies employed by the primary interactants.

There are two other mediator-discourse-specific politeness strategies to be considered that refer to threats to the face of the mediator himself/herself.

4.2.3 *Explicit mediator performatives*

Because of a mediator's particular participant status and the fact that he/she is always on the verge of speaking for himself/herself, there is an inherent danger in any mediation that the originator of the respective meanings may not be clear to the primary interactant to whom the mediation is addressed. And even if basically no ambiguity exists, the mediator may yet be held partly responsible for the meanings he/she mediates. Thus, any mediation of a face-threatening act potentially constitutes a threat to the mediator's face, too. There is, however, a conventionalised way for the mediator to distance himself/herself from the meanings of his/her mediations: the use of explicit mediator performatives like "he thinks that ...", "she would like to know", "he asks you to ...". The use of such explicit mediator performatives can be considered a politeness strategy to save the mediator's face (Knapp and Knapp-Potthoff 1985).

4.2.4 *Interactional politeness*

In all types of discourse, violations of conversational organisation constitute face-threatening acts in themselves (cf. Brown and Levinson 1987: 232f.). This points to politeness strategies that are not aimed at reducing the impact of face threats related to the particular content of the interaction, but related to the structure of the interaction itself. In mediator discourse, there is a specific type of face threat that calls for minimisation: the task of mediation may make excessive demands on the mediator, so that she/he may be found unable to cope with it. In a way, the very act of mediating is potentially face-threatening for a mediator. In this context, every action taken by a primary interactant to save the mediator's face can be considered as a form of politeness. Verbal manifestations may include the following: deliberately limiting the length of turns, repetition, finishing of the mediator's sentence by a primary interactant.

5. Concluding remarks

The analysis of the data has shown that problems in communicating politeness in intercultural communication other than those that are based on cultural differences and problems of expressing politeness in a learner language do indeed exist: problems that are inherent in a type of discourse in which politeness is expressed secondhand. Hopefully, it has also shed some light on secondhand politeness in those types of intracultural communication which involve speaking for others.

The problems manifest themselves mainly as the mediators' preoccupation with transactional meaning in their mediations to the relative neglect of politeness as a form of interactional meaning. In principle, the preoccupation with transactional meaning may be either a consequence of the difficulties inherent in the macro-level reformulation that is required for many forms of verbal politeness or rather a cause for the neglect of mediating politeness if the mediators have a higher rating of relevance for transactional meaning. In this chapter I have concentrated on the former possibility. It seems very likely, however, that the mediators' relevance structures will influence their mediations as well, and that these relevance structures vary with cultural background. As the study by Byrnes (1986) on interactional style suggests, Germans tend to be particularly biased towards the information-bearing quality of language, and it seems to me a worthwhile question for research whether mediators from other cultural backgrounds deal differently with politeness in their mediations.

In my analysis, I have tried to demonstrate that the politeness strategies listed by Brown and Levinson vary with regard to their accessibility to mediation. In this context, let me take up the question of adequacy of mediation that has been tackled before. The problem of adequacy, which has been fervently discussed in translation theory (e.g., Reiss and Vermeer 1984), enters into quite new dimensions here. Some of the questions at stake are the following: Can different politeness strategies be adequately substituted for each other? Does a reduction of the variety of politeness strategies used within a discourse – as a logical consequence of the low accessibility of some strategies to mediation – entail a reduction in the degree of politeness? Is the expectation of receiving politeness in mediator discourse the same for the primary interactants as in immediate types of discourse, or do they take into account that secondhand politeness may be "worn-out"? Can, after all, a meta-statement on the discourse-level about a primary interactant's polite verbal behaviour compensate for a failure to mediate the individual politeness strategies employed? I remember a mediator saying about a primary interactant after she had finished her mediation: "By the way, he was being very polite all the time."

8. Between matter-of-factness and politeness

Judith Stalpers

This chapter is part of a larger research project on language and culture in business negotiations.[1] The languages under study are Dutch and French, the latter as a native and as a foreign language. Although the research project involves two cultures, this study sheds more light on genre-specific differences between types of discourse than on cross-cultural differences. While there is no reason to assume that business talk is more polite than any other talk, the general nature of this kind of discourse as a goal-directed interaction in which the participants engage in order to pursue commercial interests suggests that the avoidance of impoliteness should be a high priority. I will demonstrate with one phenomenon that the rules of conduct for business talk differ from the rules of conduct for casual conversation. This shows that business talk allows for a larger degree of tolerance for behaviour, which in other contexts would more easily be considered impolite.

Discourse organisation

To understand how people organise their discourse is a complicated matter, as has been pointed out on several occasions (cf. Brown and Yule 1983 for an overview). One fruitful approach seems to be the description of how people indicate the beginning or end of a discourse unit. First, this kind of research provides insights into the kind of units that can be distinguished. Secondly, the research reveals some systematic features of the use of certain expressions which pose problems for traditional grammars because they lack a clearly defined meaning, for example, "well", "ok", "and", etc. Schiffrin (1980) uses the term "discourse bracket" for expressions whose main function is to organise the communication process rather than to add information on the subject level. The purpose of this chapter is to analyse a particular type of discourse bracket, that is, a metalinguistic expression used for indicating the opening of a particular type of discourse unit, a topic, in a particular type of discourse, business talk. The present analysis is based on eleven tape-recorded business conversations, totalling almost five hours of recording. The recordings consist of real life business negotiations among Dutch speakers, French speakers, and conversations among native and non-native speakers of French.

The use of metalinguistic expressions for establishing topic change has been described for several types of discourse (e.g., Gülich 1970; Schiffrin 1980; Scholtens and Stalpers 1982; Weijdema 1985). However, it cannot be taken for granted that the conclusions that the researchers drew about the use of such expressions in connection with topic change with respect to discourse genres such as radio interviews, classroom interaction, and panel discussions are also valid for business talk.

As the following analysis of the use of metalinguistic expressions in business talk demonstrates, the use of such expressions is the preferred way of initiating a topic change in this kind of discourse. Their use should not be seen as a strategy of dominance, but as a bald-on-record strategy, that is, a strategy that aims at maximally efficient communication.

A close look at the instances of topic conflict in my data suggests that whenever the interaction becomes problematic, interactants refer to the basic set of assumptions which have been described in previous studies for casual conversations. This leads to the conclusion that the rules of conduct in business talk allow for a broad margin in so-called bald-on-record behaviour (Brown and Levinson 1978) as long as the interactants agree with each other. As soon as the interaction becomes problematic, the rules of conduct for casual conversation are applied as the default variant, as it were.

Topic change

Unfortunately, there is not a good definition of "topic" in the linguistic literature. As Brown and Yule (1983: 70) have pointed out, the notion of discourse topic is "the most frequently used, unexplained, term in the analysis of discourse". The following is a working definition of discourse topic which is helpful to characterise and reveal some organising principles of business talk.

Each subject touched upon by the participants which calls for a solution from the parties involved constitutes a discourse topic. Examples from the data are "the things the parties want to talk about during the meeting", "the choice of products to be sold/purchased", "time of delivery", "request for changing contract conditions", etc. At times, a discourse topic is redefined when it turns out that two different subjects happen to be interconnected and need to be treated together in order to find a solution. A new topic is opened whenever the participants talk about a newly defined problem and possibilities for its solution. The definition of topic in terms of problem and solution is an analytical construct, which, however, corresponds to what speakers say about why they talk about what. Consider the following excerpt from one of the conversations:

(1) 302: B144-B147[2]
A and N are selling a piece of land

N:	*maar u neemt niet die architekt*	'but you don't take the architect
	dus die vraag	thus that question
	zit in jouw prijs zit daar die die	is in your price is that that
	die die architekt van ons eh die	that that architect of us in
	we dan toch (0.9)	your price whom we' (0.9)
A:	*nee mijnheer Ysselstein zegt dat*	'no Mr Ysselstein says
	is het probleem van de verkopers	that's the problem of the sellers'
	(...)	(...)
N:	*daarom vraag ik het toch*	'that's why I'm asking'
A:	*nee eh ja*	'no ehr yes'
N:	*ik praat alleen maar over*	'I only talk about
	problemen (Laughs)	problems (Laughs)
	dingen die we al opgelost	things which we have
	hebben zwijgen we over	solved we don't talk about'
	(Laughter)	(Laughter)

Metalinguistic expressions

By "metalinguistic expressions" I mean expressions whose subject is language. The range of phenomena that can be considered as having a metalinguistic function is very wide, as has been pointed out by Schiffrin (1980) and Weinrich (1976) among others. For the purpose of the present analysis, the set of phenomena subsumed under the notion of metalinguistic expression will be limited rather narrowly. Expressions are taken to be such expressions if and only if they contain a lexicalised item referring to talk, that is, verbs and nouns of verbal communication, such as Dutch *zeggen* 'say', French *expliquer* 'explain', *question* 'question', and terms of discourse deixis, such as French *le point* 'the point', *commencer* 'start'. Moreover, this analysis only deals with metalinguistic expressions which open a new topic. They are expressions which explicitly indicate (a) that one wants to start talking about a new problem and/or (b) what the new subject or problem is. The underlined metalinguistic expressions in examples (2) and (3) illustrate this:

(2)   302: B231–B245

Y:	*wij hebben dus eh* (1.1) *uiteraard*	'we have thus (1.1) of
	de voorwaarden	course the condition
	zij verkopen iets vrij	they sell it free
	nu hebben wij het volgende	now we have the
	en dat is een punt *dat wel*	following and that is <u>a</u>
	meespeelt	<u>point</u> which is of
		importance'
A:	*ja*	'yes'
Y:	*wanneer wij nu* (0.7) *of, tot een*	'if we now (0.7) or, come
	overeenstemming komen	to an agreement
	(...) *wij zullen slopen*	(...) we shall dismantle'

(3)   T: 211

G:	*heu autre et dernière* question	'eh another and last
	est-ce que vous avez reçu les	<u>question</u>
	documents techniques	have you received the
		technical documents'

Metalinguistic expressions and topic change

In the eleven conversations under study, there are 154 instances of topic change. Of these, 81 or 52.6% are marked by metalinguistic expressions. Table 1 gives an overview of the use of the expressions for topic openings. The figures are divided among the three types of conversations used in the analyses: native Dutch and native French conversations, and conversations among native French speakers and Dutchmen.

Table 1. *Topic changes introduced by metalinguistic expressions. Breakdown for three types of conversation.*

	Total number of topic changes	Topic changes with metalinguistic expressions
Native Dutch conversations	57	31 = 54.3%
Native French conversations	36	24 = 66.6%
French-Dutch conversations	61	26 = 42.6%
Total	154	81 = 52.6%

These figures represent the most conservative delimitation of metalinguistic expressions. If discourse deictic adjectives and adverbs, such as Dutch *volgende* 'next', French *maintenant* 'now', or French *deuxième* 'second' (cf. Gülich 1970) were included in the count, the total number of explicitly marked topic changes would be 90 instances or 58.4%. Notice that I have also excluded semantically empty instances of discourse brackets with a metalinguistic function of the kind described by Gülich (1970) and Schiffrin (1980), such as French *alors* and *bien*, or English *OK*, or other forms of marked topic change, such as pre-announcements of the kind described by Terasaki (1976), e.g., French *vous savez pas la dernière qu'il m'a faite* 'you know what he did to me'. Thus it can be said that only clear cases of metalinguistic expressions have been taken into consideration.

Preference organisation

Conversational analysts argue that there is a preferred way to organise topic change in casual conversations. The preferred way of topic change is an imperceptible drift from one topic to another, usually established by grammatically and topically connecting the new topic to previous talk. Current and subsequent topics can be found to be "natural" fellow members of some category. A succession of topics which are not linked to each other in one way or another is dispreferred. Evidence for this conclusion is the common feeling that people have difficulty bringing in a topic, because it is not related to the ongoing talk, and the tendency to use discontinuity markers in a case of non-linked topic changes. Furthermore, it has been noted that the relative frequency of marked topic introduction is seen as a feature of unskilful conversation (Sacks, cited in Levinson 1983: 313).

As we have seen above, the use of metalinguistic expressions is one type of marked topic change. For Sacks' interpretation of topic change the notion of preference is crucial. Levinson explains this notion by means of two criteria. First, "preference" is related to the notion of markedness as generally used in morphology. A preferred sequence is characterised by structural simplicity, that is, it is, as it were, the unmarked case. A dispreferred sequence, by contrast, is marked by structural complexity (Levinson 1983: 333). The other criterion of preference organisation has to do with frequency of use. Preference for one type of sequence to another "corresponds to the ranking from the most frequently used to the least used resource" (Levinson 1983: 341). From the latter criterion and from Sacks' remarks it must be concluded that the most frequently occurring forms of topic change are smooth and gradual topic changes without discontinuity markers. This seems to hold for casual telephone conversations (Sacks' material), as well as for radio interviews (Gülich 1970) and classroom discussions among university students (Scholtens and Stalpers 1982).

If we try to apply the above analysis to the data under study here, it turns out that Levinson's first criterion is not applicable. Metalinguistic expressions should be compared with other possible turn-initiation expressions, on the one hand, and topic-change sequences should be studied with regard to their structural complexity, on the other. As for the second criterion, the most frequently occurring topic opening is clearly the one which makes use of a metalinguistic expression. It would seem, then, that what is the marked and hence dispreferred method of bringing about a topic change in casual conversations is the preferred method in business talk. This contrasts with results from other kinds of spoken discourse where such topic initiations are said to be rare. However, the results are similar to certain forms of written discourse, especially explanatory scientific texts (Brown and Yule 1983: 100). That the high frequency of marked topic changes results in unskilful conversation, that is to say, in a conversation where speakers do not take into consideration possible desires of their inter-locutors, is hardly to be expected in business talk. I will come back to this point after the next section.

The manipulative character of meta-linguistic expressions

Another recurring interpretation of metalinguistic expressions concerns the alleged manipulative force of these expressions. Scholtens and Stalpers (1982) in their analysis of college classroom discussions suggest that their use is a forceful, though not compelling, strategy to open a new topic. A new topic is very likely to be accepted by fellow discussants if it is started with a metalinguistic expression. Weijdema (1985) in her analysis of TV panel discussions identifies two conspic-uous characteristics of these. The first is their evaluative function, often concerning a negative evaluation of an interlocutor's utterances (see also Schiffrin 1980). The other is their discourse-dominating function in determining the discourse topic, in turn taking and turn keeping (1985: 8), etc. Weijdema comes to the conclusion that the expressions are used, and often abused, by "verbally qualified people". She is concerned that, if not used properly, such expressions can be a form of verbal violence.

In applying this interpretation to the material under study here, we have to ask whether speakers use metalinguistic expressions in order to press a discourse topic upon their interlocutor(s). I want to argue that generally this is not the case. For a proper judgement on this issue, that is, the question of whether or not openly marked topic changes are coercive or manipulative, instances of topic conflict de-serve special attention. Topic conflicts are instances (a) where one topic is interrupted in order to introduce another, (b) where two inter-locutors start simultaneously with a new topic, and (c) where the initiation of a new topic by one interlocutor is rejected by another. Example (4) illustrates a case of topic interruption, and (5) a case of simultaneous topic start (see example (1) for a rejection of topic initia-tion).

(4)   302: B14
      Y and F are potential buyers of a piece of land. They demonstrate their trust-

worthiness by talking about their good relationship with the municipality which issues permits for construction plans.

Y:	*nou O.K. (0.6) de gemeente* *heeft vertrouwen in ons bedrijf* *uitgesproken*	'well O.K. (0.6) the municipality has shown confidence in our company'

N:	*u is plaats u heeft een* *plaatselijk bedrijf* *sorry als ik ᵣvragen mag*
	            [
		'you're a local you have a local business sorry if I may ᵣask'
		            [

F:	*nee*	'no'
Y:	*wat zegt u*	'what did you say'
N:	*u bent een plaatselijke* *aannemer of eh*	'you are a local contractor or eh'
Y:	*nee nee nee nee uit stad X*	'no no no no from city X'

(5) 102: B160

N, a wine importer from Holland, visits C's wine cellars in the Beaujolais region. He wants to import wine from C. They are talking about wine tasting. N and C then both start a new topic. C wants to talk about another of his clients, also a Dutch importer. N, however, starts to talk about having exclusive rights to import from C. He interrupts his own utterance in order to answer C's question. After that he immediately continues with his own topic.

C:	*est-ce que vous avez une* *question* *vis-à-vis de ce Monsieur* *vous connaissez cette société*	'do you have a question concerning this gentleman do you know this company'
	(1.0)	(1.0)
N:	*hum, je vous dis aussi*	'hum, I also want to tell you
	oui non je ne connais pas, *je vous dis aussi (0.5) heu* *si vous voulez travailler* *en exclus en exclusivité* *avec quelqu'un en Hollande*	yes no I do not know I also want to tell you (0.5) eh if you want to work exclus exclusively with somebody in Holland'

The data contain ten instances of topic conflict. In none of them are the conflicting topics altogether aborted. Rather interrupted topics are soon picked up again and continued. Note that in example (4) N apologises for interrupting the then current topic. Simultaneous topic initiations are resolved amicably, in such a way that both topics are dealt with one after the other. Disagreement about topic initiations are respected by the participants: example (1) is an illustration of a faulty assessment of the worthiness of the topic. Other instances of rejected topic initiations have to do with the desire on the part of the other speaker to continue the discussion of the current topic. In those instances the desired topic continuation is always accepted. After finishing with the first topic, the postponed topic change is then carried out. There is, however, one exception. Here the continuation of the current topic is delayed until the newly introduced topic has been extensively treated. This is the only instance of interactional conflict in the data. The instance is illustrated in example (6).

(6) 201: C131
R wants to continue the current topic of what to order this season. V wants to start talking about a publicity campaign. After a dispute over talking rights, V's topic is treated first, after which R's wish is also fulfilled.

1	V	*oui alors je t'expliquais tout à l'heure heu*	'well I just explained to you eh'
2	R	*tu as pas tu as pas heu dépassé les quantités-là hein*	'you haven't eh surpassed the quantities have you'
3	V	*je t'ai je t'ai fait les quantités*	'I wrote down I wrote down the quantities
4		*heu de toute façon je te confirme comme d'habitude* (0.6)	eh in any case I will reconfirm as usual' (0.6)
5		*et oui je te parlais il y a, il y a cinq minutes de la campagne de publicité* (0.6)	'and well about, about five minutes ago I talked about the publicity campaign' (0.6)
6	R	*ouais*	'yeah'
7	V	*alors*	'well'
8	R	*tu voudrais pas qu'on finisse la collection-là* (0.5)	'you don't want to finish the collection first' (0.5)
9	V	*mais je vais te dire un petit mot quand même parce que*	'but I'm going to tell you something anyway because'
10	R	*ça t'a ça t'arrange pour me pour m'entendre plus ça après non*	'that's that's alright for you so you don't have to listen to me anymore'
11	V	*non c'est pas pour t'entendre plus*	'no it's not because I don't want to listen to you
12		*non c'est surtout pour que tu*	no it's mainly that you

	saches un petit peu bon ben	know that we do
	les les efforts qu'on va faire	something
	pour vous aider à revendre	to help you reselling all
	tous ces volumes	this stuff
	(0.5)	(0.5)
13	*puisque tu aies pas*	so that you won't have the
	l'impression qu'on soit là	impression that we're only
	uniquement pour te	here
	vendre de la marchandise	to sell you goods
	(1.2)	(1.2)
14	*heu on a trois grandes*	eh we have three big
	campagnes	campaigns'

First V announces that he is going to talk about a new topic which he had already raised at an earlier stage of the conversation (line 1). R then checks what V has written down regarding the current topic (line 2). V gives an explanation whereupon he again starts to introduce the new topic (line 5). R expresses his desire to finish the current topic first (line 8). V again introduces his new topic (line 9). R challenges this topic change again by reproaching V for aborting the current topic before it is finished (line 10). In spite of the reproach, V starts to talk about his topic (line 14). R's wish to continue the current topic is acknowledged although about 4 minutes have passed in the meantime.

R's remark in line 10 supports Weijdema's observation concerning the use of metalinguistic expressions, namely that discussions tend to be dominated by those speakers who use them most. However, R's remark in line 10 is only one instance. As a matter of fact, all topics which are brought to the fore are eventually discussed. What the example does show is that topic changes are sensitive points in the interaction where irritations can be acted out, or at least, can be made explicit. As this instance of topic conflict and all other instances show, interlocutors in business conversations always get a chance to introduce a topic, regardless of whether or not the topic ties in, grammatically and topically, with previous talk.

Conclusion: Matter-of-factness

The analysis of metalinguistic expressions used for topic openings in business talk shows that topic changes carried out with their help are a common phenomenon. These marked topic changes probably indicate that topic jumps (instead of gradual changes in topic) are not at all uncommon or dispreferred in this kind of discourse. In business talk, therefore, interlocutors are not constrained by the fear of seeming awkward in making a topic jump, nor by the fear of not getting their topic into the discussion, as, Sacks argues, is the case for casual conversation.

However, instances of topic conflict show that interlocutors prefer topically coherent talk (cf. the apology in the topic interruption in example (4)), that is, a kind of discourse organisation where topics are treated one after the other. They also show that overt announcements of topic change bear the risk of being perceived as manipulative. In order to perform marked topic changes skilfully, the speaker must be aware of this risk.

If risk is involved in using this strategy, why, then, are there so many marked topic changes? One obvious answer is that they are being used for the sake of explicitness and transparency. Metalinguistic expressions signal what the speaker is going to do or what direction he wishes the discourse to take. In this sense their use is a manifestation of "bald-on-record behaviour", to borrow a term from Brown and Levinson (1978). Bald-on-record behaviour is a strategy to achieve maximally efficient communication. Grice (1975) formulated conversational maxims which supposedly enhance maximally efficient communication. Bald-on-record behaviour is speaking in conformity with Grice's maxims. Metalinguistic expressions conform with the Gricean "Maxim of Manner" which reads as follows: "Be perspicuous, avoid obscurity of expression, avoid ambiguity, be brief and be orderly" (Grice 1975: 46).

Using these expressions does not mean of course that the communication as a whole proceeds in an optimally efficient manner. Their function for the discourse as a whole, or rather for a discourse unit as a whole, can be understood in terms of a programme for the simulation of inference making. One such programme cited by Miller and Johnson-Laird (1976: 638) can play a number of different games. Illocutionary forces can be inferred more easily if, at the beginning of a game, the first move establishes its identity by means of an explicit performative (which is one type of metalinguistic expression). A discourse unit may be likened to a game, and like a game, a discourse unit can be played more efficiently if an overt announcement as to its specific character is made at the beginning. Similarly, Brown and Yule (1983: 133) argue that metalinguistic expressions used at the beginning of a discourse unit provide the interlocutors with directions concerning the type and structure of the mental representation they should construct. Such an instruction establishes a frame of reference for the appropriate props, activities, actors, technical terms, etc., through which inference-making is made easier.

It is therefore not astonishing that in business talk discourse units are opened with metalinguistic expressions. It is not due to unskilful discourse behaviour that businessmen mark topic changes, but due to the high priority of matter-of-factness. They act in accordance with, and under the mutual assumption of, the principle "time is money". It can be argued that this principle is at variance with the general expectation of polite conduct in discourse as it is assumed for casual conversation. What Sacks and others have described as the preferred manner of topic change is in line with this expectation. However, if we compare business talk with casual conversation, it would seem that certain general politeness requirements having to do with preferred indirectness are more relaxed in business talk. This would explain structural differences between business talk and casual conversations such as the high frequency of marked topic changes discussed in this chapter.

Acknowledgments

I wish to thank Florian Coulmas for his helpful comments and corrections of this chapter.

Notes

1. Fieldwork was carried out as part of the research project "Negotiating business in a cross-cultural and cross-linguistic setting" sponsored by Het Samenwerkingsorgaan Katholieke Universiteit Brabant en Technische Universiteit Eindhoven, the Netherlands, May 1983–Dec 1985.
2. The excerpts of the conversations are marked by a code, which corresponds to the numbering used in the research material. The first digit indicates the linguistic setting: "1" stands for French-Dutch conversation, "2" for native French conversation, "3" for native Dutch conversation. The conversations are transcribed in standard Dutch and French, but hesitations are marked. Pauses in tenths of a second and other contextual information are given in round brackets; simultaneous talk is indicated by square brackets.

9. Children's understanding of white lies*

Sabine Walper and Renate Valtin

The present contribution deals with a subject which has a long tradition in philosophy and literature (cf. Weinrich 1966, 1986), but has previously gone unnoticed within the field of developmental psychology. We are concerned with the tension between the norm of behaving politely and that of being honest. On the one hand, white lies contradict the normative interactional postulate of telling the truth, but on the other hand they contribute towards not hurting the feelings of *alter* in the sense of positive social behaviour (or positive politeness) and above all sparing him/her feelings of embarrassment and shame (cf. Brown and Levinson 1978).

It is an open question at what age and in what situational contexts children begin to accept white lies as an interactional strategy, and correspondingly adjust their norms of honesty. Until now lying and politeness have been investigated within different theoretical contexts. With respect to the concept of lying, Piaget's work (1973, orig. 1932) is still basic. In his studies Piaget traces a development from "moral realism" – focusing on visible external events and sanctions – to a viewpoint of subjective responsibility, which considers the intentions of the liar. Developmentally related changes in recognising the intent to deceive are foregrounded as the main topic of research (e.g., Wimmer et al. 1984). However, the ways in which children understand and evaluate possible positive functions of lying have remained virtually unconsidered in this research tradition. Piaget (1973: 332) mentions in only one footnote that children do not condemn a liar when someone lies to protect a sibling, but that they reject using this lie in their own defence.

* From a lecture held at the 36th Congress of the German Society of Psychology, Berlin, October 3–6, 1988, within the symposium "The development of interactional competence in childhood". We should like to thank Gabi Nehring for her help in data collection and transcribing the interviews, Jörg Schulz for his advice in data analysis, and Richard J. Watts for his careful translation of the German manuscript. Last but not least our special thanks go to the children and their teachers who made this study possible!

A more recent study (Peterson, Peterson and Seeto 1984), which investigates age-graded changes in judging different types of lie, also refers to an example of polite lying (or white lie). A girl asks another child what she thinks of her hairstyle, and the latter pretends to like it. For this example there were certainly no differences between children from age 5 to age 11, but it was only adults, in contrast to children, who valued the polite lie more highly. It should be noted, however, that situational variations in the politeness norm – e.g., in accordance with status differentials in interactions involving adults – were not considered, so that this finding does not offer a representative picture.

In pragmalinguistic research politeness has been addressed as mastery of the verbal register or as an interactional strategy (Brown and Levinson 1978; Lakoff 1977), but there are only few studies which look at the development of understanding and producing politeness forms in children (e.g., Ervin-Tripp 1976; Garvey 1975; James 1978). Studies on requests, orders, and questions show that, while children and adolescents can easily recognise, for instance, the social distance which is associated with certain forms of politeness behaviour, a differentiated knowledge of situational variations in the politeness norm is not acquired until late childhood (see, for example, Waller and Schoeler 1984). Even differences in social status between the requester and the addressee, which are present in children's interactions with adults (although not in the peer group), and the strength of the imposition on the addressee to comply with the request do not appear to play a role in the use of polite requests until the age of nine (Axia and Baroni 1985).

Corresponding to a more differentiated knowledge of politeness demands according to social distance or degree of social status, we should also be able to discover a weakening of norms of honesty, particularly in situations where a high degree of politeness is required. Our investigation involving children between the ages of six and ten is designed to provide answers to the following questions:

(1) Are white lies evaluated more positively with increasing age, i.e., is there an age-specific adjustment of the honesty norm in favour of the politeness norm?

(2) Do these judgements vary in accordance with contextual features of the relationship between the speaker and the addressee, and with the type of social misdemeanour that is meant to be masked through politeness? In relation to this point two dimensions of the relationship between the speaker and the addressee will be consid-

ered: (a) status differentials – is politeness towards adults evaluated more positively than politeness among peers? – and (b) the social distance or familiarity between the speaker and the addressee, on the one hand in the relationship to family members compared with outsiders, and on the other hand in interaction among friends compared with unknown peers. With respect to the type of social misdemeanour, we are concerned with whether the threatened loss of face for the addressee has been caused by herself/himself – and is thereby "repairable" – or whether the loss of face lies outside the addressee's control. The latter situation would demand a greater degree of politeness.

(3) Finally it is asked whether situational variations become increasingly important for children's judgements of white lies and/or whether aspects of context are evaluated differently by children in the various age groups.

Method

The investigation was carried out by means of structured, individual interviews with 73 Berlin primary-school children (37 boys and 36 girls), assigned to three age groups, 6-year-olds, 8-year-olds and 10-year-olds, in a roughly equal way (each group contained n>20). The method combines qualitative and quantitative procedures as is now common in research of socio-cognitive development. Each child was presented with four picture stories given in the same order, two of which offer a thematically identical initial situation which is meant to be masked by means of a white lie: in the first we have a cake that has not been baked well and in the second an ugly sweater. Boys and girls received gender-specific versions so that the protagonists in the stories were of the same sex as the children. According to the design of the experiment, each initial situation is varied with respect to the degree of familiarity between the speaker and the addressee (first, family membership vs. an unknown person, and second, a friend vs. an unknown person). In addition a distinction is made in the first initial situation with respect to status differentials (adults vs. peers) and in the second initial situation according to the controllability of the social misdemeanour.

The first two stories tell about a child (Rosa or Rudi) visiting his/her friend (Katja or Karl). A member of the host's family has baked a cake for the occasion. In the first version the sister or brother would like to give both of them a nice surprise with the cake. Despite good intentions, however, the cake is a failure: after the cake-maker has left the room, the children discover that the cake tastes terrible. When the cake-maker comes back and asks whether they liked the cake, the guest answers, "Yes thanks. It was good." The second version corresponds to the first except that this time it is the mother who has baked the cake. Within each story the subjects are first asked about the guest's (Rosa's or Rudi's) answer. Then they are asked to imagine that the child from the host's family also replied, "Yes thanks. It was good" to the question about the cake. The interview questions for the first and second part of both stories are identical each time. Thus it should be possible to compare two points: (1) both stories, one of which contains a peer as the addressee of the white lie and the other an adult, and (2) the answers given by different speakers to each of the addressees, i.e., the lie given by the guest, who is less familiar with the family situation, and that given by the child from the host family.

The second set of stories (here summarised in the girls' version) tells how both children (Rosa and Katja) go for a walk and see a friend of Rosa's in the distance coming towards them wearing a very ugly sweater. In the first version Rosa explains to Katja that this friend's parents are poor and she thus has to wear clothes handed down from her elder sister. In the second version Rosa explains that the friend has a rather odd taste in clothes and likes wearing sweaters like this even though she has other clothes she could put on. The girls meet, and Rosa's friend asks her in each version what she thinks of the sweater. Katja, who does not yet know Rosa's friend, says, "It's really nice." The subjects are again interviewed about Katja's reply and then are asked to imagine that Rosa also gives her friend the same answer. Here we are concerned with the comparison (1) between the white lie given to the poor child and that given to the child who has chosen to wear the sweater because of her bad taste, and (2) between the white lie given by Katja, who doesn't know Rosa's friend, and that given by Rosa.

At the end of each story a set of comprehension questions is first given to insure that the discrepancy between the speaker's opinion and his/her answer has been recognised and that the cake-baker and the sweater wearer, on the other hand, does not realise this. The interview following this set of questions probes for the possible motive behind the answer, for the evaluation of the answer, for the reasons for this evaluation, etc. In addition to the separate judgements, the children are required to compare explicitly which character is more likely to tell the truth and to whom the truth is more likely to be told.

Results

Before turning to the results, we should mention that almost without exception all the children understood the motive behind the lie. Even those who at first said that they did not know, said, in the course of the interview, that the truth would have been unpleasant for the addressee.

1. On the role of intra-family intimacy and age-graded status differences: The cake stories

We shall first look at the evaluations given by the children from individual age groups for each of the four situations in the cake stories. Figure 1 (p. 237) shows the ratings for lies directed at an unfamiliar peer and a sibling on the left, and those directed at an unfamiliar adult and the child's own mother on the right of the diagram. The scale of answers ranged from "very bad" (two devils), "rather bad" (one devil), "neither bad nor good" or "both good and bad" (no symbol), through "rather good" (one angel) to "very good" (two angels). Before the presentation of stories began, the scale was explained to the children and tested out on examples chosen by the children themselves.

In order to test the expected effects of age and social context, a mixed model analysis of variance was calculated. The three age groups represent the between-subject factor, and the four evaluations represent the within-subject factor. In addition, gender was included as a factor, since the results of a pilot study led us to expect gender-typical differences. In the present experiment, however, no influence of this kind is evident (neither as a main effect nor in interaction with age or situation; p>.20). As we expected, there are significant main effects for both age (F=5.25, df=2, p=.008) and situation (F=3.61, df=3, p=.014). The interaction effect, however, is statistically insignificant.

Figure 1 (p. 237) shows that the most positive evaluations are given by the ten-year-olds. Special post-hoc contrasts between the age groups show that the evaluations of the two younger groups score significantly lower than those of the ten-year-olds (over all situations: F=10.493, df=1, p=.002), whereas there is no difference between the two younger groups (F<1, df=1, n.s.).

This is true above all for the first and third situations (F=4.56, df=2, p=.014 and F=6.35, df=2, p=.003), i.e., for those contexts in which an unfamiliar host is the addressee. Where politeness with respect to a sibling is concerned, the age effect is only marginally significant (F=2.71, df=2, p=.074), and with respect to the mother it is missing completely (F=1.37, df=2, n.s.). We can thus conclude that the increasingly positive evaluation of white lies is situation-specific to the extent that it does not occur for contexts of great intimacy, viz., for the child's relationship with his or her own mother. At the same time the lack of an interaction effect between age and situation indicates that even the latter context variant does not deviate significantly from the general age-graded trend.

If we now look at the pattern of evaluations for each age group, it is clear that the six-year-olds do not distinguish between the four situations, while the eight- and ten-year-olds follow the same pattern. However, only the oldest group yields reliable situation-specific evaluations (F=3.94, df=3, p=.009), whereas the situation factor for the eight-year-olds does not reach the 10% level of significance (F=1.92, df=3, p=.128; six-year-olds: F<1, df=3, n.s.). Hence, even if these context factors only appear to become significant between eight and ten years of age, it is still true that the main effect of the speaker-addressee relationship is far stronger than the age specificity of situational influences.

What, then, are the situational differentiations to be found for the ten-year-olds? Special (orthogonal) contrasts show that the evaluations do not vary according to status differences between speaker and addressee (t<1, n.s.), but certainly according to social distance or intimacy (t=2.71, p=.008). Essentially this can be attributed to the situation in which an adult is the addressee (t=3.18, p=.002): the white lie aimed at the host's mother is most positively evaluated, that aimed at one's own mother most negatively. On the other hand, among peers the familiarity of the addressee does not seem to play a significant role (ten-year-olds: t=1.17, p>.20).

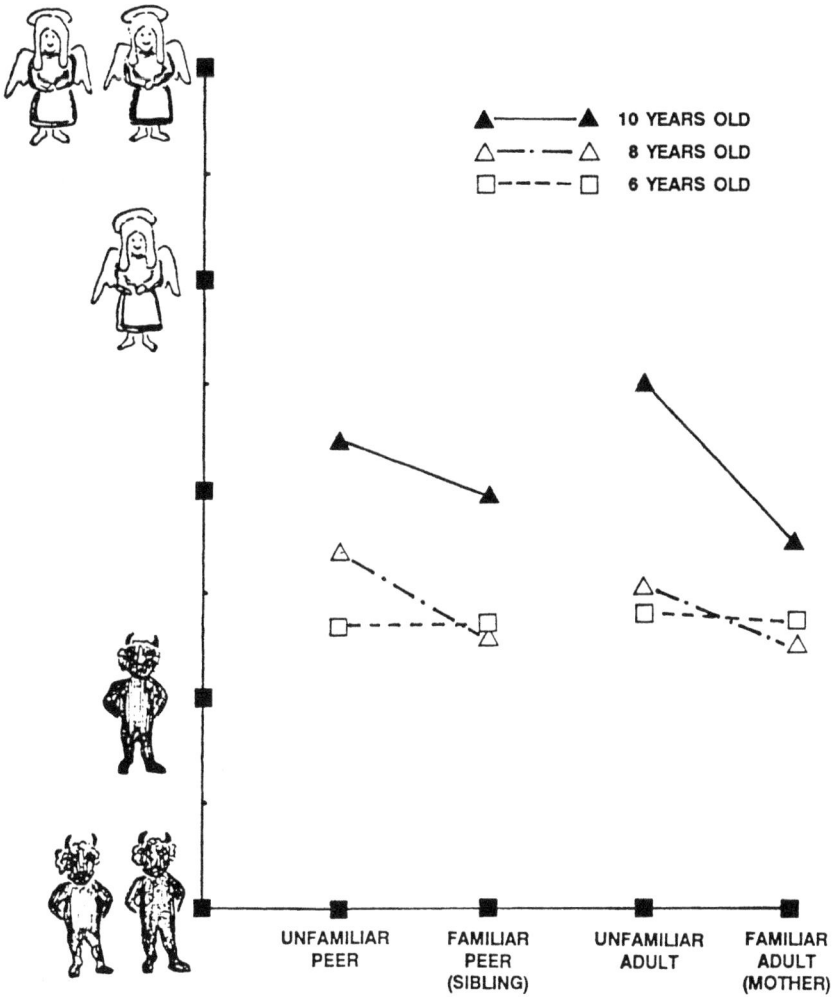

Figure 1. Evaluation of white lies according to familiarity and age-graded status of addressee given by children aged 6, 8 and 10 years.
Note: symbols of evaluative rating were: two angels=very good; one angel=good; no sign=neither good nor bad or both to the same extent; one devil=bad; two devils=very bad.

These findings are supported by the children's arguments for and against white lies. The reasons they provided as to why the relevant evaluation was chosen were ordered into three categories: explanations that speak (1) only against, (2) only for, and (3) both for and against white lies. These and the following analyses of the cake stories are summarised only briefly here, since they have been discussed in more detail elsewhere (Walper and Valtin 1988).

The prototypical politeness situation – interaction with someone else's mother – yields the clearest age differences in the reduction of arguments against lying and the increase of reasons for lying. Whereas 73.7% of the six-year-olds and 58.3% of the eight-year-olds argue strictly against lying, only 9.5% of the ten-year-olds do so. 26.3% of the six-year-olds, 20.8% of the eight-year-olds, but 61.9% of the ten-year-olds argue for lying. It is only the eight- and ten-year-olds (20.8% and 28.6%) who give mixed reasons, such reasoning being very rare among the six-year-olds.

When we consider white lies given to an unfamiliar peer, the age trend looks rather different. Here, above all, mixed arguments increase (from 8.7% with the six-year-olds to 43.5% and 45.5% with the eight- and ten-year-olds) well in line with conflicting contextual dimensions: on the one hand a lack of intimacy speaks in favour of politeness, on the other hand peer status makes it less necessary. And even for lying to one's own mother age-dependent differences in the type of counter-arguments are in evidence. Whereas a clear majority of the two younger groups argue in a prescriptive way against lying (81.3% and 78.9%), the majority of the ten-year-olds (60%) appeal to the fact that, because of the type of relationship, lying is not necessary.

The answers to the question by whom the cake-maker would prefer to be told the truth about the cake failure, i.e., whose insult would be easier to accept (the addressee's perspective) and which of the two children can more easily tell the truth (the speaker's perspective) are particularly revealing. With respect to the speaker's perspective all the age groups are largely in agreement that it is the family member rather than the guest who should tell the truth. Although a preference for openness within one's own family increases slightly with age (for the adult situation from 58.3% with the six-year-olds to 81.8% with the ten-year-olds), these differences are statistically insignificant.

If we take the addressee's perspective into account, there certainly are age-specific differences. Whereas in both younger groups about half the children think that it does not make any difference to the cake maker who tells him the unpleasant truth, the number of such arbitrary evaluations falls to around 10% with the ten-year-olds (9.1% and 13.6%). The majority of the ten-year-olds realise that it is less painful for the addressee if the truth, as it were, remains within the family, i.e., if the visitor displays polite reticence and leaves the child of the host family to make the revelation. This is the case in both situations, whether the addressee is a peer or an adult. An appreciation of threatened loss of face, in particular with respect to unfamiliar people – or, vice versa, an appreciation of the protective function of an intimate relationship in which openness is possible and valued – only seems to be present with the ten-year-olds.

Intra-family relationships offer only one case of intimacy. Friendships as another example may be subject to different norms, viz., those of reciprocal protection and positive attraction. If we follow Selman's analyses of the development of mutual understanding in friendship relationships (Selman 1981), friendships are, from the point of view of the preschool child, determined first and foremost by the physical proximity of the playmate (stage Ø). As the development of the ability to differentiate and coordinate social perspectives progresses, friendships are seen as a one-sided adaptation of the one to the needs of the other (stage 1), followed by a concept of reciprocal "good weather" cooperation (stage 2). At this stage the subjective needs and feelings of both parties are increasingly recognised and respected, but, at the same time, infringements of the rule of cooperation, conflicts and argument cannot yet be adjusted by a basic continuity of relationships. In these developmental stages it seems more than questionable whether openness, which implies criticism by the partner, is accepted among friends more than among strangers. Only in adolescence, with an increasing understanding of intimacy and trust (stage 3: "intimate and mutually shared relationships") and finally with a view of an autonomous friendship relationship that is seen as a supportive arena for the development of independent personalities (stage 4) could we say that it becomes less important to uphold *alter*'s face and protect her/him from unpleasant truths.

We therefore need to ask whether reduced social distance in friendships when compared with unfamiliar peers plays another role than that which was previously displayed for intra-family intimacy. The sweater stories should clarify this and the question as to whether the cause of imminent loss of face plays a role.

2. On the role of friendship and a lack of control over the social misdemeanour: The sweater stories

Recall that the sweater stories yield, on the one hand, variations relating to the reasons for the social misdemeanour that has to be masked – in the first case the reason for the ugly sweater is the child's unsought social situation, her/his poverty, which leaves the child with no other option but to wear the sweater, and in the second case the child has chosen the sweater in accordance with her/his own taste although other options were open. On the other hand, the stories concern the contrast between a white lie told to an unfamiliar child and one told to a friend. Figure 2 (p. 242) shows the relevant mean evaluations of white lies for each of the age groups, on the left the lie told by the stranger and that told by the friend to the poor child, on the right the lie told by the stranger and that told by the friend to the child who has made the conscious choice to wear the ugly sweater.

In order to check interactions between both kinds of situational variation, a four-factor analysis of variance was chosen here. The controllability of the social misdemeanour and social distance – here friendship vs. unfamiliarity – represent the two within-subject factors, and age and sex the two between-subject factors.

2.1 Age and situational differences in evaluations of the lie

As was expected, the analysis of variance yielded a significant main effect for age ($F=4.18$, df=2, p=.019), whereas sex once again showed no effect (both as a main and also an interaction effect: $F<1$, n.s.). Again it is the difference between the ten-year-olds and the two younger groups that catches our attention ($F=6.81$, df=1, p=.011), whereas the younger age groups do not differ ($F=1.85$, df=1, n.s.). In other words, once again it is only with the ten-year-olds that we find a more positive evaluation of white lies.

Of the two contextual dimensions it is exclusively the controllability of the social misdemeanour that has a significant main effect on the evaluation of white lies ($F=10.71$, df=1, p<.002). Lying to a poor child about her/his ugly sweater is always more positively evaluated than lying about differences in taste. Even the interaction of this situational aspect with age is significant ($F=4.36$, df=2, p=.016), which strongly suggests that the controllability of the social misdemeanour is considered very differently between the age groups. Social distance, either taken singly (F<1, n.s.) or in interaction with age (F=1.62, df=2, p>.20) or sex (F<1, df=1, n.s.), is not important. Its influence appears only in interaction with the controllability of the social misdemeanour (interaction effect of both context dimensions: F=7.25, df=1, p=.009).

Let us first look at the reciprocal dependence of both context dimensions. Figure 3 (p. 243) shows that controllability, or responsibility, primarily becomes important among friends. White lies told to a friend are clearly more positively evaluated if the reason for the ugly sweater is poverty, whereas this differentiation plays no role among strangers. At the same time the function of the friendship relationship is inverted in accordance with imminent loss of face: whereas in the case of poverty the friend's protection through a white lie is more positively evaluated than the protection of the unknown peer, in questions of taste the politeness norm is dominant with respect to strangers. However, these latter differences are less pronounced than the situational differentiation within the friendship relationship.

It is striking that a greater amount of consideration is paid to the poor friend. Given the plight of poverty and the smaller amount of social distance, it seems to be empathy and sympathy for "significant others" that motivates the preference of a white lie. By contrast, greater openness among friends is more likely to be revealed when the friend is able to influence the situation her/himself, i.e., by "repairing" the situation through the choice of a better sweater.

Let us return to the context differentiations as they are reflected in the respective judgements of the individual age groups (see Figure 2). Although the relevant mean scores suggest that above all the eight-year-olds treat a poor friend with particular consideration, the three factor interaction between both context dimensions and age is statistically non-significant (F<1, df=2, n.s.). However, more information is yielded by special contrasts which were calculated for the three age groups separately. The first contrast concerns the dimension of the controllability of the social misdemeanour (averaged across the variations of social distance), the second concerns the distinction between the unfamiliar peer and the friend in the first story – i.e., in relation to the poor child – and the third concerns the corresponding distinction in the second story, i.e., related to the free choice of an ugly sweater. In order to better estimate the individual and the joint relevance of the individual contrasts, they were treated as dependent variables in multivariate analyses of variance which were carried out separately for

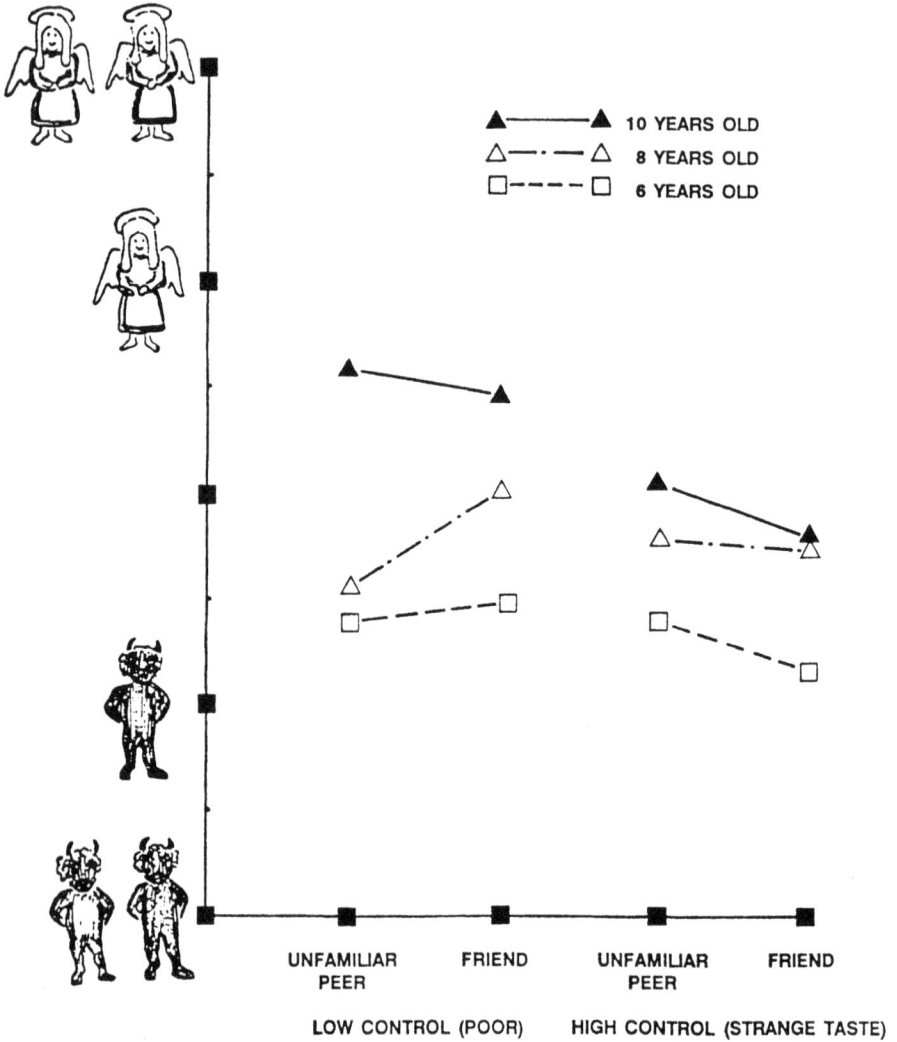

Figure 2.   Evaluation of white lie according to familiarity of the addressee and his/her control of the social misdemeanour given by children aged 6, 8, and 10 years.
Note: Symbols of evaluative rating; see note to Figure 1.

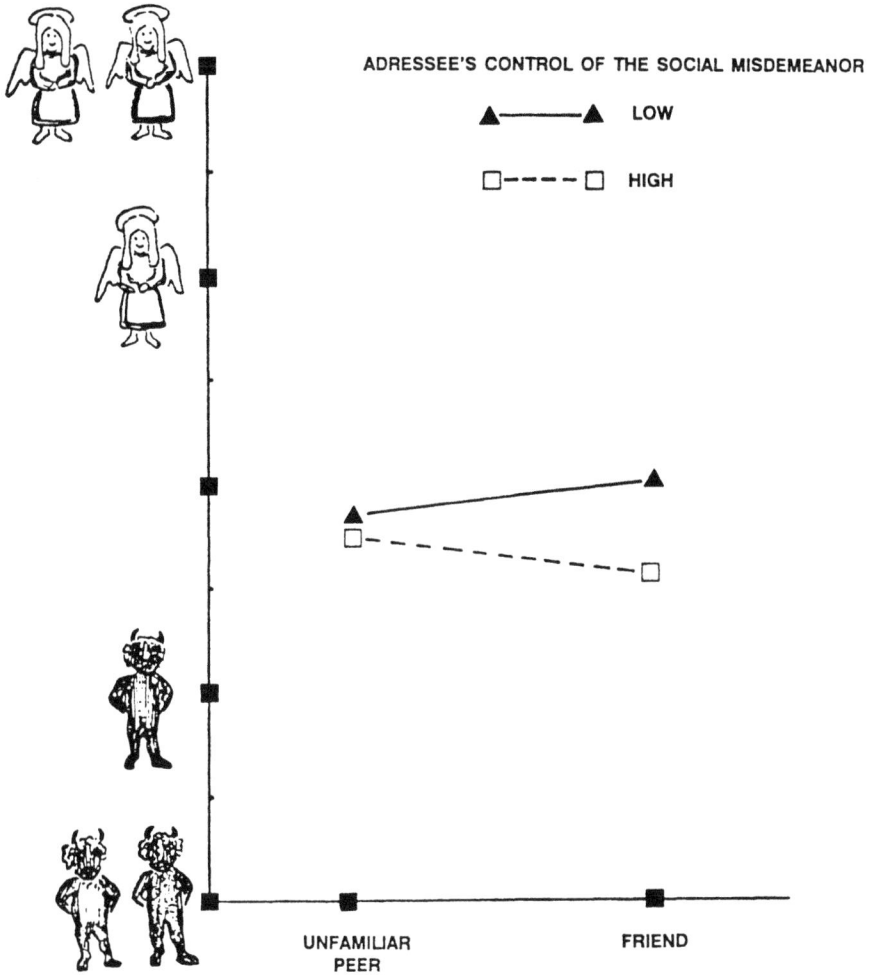

Figure 3. Effects of the addressee's control of the social misdemeanour as modified by familiarity between speaker and addressee.
Note: Symbols of evaluative rating; see note to Figure 1.

each age group. In doing so, sex was no longer considered, since it had proved to be irrelevant.

The results show that none of the three contrasts yields important differences in the evaluation of white lies for the six-year-olds (multivariate: $F=1.34$, $df=3$, $p>.20$; univariate in each case $F<1.27$, n.s.). For the eight-year-olds there is a significant multivariate effect ($F=2.92$, $df=3$, $p=.041$), which is, however, uniquely derivable from the differentiation between the friend and the unknown peer in the case of low controllability of the social misdemeanour, i.e., in the case of poverty. Both the other contrasts are unimportant for this age group (in each case $F<1$, n.s.). With the ten-year-olds the multivariate effect of the three contrasts is highly significant ($F=7.29$, $df=3$, $p=.001$), but even here only one aspect is relevant, viz., the differentiation with respect to the controllability or direct personal responsibility for the social misdemeanour causing the white lie ($F=19.28$, $p=.000$). It is only with this oldest group that the differentiation between social fate and questions of good taste in evaluating white lies really comes out clearly.

2.2 Arguments for and against the lie

Once again these results are complemented by the children's arguments for and against white lies. Figure 4 (p. 245) shows that strict counter-arguments in all four situations of the sweater story decrease with age. However, consistent with the evaluations, this trend is only statistically significant for those contexts in which the addressee is hardly in control of the social misdemeanour, i.e., the lie told to the poor child (in the case of an unfamiliar peer: $x^2=15.48$, $df=2$, $p<.001$; among friends: $x^2=7.13$, $df=2$, $p=.028$; correspondingly with a high degree of control: $x^2=4.48$, $df=2$, n.s. and $x^2=4.95$, $df=2$, $p=.084$). Most striking are the age differences in the case of the ugly sweater of a poor unknown peer (situation 1). Whereas in this case 68.4% of the six-year-olds are strictly against lying, only 9.1% of the ten-year-olds are. Of the four situations this is the one for which the white lie is most positively evaluated by the ten-year-olds (cf. Figure 2, p. 242).

If we go on to compare the respective answers of the ten-year-olds, the lie told to the poor child is rejected far more rarely (9.1% and 18.2%) than in the case of a high degree of controllability, i.e., in questions of good taste (31.8% and 36.4%). This confirms that for the older children above all the situation of the social misdemeanour or its

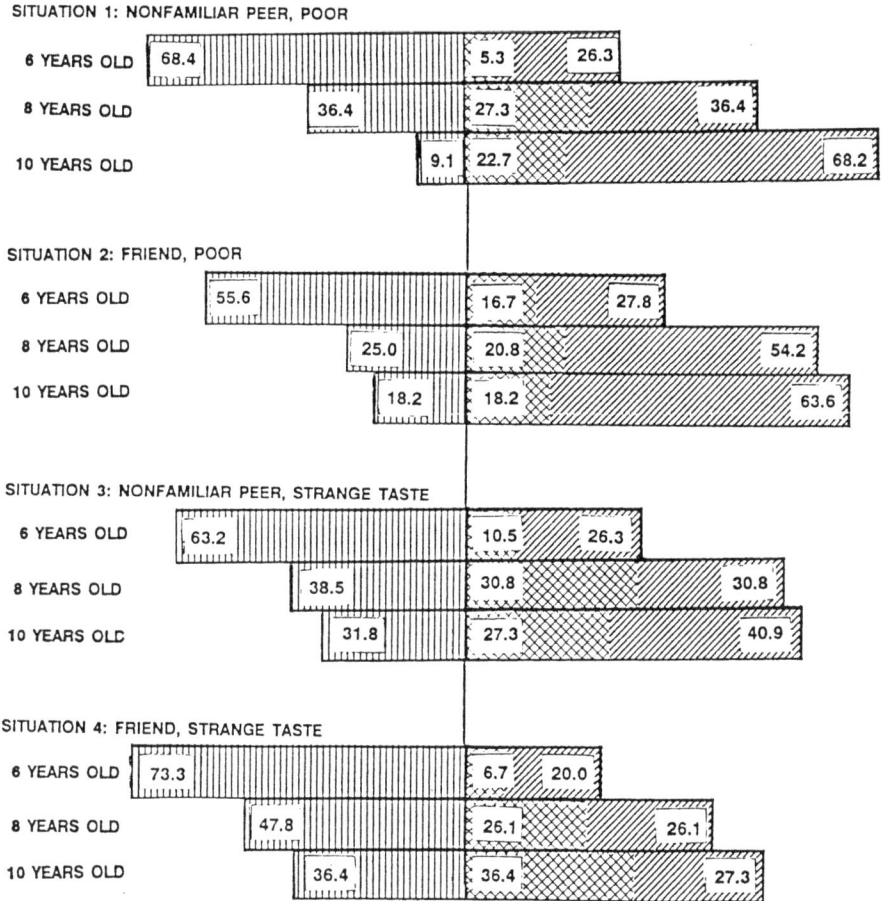

Figure 4. Percentage of children arguing against and/or in favour of a white lie among 6-, 8-, and 10-year-old children.

cause and the degree to which it can be influenced is relevant. In no other age group are these differences so noticeable. The fact that the eight-year-olds, in their evaluations, above all respect the protection of the poor friend compared with the unknown peer corresponds to a certain extent to the way they justify their evaluation. Whereas 54.2% of the eight-year-olds argue strictly in favour of the white lie in the case of the poor friend, only 36.4% do so when an unknown peer has no other option but to wear the ugly sweater. In questions of taste they do not particularly favour a lie either told to a friend or told to a stranger (26.1% and 30.8%).

2.3 Specific comparisons

Who should tell the truth to whom? If we focus on comparisons between the two stories, the differentiation between poverty and questions of taste yields a somewhat different picture. As Table 1 (p. 247) shows, the overall majority of both the eight-year-olds and the ten-year-olds prefer the child with the peculiar taste in sweaters when they have to decide to whom they would rather tell the truth (non-intimate speaker: 84.6% and 94.5% of the eight- and ten-year-olds; correspondingly among friends: 92.3% and 90.9%). In comparison the six-year-olds are indecisive somewhat more frequently (with respect to strangers: 27.3%; among friends: 18.2%) or even prefer to choose the poor child, often combined with the offer to give her/him a more attractive sweater of one's own (with respect to strangers: 18.2%; among friends: 27.3%). If we contrast the two latter choices ("makes no difference" or "telling the poor child") with choosing the child with peculiar taste as addressee, the difference between the age groups is highly significant, not only with respect to honesty among friends ($x^2=13.01$, df=2, p<.002) but also with respect to the unfamiliar child's answer ($x^2=11.83$, df=2, p<.003). Put differently, if this contextual aspect is explicitly thematised, the eight- and ten-year-olds do not differ in their judgements. But if it remains implicit – as in the individual evaluations – it is not taken into consideration by the eight-year-olds.

How is the role of social distance represented in the explicit comparisons? Table 2 (p. 248) shows for each age group the relative proportion of decisions as to whether one should rather tell the truth to the unfamiliar child or to the friend (speaker's perspective, lefthand column) and for whom it is less painful to hear the truth about the ugly sweater (addressee's perspective, righthand column). It is very clear that with an increase in age it is in no way the politeness norm towards strangers that is valid, but the very opposite. The interaction with the unknown peer – the non-committal relationship – is always preferred as the context in which the truth can more easily be said and accepted. If the six-year-olds clearly prefer their friend for talking openly about the ugly sweater, the ten-year-olds more frequently choose the un-familiar peer.

Table 1. Percentage of children per age group who prefer to tell the truth either to the poor peer or to the peer with strange taste if the addressee is (A) unfamiliar or (B) familiar to the speaker

	(A) Unfamiliar addressee			(B) Familiai addressee		
	6 years	8 years	10 years	6 years	8 years	10 years
No preference	27.3	7.7	4.5	18.2	3.8	9.1
Poor peer	18.2	7.7	0.0	27.3	3.8	0.0
Strange taste	54.5	84.6	94.5	54.5	92.3	90.9
Total	100.0	100.0	100.0	100.0	100.0	100.0

This trend is a little weaker in the case of the speaker's perspective. Telling the the truth to the unfamiliar child is more frequently preferred with increasing age if the addressee is poor and does not bear the "responsibility" for the ugly sweater her/himself ($\chi^2=6.44$, df=2, p=.040). However, in questions of taste the judgements of each age group only tend to diverge ($\chi^2=4.69$, df=2, p=.096).

However, as in the cake stories, age exerts a significant influence when the addressee's perspective is concerned ($\chi^2=12.38$, df=1, p=.001 and $\chi^2=11.83$, df=2, p<.002; cf. the righthand column of Table 2). In each case more than 60% of the ten-year-olds state that a negative judgement by a stranger is less hurtful than one by a friend. The six-year-olds, on the other hand, are rather of the opinion that it does not matter to the addressee who passes on the unpleasant message (in the case of poverty: 36.4%; in the case of questions of good taste: 33.3%), or that is less hurtful if the friend does so (45.5% and 52.4%).

Table 2. Percentage of children per age group who prefer the friend or the unfamiliar peer to tell the truth if the addressee (I) has low control (poor peer) or (II) has high control of the social misdemeanour (strange taste), each judged from (A) the addressee's and (B) the speaker's perspective

(I) Addressee with low control (poor peer)

	(A) Speaker's perspective			(B) Addressee's perspective		
	6 years	8 years	10 years	6 years	8 years	10 years
No preference	16.7	3.8	9.1	36.4	40.0	0.0
Friend	58.3	73.1	36.4	45.5	28.0	31.8
Unfamiliar peer	25.0	23.1	54.5	18.2	32.0	68.2
Total	100.0	100.0	100.0	100.0	100.0	100.0

(II) Addressee with high control (peer with strange taste)

	(A) Speaker's perspective			(B) Addressee's perspective		
	6 years	8 years	10 years	6 years	8 years	10 years
No preference	13.6	12.0	0.0	33.3	30.8	4.2
Friend	59.1	60.0	45.5	52.4	26.9	33.3
Unfamiliar peer	27.3	28.0	54.5	14.3	42.3	61.9
Total	100.0	100.0	100.0	100.0	100.0	100.0

The discrepancy between the two perspectives observable among the eight-year-olds is striking. Whereas the majority of them claim that one should be more open towards a friend, they do not in any way see the friend as the person more likely to accept a negative judgement. Like the six-year-olds they are largely indifferent with respect to the addressee's perspective (40% and 30.8%), but they also more frequently prefer the stranger as the person who is less likely to take an unpleasant judgement to heart (32.0% and 42.3%).

Some final remarks

Summing up, our older age group does not appear to hold with the dictum in Goethe's *Faust*, "In German one lies when being polite." The results show rather that with increasing age the honesty norm may be qualified in relation to situation-specific politeness norms which are taken into account to respect and protect the feelings of the addressee. The range of non-controversial politeness that is not considered to be an outright lie increases and thereby yields greater flexibility for the choice of context-appropriate interactional strategies. Most likely, the decisive underlying factor can be found in the development of role-taking abilities which allow one to infer and take into consideration the needs and wants of interacting individuals and to co-ordinate different perspectives (cf. Silbereisen 1986; Edelstein and Keller 1982; Valtin 1982). More specifically, taking a social perspective should enable the children to shift their focus from the active speaker and to consider the addressee's point of view as well. Such increasing interpersonal competence and understanding also contributes to developmental changes in how social norms and conventions are conceptualised. As outlined by Turiel (1977, 1978), children's early understanding of social conventions is largely based on rules and sanctions as given by social authorities, while throughout childhood a more flexible person-orientation is developed. Taking into account the personal needs and claims of interacting individuals, social conventions are then understood as being based on mutual expectations.

One aspect to be mastered in this process is to infer the hidden situational demands which determine each participant's expectations. According to the findings of our study, the eight-year-old children only took into account the poverty of the child who wore the ugly sweater, when a comparison of both conditions was directly asked for. This finding is in line with results of a study by Pearl (1985). Younger children understood the other's need for help only when the cue was made explicit. Only older children were also aware of the actor's problems irrespective of the nature of the cue (explicit vs. implicit). Again, the crucial factor here is probably the development of role-taking abilities.

In this study individual variants of intimacy/familiarity between speaker and addressee have been shown to exert a characteristically different influence in each case. The intimate relationships within the family constrain the children of the age groups considered here to show more openness, whereas the opposite is the case for friendships. Relationships among friends rather seem to represent that area in which social competences of respect, consideration and empathy are practised and developed, during which honesty – to begin with – can be given less weight.

Sullivan (1953) and Youniss (1978) have already pointed out that friendship provides the prototypical example of symmetric relationships that foster reciprocity, mutual understanding and respect to a higher degree than the complementary reciprocity towards adults or parents. Hence, friendship is seen to have a crucial function in the social and moral development of children and adolescents, providing the ground for a unique experience of solidarity, co-operation, and intimacy. As Sullivan (1953: 245) pointed out:

> All of you who have children are sure that your children love you; when you say that you are expressing a pleasant illusion. If you will look closely at one of your children when he finally finds a chum – somewhere between eight-and-a-half and ten years – you will discover something very different in the relationship, namely, that your child begins to develop a real sensitivity to what matters to another person [...] not [...] "what should I do to get what I want?" but instead "what should I do to contribute to the happiness or to support the prestige and feeling of worthwhileness of my chum?"

That politeness presumably plays a special role in the development of friendship expectations may be concluded from the studies about children's concepts of friendship. Children aged nine to eleven years (corresponding to our older age group) regarded "being nice" as an important mechanism for building up friendship relations (Selman 1980; Fatke and Valtin 1988) and expected their friends to be non-aggressive, co-operative and supportive (Bigelow 1977) – expectations that ask for, and foster, politeness to a higher degree than openness, at least in such cases where the feelings of the other may be hurt.

Within the age range studied here, openness among friends does not increase, even when it is only differences in personal preferences that are thematised and *alter*'s face can be maintained by referring back to something non-committal such as questions of taste. At best a divergence from the general age trend is indirectly indicated for this situation. If the speaker is put into the position of having to choose explicitly between an intimate or a non-intimate addressee in questions of taste, the preference for protecting a friend and being more open towards a stranger does not substantially increase with age. If the comparison is not forced but the subject is asked for her/his individual evaluation of white lies, friends even enjoy the respect of this face saving strategy somewhat less than strangers.

It must remain an open question at which point in social development the politeness norm is given more weight towards strangers than in friendship relationships and whether in the course of these changes the kind of social misdemeanour (repairable vs. uncontrollable) plays a role. In a study not yet fully completed (for first details see Fatke and Valtin 1988) only adolescents and adults, but not younger children, expected from their friends, besides trust and acceptance, openness and honesty. The willingness to give and receive criticism, even in the case of "unpleasant truths", was seen as an important criterion of friendship relations. However, some tactfulness was appreciated, as a fifteen-year-old girl argued: "I wouldn't say to my friend 'You are too fat' but 'Let's go on a diet together!'"

Further research will have to clarify whether specific forms of politeness can be differentiated in accordance with the event and the context – that which is genuinely pro-social in that it takes into consideration the plight of others, and that form which tolerates divergent opinions and maintains respectful distance in personal questions. It is already clear in the present material that both types of politeness take on a different function in the context of different social relationships.

Part 3: Politeness in a Non-Western Cultural Setting

10. The metapragmatics of politeness in Israeli society*

Shoshana Blum-Kulka

1.Introduction

In recent years politeness phenomena have become central to discussions of human interaction as such. In contrast to the Western folk etymology of the term, which usually equates politeness only with the icing on the cake of social interaction, current theories of politeness see it as basic to human interaction. Following the Goffmanian tradition, politeness thus becomes essential to the production of social order, and a precondition of human cooperation. As Gumperz notes in his introduction to the new edition of Brown and Levinson's influential work on universals of politeness phenomena, "any theory which provides an understanding of this phenomenon at the same time goes to the foundations of human social life" (Gumperz, Foreword to Brown and Levinson 1987: xiii).

Yet despite the richness of the recent literature in sociolinguistics and pragmatics on the topic (almost every issue of the *Journal of Pragmatics* or *Language in Society* in 1987/88 features at least one paper concerned with politeness), neither the motivating factors behind the phenomenon nor the cross-cultural validity of its linguistic expressions are as yet very well understood.

One of the central themes running through recent discussions of politeness phenomena is the question of universality: Are there any universal principles of politeness? How do such universal principles, if shown to exist, relate to observed differences between cultures in both perceptions of the concept and interactional styles?

The purpose of this chapter is to explore these questions; my main focus here is to try to unveil the role of culture in negotiating perceptions of politeness and in accounting for culturally coloured ways of

* This project was supported by grant No. 87-00167/1 from the Israel-American Binational Science Foundation (BSF).

speaking. The analysis is derived from two sets of semi-structured interviews on notions of politeness, complemented by empirical findings on speech-act realisations across different cultures (Blum-Kulka, House and Kasper 1989) and from a study of family discourse in three cultural groups (Blum-Kulka 1990). The first set of interviews was conducted by graduate students taking a course in Language and Social Context at the Hebrew University. As part of the class assignment, students were asked to interview in pairs two Israeli families (children included) of their acquaintance. Interviews were audio-recorded and fully transcribed. Fifty-two families were interviewed this way, representing a wide spectrum of Israeli society. Families varied in terms of parents' ages (from early twenties to late fifties), socio-economic status (lower to upper middle class) and degree of religious observance. Students were advised to choose families sharing their own cultural background. Most, as native-born Israelis, approached native Israeli families; a pair of Argentinian students interviewed two immigrant families from Argentina, and two students of British origin interviewed two families of similar background.

The second set of interviews was conducted with 24 Jewish families (eight Israeli, eight American, and eight American immigrants to Israel) taking part in a cross-cultural family discourse project (Blum-Kulka 1990). The student interviews elicited definitions and descriptions of polite and impolite speech and behaviour, asked for verbalisations and evaluations of modes of situated speech performance, and encouraged exemplification via personal narratives (see Appendix). The family-study interviews focused on the pragmatic socialisation of children.

The following is an attempt to explore a native, metapragmatic point of view, as related to both theories of politeness and actual speech behaviour. The discussion is organised in three sections: section 2 describes the metapragmatics of politeness in Israeli society as revealed through the meaning clusters associated with the term; section 3 analyses the ways in which expressive modes are filtered through social differentials in this society; and section 4 relates the metapragmatics of politeness in Israeli society to a conceptual framework proposed for pin-pointing the role of culture in the construction of politeness systems.

2. Metapragmatic definitions: "I don't think it's polite to be hypocritical"

2.1 *The semantics of politeness*

The first part of the interview focused on perceptions of the notion of politeness expressed in Hebrew by the words *nimus* and *adivut*. In asking for definitions and examples of applicability, we did not limit our informants in any way. It should be noted that in this metaprag-matic mode, informants tend to evoke normative descriptions of the phenomenon and engage, to a degree, in positive self-representation (a polite act in its own right) by coming up with what seems to them socially acceptable definitions.

Both *nimus* and *adivut* are translation equivalents of 'politeness'. Both terms acquired their current meanings relatively late; *nimus*, which comes from the Greek *nómos* (meaning 'order', or 'custom'), became a translation equivalent to 'politeness' only in the Modern Hebrew of this century. The second term, *adivut*, was coined from Arabic again in Modern Hebrew. No clear distinction was drawn by the interviewees between the two terms denotatively, though there is some suggestion of a difference in connotations. The first term, *nimus*, is more readily associated with etiquette and formal aspects of politeness than the second; we noticed a certain ambivalence in attitude in relation to *nimus* and what it stands for. As will be shown, *nimus* is not always seen in a positive light. *Adivut,* on the other hand, is the term used publicly in slogans calling for politeness in bureaucratic settings and on the road (for example, *taxarut hanehag headiv* is the competition for the 'polite driver'). This term seems to have acquired none of the negative undertones sometimes associated with *nimus*.

In definitions offered for both terms "politeness" is positively associated with tolerance, restraint, good manners, showing deference and being nice to people, but is simultaneously referred to in a nega-tive manner as something external, hypocritical, unnatural. Hence, though Israeli definitions echo Western folk-etymology notions of politeness, a cultural caveat is added to its traditional connotations. The metaphors used colourfully express the association of the notion with decorum, often with a slightly negative connotation. Politeness refers to "external manners used as an envelope that's supposed to leave each of the parties involved in an interaction unhurt, not penetrating the space of the other"; "politeness is like the icing on the cake; it's the icing on spoken language"; "it's the grease which makes the wheels of society go around" and "smooths out the rough edges of daily life."

It is interesting to note that from a historical perspective, these notions of politeness are deeply embedded in the history of Western civilisation. In his highly influential treatise on politeness in the 16th century, *De civilitate morum puerilium* ('On civility in the manners of children'), Erasmus of Rotterdam (cited by Elias [1939] 1978) advises the young noble "to not do or say anything that the other might find offensive." As a sociologist of culture, Norbert Elias views this treatise as seminal in shaping European society's self-consciousness as "civilised" compared to earlier societies or "more primitive" contemporary ones. The norms for interpersonal conduct, namely manners, play a central role in the French notion of *civilité*, the German *Kultur* and the British *civilisation*. To show why manners are so important in this context Elias quotes in great detail extracts from the European prescriptive literature on the subject in several chapters of his book, tracing the development of norms for table-manners, bodily postures in public and, most relevant for our purposes, speech style. The Israeli metaphors for politeness in part evoke this tradition; in Israel, as elsewhere, "politeness" is associated with "civilised" forms of behaviour.

In the framework suggested by Janney (1988) this body of literature on manners would represent the development of a European system of "social politeness". Janney suggests that politeness encompasses both a normative dimension, embodied in "social politeness", and a more flexible interpersonal dimension, represented by the notion of "tact" (cf. Janney and Arndt, this volume). While the distinction can be useful in providing different perspectives for empirical studies of politeness, as done by Fraser (1990), theoretically it fails to account for the culturally embedded relationship between the two aspects. In the final analysis, systems of social politeness seem to represent *culturally coloured interpretations of basic notions of tact,* (e.g., face concerns) *as conventionalised in any given culture or even speech event type.* As suggested already by the semantic definitions offered for the term "politeness" by Israelis, the constituents of "tact" and its appropriate modes of expression are very much subject to cultural interpretation.

2.2 *Scope: public versus private domains*

All aspects of social life are amenable to politeness considerations. To be polite is "to adapt yourself to different situations," to behave "according to the expectations of the place."

Yet an important distinction is drawn between the public and the private spheres of life. The politeness requirement for public life is inferable from recurring complaints concerning the "impolite" behaviour of the Israeli in public places; street behaviour is found lacking in restraint (loud voice, bad language) and consideration (not queuing, pushing and shoving), and public service deplorable (phone operators in government offices). The underlying notion of politeness expressed by these complaints is the socially normative traditional one; it is the lack of clear conventions for politeness as a socio-cultural code which is complained about (*ein defus adivut yisraeli*, i.e., 'there is no Israeli pattern of politeness'). In Ide's (1987) terms, Israeli public life is emicly perceived as low in discernment (i.e., obligatory scripts for polite behaviour) and high in (im)polite volition.

It is when Israelis are called upon to formulate their ideas and feelings of politeness in the private sphere that a strong cultural bias emerges. Among friends and family some find politeness completely irrelevant, others severely restrict its appropriate modes of expression. The "irrelevance" argument rests on associating politeness with a distancing function: "Between husband and wife there is great intimacy and politeness does not really matter." As noted by Garfinkel (1967), politeness intuitively tends to be associated with formality; hence politeness is juxtaposed with informality: "You have to be more polite to people who are less close, in the family there is less formality." At home "you have to feel at home." What is called for in the family, then, is *hitxasvut* 'consideration'; "you have to speak in a way that shows that you really care, not because of something external." Sometimes to show a caring attitude to a friend is to say it as it is, even if the things said are not the most flattering ones; this is the *dugri* 'straight' mode Katriel (1986) analyses in depth, captured in the interviews by the young man who said, "I don't think it's polite to be hypocritical."

Especially revealing in this context are the verbalisations of children participating in the interviews. Roy's (aged 11) expectations for politeness from people around him include the school principal and his teacher, who should greet him with *shalom* and 'good morning' when he comes to school; he complains of being greeted "politely" only by the school superintendent. In a similar vein, Ran (9) includes in his expectations of polite behaviour his mother, who should greet him when he comes home from school and ask specific questions about his day. Maayan (7) says it is polite to say "thank you" and "please" but also "it was good" after a meal, and "to hug my Mommy."

As could be expected from the literature (Bates 1976), children associate politeness primarily with the conventional formulae of saying "please" and "thank you"; but, interestingly, they also associate politeness with the expression of positive attitudes. To be polite is also to praise your mother for her cooking, to show her your love. This notion of politeness as the expression of positive beliefs is captured in Hebrew by the cultural notion of *lefargen* meaning roughly 'to indulge, to support, not to begrudge', a notion that Katriel (forthcoming) claims goes beyond mere *nimus* 'politeness' for Israelis.

Several theoretical issues are echoed in this rhetoric of politeness; one is the search for the most relevant social differentials in distinguishing types of polite behaviour. For Israelis, the relevant distinction is a Goffmanian one: it is "frontstage" behaviour in public which is clearly distinguished from "backstage" behaviour between friends and at home (Goffman 1959). A second issue concerns the dialectics of interactional harmony versus instrumentality; Israelis are aware, with Leech and Brown and Levinson, that politeness indexes a "show of consideration" (i.e., redress to face), that it works "to keep peace" (i.e., harmony). But they are also keenly aware of the risks involved in the strategic dimension of politeness; politeness is "a diplomatic way of getting things," yet too much "diplomacy" is suspected of being flattery, if not manipulativeness.

The third issue concerns the depth and scope of the phenomenon: is it indicative of decorum only, in the European tradition of "civilised behaviour" (Elias 1939/1978), or does it reflect values, and hence personality? Israelis who reject politeness as something artificial, external, "hypocritical", are in effect subscribing to the latter view. It is in the name of distancing the new personality of the Israeli from that of the diaspora Jew that the founding fathers of Israel called for the creation of a new type of person and of a mode of communication to fit this new conception of self. As Katriel (1986: 17) says, "The Israeli Jew was to be everything the Diaspora Jew was not. In communicative terms, this implied the rejection of ways of speaking associated with European genteel culture and Jewish Diaspora life in particular".

She cites the labourer-philosopher A.D. Gordon (1856–1922), whose teachings had a lasting influence on the Israeli Socialist Zionist movement, to the effect that in reviving the Hebrew language, the Jews of Israel should replace the decadent European ways of speaking that involve "twisting the forms of speaking for purpose of showing respect" by a style which is "more natural and closer to truth," indicative of a "true, internal politeness deriving from a pure source – from the pure heart of the simple soul – politeness which makes no recourse to fancy expressions either in speech or writing" (Gordon 1943: 254, cited in Katriel 1986: 22–23).

The fourth issue, brought up by the children, is whether it is conceptually valid to distinguish between "polite" and "impolite" illocutions; are certain speech acts (such as criticism) impolite by their very nature, regardless of their manner of expression? Israeli children answer positively; in this they confirm Leech (1983) against Fraser (1990) in intuitively classifying speech acts as polite or impolite not only by their way of expression but also by their underlying intent, or illocutionary point.

2.3 *Indicators: verbal and non-verbal means*

Politeness is expressed by both verbal and non-verbal means. Israeli informants confirm Arndt and Janney (1987) in their emphasis on the importance of non-verbal behaviour: "Sometimes a pat on the shoulder means more than a thousand words." To be polite is also "to look your interlocutor in the eye," "to smile." The European tradition of politeness as publicly "civilised behaviour" (Elias 1939/1978) and Goffman's notion of "demeanour" (Goffman 1967) are echoed in the inclusion of table-manners and dress in the spheres mentioned. To be polite is to adhere to behaving in a decorous manner reflecting on self: using your utensils, "not to lick your fingers while eating" (Roy, 11), even not to dress sloppily.

Ways of speaking are very important. Tone of voice, formal markers ("please", "thank you") indirectness ("allowing the other an out so he doesn't feel imposed on") as well as directness ("between friends it's polite to say exactly what you feel"), taciturnity ("it's sometimes polite to keep silent") as well as a socially differential attitude to volubility ("to a stranger I would give many more reasons in asking for a favour"), are all mentioned as politeness indicators.

In terms of Grice's maxims of communication (1975), these

comments show that both cooperativeness and the four maxims are amenable to politeness evaluations: basic cooperation is essential ("it's impolite when people do not answer"), the sub-maxim of Manner is implemented in judging politeness by appropriate levels of directness, that of Quantity in relation to the dimension of taciturnity versus volubility (Scollon and Scollon 1981), and for this culture the maxim of Quality can be interpreted to mean an equation of sincerity with politeness.

The sub-maxim of Relevance did not come up in this metapragmatic mode, but it does figure in metapragmatic comments made by parents to children in the course of dinner-table conversations (Blum-Kulka 1990). In both Israeli and American families, parents socialised children to politeness by comments in regard to behaviour ("use your knife and fork"), turn-taking ("don't interrupt"), adherence to all four Gricean sub-maxims and use of language (grammaticality and pronunciation). Adherence to the sub-maxims is expressed via comments in regard to Relevance ("you didn't answer Mom's question"), Manner ("don't be impertinent"), Quantity ("we heard that"), and Quality ("are you sure you saw a giant turtle?").

But there is a revealing difference between Israelis and Americans with regard to aspects of polite talk emphasised: while the two groups pay equal attention to socialising children to learn to adhere to Gricean maxims, in American parents' discourse the next most prevalent type of comment relates to turn-taking. Children explicitly bid for a turn ("can I say something?"), and parents navigate "fair" division of floor-space ("it's not your turn. Let David speak now"). The Israeli parents, on the other hand, stress "correct" use of language. The talk-space allocated in American families to meta-turn-taking talk is taken up in Israeli families by metalinguistic talk (for details see Blum-Kulka 1990).

This study complements the metapragmatic rhetoric of the interviews in interesting ways. First, there are areas of overlap; non-verbal "polite" behaviour is both mentioned in the interviews and attended to in the families; so are conversational norms as related to the four maxims, confirming the cultural relativity attached to their interpretation (Blum-Kulka and Olshtain 1986). It is not by chance, though, that the attention paid to turn-taking rules in the Israeli families is negligible; we know from the interviews that formal aspects of politeness are treated with ambivalence in this society. On the other hand, being only first-generation or at most second-generation native speakers of

Hebrew (revived as a spoken language only in this century), Israeli parents are quite self-conscious about normative language use (Rabin 1976), transmitting this self-consciousness to their children.

3. Expressive modes and social differentials

In this section I analyse the responses given by informants to questions asking them (a) to react to indirect formulations of speech acts in specific situations and to suggest alternatives and (b) to exemplify requests in the family (to spouse and children), between friends and to a stranger, specifying their politeness rationale (see Appendix). Where empirical data are available, interview responses will be compared with observed linguistic behaviour in Israeli society. Hence, the Israeli interpretation of politeness is captured here by "what people say they do with words" (Verschueren 1985) as well as by what they actually do.

3.1 *Directness and indirectness revisited*

It should be noted that "directness" as used in the literature often confuses two related, but still different dimensions: (a) choice of form ("close the door" as opposed to "the door is open") and (b) choice of illocution. The first dimension realises the Gricean sub-maxim of Manner; it relates to the way in which a speech act is formulated. The second is related to the sub-maxim of Quantity: it is the choice between silence and speech.

Choice of form reflects the speech act's degree of illocutionary and propositional transparency (Weizman 1989). This dimension of cross-linguistic variation is widely documented in the literature; it has been repeatedly shown that languages around the world provide their speakers with rich repertoires of "direct" and "indirect" verbal means for expressing given illocutions, and that cultures vary in preferences shown for choices along this continuum (see, for example, the cross-cultural speech act realisation study results in Blum-Kulka, House and Kasper 1989). When compared with speakers of French Canadian (Québecois), German, Australian English and Argentinian Spanish, Israeli speakers come out second in directness, surpassed only by speakers of Argentinian Spanish. Yet it is a highly differential use of directness: Israelis, as well as Argentinians, vary levels of directness by situation more than members of the other cultures studied (House 1989).

The interviews enrich these findings by the rationales provided for the need for illocutionary and propositional transparency: "You have to be direct and say what you want because otherwise you won't be understood." This emphasis on the need for clarity even leads to a dissociation of politeness from indirectness: "You can say something directly and impolitely or indirectly and impolitely."

Indirectness *per se* may backfire in two ways: (a) by excessive cognitive burdening (cf. Blum-Kulka 1987) and (b) by inviting conversational implicatures. Israelis are sensitive to both dangers; talking about their experiences as participant-observers of other cultures, our informants tended to evoke the first: "They talk much more politely and therefore you can't understand what they mean; I often failed to understand if it's 'yes' or 'no'." This aspect is called forth in the justification given for high levels of directness with children; a parent should be "assertive but clear." And, indeed, this dictum of clarity in parent-child interaction is adhered to in both American and Israeli families (Blum-Kulka 1990).

The danger of being suspected of inviting face-damaging conversational implicatures (such as of being sarcastic) came up in the interviews in three instances. In the first, a secretary is told by her boss, upon leaving the office, "You left the door open." Our informants found this indirect request extremely impolite, even "humiliating" and "offensive". The suspected sarcasm seems to be motivated here by the request being phrased as a complaint in regard to unperformed duties and obligations (Labov and Fanshel 1977), the implication being, "You should have known better (than to leave the door open)."

The second instance depicts a non-standard request between husband and wife; informants here stressed the vulnerability of style to misinterpretation: "Especially between husband and wife one should be careful because there is high vulnerability." Israeli informants here echo Tannen (1986) in showing a high degree of awareness of the risks of misunderstanding in symmetrical intimate relations. Analysis of family talk indeed shows that misunderstandings that occur as a result of excessive indirectness between husband and wife are extremely difficult, if not impossible, to repair (Blum-Kulka and Weizman 1988). To avoid such risks, informants recommend the use of conventional indirectness. By asking your spouse if he or she could or would replace you at a meeting with the teacher of your child "you leave her the option to refuse," "you do not force him to do it." Conventional indirectness is hence perceived as the optimally polite strategy, making a bow to face, while being free of ambiguity and the suggestion of manipulativeness.

This recommendation is confirmed empirically in two ways: in judgement tests, Israeli subjects find conventional indirectness to be far more polite than hints (Blum-Kulka 1987). In elicitation tests, conventional indirectness is the dominant strategy in Hebrew both for non-standard requests between spouses (Blum-Kulka 1982) and in requests for a favour between student-friends (to borrow lecture notes) and between neighbours (for a ride home after a meeting) (Blum-Kulka 1989).

The third instance of indirectness in the interviews depicted a negative illocution: a friend's new haircut is reacted to with "it's quite nice"; is this polite? Informants generally agreed that it is not; friends are entitled to hear what you really think *bexenut* 'sincerely'. But it should be said with tact and care (*bizhirut*, 'carefully'). Not being sincere in expressing a critical attitude invites the implicature of irony. Yet the rejection of indirectness for expressing critical attitudes is not universally applicable. To an acquaintance, "one should not say anything," or even violate the maxim of Quality and give a compliment.

The social differential drawn on is not merely that of social distance; underlying "friendship" is the dimension of affect: it is people who are emotionally close who deserve in this culture the politeness of *dugriyut* (cf. Katriel 1986) for both positive and negative attitudes. This example further illustrates how directness is related to the maxim of Quantity, to the choice between silence and speech as well as to degree of verbosity and informativeness.

Politeness can find its expression in the act of not saying, at the level of *dire et ne pas dire* as aptly captured by the title of Ducrot's book (Ducrot 1980). The tension between silence and speech is not confined to the expression of negative attitudes: it represents the dilemma of expressing or not, in Leech's terms (1983), both polite and impolite illocutions. It is in this domain that the greatest degree of both cross-cultural and individual variation is to be expected. Israelis, for example, share with Apache Indians (Basso 1979) a critical attitude towards American patterns of phatic greeting and leave-taking talk. Where American norms call for formulaic expression of polite illocutions, Apache norms call for silence, and Israeli norms vacillate between silence and brief, "sincere" talk.

Occasions calling for a show of gratitude and appreciation are another case in point. An Israeli teenager interviewee noted critically the profuse thanks of an American friend of hers staying in her home for a while; she would have just said, "Thank you."

The expression of impolite illocutions distinguishes cultures and individuals even more sharply; for acts threatening the other's (positive) face, Israelis can view as polite the expressing of unpleasant "truths" (recall the hairdo example) where other cultures would view it as impolite; for acts threatening the positive face of self, they often recommend avoidance as the preferred strategy. It is in relation to this issue of the performability of self-threatening acts that we note the widest range of individual differences; on many occasions, an example of a favour asked from a stranger or friend given in the course of the interview by one of the participants would be reacted to with "I would never ask/ mention that", or even "asking favours is not in my lexicon."

3.2 *Mitigation: cultural styles of redress*

The means available for indexing the politeness of speech acts, as documented for requests and complaints (Blum-Kulka, House and Kasper 1989; Olshtain and Weinbach 1987), fall into two basic dimensions:

1. choice of strategy at a particular level of directness
2. internal and external modifications

The first dimension relates to choice of form and illocution, as discussed above. The second dimension represents types of mitigation independent of choice of strategy (Faerch and Kasper 1989). Hence, *mitigation can index politeness regardless of levels of directness*. The independence of these two dimensions becomes particularly poignant through Israeli views on politeness. While the two meanings of "directness" are related to the maxims of Manner, Quantity and even Quality, mitigation is the expression par excellence of Manner: it encompasses the repertoire of verbal and non-verbal means available for modifying polite attitudes.

The two types of mitigation differ in the means used, in their positive versus negative politeness orientation, in the types of attitudes indexed, and in the interactional functions served by each.

a) Means: "Internal modification" (so called because it acts on the strategy proper, or the Head Act) includes syntactic (modals), lexical (hedges and minimisers) and phrasal (consultatives and understaters) components (for a taxonomy see Appendix to Blum-Kulka, House and Kasper 1989). A parallel set of verbal means serves to modify all face-threatening acts; hence the salience of hedges and subjectivisers in discussions of linguistic politeness (e.g., Brown and Levinson 1987). In spoken language paralinguistic and kinesic means can replace the verbal ones; tone of voice and a shift to a questioning intonation may convey polite attitudes with a force similar to that of verbal modifications (Arndt and Janney 1987; Grabowski-Gellert and Winterhoff-Spurk 1987).

External modification acts as a supportive move to the strategy proper. For requests, these include checks on availability, attempts for a precommitment, as well as justifications and grounders preceding or following the act (Edmondson 1981; Faerch and Kasper 1989).

b) Orientation and attitude: The two types of modification differ in politeness orientation; while internal modification largely redresses face by stressing in-group membership, the hallmark of positive politeness, external modification, appeals to the interlocutor as a rational agent in need of persuasion as required by the independence tenet of negative politeness. Addressing a spouse or a child by a nickname and using slang can be polite by stressing in-group affiliation; prefacing or following a request with the reasons, on the other hand, is polite by paying homage to the hearer's image as a rational being asked to act out of conviction. The same strategy for apologies redresses face by augmenting the speaker's recognition of the severity of the offence. Internal modifiers can easily index affect and involvement; external modifiers are by definition other-oriented, deference-indicating devices.

c) Interactional functions: Minimising distance and imposition. While Israeli speakers draw on both sources of mitigation, it is the *salience of positive politeness markers* which is particularly culture specific. Asked, for example, how they would upgrade the politeness of a bald on-record command (previously judged impolite) to a child or a spouse, Israeli informants almost invariably rephrased the request by adding an endearment or a nickname, changing the assertion to an interrogative, softening tone of voice, and adding an appealer. For example, in talking to a 10-year-old at dinner, it would be impolite to say "bring the pitcher from the kitchen"; a "nice" way of asking would be: *ruti'le, tavi'i et hakumkum, tov?* 'Rutile, get the pitcher, OK?'.

Between spouses, endearments and pre-requests are used: *noga, motek, ta'asi li tova?* 'Nogah, darling, will you do me a favour?'.

The prevalence of nicknames is of particular interest in this context. In family discourse their use differentiates Israeli from Jewish-American (both middle-class) families in our sample (Blum-Kulka and Katriel 1991). While in the former they are used excessively, with up to five or six innovative nicknames addressed to one child per dinner, in the latter their use is scarce and unpopular. American parents soften bald on-record commands by transforming them to conventionally indirect strategies ("could you get the pitcher?") (Blum-Kulka 1990). Thus, in contrast to the Americans, Israelis show a strong tendency towards positive politeness forms of mitigation, suggesting their use as a strategic device in talking to both friends and strangers. In examples given for "polite" ways for asking a neighbour for a favour, again the use of endearment suffixes as openers was the dominant feature of many requests (saying *talcik* for *Tal, dubik* for *Dov*). Humour and slang are also part of this repertoire of solidarity politeness. One of our young male informants volunteered the following example: "If I am dying for a cup of coffee, I'll try to convince my secretary to make me one by using humour, saying something like 'if you make me a cup of coffee, I'll be your slave for the next two years'."

The following example from the transcripts illustrates the degree of awareness that accompanies the use of this style. The couple interviewed are both academics, have three young children (aged 2, 7, and 10) and hold professional jobs. Asked to give an example of a situation where politeness is an important consideration at work, the following conversation between the couple ensued:

> Husband: Today, for example, I had to turn to my boss: "look, we have a problem, because the mother of our *metapelet* ('house-keeper/ nanny') died – it will be a problem for us all week, we need, actually, to pick up the baby from nursery school before the boys come home; so would it actually be possible to leave and arrange this?" It's important to involve him in the problem to avoid questions, so he understands.
>
> Wife: I noticed that when you talked to the boss you said "baby". Michal is two-and-a-half and we don't refer to her as "baby" any more; you used that to gain empathy, identification, involvement. That always works.

The mixture of politeness styles used in the request cited shows that negative and positive politeness are not necessarily mutually exclusive:

the strategy opted for is conventionally indirect ("would it be possible") modified via both external (grounders) and internal means ("baby"; the repeated use of a discourse filler *pashut*, translated as 'actually'). In phrasing the request, the husband seems to rely on the power of explanation as an imposition-minimiser. The wife, on the other hand, points out to him that he combines this strategy with markers of solidarity meant to minimise distance.

This example further illustrates that forms of external modification by way of justifications, explanations and grounders are related to the notion of volubility: politeness in certain circumstances is directly linked to quantity of verbal effort invested in performing the speech act. There are situations where one needs to display politeness by investing in words. The degree of informativeness thus becomes a measure of "external" redressive action, on a par with internal types of modification.

d) The social differential of mitigation: Within Israeli society, the positive politeness-oriented style of mitigation is pervasive in intimate relationships. As documented for family discourse (Blum-Kulka 1990), in this role-constellation one of its main functions seems to be to gain cooperativeness by stressing affect. In symmetrical relations between friends both styles seem legitimised; informants stressed metacommunicatively the importance of negative politeness markers ("you should show respect/leave the other an out") while in their actual examples they frequently mixed the two mitigation orientations. In this role-constellation both distance-minimisation and imposition-minimisation are called for; cooperativeness is sought for both via symbolic upholding of social proximity as well as by appeal to reason. The same double function and use comes up in relation to strangers, but it is in this role-constellation that we find the least agreement between informants. Lacking conventional cultural scripts for behaviour in public, Israelis alternately rely either on the ethos of solidarity or on individuated scripts true to personality. The ethos of solidarity legitimises approaching strangers in cases where members of other cultures might not; individual differences will determine both the performability and the manner of such acts. Thus, both avoidance ("wouldn't do it"), volubility ("I would explain more than to a friend") solidarity ("I would be very friendly"), as well as formal deference ("I would be much more formal than usual") can be mentioned as polite strategies in performing one and the same imposing speech act.

4. Theoretical implications: Culture's constructivist role

Incorporating the native point of view, as attempted in the previous sections, has led me to adopt a "constructivist position" (Bruner 1986) in regard to politeness. On a theoretical level this means that systems of politeness manifest a culturally filtered interpretation of the interaction between four essential parameters: social motivations, expressive modes, social differentials and social meanings (Figure 1, p. 271). Cultural notions interfere in determining the distinctive features of each of the four parameters and as a result, significantly effect the social understanding of "politeness" across societies in the world.

4.1 *Social motivations*

Consider first the issue of social motivation. Why be linguistically polite? In other words, why do languages around the world provide their speakers with alternative modes of expression for both propositional and relational attitudes, assigning social values to their choices?

In the Goffmanian tradition, the answer is phrased in terms of the individual striving to maintain "face", which Goffman defines as "the positive social value a person effectively claims for himself by the line others assume he has taken during a particular contact" (Goffman 1967: 5). Brown and Levinson's (1987) theory of politeness rests on explicating the particulars of face-wants that politeness strategies are meant to satisfy. Politeness is viewed as the intentional, strategic behaviour of the individual meant to satisfy self and other face-wants in case of threat, enacted via positive and negative styles of redress. This basic notion of politeness as redressive action aimed at reestablishing or preserving interactional harmony is also at the heart of Leech's (1983) theory of politeness.

Our findings suggest that it is already at the deep level of the nature of face-need that cultures differ: the constituents of face-wants are not necessarily universal. Consider two cultures as different as the Israeli and the Japanese. The metapragmatics of politeness in Israeli society discussed above, Katriel's (1986) work on the notion of *dugriyut* 'straight talk' as well as our work on requesting behaviour in Israeli culture (Blum-Kulka, Danet and Gerson 1985; Blum-Kulka and House 1989) combine to show that for Israelis an emphasis on sincer-

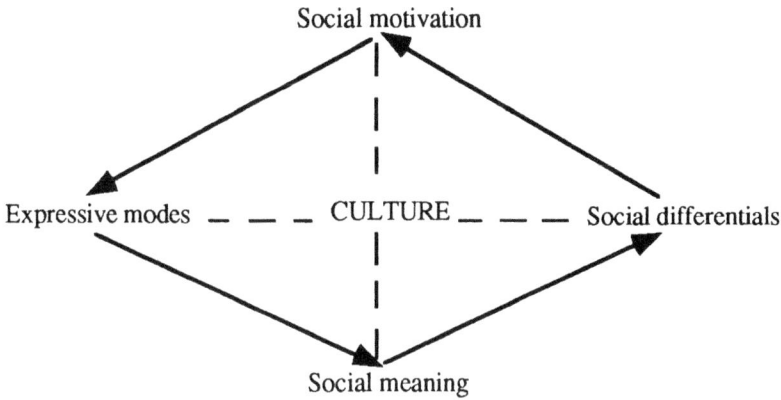

Figure 1. Culture's constructivist role

ity and truthfulness in interpersonal relations overrides the importance of avoiding infringement on the other. The result is the licensing and even positive evaluation of high levels of directness in (especially) private speech. Students of Japanese society, on the other hand, challenge the very presupposition that the basic unit of that society is the individual whose needs for non-imposition politeness strategies are meant to satisfy. As pointed out by Matsumoto (1986) and Ide (1987), the concept of "face" in Japan is fundamentally different from that in the Western world: for the Japanese, it is the acknowledgement and maintenance of the relative position of a member to others, rather than the preservation of an individual's own territory which governs all social interaction. Being polite for the Japanese means paying tribute to members' proper place in society, preserving the necessary frames that signify belonging and fitting in with others.

4.2 *Expressive modes*

Expressive modes encompass potentially all verbal and non-verbal elements available for communication. For marking politeness, two sources of cross-linguistic diversity seem especially noteworthy: availability of means and obligatory versus optional choice.

First, consider the cross-linguistic diversity in the availability of linguistic means. The process of mapping basic social needs with linguistic forms will obviously be constrained by the pragmalinguistic repertoires available in any specific language. The domain of socially deictic phenomena is particularly revealing in this context; as amply demonstrated, languages differ in the types of social information formally grammaticalised or lexicalised (e.g., Silverstein 1989). In Japanese, for example, a distinction is drawn between in-group and out-group reference, which is encoded in both nominal and verbal elements (Wetzel 1985). Wetzel (1985: 156) concludes that the Japanese "think about and cognitively represent social situations in terms of their group rather than individual identity," a cognitive habit "that manifests itself in situationally dependent linguistic choices not typically found in Western countries" (1985: 156). A further example would be the distinction between married/unmarried in addressing women, encoded in the choice between Miss and Mrs in English; the feminist protest against the use of this distinction (replaced by the neutral Ms in current American practice) shows that actual use of encoded distinctions might be a matter of dispute.

Hence, even more important than availability is the issue of obligatory versus optional choice. As long as speakers of English had to distinguish between *Miss* and *Mrs* they necessarily conveyed deference to a woman's marital status. Similarly, contextual variables governing choices in languages possessing a T/V system as described in the literature (e.g., Ervin-Tripp 1972; Friedrich 1966) create structured networks for the types of social information *needed to be conveyed as part of the politeness system*. Thus addressing an older addressee by "T" in Yiddish would convey an impolite attitude, while addressing a familiar person by "V" might invite a conversational implicature of deliberate impoliteness (Slobin 1963).

Optional choices for politeness across languages can be subsumed under the notion of "strategic choice". Thus, the full gamut of negative and positive politeness strategies elaborated by Brown and Levinson (1987) is claimed to be available to individual speakers across diverse languages where choices within this realm are a matter of situational assessment in terms of social distance, social power and the extremity of the intentional act.

The expressive modes of Modern Hebrew, as captured here, should be understood in the historical context of the revival of Hebrew as a spoken language. As Rabin (1976: 158) says, "conversational Hebrew is a well established form of language, expressive, forceful and pliable" that "has a range of registers and a scale of social varieties". Yet in encoding its social differentials Modern Hebrew had to recreate its own ways of expression in a way that would be true to the national and socialist ideologies strongly associated with its revival. As a result, it rejected types of obligatory politeness markings (such as T/V) felt to be unnatural to the spirit of this language and society. The distinctions that did develop draw on the full gamut of markers available in other languages: as discussed above, they include the dimension of indirectness, forms of address, degree of verbosity, and types of mitigation. But in sharp contrast to a language like Japanese, the sociolinguistics of politeness in this society is governed by a tacit system of norms (not yet fully documented) which leaves ample room for optional choice.

4.3 *Social differentials*

The cultural factor intervenes at the level of situational assessment in several ways. Even if we assume with Brown and Levinson that the three social parameters of distance, power and extremity suffice to explain strategic variation in choices of politeness strategies, we have to allow, as does their theory, for cultural variation in the relative weight of these factors for predicting politeness. The cultural bias of the Israeli system is expressed strongly in regard to weighing social distance and degrees of imposition, as well as in reinterpreting the relationship between the two. While social power is empirically shown to be of predictive significance for explaining sociolinguistic variation in Hebrew, social distance is not (Blum-Kulka et al. 1985). This result can be interpreted to mean that Israeli society is positive politeness-oriented by social orientation, motivated by the trend towards minimising social distance and degrees of imposition.

While the Israeli metapragmatics of politeness discussed here partly confirm this trend, they modify this generalisation in two ways. First, it should be noted that on the macro, societal level, the relevant distinction to be drawn in terms of social distance is between the "public" and the "private" domain, with distinct styles of interaction expected from each. For the public domain a longing is expressed for less minimisation of social distance and more formal enactments of politeness. In the private domain, the prevalence and justification for positive politeness are strongly reasserted. In this style, indexing affect is of particular importance; as claimed by Brown and Gilman (1989), "affect" seems equally as important as distance, power and imposition in accounting for politeness. Second, on the micro, personal level, the notion of imposition seems more critical than social distance *per se*. Both with regard to strangers and friends, we found sharp interpersonal differences in defining performable speech acts; things one speaker finds easy to say or ask, others would not even attempt. Yet, from a cross-cultural viewpoint, and especially in friendly relations, performability (with low estimates of imposition) seems higher than elsewhere.

The following example is illuminating on this point. An Israeli woman of British origin, having lived in Israel for 7 years, expressed her amazement at the kinds of favours Israelis ask from each other, favours she would never ask. For example, asking your neighbour to pick up your child from school together with his or her own (unless you have a regular pre-arrangement), or keeping an eye on your infant while you "run to the grocer's" are outside the scope of performable requests for her, but "normal" favours among her Israeli friends.

A further source of cross-cultural variation on the situational dimension is the degree to which linguistic politeness is conventionalised relative to culture and situation. As Sachiko Ide (1987) argues convincingly, cultures may differ in the relative weightiness granted to volition, namely individual strategic manipulation, as opposed to what she calls "discernment" (and I refer to as "convention"). She claims that in Japanese, the expression of linguistic politeness is much more situationally conventionalised than, for example, in the English-speaking world. This means that in many situations the Japanese speaker will opt for culturally determined situationally appropriate scripts, where the Western speaker will need to make in situ decisions of appraisal and strategic choice. For the Japanese, "discernment" is linked to a generally high degree of obligatory linguistic choice; but "scripted" versus "unscripted" linguistic behaviour can just as well distinguish between situations in cultures with less rigid linguistic politeness systems (House 1989). The "lack of an Israeli pattern of politeness" is remarked on by one of the informants, thus lamenting the lack of scripts, or more precisely, the unbalanced proportions, in his view, between conventionalised and non-conventionalised types of situational politeness.

And yet certain speech domains are governed by a high degree of conventionalisation. Within the private domain, family discourse provides such an example of the interaction between the effect of speech event conventions and culture in determining the nature of politeness. Within the family parents and children are bound to each other by asymmetrical yet highly intimate affective relations; the conventional enactment for this relational configuration is a highly "direct" style. We found high levels of directness in both American and Israeli families' dinner-discourse. Yet it is not a style devoid of politeness; first, given the role-constellation, the informal key and "backstage" (cf. Goffman 1959) nature of the event, directness in this context does not necessarily encode lack of politeness. Furthermore, family discourse is rich in mitigation; half of the direct request strategies used are downtoned or embedded in explanations and justifications. But despite the common speech event characteristics of the system, cultures do differ. American family discourse is the less direct of the two, and shows a preference for conventional forms of mitigation. Israeli families, on the other hand, prefer positive politeness-oriented types of mitigation, such as nicknaming (Blum-Kulka 1990).

4.4 *Social meanings*

The fourth dimension of the model relates to the social meanings attached to choices of linguistic encoding in particular situations or speech events. In other words, it is the degree to which any linguistic expression is deemed polite by members of a given culture in a specific situation. On the one hand, appraisals of politeness will be motivated by cultural determinants of face wants and variable degrees of linguistic conventionalisation. On the other hand, they will be affected by culturally coloured definitions of the situation, with the result that similar linguistic choices can carry very different values of politeness in the same situation across different cultures. If the dimension of social motivation answers the "why" of politeness, that of "expressive modes" and "social differentials" the "how" and "when" respectively, the fourth dimension labelled "social meaning" answers the "what for" question. It is this dimension that serves as the selection principle for inclusion of verbal and non-verbal variations in the class of "politeness phenomena". Included will be those phenomena which are amenable to judgments of "politeness", i.e., types of social verbal and non-verbal behaviour interpretable along the continuum of meaning clusters associated with the concept. I propose to view this continuum as composed of three zones, each subsuming a range of social meanings, as presented in Figure 2 (p. 276).

IMPOLITE   POLITE   EXTENSIVELY
                                    POLITE

improper - rude   appropriate -   strategic-manipulative
   "foreign"   tactful   "foreign"

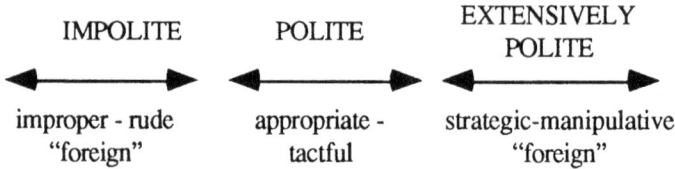

Figure 2. The scale of social meanings

The central zone is that of "polite" behaviour; included in this zone is the range of cultural expectations for what constitutes appropriate social behaviour relative to changing social situations. Since such expectations are usually tacit, polite behaviour is largely taken for granted, at most noticeable as showing an actor's "tactfulness". It is deviations from the cultural norms which will arouse attention; thus, non-fulfilment of a given politeness rule, such as using a "wrong" term of address, carries with it two potential social risks. The first risk is that of being judged as lacking in social manners, or more extremely, of being attributed negative personality traits (such as a "non-considerate" or "tactless" person). The second risk is the graver one; it is derived from the power of politeness to invite conversational implicatures. In summing up the power of his model of the Cooperative Principle plus the four sub-maxims, Grice (1975: 47) notes that "there are, of course, all sorts of other maxims (aesthetic, social or moral in character), such as 'Be polite', that are also normally observed by participants in talk exchanges, and these may also generate non-conventional implicatures". Deviance from "normal" politeness, especially by excess, might invite such implicatures. Minimally, participants in an exchange will just notice if undue effort is being invested in "being polite"; maximally, they will attribute to the speaker a hidden agenda of some sort. For example, a wife might interpret her husband's extremely polite behaviour to her mother as a sure indicator of his dislike for his mother-in-law; within any given role-relationship "unusual" politeness, by a child to a parent, say, or between spouses or friends, might be suspected as an attempt at manipulation. One type of attribution, though, seems common to deviance from cultural norms of politeness both by diminished and excessive use: if the person in question is clearly an outsider to the culture, he or she might be excused as "foreign", the label cancelling all other attributions. But of course, as we know from the rich literature on ethnic and cross-cultural miscommunication (e.g., Gumperz 1982; Knapp et al. 1987), in actual discourse the excuse for "foreigners" is barely granted even to tourists, while in practice perceptions of the behaviour of the foreigner as deviant most often lead to cultural stereotyping.

It is a matter for cross-cultural research to compare the borderlines within the politeness continuum across cultures. Within the emic viewpoint on Israeli culture explored here, it is the cutting points between "impolite" and "polite" and "polite" and "extensively polite" which are of particular interest. We have seen that both ends of the continuum encompass judgments made equally by type and mode of illocution; a speech act thus can be considered impolite because it defies culturally interpreted face concerns, or because it deviates from culturally conventionalised ways of expression. Thus, both not siding with a friend directly in expressing a critical attitude, as well as avoiding the expression of a positive attitude might fall within the range of impoliteness. It is the "extensively polite" end of the continuum to which Israelis are particularly sensitive; upholding clarity, they reject forms of indirectness thought overtly cognitively burdening. Evoking their belief in sincerity, they shun forms of indirectness suspected of being manipulative. Between the two extremes lies the wide range of ways of speaking tacitly felt to be appropriate or polite.

5. Conclusion

The folk-notions of politeness discussed here validate many of the theoretical concerns discussed in the literature. The association of the notion with social appropriateness ("manners"), self-restraint and generally decorous behaviour continue the European social-perspective tradition of politeness (Elias 1939/1978). Linking politeness with deference and consideration in interpersonal relations reveals an awareness for face-concerns or interpersonal harmony, as formulated by Brown and Levinson and Leech. Even the expressive modes mentioned could be categorised along the strategies for redressive action listed for positive and negative politeness by Brown and Levinson.

And yet the attitudes expressed are deeply embedded in cultural traditions; that is why the word denoting the phenomenon under consideration carries with it a slightly negative connotation. While the need to express face-concerns is readily acknowledged, the nature of these concerns and the appropriate ways to address them in different situations are often highly culture specific. As a relatively "young" cultural group, native Israelis seem to be extremely sensitive to the range of social meanings attributable to communicative modes. Such meanings can range from (possibly unnoticeable) social inappropriateness to attributions of strategic or even manipulative intent. It is the fear of the second and third types of meaning which seems to motivate many aspects of Israeli interpersonal discourse. Israelis solve the clash between values such as naturalness, sincerity, truthfulness and clarity – all important values in this culture – and the perceived dictum of politeness as the non-sincere language of redress by implicitly redefining the notion of politeness while explicitly shunning the name.

Within this redefined notion, the rich range of registers and scales of social varieties of Modern Hebrew are used differentially to mark status, to defer to, and minimise, social distance, to index affect and acknowledge impositions. As Brown and Gilman (1989) argue, all four are essential for politeness. In incorporating all four parameters into its system of politeness, Israeli society does not differ from others around the world. Here, as elsewhere, degree of politeness varies by situational perceptions. Yet in fitting styles of expression to speech events, again cultural preferences emerge. In family discourse, status differences and intimacy come into play; here politeness is expressed via mitigation rather than by indirectness. Mitigation, especially if positive politeness-oriented, also figures strongly both in expectations and actual use in relations of friendship. It is in norms of politeness for behaviour in the public arena that Israeli present-day culture seems less consolidated; the metapragmatic discourse of informants admits to the lack of cultural scripts in this area and expresses a longing for both deference and demeanour, very much in the Western meanings of the terms.

Appendix

1. Guidelines for student politeness interviews

The purpose of the student interviews was to explore the notion of politeness in contemporary Israeli culture. In formulating the questions, I utilised information derived from previous sociolinguistic studies on language use and attitude in Israel. Students were given guidelines on interviewing in pairs native Israeli families; no limits were set on choice of population except that of being native-born and Israeli-educated.[1]

The following types of information were gathered in each interview:

A. Background of informants: education, profession, native language, ages of children, ages of parents, religious observance.

B. Issues addressed in open-ended questions:
   1. Identification of the semantic field and connotations associated with the Hebrew terms *adivut* and *nimus*.
   2. Identification of the negative and positive collocational sets associated with the terms (polite/impolite deeds/people/-speech).
   3. Exploration of the expectations held for politeness in different types of social context.
   4. Exploration of attitudes and beliefs held in regard to politeness in the family. Interviewees were asked to exemplify their comments by personal narratives.

C. Semi-structured questions probing attitudes to indirectness and politeness. Questions had the following pattern:
   "Would you consider it polite if -----------------; could you elaborate what made you say so?" For example:
   – If a boss, on leaving his office, says to his secretary, "You have left the door open."
   – If a friend reacts to your new hairdo with "It's quite nice."

D. Semi-structured questions eliciting request realisations in different social contexts. The format used was: "How would you ask x to do/for y; do you consider this a 'polite' way to ask? Why?"
   Examples:
   – How would you ask your husband/wife to replace you at a meeting with the teacher of your child?
   – How would you ask your boss if you had to leave work suddenly?

Interviews ended with a general discussion on politeness in Israel.

2. Family interviews

The topic of "politeness" figured as part of an extensive ethnographic interview with American, Israeli and Israeli-American families previously taped at the dinner table. with regard to politeness, the focus was on the pragmatic socialisation of children, asking parents to verbalise their expectations and educational customs in this domain.

Notes

1. These strictures did not apply to students who themselves were not Israeli natives; immigrant students (i.e., from Argentina and England) were asked to interview families of their own linguistic background.

11. The concept of politeness: An empirical study of American English and Japanese

Sachiko Ide, Beverly Hill, Yukiko M. Carnes, Tsunao Ogino,
Akiko Kawasaki

Introduction

In a previous study on linguistic politeness in Japanese and American English, Hill et al. (1986) assumed a more or less common concept of the term "politeness". However, the equivalence across cultures of the key term itself needs to be questioned. The purpose of the study, therefore, is to investigate how politeness is conceptualised by Americans and Japanese.

"Politeness" itself is a neutral concept, which we use as the label for a scale ranging from plus- through zero- to minus-politeness. Thus, "polite" refers to plus-valued politeness, "impolite" means minus-valued politeness, and "non-polite" marks the neutral or zero-valued center of the scale.[1]

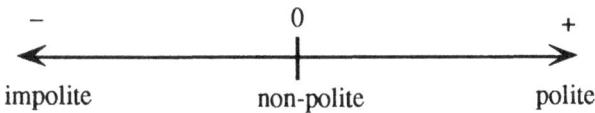

Figure 1. Scale of politeness.

As discussed by linguists, however, "politeness" usually refers to the positive end of the scale.[2] Lakoff (1989: 102), for instance, defines politeness "as a means of minimising the risk of confrontation in discourse." Fraser and Nolen (1981: 96) state that "to be polite is to abide by the rules of the relationship. The speaker becomes impolite just in cases where he violates one or more of the contractual terms." According to Brown (1980: 114), "What politeness essentially consists in is a special way of treating people, saying and doing things in such a way as to take into account the other person's feelings." What is common to these varying definitions is the idea of appropriate language use associated with smooth communication. This smooth communication is achieved "on the one hand through the speaker's use of intentional strategies to allow his utterances to be received favourably by the addressee and on the other by the speaker's expression of the expected and prescribed norms of speech" (Ide 1988: 371).

Concepts of politeness thus defined by researchers may be applicable to any possible culture. However, we cannot assume that the concept of "politeness" is fully equivalent to the concepts of corresponding terms in other languages, since language itself is the door to a concept in people's minds. Our assumption underlying this contrastive survey was that concepts of terms lie in the minds of native speakers. The focus of this study is to compare the American English concept of "polite" with the Japanese concept of the corresponding *teineina*.

Method

Knowing that multivariate analysis of quantitative data will yield correlations of items in visual form, we designed a survey which would allow us to plot the concepts of 'polite'/*teineina* relative to other concepts in English and Japanese which evaluate human behaviour.

American and Japanese versions of the questionnaire were prepared. In order to avoid the distortions of direct translation, comparable English and Japanese versions were developed through joint workshops by bilingual and bicultural members of the research group. After field testing, the two versions were further modified in order to achieve comparability.

Subjects were 219 American and 282 Japanese college students.[3] Each subject was given a grid containing descriptions of fourteen interactional situations and a list of ten adjectives evaluating human behaviour. The interactional situations consisted of behaviours or verbal behaviours in six kinds of speech acts: (1) rejection, (2) request, (3) compliance, (4) protest, (5) invitation and (6) apology. The situations were varied as much as possible to balance the questionnaire cross-culturally. Categories of situations were distributed as follows: (1) situations polite for both Americans and Japanese, (2) polite for Americans but non-polite for Japanese, (3) polite for Americans but impolite for Japanese, (4) non-polite for Americans but polite for Japanese, (5) non-polite for both Americans and Japanese, (6) non-polite for Americans but impolite for Japanese, (7) impolite for

Americans but polite for Japanese, (8) impolite for both Americans and Japanese.[4]

Subjects were asked to imagine themselves in each situation. Then they were asked whether each of the 10 adjectives would represent their own feelings if the words/action of the other person in the description had been directed toward them: YES/NO/NA ("can't say either positive or negative"). (See Appendix A for the full English version.)

	P?	R?	C?	F?	Pl?	C?	A?	O?	Co?	Ru?
3: Suppose you were an assistant professor. You made a critical comment on a student's term paper and asked him/her to rewrite a section. The student replied...										
(A) "I'm sorry. I do see your point. I'll give it another try.'	Yes	Yes	Yes	Yes	Yes	Yes	Yes	Yes	Yes	Yes
	No	No	No	No	No	No	No	No	No	No
	NA	NA	NA	NA	NA	NA	NA	NA	NA	NA
(B) "I see. I'll give it a try."	Yes	Yes	Yes	Yes	Yes	Yes	Yes	Yes	Yes	Yes
	No	No	No	No	No	No	No	No	No	No
	NA	NA	NA	NA	NA	NA	NA	NA	NA	NA

P?=polite?, R?=respectful?, C?=considerate?, F?=friendly?, Pl?=pleasant, C?=casual?, A?=appropriate?, O?=offensive?, Co?=conceited?, Ru?=rude?

Figure 2. Two sample situations from the questionnaire.

Results

Subjects' responses are diagrammed in Appendices B and C. Since both situations and adjectives were specifically selected for cross-cultural comparability, we may read the differences in responses between American and Japanese subjects as differences in their respective evaluations of speech acts in terms of the given adjectives.

Examining patterns of responses, we find that the Japanese show a greater average number of NA responses than do the Americans: 21.5% of Japanese responses vs. 9.9% of American. This difference is significant at the 0.01 level. Compared to the American subjects the Japanese appear to find it easier to choose the indecisive responses

(NA).[5] In the majority of cases, we also see a greater "yes" portion in the American responses. Further, the Americans show near-unanimous agreement across some interactional situations like 2A, 2C, 4C, 5A, 5C and 6A, while the Japanese show greater complexity in the evaluation of these behaviours.

Multivariate analysis was applied to the data in the following process: (1) 10 adjectives with affirmative answers and 10 adjectives with negative answers were arranged making a list of 20 adjectives. (2) A crosstable of 20 adjectives and 14 interactional situations was made. (3) Using a method of quantification of the crosstable, correlations between adjectives and situations were computed. (4) These correlations were converted into relative locations in a two-dimensional Euclidian space, yielding Figures 3a/b and 4a/b (p. 285–288).

The analysis plots the degree of similarity of the ten adjectives as calculated from response data. In the figures, we may compare the position of the two key terms, "polite" and *teineina* relative to the other nine terms in the respective languages. The individual correlations appear at the tops of the figures.

The cumulative variance for each axis is as follows:

Horizontal (first) axis: Japanese 0.755   Americans 0.923
Vertical (second) axis: Japanese 0.134   Americans 0.033

The closer the number is to 1.0, the more the data are to be read as being accounted for by that axis. In the Japanese case, we see 75.5 percent of the data are explained by the first axis, while in the American case, it is 92.3 percent. Looking at the second axis, we find some explanatory meaning (13.4 percent) in the Japanese case, but almost none (3.3 percent) in the American case. In other words, the American case is clearly one-dimensional, while the Japanese case is more or less two-dimensional .

Now we may turn to the question of the "meaning" of the axes. The numbers (1–9) and letters (A–K) in Figure 3a/b correspond to those of Figure 4a/b. The circles represent "yes" responses and the triangles "no"s. The lines drawn between "yes"s and "no"s show the dimension of the concepts. In both the Japanese and the American cases, we may interpret the left half of the horizontal axis as meaning "good" and the right half as "bad". The meaning of the second, vertical dimension evi-

Code	Sym	Name	Total	1	2	3	4	5
11	1	Polite-yes	2052	-0.437	0.040	-0.035	-0.008	-0.0(
12	2	Polite-no	667	1.304	-0.096	0.084	0.010	-0.09
21	3	Respectful-yes	1744	-0.442	-0.011	-0.063	0.010	0.0(
22	4	Respectful-no	714	1.243	0.038	0.093	-0.003	-0.02
31	5	Considerate-yes	1990	-0.413	0.030	-0.028	0.004	-0.0(
32	6	Considerate-no	677	1.200	-0.005	0.087	0.069	-0.01
41	7	Friendly-yes	1864	-0.364	0.168	0.052	-0.004	-0.02
42	8	Friendly-no	443	1.095	-0.296	-0.089	-0.104	-0.0(
51	9	Pleasant-yes	1843	-0.435	0.113	-0.016	-0.037	-0.08
52	A	Pleasant-no	730	1.119	-0.172	0.029	0.036	0.0:
61	B	Casual-yes	1969	-0.018	-0.001	0.161	-0.075	0.0(
62	C	Casual-no	543	0.252	-0.030	-0.422	0.180	-0.0(
71	D	Appropriate-yes	2104	-0.322	-0.136	-0.027	-0.006	0.04
72	E	Appropriate-no	647	1.024	0.336	0.080	0.103	0.0(
81	F	Offensive-yes	468	1.240	0.231	-0.118	0.003	0.1(
82	G	Offensive-no	2349	-0.259	-0.080	0.018	0.012	0.0(
91	H	Conceited-yes	306	1.167	0.215	-0.449	-0.327	0.09
92	I	Conceited-no	2375	-0.188	-0.044	0.047	0.022	0.01
101	J	Rude-yes	487	1.291	0.074	-0.026	-0.002	-0.0:
102	K	Rude-no	2339	-0.280	-0.045	0.004	0.013	0.04

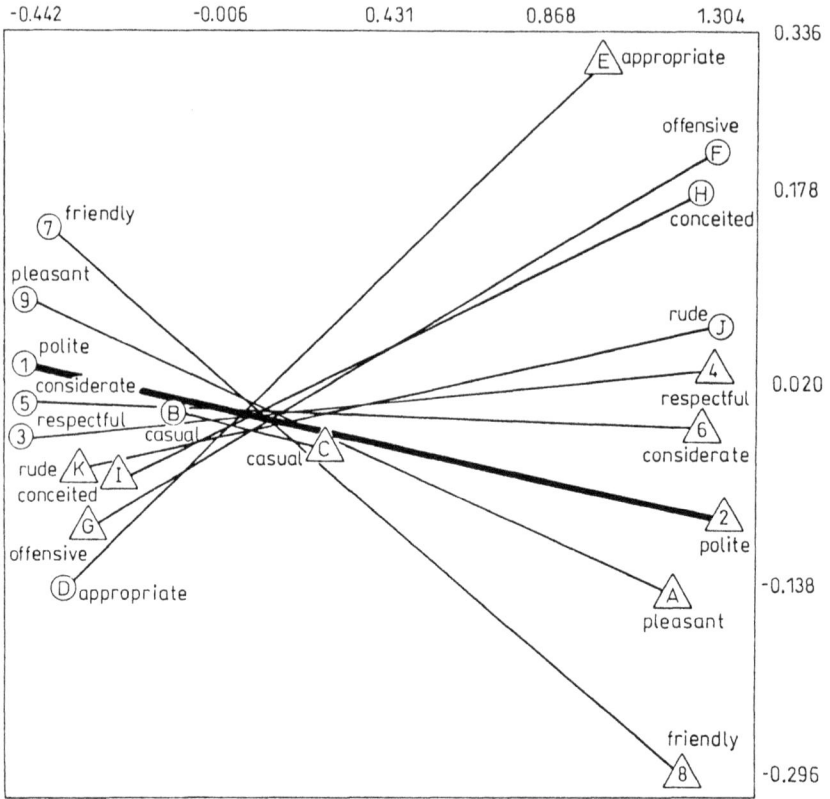

Figure 3b. Multivariate analysis of adjectives – American English

Code	Sym	Name	Total	1	2	3	4	5
11	1	Teineina-hai	2035	-0.508	-0.144	0.064	0.062	0.027
12	2	Teineina-iie	1092	0.930	0.112	-0.063	-0.060	-0.201
21	3	Keii no aru-hai	1598	-0.566	-0.170	0.134	-0.033	0.054
22	4	Keii no aru-iie	1307	0.794	0.087	-0.088	0.080	-0.085
31	5	Omoiyari no aru-hai	1544	-0.522	0.215	0.185	0.225	-0.132
32	6	Omoiyari no aru-iie	1105	0.720	-0.101	-0.117	-0.021	0.113
41	7	Sitasigena-hai	1753	0.107	0.611	0.004	-0.030	0.095
42	8	Sitasigena-iie	1288	-0.028	-0.567	-0.061	-0.031	-0.042
51	9	Kanzi yoi-hai	2030	-0.504	0.064	0.093	-0.050	0.004
52	A	Kanzi zoi-iie	1078	0.871	-0.120	-0.093	0.097	0.027
61	B	Kidoranai-hai	2281	-0.057	0.130	-0.049	-0.100	0.030
62	C	Kidoranai-iie	733	0.267	-0.187	0.091	0.059	-0.013
71	D	Tekisetuna-hai	2093	-0.318	-0.118	-0.125	0.049	0.019
72	E	Tekisetuna-iie	842	0.766	0.011	0.165	-0.068	-0.047
81	F	Kanzyou wo kizutukea-hai	408	0.963	-0.078	0.041	0.347	0.362
82	G	Kanzyou wo kizutukea-iie	2904	-0.171	0.013	-0.034	-0.065	-0.048
91	H	Unuborete iru-hai	504	1.060	-0.266	0.529	-0.256	0.074
92	I	Unuborete iru-iie	2819	-0.205	0.011	-0.106	0.001	-0.008
101	J	Bureina-hai	529	1.225	0.128	0.206	0.097	-0.025

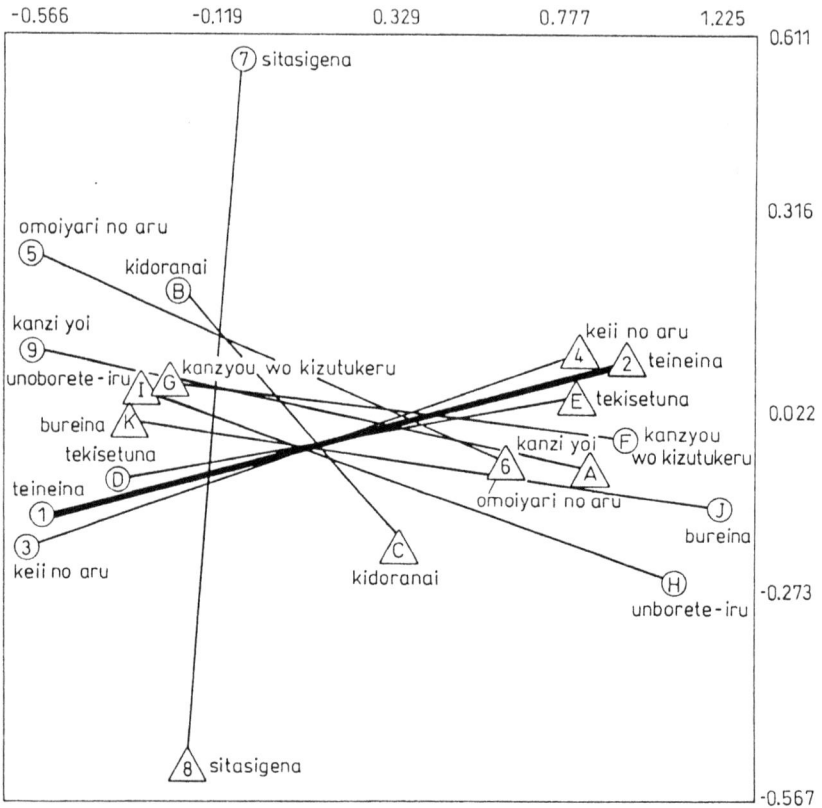

Figure 4b. Multivariate analysis of adjectives – Japanese

dent in the Japanese responses can be characterised as "friendly" (upper half) and "non-friendly" (lower half).

This means that Americans exhibit unilateral judgement of various concepts of evaluation while the Japanese judge in terms of two dimensions. The relationship of the "good" axis and the "friendly" axis seen in the Japanese conceptualisation is that of discrete, but not opposing concepts. We conclude that the Japanese have an evaluation scale with at least two levels, which are not contradictory but co-exist in their minds.

This discrete but non-opposing structure of concepts of evaluation must represent Japanese patterns of behaviour, as indeed we read in an anthropologist's description of characteristics of the Japanese ethos. Lebra (1976: 8) states that "the Japanese ethos has more affinity with interactional relativism than with unilateral determinism, whereas traditional Western culture comes closer to the latter than the former." According to Lebra unilateral determinism seems to entail epistemological and ideological compulsions to differentiate or separate one element from another, such as "good" from "bad". Interactional relativism by contrast, tends to suppress such distinctions and tends to connect things that appear as discrete but not opposing concepts like *teineina* and *sitasigena*. The relation of concepts in unilateral determinism is differentiation and separation whereas that of interactional relativism is interlocking and fusion. In Figure 3a/b, "polite" and "friendly" are mapped together as "good" concepts separate from minus "polite" and minus "friendly", which are "bad" concepts. On the other hand, in Figure 4a/b *teineina* and *sitasigena* are mapped as discrete concepts but do not stand in a plus/minus relation.

Quantitative evidence for the closeness of the adjectives was obtained by computing correlation coefficients of adjectives with the key terms "polite/*teineina*".[6] Table 1 (p. 290) shows adjectives arranged according to the rank order of the correlation coefficients in each language.

Examining the relative positions of adjectives in the Japanese data in Figure 4a/b, we find that *sitasigena* (corresponding to "friendly") is in a different dimension relative to the key term *teineina* (the corresponding term to "polite"), while in the American data in Figure 3a/b "polite" and "friendly" are found on neighbouring places along the same dimension. This outstanding difference in the two figures is confirmed by the difference in the relevant correlation coefficients: -0.3213 for *teineina – sitasigena*, but + 0. 9103 for "polite–friendly".

Table 1 quantitatively demonstrates the two-dimensionality of the Japanese data compared to the American (the lines connect the corresponding English and Japanese terms).

Table 1.   Rank orders of correlation coefficients of "polite"/"teineina" to adjectives in their respective languages.

Americans		Japanese	
	POLITE		TEINEINA
respectful	0.9892 ——————	keii no aru	0.9697
considerate	0.9868	kanzi yoi	0.9108
pleasant	0.9713	tekisetuna	0.8544
friendly	0.9103	omoiyari no aru	0.7496
appropriate	0.8826	kidoranai	0.2816
casual	0.1204		
		sitasigena	-0.3213
conceited	-0.7995 ——————	unuborete-iru	-0.6848
offensive	-0.9189 ——————	kanzyou wo kizutukeru	-0.7078
rude	-0.9545 ——————	bureina	-0.7880

The "respectful"/*keiinoaru* pair ranks first in degree of correlation with the key terms "polite"/*teineina*. To this extent, the Japanese and American concepts of politeness are similar. But out of the second and third highly correlating terms ("considerate" and "pleasant" vs. *kanziyoi* and *tekisetuna*), "pleasant" and *kanziyoi* are corresponding adjectives, but "considerate" and *tekisetuna* are not. This disparity may be taken as marking another important difference between the Japanese and American concepts.

Tekisetuna is the adjective used in Japanese to evaluate behaviour in the light of worldly criteria, i.e., *wakimae* (discernment), which is the key concept of linguistic politeness in Japanese (see Hill et al. 1986 and Ide 1989). In other words, whether one observes *wakimae* or not is evaluated in terms of *tekisetuna*. On the other hand, "considerate", which lies very close to the key English term "polite" (correlation coefficient 0.9868), is used to evaluate behaviour which is careful not to hurt or inconvenience others,[7] or has regard for another's feelings, circumstances, etc.[8] In other words, considerate behaviour depends upon an actor's volition rather than upon discernment. From these differences of neighbouring adjectives we may infer that *teineina* is oriented to *wakimae*/discernment, while "polite" is oriented to volition. As discussed in Hill et al. (1986), the concept of "volition" is one of the two major aspects of linguistic politeness prevalent in the West, the other being *wakimae*.

Implications for linguistic politeness

The major finding obtained from this study is the cross-cultural difference between the relation of "polite" to "friendly" on the one hand and of *teineina* to *sitasigena* on the other: i.e., "polite" and "friendly" pattern in the same dimension while *teineina* and *sitasigena* fall into different dimensions. This difference may help to explain some of the questions underlying studies of linguistic politeness of Japanese and Americans.

1. *The choice of TLN vs. FN by Americans and Japanese*

TLN (title plus last name) and FN (first name) in English are distinct linguistic forms used for address. TLN is the formal and polite form to be used to convey a polite or formal attitude of the speaker, whereas FN is the informal and casual form which conveys a friendly attitude of the speaker. In a culture like that of the U.S., where "polite" and "friendly" are perceived as more or less similar concepts, it is easy for speakers to switch from TLN to FN. FN, which conveys a friendly attitude, can be used without great offense to address a person to whom a polite or respectful attitude is expected. However, in Japanese culture, polite and friendly are discrete concepts. Therefore, a Japanese who can speak English tends to keep a distinction between a polite form TLN and a friendly form FN, in accordance with the Japanese concepts *teineina* and *sitasigena*. For such a person, learning to use FN like an American means learning the American conceptual structure of "polite" and "friendly".

2. *Co-occurrence of* teineina *and* sitasigena

Identifying the discrete relation between *teineina* and *sitasigena* might lead us to conclude that these two concepts never co-occur. However, the fact is that they do co-occur, because they are not in a contradictory relation, as are "polite" and "impolite", but simply in different dimensions.

It is a general rule that the use of honorifics maintains the distance of the speaker toward the addressee or the referent, while the use of sentence final particles shortens the distance. Thus, honorifics and sentence final particles are supposed to function in a reverse way in terms of distance of interlocutors.

However, we sometimes observe that these two do co-occur. Note the example sentence below. This is an utterance by a woman of the educated class to another educated woman in the neighbourhood.

> *Doko   ni irrasyai   masu   no*
> where   to go REF HON   ADD HON   SFP
> 'Where do you go?'

In this utterance, the speaker's sense of distance towards the addressee is expressed by referent (REF) and addressee (ADD) honorifics (HON) together with a sense of beautification, which is derived from the distance created by polite forms, i.e., honorifics. At the same time, the speaker's sense of friendly attitude is expressed by the sentence final particle (SFP) *no*. In terms of the function of distance, the co-occurrence of honorifics and a sentence final particle, as seen in the example sentence, may look contradictory. Instead, for smooth interaction, even in a *sitasii* (friendly/intimate)[9] context where a sentence final particle is appropriate to mark the short distance between interlocutors, it is generally expected that one will practice occasional use of honorifics. This use of honorifics to imply politeness in a friendly relationship is appreciated among Japanese to the extent that we have the saying "There is a courtesy in '*sitasii* terms'." This represents the spirit of interlocking and fusion of two discrete concepts, *teineina* and *sitasigena*, as we see in Lebra's description of Japanese ethos.

Conclusion

Using native-speaker judgments, we have demonstrated that among groups of American English and Japanese speakers, the seemingly corresponding terms "polite" and *teineina* differ in their conceptual structure. For the American subjects, the adjectives "polite" and "friendly" correlate highly when applied to certain behaviours in specific situations. For Japanese subjects, however, *teineina* and *sitasigena* fall into different dimensions when applied to the same cross-culturally equivalent situations. This finding supports our general thesis that studies of cross-cultural politeness cannot assume equivalence of key concepts, but must identify structural patterns of similarities and differences.

Notes

1. We avoid the more natural terms "positive politeness" and "negative politeness" because these have already been employed by Brown and Levinson (1978) for different purposes.
2. The conceptualisation of politeness is coloured by its adjectival form "polite", since "politeness" is derived from the adjective form. "Politeness" is – or should logically be – neutral concerning the degree of being "polite", just as "height" is neutral concerning the degree of being "high". It is in adjective forms like "high" and "polite" that we attach a positive value to the neutral concept.
3. American subjects were male and female undergraduates at George Washington University. Japanese subjects were male and female undergraduates at Nagoya University and Tsukuba University.
4. A potential ninth category "impolite for Americans but nonpolite for Japanese" is omitted because we could imagine no such examples suitable to the framework of our study.
5. In any survey of questionnaires given to Japanese we tend to receive a good portion of undecided responses. This may be a general characteristic of response patterns among Japanese. In reviewing Rorschach-test results, de Vos and Bordens (1989: 151) note that Japanese subjects were more likely than American subjects to give no response "when they were unable to give that they believed to be a satisfactory response." They attribute this to a strong drive for intellectual organisation among Japanese subjects, as manifested in their preference for "a single well-integrated response".
6. The numbers were computed based on the correlation with "polite"/*teineina* of "yes" and "no" responses for each pair of adjectives. The closer a number is to 1.00, the closer the relation of an adjective to "polite" or *teineina*.
7. *Oxford advanced learner's dictionary.* New edition. (Oxford University Press, 1989).

8. *The Random House dictionary of the English language.* (New York: Random House, 1968).
9. *Sitasigena* was chosen for the purpose of the questionnaire, as an adjective corresponding to friendly, because it is the form describing the mood of someone else's behaviour rather than the subjective mood of the speaker. *Sitasii*, instead, is the form representing the speaker's subjective psychological feeling.

Appendix A: English version of the questionnaire

I am a sociology graduate at the George Washington University, Washington, D.C. I am helping a group of Japanese and American sociolinguists in their cross-cultural survey of the "image of politeness". The purpose of the survey is to understand how people interpret the behavior of others in a given situation and how the "image of politeness" is structured in different societies.

We believe that by identifying the differences and similarities in the pattern of "image of politeness," we will be able to minimize possible misunderstanding between the people of different countries, and thus to contribute to better cross-cultural communication.

Your contribution to this end is a valuable one. We appreciate your helping us by filling out the attached survey form, which will not take you more than fifteen minutes. Thank you very much.

* * * * * * * *

I. Please provide the following information about yourself.
a. Gender:_____ b. Age: _____
c. Place where you lived longest: _____
d. Student status: (Please circle an appropriate number.)
1. Freshman 2. Sophomore 3. Junior 4. Senior

II. INSTRUCTIONS:

Listed below are (1) interactional situations you may encounter; (2) some examples of what a person might do or say to you in a given situation; and (3) adjectives which you might use to describe the conduct/verbal expression of the person. Please read them carefully. Then, circle the appropriate answer for each of the adjectives based on HOW YOU MIGHT INTERPRET THE DESCRIBED BEHAVIOR HAD IT BEEN DIRECTED TOWARD YOU.

The answer category, "NA" stands for "Can't tell either Yes or No."

Interactions:

1: You and your close friend planned to go to see a movie one evening. That morning, your friend called you and postponed the date because...

    (A)   he/she was asked out for dinner by his/her boyfriend/girl-friend.

    (B)   something urgent had turned up.

2: You were at the laundromat on a busy evening. One of the machines being used by a student stopped working. The student walked up to you and...

    (A)   asked you to let him/her borrow your pen to write a note of warning for other customers.

    (B)   said to you, "Got a pen I can use?"

    (C)   said to you, "Excuse me. Do you have a pen I could use for a minute?"

3: Suppose you were an assistant professor. You made a critical comment on a student's term paper and asked him/her to rewrite a section. The student replied...

    (A)   "I'm sorry. I do see your point. I'll give it another try."

    (B)   "I see. I'll give it another try."

4: Again, suppose you were an assistant professor. You gave a student a C on a term paper. The student came to you and...

    (A)   asked the reason why the paper was a C.

    (B)   said to you, "What's wrong with this term paper? You only gave it a C. I worked hard and it should get at least a B."

    (C)   said to you, "I'd like to ask you about my term paper. The C was a little disappointing after all the care I gave it. I wonder if you could show me where I went wrong."

5: Your male friend has just gotten married.

    (A)   He invited you and your friend for dinner to meet his wife.

    (B)   He said, "My wife can't cook very well, nor is she a good housekeeper. But I do hope you and your friend will come to dinner next Saturday."

    (C)   He said, "My wife loves to cook. We'll both enjoy having you and your friend for dinner next Saturday."

6: You were late for your appointment by fifteen minutes. You apologized to your friend upon your arrival.

    (A)   Your friend responded, even though he/she was there on time, "Don't worry. I've just gotten here too."

Appendix B: American subjects' choice of adjectives for interactional situations

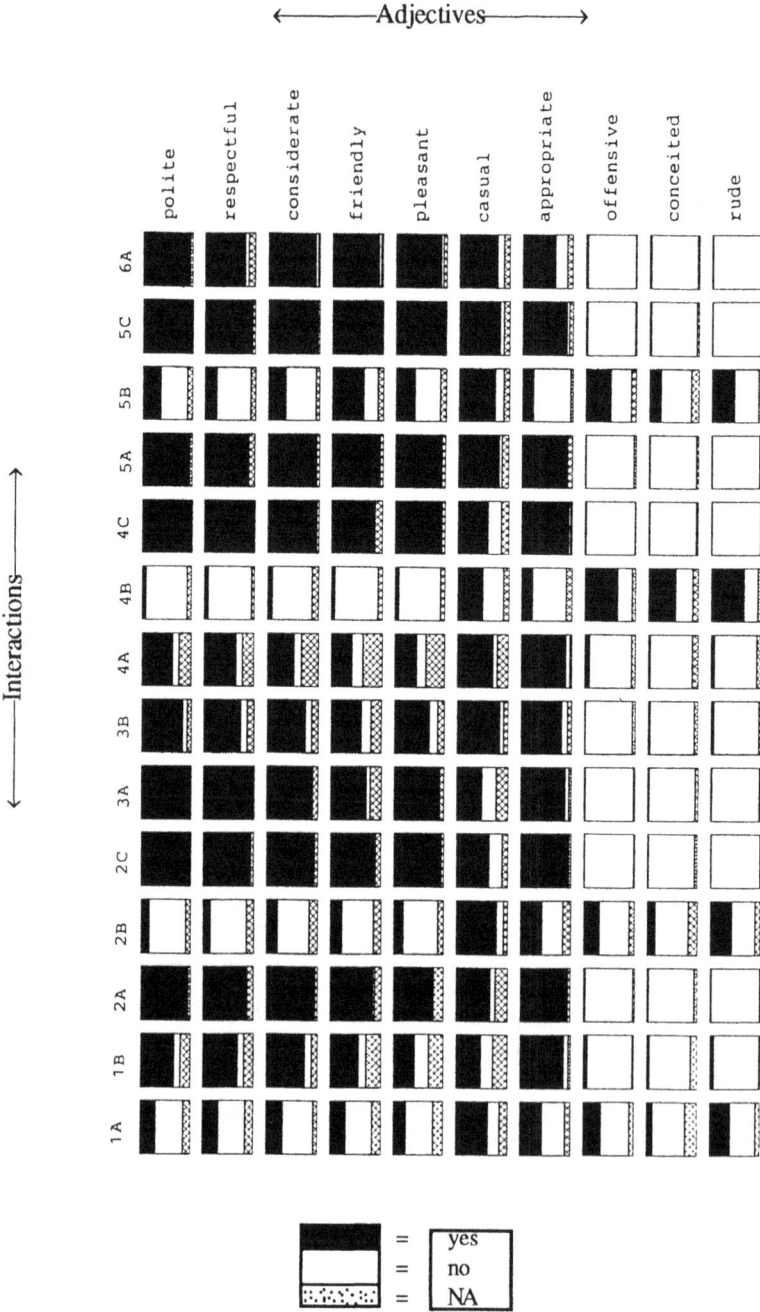

← ———— Adjectives ———— →

polite · respectful · considerate · friendly · pleasant · casual · appropriate · offensive · conceited · rude

Interactions: 6A, 5C, 5B, 5A, 4C, 4B, 4A, 3B, 3A, 2C, 2B, 2A, 1B, 1A

■ = yes
□ = no
▨ = NA

Appendix C: Japanese subjects' choice of adjectives for interactional situations

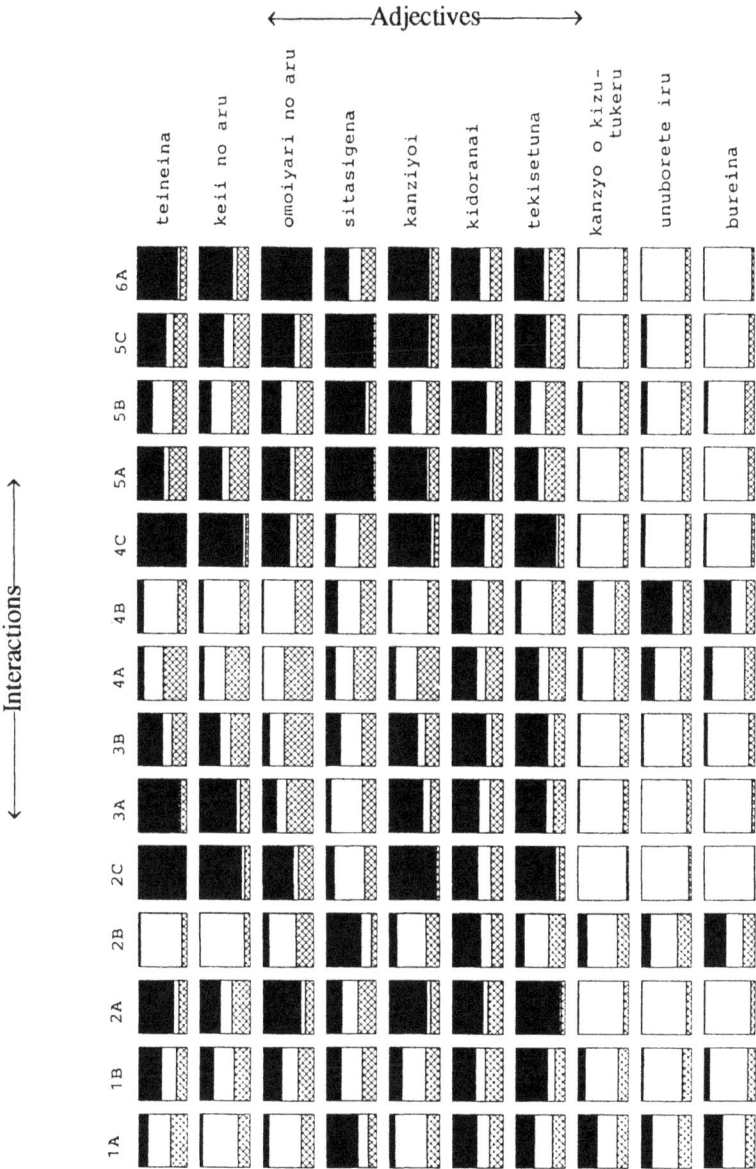

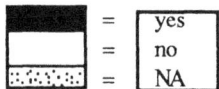

12. Linguistic etiquette in Japanese society

Florian Coulmas

Prologue: A story of language and violence

On May 30, 1975, Mr. Tanaka and Mr. Yamada, two young employees, went to a bar as they often did after a long work-day. They were colleagues. A couple of hours later, Mr. Yamada was dead.

What had happened? On the way home, under the influence of the alcohol consumed in the bar, Mr. Yamada had called his colleague *Tanaka-kun*. This made Mr. Tanaka so angry that he hit Mr. Yamada's head against the wall of the railway station where they were waiting for the train, causing him fatal injuries. This at least was Mr. Tanaka's explanation of the accident.[1]

One of several suffixes, *-kun* is used among male students or when addressing, or talking about, an inferior male person. Mr. Yamada had entered the company earlier than Mr. Tanaka, but the latter was three years older than the former. The social relationship between the two was, therefore, of a kind where the correct choice of term of address is a potentially sensitive issue. In any event, Mr. Yamada was in no position to call his colleague *Tanaka-kun*.

Obviously, not every incorrect use of a term of address or honorific forms has such catastrophic effects. To be sure, this is a very unhappy and extreme example, but it shows that Japanese linguistic etiquette is an affair with some consequence. The two speakers knew each other well, worked for the same company, were on friendly terms and separated by only three years. Yet, inappropriate speech which did not even involve any rough language was instrumental in making the addressee lose control.

Objectives

Honorific language use in Japanese is a well-researched area both of Japanese linguistics and sociolinguistics in general. To those familiar with this research the present paper offers little that is really new.

However, most of the pertinent works are not accessible to the reader with no knowledge of Japanese. My purpose here is, therefore, a modest one, but it may nonetheless be worth pursuing in the context of the present book. If I succeed in explaining to the non-specialist the basics of how Japanese honorifics work and, maybe, add some observations that strike the outside observer, I will have achieved my objective. For a better understanding of the important role honorific speech plays in Japanese society a brief look at the literature may also be useful.

Japanese literature on honorifics

The many Japanese publications about honorific speech fall into three categories. First, there is a considerable amount of solid sociolinguistic research, the most important of which grew out of Japan's long tradition in dialectology. Mention should be made in particular of the outstanding work of Nomoto and his associates at the National Language Research Institute (NLRI), which consists largely of long-term surveys of honorific-language use in various parts of the speech community, some ranging over two to three decades. As far as I know, long term studies of this kind are not available for any other language. The NLRI has also carried out contrastive studies on linguistic etiquette, especially on Japanese and German (Sugito 1987). These various research activities are succinctly summarised in Minami's excellent 1987 book. A recent account of some of this work in English is Egawa et al. (1986), cf. also Neustupný (1972), Peng (1975).

Another strand of sociolinguistic research developed under the influence of US-American paradigms. In this connection much attention has been paid to gender differences in language use, an important aspect of proper usage long recognised in traditional scholarship (cf. Ide 1979; Ide et al. 1986; Jugaku 1979). It is a peculiar and somewhat unfortunate feature of these two schools of thought – the "traditionalists" and the "American disciples" – that they take very little notice of each other.[2]

Secondly, there are a number of publications which fall into the category of what might be called auto-exotism, stressing as they do the peculiarity and uniqueness of the Japanese and the Japanese language.

The influential Japanologist Kindaichi gives expression to this attitude with characteristic candor: "Japanese has a unique position among the languages of civilised countries. That is to say, there is absolutely no other language of a similar kind" (Kindaichi 1957: 10).[3] Similarly, Toyama observes: "The honorific system the Japanese language has developed is so fine as cannot be found in the language of any other country" (Toyama 1978: 6). The interest that some Japanese scholars take in their own race, language, and culture on the basis of this presupposition has developed into a new brand of ideologically informed scholarship known as *Nihonjinron* 'theory of Japaneseness'. While it contributes little to real knowledge, it is an interesting object of social and sociolinguistic study in itself, because it encapsulates popular beliefs and attitudes. Miller (1982) offers a critical, if sometimes overstated, account of the mystifying attitude some Japanese scholars hold towards their language, and Mourer and Sugimoto (1986) is an excellent study of the significance of the ideologeme of uniqueness in Japanese society, past and present, and how it is unwarranted. The leading dialectologist of Japanese, W. A. Grootaers, has tirelessly attacked the prejudice of the incomparability of the Japanese language as being founded in ignorance (e.g., Grootaers 1982), and Neustupný (1974) puts the system of Japanese honorifics into perspective with other similar systems.

Thirdly, there are numerous publications dealing with honorific speech in a normative manner. These publications are sometimes dismissed as falling outside the domain of proper linguistic scholarship; however, such a lofty attitude can hardly do justice to them. Two points should be noted in this connection: (1) there is a long-standing tradition of language cultivation in Japan which has always been supported by language experts who have never been affected by the modern Western credo that linguists should discover rather than stipulate norms, and who believe that language is both a natural asset and a deliberately created instrument. This tradition is associated with the notion *gengo seikatsu* 'the life of language' (Haga 1988).[4] (2) Many of the present-day authors in this field are highly qualified academics who exercise an influence on the development of the language, however indirectly, through their writings or through their advice to various government institutions such as the Ministry of Education (Monbusho) or the Agency of Cultural Affairs (Bunkacho). Language guidance and the normative attitude towards linguistic usage are integral parts of the sociolinguistic landscape of Japan which should thus be taken into account in a treatment of linguistic etiquette in Japanese society (see below).

Honorific speech and Japanese society

Like Javanese, Madurese, Korean, Thai, and many other Asian languages, Japanese is a language in which social meaning is codified in an intricate manner by morphological means largely reserved for this purpose rather than grammatical forms serving other functions (Neustupný 1974). The system of Japanese honorifics is elaborate and not easy to master. As indicated by the above example, it is an object of considerable concern to many members of the speech community, and for those trying to become proficient in the language it is one of the biggest stumbling blocks. An opinion poll of the Japanese national broadcasting station NHK reveals that as many as 75% of the Japanese wish to improve their command of the language. The only thing which the Japanese are more concerned about is their health.

It should be noted that honorific expressions in Japanese are not stylistic frills which, for the sake of efficiency or any other reason, could easily be left out. Many aspects of honorific speech are encoded in the grammar and would be hard to avoid. Except for dialects, the only variety of Japanese where honorifics are left out or systematically distorted, therefore, is foreigner talk and Japanese spoken by not very advanced learners. The following quote from a documentary account of the misery brought about by the bombing of Hiroshima illustrates that proper honorifics are second nature to the speakers, which is not even shed off under extreme pressure: "From every second or third house came the voices of people buried and abandoned, who invariably screamed, with formal politeness, *Tasukete kure!* 'Help if you please!'" (Hersey 1946: 46).

A more recent example of a similar kind involves the catastrophic accident of a Japan Airlines jumbo jet which crashed into Mt. Ogura in August 1985 killing 520 passengers and crew members. The transcripts of the last words of the desperate crew who were struggling to keep the damaged plane aloft exhibit appropriate honorifics. The entire transcript covers 32 minutes of conversation between the pilot (CAP), the co-pilot (COP), the flight engineer (FE), the purser (PUR), and a stewardess (STW). All the speakers are aware that there is an emergency. What follows are a few excerpts only. Honorific forms are romanised. A structural analysis of these forms is provided below (p. 304f). The transcript was published (in Japanese letters) in the daily *Asahi shinbun*, August 28, 1985, p. 22.

Interphone
STW: *sutichi-o oshite iru* kata-*ga* irassharun desu *ga, yoroshii*
    'A passenger is pressing the call button, would it be all
    desh*ōka*
    right [to attend to him]?'
CAP: *ki-o tsukete tebayaku, ja, ki-o tsukete* o-*negai shi*masu
    'Be careful and do it quickly, well, please be careful.'
STW: *hai, arigatō* gozaimashita
    'Yes, thank you.'

Cabin Announcement
STW: ...o-*kyaku*sama-*ni* o-*negai* itashimasu o-*kosama tsure no*
    'This is a request to all passengers. Passengers with
    o-*kyaku*sama *dōzo chikaku no kata osore irimasu ga*
    children, and will those sitting close by kindly excuse,
    o-*kosama...yōi-o* o-*negai shi*masu.
    please prepare for the children's ...'

Conversation in the cockpit
FE: *orutānēto ichi ni setto shi*mash*ōka*
    'Shall I set [the flaps] on the alternate position?'
CAP: *hai, chotto matte...*
    'Yes, wait a second ..'
(...)
CAP: *oi yama da zo motto okose kontorōru tore migi*
    'Look, a mountain! Pull 'er up more! Take the controls, right
CAP: *raitotān, okose, yama no butsukaru zo*
    turn right, pull 'er up, we're going to crash into the mountain.'
COP: *hai*
    'Yes.'
CAP: *makkupawā*
    'Maximum power ..'
COP: *makkupawā*
    'Maximum power ..'
(...)
CAP: *migi, migi, atama sagero*
    'Right, right, bring the nose down!'
COP: *zenzen kiki*masen
    'It doesn't work at all.'
CAP: *atama sagero*
    'Bring the nose down!'
COP: *yōshi*

'Yo-ho!'
CAP: *iku zo*
'Let's go!'
FE: *fukashi*mashōka
'Shall we race the engines?'
CAP: *pawā pawā*
'Power, power!'
COP: *hai*
'Yes.'
CAP: *fukashi*mashō, *fukashi*mashō
'Let's race the engines, let's race the engines!'
COP: *supiido dete*masu
'We are gathering speed.'
CAP: ...*ganbare*
'Hold out!'
COP: *hai*
'Yes.'
CAP: *atama sagero, ganbare, ganbare*
'Bring the nose down, hold out, hold out!'
COP: *kaji ippai* desu
'The rudder is fully out.'
FE: *supiido ga hette* imasu. *supiido ga... pawa-de supiido-o*
'We are losing speed. The speed... we are controlling the
*kontorōru shi*masu *ga ne. pawā kontōru-wa ii* desu *ka,*
speed with the power, okay? Is the power control all
pawā kontorōru-wa kyapputen
right? Captain, the power control ..'

CAP: *hai*
'Yes.'

If it is true at all that social relationships are reflected by honorific language use, then the above transcript furnishes one example. Notice that the pilot uses fewer honorifics than the other speakers. He occupies the highest rank in the hierarchy. The stewardess who is the lowest in the hierarchy and female uses honorifics most, both in the exchange with the pilot and in addressing the passengers. The flight engineer ranks lowest among the speakers in the cockpit and, accordingly, uses a polite style. What this example shows more than anything else is that in Japanese the use of honorifics is in some measure normal rather than being associated with special occasions or speakers.

In this connection it is also noteworthy that honorific speech is no matter of ideological controversy. Not even those who, like the communists, could be expected because of their political orientation to view honorific speech as a remnant of feudal society would ever try to rid their own speech of honorifics.

However, although the use of honorifics in Japanese comes, as it were, naturally, many Japanese feel that their mastery of language etiquette is imperfect.[5] Not surprisingly, many of those who deal professionally with the language cash in on this feeling of insecurity. The market is flooded with popular guide books on how to master or improve one's linguistic skills. There are also numerous "speech clinics" as well as radio and television programmes designed to help people improve their honorific speech. The language of politeness is big business for the publishing industry which produces new books on the topic regularly every spring when college graduates enter the work force. They sell by the tens of thousands. While this observation is more interesting, maybe, to the sociologist of language than to the student of linguistic politeness, it can be taken as a clear indication that the system of Japanese language etiquette requires conscious attention and training.

There is another reason, however, for the widespread insecurity about proper honorific speech. After World War II, the recognised conventions have undergone major changes reflecting changes in Japanese society. A recent book on the subject offers the following explanation: "When was it then, that the sense for linguistic politeness became so weak among modern people, especially the youths? While the exact time cannot be pinpointed, one might say, roughly, that deficiencies in honorific language came along with the democratic education after the war" (Sakazume 1985: 2). The author goes on to speculate that the confusion in honorific language use can be attributed to the diversification of values in post-war Japanese society. Lewin (1969) is more specific in his account of how the use of honorific language changed in Japan after the war, and what was at the bottom of the ensuing confusion. While honorifics used to be employed as markers of social rank and status, he explains, they were transformed into a means of indicating mutual respect in the wake of the democratisation of society. In many instances this meant that only the function changed, while the form remained the same.

That this should cause some disorientation is hardly surprising.[6] Somewhat simplistically it can be said that the change involved a shift in emphasis from using language to indicate one's position in the social hierarchy as well as that of the addressee to using language as a means of being considerate and obliging towards the other. This is not to say that social hierarchy has become unimportant in present-day Japan, but the various means of honorific speech are being used more for differentiating formality, respect and intimacy, and less for social discrimination. This process has been described as bringing about an increase in the use of polite forms (Watanabe 1977) which can be explained, again somewhat simplistically, by the fact that social discrimination had been replaced by treating the interlocutor as one's superior as the guiding principle of honorific usage (Kishitani 1969).

An important lesson that can be learned from the post-war changes in Japanese honorific usage is that it is extremely difficult to draw any direct conclusions from the linguistic means of expressing politeness to the social organisation of the speech community at a given time. Today, Japanese society is no less democratic than the capitalistic countries of Europe and North America. Yet, the linguistic system of courtesy which by many of its features betrays its origin in a highly stratified court society is largely intact. Language change cannot be assumed to be synchronous with, or even mono-causally determined by, social change, which is maybe yet another reason why a speech community can hardly be expected to sustain an intricate system of honorifics such as the Japanese without a certain measure of normative support.

Normative attitudes

As indicated above, correct language use is a matter of keen public interest in Japan, and those who are able to make informed judgments about it enjoy much more prestige than their colleagues in Western countries. There is not only wide agreement that questions of correctness can be decided, but also that this is desirable. Thus, notwithstanding its apparent openness to rapid inadvertent language change, the speech community can be said to possess a highly developed norm consciousness and the willingness to adhere to normative directives. This holds in particular for honorific usage.

A comparison of two normative documents concerning honorific language can help demonstrate the importance attributed to it by the Japanese speech community and the state.

First consider some excerpts from a decree entitled *Reihō-yōkō* 'The essential points of etiquette', which was issued by the Ministry of Education on April 1, 1941, when Japanese militarism was at its prime and Japan was the most powerful country in Asia. Some of the provisions of this decree clearly testify to the authoritarian attitude the representatives of the state at the time intended to inculcate in the public.

> *The essential points of etiquette*, a decree issued by the Ministry of Education 1941:
>
> #1. Proper honorific language is to be used to superiors.
> #2. Generally, the term for self-reference is *watakushi*. To superiors one may use family or first name. Men may also use *boku* when talking with equals, but not to superiors.
> #3. Terms of equal address must be appropriate with respect to rank. Equals can be addressed with *anata*; men may also use *kimi*.
> #4. Appropriate honorific language is required for referring to third persons. When conversing with a superior, honorific expressions referring to third persons can be omitted even if the person referred to is superior in rank to the speaker.
> #5. When talking to others about one's own relatives or other personal matters one must not use honorific words.
> #6. In response to a question or a summons one has to say *hai*, especially to superiors it is not good to say *ee*.
> #7. *To* superiors one should, whenever possible, use forms such as *gozaimasu, arimasu, mairimasu, itashimasu, zonjimasu, mō shimasu, itadakimasu. Desu, morau, kureru*, etc. must not be used to superiors.
> #8. As a general rule, o- and *go*- are to be prefixed to things of others and to be omitted when referring to one's own things.
> #9. The standard language shall be used as much as possible.

Five of the above nine clauses explicitly refer to the notion 'superior', and in another, #3, it is implicit. Clearly, recognition of social rank was the key to the prescribed honorific usage at the time, and the social universe was conceived first and foremost in terms of superiors and inferiors. It is of more than cursory interest that later deliberate measures were taken to revise what appears to be the basis of the system. Again this testifies to the general belief that deliberate intervention into language use both with respect to detail and basic principles is feasible.

To illustrate the kinds of revisions which were recommended and the questions for which advice was felt to be necessary, consider next some excerpts from a memorandum entitled *Kore kara no keigo* 'Honorific language from now on' (Monbushō 1954) which was officially released in 1952. Japan found itself in a very different position then. The American occupation had come to an end and the effects of various social and educational reforms were strongly felt. Japan was trying to become a peaceful and democratic country amenable to the USA. The purpose of this memorandum, as stated in the preface, was "to consider the most common problems of everyday language use to put together those speech forms which are advisable from now on."[7] It lists a number of general principles as well as specific provisions concerning basically the same topics as the 1941 decree, that is, self and other reference, terms of address, plural forms, honorific prefixes, conversational style, the description of actions, the combination of the copula *desu* with adjectives, salutations, language use in education, language use in the media, and language use concerning the Imperial Household.

The intended change in the social meaning of honorific language use is stated in one of the general principles:

> #2. To date, honorific language has developed primarily based on relations between upper and lower social ranks; however, from now on it shall be based on the principle of mutual consideration and fundamental respect for every individual.

Thus the idea was to transform what used to be an asymmetrical system into a symmetrical one where human dignity is given priority over social standing. How this affects linguistic usage is revealed by some of the specific provisions. Consider, for example, those provisions regulating self and other references:

I. Words for person reference
A. Self-reference
1. The standard form shall be *watashi*.
2. *Watakushi* is the term for formal occasions.
   Note: the female variants *atakushi, atashi* are also recognised, however, as a matter of principle, *watashi* and *watakushi* shall be the standard forms for both men and women.
3. *Boku* is used by male students, but care should be taken in their education that they change to using *watashi* upon entering society.
4. The use of *jibun* 'self' instead of *watashi* should be avoided.
B. Other-reference
1. The standard form shall be *anata*.
2. Instead of forms such as *kiden* ('you' to superiors) and *kika* ('you' to inferiors) which have been used so far, *anata* shall be used in both official and personal letters.
3. *Kimi* 'you' and *boku* 'I' shall be used in intimate relations only, while *watashi* and *anata* shall be the standard forms of common

usage. Accordingly, *watashi* and *anata* shall also be used instead of *ore* 'I' and *omae* 'you.'

As long as they were used, *kika* and *kiden* were considered respectful terms. The purpose of the reform intended by the memorandum, therefore, was not to replace non-honorific forms by honorific ones, but rather to eliminate asymmetrical terms testifying to social inequality. The easiest way to achieve this was to designate *wata(ku)shi* and *anata* as the desired standard forms. A similar tendency can be observed in the provisions for titles.

II. Titles
1. The standard form shall be *san*.
2. *Sama* is the form for formal occasions; it also occurs in fixed expressions, but it is to be used primarily for the addressee of a letter. It is advised that in future the term *dono* of official letters is also replaced by *sama*.
3. *Shi* is used in writing, and generally *san* is used in speech.
4. *Kun* is used among male students. It is also used to address relatively young people; however, as a matter of principle, *san* is used in conversations in public. Note: So-and-so-*kun* is a special term of address in the Diet.
5. *San* should not be attached (by speakers of either sex) to professional titles such as *sensei* 'professor,' *kyokuchō* 'chief of bureau', *kachō* 'section chief', *shachō* 'president' (of a company), *senmu* 'director', etc.

These regulations are quite specific. What is said about *kun* (4.) to some extent explains why using this term can be a delicate matter. Great care must be taken to avoid any apparent confusion between the factors of familiarity and rank which determine its symmetric and asymmetric use.

In the 1952 memorandum it was also felt necessary to eliminate asymmetric features from conversational style. One and the same style was recommended for all members of society.

V. Conversational style
From now on the basis of conversational talk shall be the *desu/masu* style.
Note: While this shall be the received basis of regular conversation between members of society, the use of other styles such as *dearimasu* for lectures, *gozaimasu* for formal occasions, as well as *da* for intimacy shall not be restricted.

More obviously than other clauses this one shows that the authors of the memorandum foresaw certain difficulties for the realisation of their recommendations. Although they favoured one particular style for regular use, they did not prescribe others, probably because such a prescription was considered both pointless and difficult to enforce.[8]

Finally, consider the provisions for language use at school. Although they concern language use rather than instruction, their significance in the present context is twofold: (1) The school is the most important social agent for perpetuating the honorific system of Japanese (Mizutani 1979: 168). (2) The fact that the school is needed for this purpose says something about the complexity of the system.

IX. Language use at school
1. Because female teachers from kindergarten through high school have a general tendency to overuse the (honorific prefix) *o-*, they should pay attention to this point.
2. It is desirable that in principle the *desu/masu* style is used between teacher and pupil.
    Note: This shall not impede use of the familiar *da*-style.
3. The honorific style of pre-war times which always made use of (exalting forms such as) *osshatta* 'said' and *o-...ni natta* 'did' when speaking to parents and teachers made the impression of excessive formality. However, the post-war style which, as a reaction against this, uses only (plain forms such as) *itta* 'said' and *naninani shita* 'did something' seems to go a little too far in the opposite direction. A middle course should be found, for example, (the respectful forms) *korareta* or *mieta* 'came' rather than (the plain form) *kita* 'came.'

From the above it should be obvious that the official norms for honorific language use were strongly affected by the social restructuring of Japan after the Pacific war, which betrays a belief in the relatedness of linguistic etiquette and social structure. Whether, or to what extent, the 1952 memorandum really had an effect on speech behaviour is not for me to judge. However, its normative potency is still recognised by several important language users such as the national broadcasting station and writers on the subject. For example, Sakazume evaluates the memorandum as follows: "To be sure, there is a great variety of conventions of honorific language which to learn one by one may be quite troublesome. However, mastering the fundamentals touched upon in this book and acquiring a firm sense of honorific language is not all that difficult. Many years have passed since the memorandum *Kore kara no keigo* was first promulgated in 1952, but most of its contents are still valid today" (Sakazume 1985: 197).

Nevertheless, there are reasons to doubt that the important shift from hierarchy to symmetry as the underlying principle of honorific language use intended by the memorandum has been absorbed fully by the speech community.[9] A quarter century after the said memorandum, the Japanologist Mizutani explains the basic principle of honorific language as follows: "We Japanese have a strong sense of the relative relationship to the listener, and honorific speech forms are based on whether the listener's position or social status is above or below oneself" (Mizutani 1979: 151). Accordingly, *meue* 'one's superior' and *meshita* 'one's inferior' (lit. *above and below one's eyes,* respectively) are still crucial notions for explaining the norms of proper honorific usage.[10]

Another factor determining the choice of honorific expressions which, if anything, has become more important as a result of the postwar changes is group membership. This can be understood as an extension of the division between self and other. The general principle is that reference to self and members of one's own group – i.e., family, school, company, etc. – is modest/humble when talking to others, whereas reference to others is respectful. This seems like a simple enough principle; however, as it interacts with the superior-inferior distinction, it implies different forms for the same referent depending on the perceived relationships between speaker, addressee, and third (i.e., talked-about) person. For example, in response to a customer's question concerning her boss, a secretary would refer to her superior by name only because she and he belong to the same group, while she could never address him by name.

Customer:	*Tanaka-san-wa*	*Pari*	*kara*	*kaette*	*irasshaimasuka*
	Mr. Tanaka-Topic	Paris	from	returned	is [+ respect] Q
Secretary:	*Tanaka-wa mada*		*kaette*	*orimasen.*	
	yet		returned	is not.	

Addressing someone by (first or last) name only indicates intimacy, while referring to someone by name only merely indicates group membership as well as the required awareness that honorifics are inappropriate when referring to in-group members toward outsiders.

These distinctions are neutral with regard to speaker's sex, but others are not. Indeed, gender is yet another factor which is traditionally recognised as part of the normative framework of honorific speech. Generally speaking, morphologically relatively polite expressions are considered appropriate for female speakers. Because of the relational nature of honorific speech such findings could be interpreted as evidence of the subservient position of women in Japanese society. Although this view can hardly be rejected offhand, one should not jump to conclusions. Rash inferences from linguistic observations to social facts can be avoided if, instead of saying that women are forced to be more polite, gender differences are taken to indicate that the same level of politeness is achieved by women on a higher level of linguistic formality than by men (cf. Ide et al. 1986). It should also be noted that gender differences in speech decrease both with social standing and with relative politeness. That is, differences between the speech of male and female speakers become less marked as you go up in the social hierarchy, on the one hand, and as the politeness level increases, on the other hand. Although there is no empirical evidence to support this claim, this seems to be true for all social classes.

In sum, there are three main parameters on which the norms for proper honorific speech are based. These are:

superior vs. inferior (i.e., relative status)
in-group vs. out-group (i.e., group membership)
male   vs. female (gender)

Usually, all of them have to be reckoned with at the same time. Training of honorific speech according to this normative framework begins at an early age in the family. However, the individual enters into many kinds of social relationships for the first time only after graduating from high school or college when he or she gets out into society.[11] This explains why deliberate instruction in honorific speech is considered necessary until a relatively advanced age. The school is the most important norm-enforcing agent, but not the only one. Special training sessions on honorific speech are quite common for new employees in banks, retail businesses and other branches of the private sector involving much customer contact, as well as the civil service. The following account of the systematic foundations of Japanese honorifics as it is presented in traditional textbooks may help explain why this should be necessary.

The basic model of the Japanese honorific system

Traditionally, the Japanese honorific system is taught as consisting of the trichotomy of *teineigo* (polite forms), *sonkeigo* (respectful or exalting forms), and *kenjōgo* (modest or humble forms), with *bikago* (beautifying or soft terms) sometimes subsumed under *teineigo* and sometimes treated as a separate, fourth category. A functional distinction between addressee and referent-related expressions cuts across this trichotomy as follows in Figure 1.

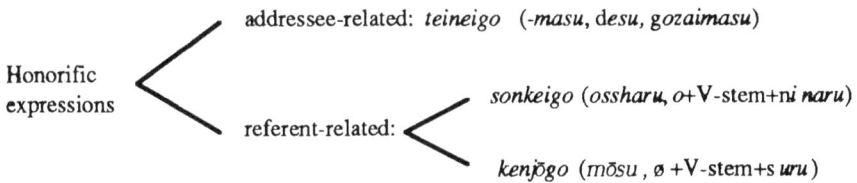

Honorific
expressions

addressee-related: *teineigo* (*-masu,* d*esu, gozaimasu*)

referent-related:

sonkeigo (*ossharu, o*+V-stem+n*i naru*)

kenjōgo (*mōsu ,* ø +V-stem+s *uru*)

Figure 1. *The basic model of the Japanese honorific system.*

Addressee-related expressions are used irrespective of the subject matter referred to and allow speakers to differentiate their speech on a scale of formality and familiarity, that is, to indicate the kind of relationship they wish to maintain with their interlocutors. This is done by choosing between a variety of styles, such as intimate, obliging, polite, and formal (written). The most important linguistic means are the copula verbs *da, desu,* and *dearu,* the verb *gozaru,* and the auxiliary *-masu.* A few examples in Table 1 may serve to illustrate this point:

Table 1. *Addressee-related differentiation of predicates.*

neutral	polite	meaning
Samui.	*Samui desu.*	'It is cold.'
Taberu.	*Tabemasu.*	'He eats.'
Are wa gijidō da.	*Are wa gijidō de gozaimasu.*	'That is the Diet building.'

Referent-related expressions, on the other hand, enable the speaker to refer to objects, events and actions in different ways. For instance, kinship terms are systematically paired to distinguish between the speaker's relatives and those of others he refers to. Similarly, except in frozen expressions, the prefixes *o-* and *go-* are used mostly to refer to things of others.

Lexical differentiation is also available for the verbal representation of a number of common actions such as eat, go, say, etc. For example, the same movement "go" can be described by the neutral verb *iku*, the exalting verb *irassharu*, or the humble verb *mairu*. This differentiation concerns the agent rather than the speech act's addressee, although both may of course be identical. Accordingly, the speaker's action is described using a humble verb, whereas an exalting verb is used whenever there is a reason to show respect to the agent, for example when s/he happens to be the addressee. This implies that humble verbs are never used with a second-person subject, and exalting verbs are never used with a first-person subject, a point which is of considerable functional importance because the subject position in Japanese sentences is more often than not left empty. Thus, rather than belonging to the stylistic domain only, these lexical distinctions have a grammatical function, indicating, as they do, who the agent of a given action is (cf. Coulmas 1980). Thanks to the in-group/out-group distinction both exalting and humble verbs can also occur with third-person subjects when the action of an in-group member is described (humble) to an outsider or an action is attributed to a member of the addressee's group (exalting). The basic tripartite pattern is illustrated for some common verbs in the Table 2.

Table 2. *Referent-related differentiation of predicates.*

neutral	exalting	humble	meaning
iu	*ossharu*	*mōsu*	'say'
iku	*irassharu*	*mairu*	'go'
kuru	*irassharu*	*mairu*	'come'
suru	*nasaru*	*itasu*	'do'
taberu	*meshiagaru*	*itadaku*	'eat'

Where no lexical differentiation is available, the same distinction can be made by means of morphological patterns. Thus the pattern *o*+verb stem+*ni naru* fulfils the same exalting function as lexicalised exalting verbs, and the corresponding pattern *o*+verb stem+*suru* fulfils the same function as lexicalised humble verbs. Both *naru* and *suru* are to be translated as 'do, make', although *naru* actually means 'become' and thus lends greater indirectness to the exalting expression in which it is used. An additional morphological strategy is using the passive form of the verb with non-passive meaning, which again makes the speech act more indirect. Accordingly, this is considered another exalting form. For verbs such as *kaku* 'to write' with no lexicalised exalting form and humble counterparts there are thus the following basic forms of referent-related differentiation: *kaku* (neutral), *kakareru* (exalting 1 [passive]), *o-kaki ni naru* (exalting 2), *o-kaki suru* (humble).

Referent-related differentiation and addressee-related differentiation are descriptive categories which in actual practice are, of course, always used together. Combining referent- and addressee-related differentiations we arrive at tables 3a and 3b for predicates differentiated through lexical and morphological means.

Tables 3a and 3b combine referent- and addressee-related predicate differentiation:

Table 3a. Referent-related differentiation lexicalised

		referent-related		
		neutral	exalting	humble
addressee-related	neutral	*iu*	*ossharu*	*mōsu*
	polite	*iimasu*	*osshaimasu*	*mōshimasu*

Table 3b. Referent-related differentiation through morphological means

		referent-related				meaning
		neutral	exalting 1	exalting 2	humble	
addressee-related	neutral	*kaku*	*kakareru*	*o-kaki ni naru*	*o-kaki suru*	'write'
	polite	*kakimasu*	*kakaremasu*	*o-kaki ni narimasu*	*o-kaki shimasu*	

Morphologically structured honorific forms can be constructed for all verbs, although they are not used with all verbs. For example, instead of the regularly structured exalting form *o-mi ni naru* of the verb *miru* 'to see', the supplemental form *go-ran ni naru* is used, which does not belong to the paradigm.

It should be emphasised that the types of honorific expressions distinguished so far constitute no more than the groundwork of the system. A great variety of combinations of these linguistic means are possible and actively exploited for subtle distinctions (cf. p. 317f below). Of special importance are a number of movement verbs and the verbs of giving and receiving which are used in combination with other verbs to mark aspect and the direction of an action, as well as to symbolically encode the relationship between agent and patient as being on an equal footing, or being characterised by a social gradient from higher to lower or from lower to higher. This conforms with the general patterns of lowering oneself and elevating the other.

When more than two speakers are involved in a conversation or where in addition to speaker and addressee others to whom speaker and/or addressee are socially related in one way or another are referred to, the correct choice of forms can be a tricky business. Therefore, usage often deviates from the norm.

Problems of usage

From the foregoing it should be clear that in Japanese three social factors are decisive to answer the by now classic question of sociolinguistics, "Who says what how under what circumstances to whom?" These factors are social rank, group membership, and gender. The following example (adapted from Yoshizawa 1981: 72ff.) illustrates some of the problems which may arise in reckoning with these factors because of the great variety of structurally determined choices.

Let us assume that the communicative task at hand is to convey the message that Mr. Katō should come to a conference room for a meeting, that the speaker is Mr. Tanaka's secretary and the addressee is Mr. Katō, who, like Mr. Tanaka, is a section chief of the company for which both of them work. In English this message might be phrased like this:

"Section chief Tanaka said you should please come to the conference room."
Holding the syntactic pattern invariant, this sentence still has a number of possible Japanese counterparts. The assumed pattern is as follows. The first part, which contains the subject of the matrix clause as well as a locative phrase which belongs to the embedded clause, will be the same throughout:

Tanaka kachō	*ga*	*kaigishitsu*	*ni*
Section chief T.	subj.	conference room	to

The five positions that follow express, in this order, (1) the movement "to come", (2) a desire to receive, that is, a request, (3) a quotative, (4) the act of saying and (5) the sentence closure by means of a finite copula or auxiliary verb. Positions 1, 2, 4, and 5 vary, thus yielding a set of possible choices some of which are listed below.

	'come' 1	'request 2	quot. 3	'say' 4	finite verb 5
(a)	*kite*	*kudasai*	*to*	*itte*	*(i)mashita*
(b)	*kite*	*itadakitai*	*to*	*itte*	*(i)mashita*
(c)	*kite*	*itadakitai*	*to*	*itte*	*oraremasu*
(d)	*kite*	*itadaku*	*yōni*	*onegai sarete*	*imasu*
(e)	*kite*	*itadakitai*	*to no koto*	*desu*	
(f)	*kite*	*hoshii*	*to*	*osshatte*	*(i)mashita*
(g)	*kite*	*hoshii*	*to*	*itte*	*(i)mashita*
(h)	*kuru*	*yōni*	*to*	*mōshite*	*orimashita*
(i)	*korareru*	*yōni*	*to*	*itte*	*orimashita*
(j)	*oide*	*itadakitai*	*to no koto*	*desu*	
(k)	*oide*	*itadakitai*	*to*	*mōshite*	*orimashita*
(l)	*oide*	*kudasai*	*to*	*mōshite*	*orimashita*
(m)	*irashite*	*itadakenai*	*deshōka*	*to no koto*	*deshita*
(n)	*irashite*	*kudasai*	*to*	*mōshite*	*orimashita*
(o)	*o-koshi*	*itadakitai*	*to*	*itte*	*orimasu*
(p)	*go-sokurō*	*kudasai*	*to no koto*	*desu*	

A simple criterion of scaling politeness is length. Generally, there is a direct correlation between the length of an expression relative to others with similar content and the degree of its politeness. Thus phrasing the request (2) as a negative question in the potential mood as in (m) is more polite than making a direct request as in (n). Indirectness is another criterion which in Japanese, as in several other

languages, correlates with politeness. For example, instead of referring to the request as a speech act by the other section chief, it can be
referred to as a fact using the quotation form *to no koto desu,* where *to*
is the quotative particle, *no* is a case marker for genitive-possessive,
and *koto* means 'thing, fact'. Thus, the content of the speech act referred to is, as it were, reified.

   Considering the position where variation occurs, first the desired
movement of the request's addressee can be referred to in various
ways. The form *kite* (a-h) is unproblematic as it is neutral on the level
of subject-related differentiation and, being the subjunctive, that is, a
non-finite form of *kuru* 'come', it is also neutral on the level of partner-related differentiation. *Oide* (j-l), by contrast, is an exalting form
marking respect for the agent who in this case is the addressee. The
same holds true for *korareru* (i), the passive of *kuru,* which functions
as the exalting form. *Irashite* (m, n) is the subjunctive form of the
exalting verb *irassharu* 'come, go, be'. Finally, *o-koshi kudasai* and
go-sokurō kudasai are exalting routine formulae, where *o-* and *go-* are
honorific prefixes, *koshi* is the nominalised stem of the verb *kosu*
'pass, move', *sokurō* is a noun which means 'the trouble of going
somewhere', and *kudasai* is the imperative form of *kudasaru* 'give'.

   Next, the options in (2) include the verb forms *kudasai, itadakitai,*
and *itadakenai,* the adjective *hoshii* 'desired', and the conjunction *yōni*
'in such a way that'. Choosing either of the latter two precludes any
problems with regard to appropriate honorifics. *Itadaku* 'receive' is a
humble verb and slightly more polite than *kudasaru* 'give' (where the
giver is superior). *Itadakenai* is the negative potential form. *Tai* is an
auxiliary adjective expressing a desire to do something. Thus what is
literally said in (b), (c), (e), (j), (k) and (o) is that the speaker of the
reported speech act wishes to receive something, namely the
addressee's coming to the conference room, whereas in (a), (l), (n)
and (p) it is said that the addressee should give his coming to the conference room.

   Proceeding now to position (4), the appropriate choice of
honorifics is more difficult. Recall that the problem is that the speaker
has to convey a request by her (or his) superior to another superior of
equal rank who, however, belongs to a different section of the
company than she does. In (4) she has to refer to her immediate superior's speech act while addressing an out-group superior. As pointed
out above (p. 314), there is a choice between a neutral, an exalting and
a humble verb for 'say', all of whose variants occur under (4). The

neutral verb *iu* is used in (a), (b), (c), (g), (i) and (o), the humble *mō su* in (h), (k), (l) and (n), and the exalting *ossharu* in (f). In the other cases the choice between these three is avoided; (d) contains a polite form of *negau* 'ask, request', and the rest make use of the nominalisation construction mentioned above. If the speaker does not decide to avoid the problem by choosing the neutral verb or another construction, the choice is thus between the humble and the exalting verb. Since these are, so to speak, two opposite extremes, no confusion should be expected here. The appropriate form is *mōshite,* that is, the subjunctive form of the humble verb *mōsu,* because the speaker belongs to the same group as the agent of the verb, speaks on his behalf to an out-group superior, and should therefore refer to the action as if it were performed by herself. However, faced with the choice between *mōsu* and *ossharu* in a situation like the one under discussion here, 50% of the respondents of a survey on honorific language use favoured the inappropriate *ossharu* (Yoshizawa 1981: 72). By using *ossharu,* the speaker symbolically elevates the agent of the saying. This choice, if understandable, is at variance with the norm. It is triggered, maybe, by the fact that the agent is the speaker's superior. The most likely explanation for the confusion is that the determining factor of rank interferes with that of group membership.

Finally, a choice is to be made for the finite form of the matrix verb, which is another critical point with respect to honorifics because it is here that the partner-related differentiation becomes most salient. Since the interlocutor is both out-group and superior, there is no question that a polite form is to be used. This criterion is met by all forms listed under (5), since they all belong to the polite *desu/masu* style, *mashita* and *deshita* being the past-tense forms of the auxiliary *masu* and the copula *desu,* respectively. Yet, there is still a choice between several variants: *oru* (c), (h), (i), (k), (l), (n) and (o) is the humble equivalent of *iru* 'be', which appears in the polite forms *imasu* (d) and *(i)mashita* (past tense, contracted). Since the speaker is addressing a superior, *oru* in its polite form *orimasu* or *orimashita* would be the favoured choice according to the norm.

To sum up, while (f) violates the norm, the other varieties are more or less acceptable. Some are somewhat pleonastic, for instance (c), and others are admittedly unnatural and could not be expected to occur, notably (d) and (h). The more important point, however, is that the speaker has to make options at several points choosing from a rich repertoire of grammatical means. The example under consideration here is relatively simple, and the multiplicity of choices is, of course, much greater. Moreover, the relevant components of the situation could be changed to make other choices possible and necessary. For example, the agents of the reported request and the desired movement could be of unequal rank, and the speaker could be of equal or higher rank than the addressee, etc. While some of the resulting choices could be circumvented, others have to be made which, apparently, not all native speakers of Japanese always find easy.

Conclusion

The honorific system is a part of the Japanese language. Its basic aspects are essential for proper usage and should not be thought of as a dispensable stylistic refinement. This is often obscured by the complex framework necessary for the description of Japanese honorifics. "Exalting" and "humble" are rather grand terms to describe an everyday phenomenon. They suggest that the forms so described are used, maybe, under special circumstances. However, quite the contrary is true. They are an essential part of linguistic conduct at all times, in most cases because their omission would render the utterance incomprehensible or provoke misunderstanding. The use of exalting and humble expressions is by no means restricted to formal relationships between interlocutors. Very often they serve referential rather than stylistic functions, although, the system being as it is, stylistic distinctions can simply not be avoided.

Humble and exalting expressions are not required by etiquette in intimate relationships, yet they are often used there for purposes other than expressing respect or marking social distance, that is, relation to a given group. The interplay of subject-related and partner-related differentiations allows for fine nuances in attuning one's speech to a given situation and interlocutor. For example, putting an exalting verb (subject-related) in plain style (partner-related), a combination often used by female speakers in familiar or intimate relationships, indicates both intimacy and a sense of decorum which is not suspended in informal situations.

It is maybe due, in part, to the fact that virtually every Japanese utterance is to be described as containing honorifics and to the misleadingly pompous descriptivist terms whose true significance is hard to appreciate on the basis of a theoretical account alone, that Japanese culture has a reputation for being very polite. This, I think, is a rather meaningless supposition, for the simple reason that, unless the notion is watered down to something like general consideration and benevolence, politeness is necessarily defined within the framework of a given culture.

Comparing politeness across cultures presupposes a position or rather some measure which is independent of any culture. However, a question which in one interpretation does make sense is that of whether or not a given language is more or less polite than another. A sensible answer to this question has to refer to the language system rather than to language use. In this sense Japanese can be described as a polite language, because there are relatively many structural means which are employed for the sole purpose of marking honorific distinctions.

The assumption underlying this claim is, of course, that there is a difference as it were between canonical and derived functions for which certain grammatical means are used. For example, interrogative mood is canonically related with questions, but in many languages it is used in a derivative way to make polite requests. Some languages have no grammatical mood, others have no or only sparse grammatical means which are canonically related with the expression of politeness. Although the honorific system described above is certainly one of the more highly developed ones, speakers of Japanese make use of both canonical and derived means for the expressions of politeness. [12]

Whether or not the speakers of Japanese are very polite or whether politeness is highly valued in Japanese society are entirely different questions which can only be answered on the basis of a detailed analysis of social structure and conduct as well as the historical background of Japanese etiquette in the Confucian ideology imported from China. Obviously, this is quite beyond the scope of the present paper. What is intended with the above description of the structural basics of Japanese honorifics and some of the problems of proper usage is merely to demonstrate that the linguistic apparatus available to the Japanese for the expression of politeness is fairly elaborate and that this apparatus occupies an important position in the perceived as well as the actual organisation of Japanese society.

Acknowledgements

I am grateful to Sugito Seiju who was kind enough to read this paper.
Discussing it with him helped me to improve it. He also provided
some pertinent references.

Notes

1. This event was reported in a program of NHK educational television of May
    27, 1982, entitled *Kun to yobimasu-ka* ('Do you use -*kun*?'). Cf. also Sugito
    (1976).
2. In 1987, a symposium took place in Tokyo with the explicit purpose of
    bringing together these two schools of thought. The proceedings were pub-
    lished in a special issue of *Gengo Kenkyū* (*Language Research*) in 1988.
3. All translations from Japanese sources are mine.
4. For a critique of modern Western linguists engaging in prescriptive linguis-
    tics cf. Coulmas (1989).
5. According to a survey by the National Language Research Institute carried
    out in 1981–82 only 14% of the subjects were confident that they had a good
    command of honorific speech. Another interesting finding of the same survey
    is that this figure is considerably lower than the corresponding figure of a
    survey carried out twenty years earlier (KKK 1983: 109f).
6. That there is great insecurity and confusion about honorific speech is ac-
    knowledged in both popular and scholarly treatments of the subject. Changes
    and mistakes characteristic of the first decade after World War II were dis-
    cussed at length in Miyaji (1957). The new encyclopedia of the Japanese lan-
    guage includes a page-long article on the confusion of honorific speech in the
    second half of the twentieth century (Kindaiti-Hayasi-Sibata 1988: 644f.).
    Most popular books on the subject cite the many mistakes they have ob-
    served in honorific-language use and the continuing demand for instruction as
    the rationale for their once again tackling this much belaboured topic.
    Surprisingly, there are nonetheless some linguists who prefer to ignore this
    evidence of linguistic insecurity, or worse, brush it aside as having to do
    with rural and less educated people only, thus allowing their bourgeois bias
    to dominate their scholarship.
7. All quotes are from Mombushō (1954).
8. Japanese has undergone a number of considerable stylistic changes since the
    Meiji period (1868–1911) when the country was set on a course of rapid
    modernisation (Westernisation). These changes had to do, most of all, with

narrowing the wide gap between spoken and written Japanese. In a sense, the reforms initiated after World War II can be understood as the logical conclusion of what was begun during the Meiji period (cf. Coulmas 1990).

9. Miyake (1961) provides an early assessment of the effects of the 1952 directives by the Ministry of Education showing in some detail why they were not altogether successful.

10. Socially, many relationships are conceived in terms of the seniority principle which finds expression in the paired notions of *sempai* 'one's senior' and *kō-hai* 'one's junior', literally, 'the one who came first' and 'the one who came later.' *Sempai* and *kōhai* are used both as descriptive terms and as terms of address. Among students, members of sports clubs, employees of the same company and other groups, social relationships are conceived in terms of this dichotomy.

11. *Shakai ni deru* 'get out into society' is a revealing expression. Somehow, students are not considered to be full members of society, and their speech, a student jargon lacking many essential features of prescribed honorific language, sets them apart. Once they 'enter' society, however, they are expected to conform to the norm. Thus speakers in the age bracket between 30 and 50 were found to be most accurate and skilful in honorific usage (KKK 1983).

12. A somewhat curious example of the derived use of a grammatical means is the past-tense form of verbs which in a northern dialect of Japanese is used as an additional politeness marker. Thus instead of standard *ohayō gozaimasu* 'good morning' speakers would say *ohayōgozaimashita*, where *mashita* is the past-tense form of the auxiliary *masu*. Similarly, they would identify themselves on the telephone in the past tense, *Moshi moshi, Tanaka deshita*, lit. 'hello, this was Tanaka', where obviously no past-time reference can be intended.

13. Politeness in Thai

Manfred Kummer

> When you bow
> Do bow low
> (Chinese saying)
>
> Politeness is but a strategy for avoiding that others feel despised
> (John Locke)
>
> Im Deutschen lügt man, wenn man höflich ist
> (Baccalaureus in *Faust* by J. W. von Goethe)

In the above quotations politeness seems to be regarded as a diplomatic strategy of communication. It is used under the constraints of the respective culture values. The means of expressing politeness vary widely from one culture to another and the concepts of what politeness is can be very different. Judging by outer appearance, Thai people seem to be very considerate in expressing verbal and nonverbal politeness. Their behaviour will strike foreign visitors to Thailand as charming and graceful: smiles all the time, bowing to each other with the palms of their hands placed together (*wài*), uttering particles in their melodious tonal language. Yet these signs can be deceptive.

What is considered polite in exchanging greetings, asking favours and offering apologies in Thai can be explained as an elaborate system of grading interpersonal factors as age, kinship, educational background and professional position (see Figure 1 p. 326). The means of expression are chosen with respect to the partner out of a rich repertoire of *pro*-forms such as personal pronouns, kinship terms, titles, names and nicknames. A series of final and isolated particles have the functions of lending illocutionary force to a message, expressing emotions and giving social indications.

According to Leech, politeness can be measured by applying the criteria of scales of expressives. Leech sets out from Halliday's concept of functionalism and proceeds from an interpersonal aspect, examining the conditions of expressing attitudes, feelings and emotions (Leech 1983: 56). This approach is derived from Searle's concept of

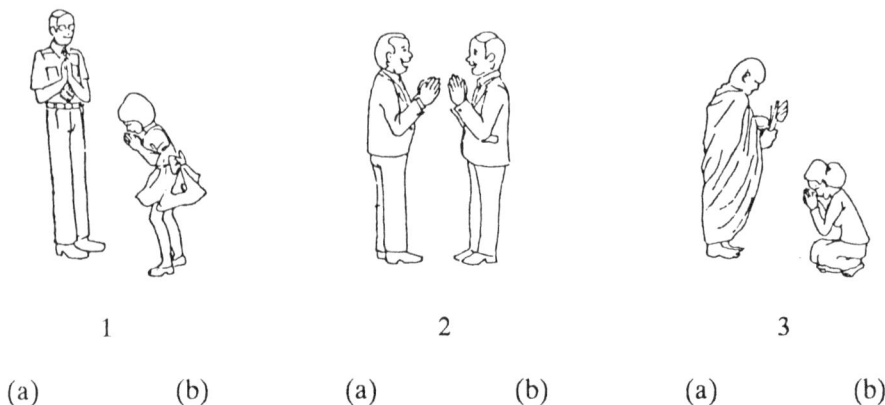

Figure 1. The traditional Thai way of greeting

The wài *is depicted above in three different social situations. In 1, for example, there is a teacher in the act of communication with his student (b). The two gentlemen 2(a) and (b) are communicating on the same level. The priest 3(a) is addressed by a student (b). As a rule, the higher the rank of a person the higher his/her head can be raised and the lower and more relaxed the hands can be held. Note that in a combination of, for example, 3(a) with 1(a) the priest will remain as with 3(a) and the teacher will bow similar to 1(b) and 3(b) may bow to 2(a) or (b) like 1(b) to 1(a).*

"regulative rules" (1983: 20–21). Two of the scales introduced for measuring politeness fall under the maxims of Tact and Modesty. Politeness in English, for instance, can be shown to grow proportionately with the decrease in directness. The two ends of the range are marked by the utterances "Answer the phone!" on the one hand and "Would you mind answering the phone?" (1983: 108), on the other. Regarding the Modesty Maxim, a "minimised praise of self" goes with a "maximised dispraise of self". Leech cites part of a dialogue in which two Japanese ladies perform a "pragmatic paradox" by denying the truth of a compliment (1983: 136–137). Leech points out the relativity of the maxim when he comments:

It appears that in Japanese society, and more particularly among Japanese women [...] the Modesty Maxim is more powerful than it is as a rule in English-speaking societies, where it would be customarily more polite to accept a compliment "graciously" (e.g., by thanking the speaker for it) rather than to go on denying it.

In Thai culture, such a performance of modesty will be considered strange and exaggerated. In this case, Thai people would act and think rather as Europeans would do.

As a rule, Thai expressives – verbal or nonverbal – are directed towards a communication partner in a dyadic system. The use of words is dependent on a network of relationships which must be tentatively explored during the first sequences of a conversation if the partners meet for the first time. Thai focuses on forms that express volition, impositions, interrogations and many degrees of social and emotional signals which must be chosen according to the characteristics of the partners. Therefore, a Thai person must be aware of his/her position in relation to that of his/her communicative partner.

In Leech's book, cited above, the author touches on the interesting case of the use of the pronouns 'tu' and 'vous' in French which can be paralleled by the German 'du' and 'Sie'. Leech deals with such forms in connection with the scales of social distance. The distribution of words is seen by the relationship of power to the solidarity factor (or the social distance). Leech (1983: 130) refers to Brown and Gilman (1960) that "French mountaineers shift from 'vous' to 'tu' after a 'certain critical altitude' is reached." This implies that the expressives can change on a continuum and move on a scale according to the situation and subjective personal factors. It is the situational circumstances that prompt a change of relationship and hence a corresponding choice of expressives. The Thai sets of expressives (e.g., in the use of personal pronouns) are meant for a rather fixed relationship between partners. This will be elaborated later.

In reference to the modesty scales, we can notice a Thai affinity to certain forms (1983: 135–136). Modesty is observed in a country where Buddhism plays a dominant role (more than 90% of the Thai population are Buddhists). Buddha taught modesty. In a world which is plagued by everlasting suffering and numerous misfortunes, praise for good fortune is immediately played down:
- "What a lovely baby your daughter is!"
- "Oh no, she is but an ordinary tiny tot!"

Or the answer could be put as mitigated disagreement:
  - "What a most wonderful country you live in!"
  - "Yes, it's not such a bad place."
Another popular strategy in Thai is the avoidance of negative replies. Kimsuvan (1984: 131) gives an example. A German teacher in Thailand asked a Thai friend to inquire about an old-fashioned stool in a Buddhist temple. He was interested in purchasing this piece of furniture, which was obviously no longer in use and about to be discarded. The Thai gentleman said that he would see to it and the German waited for a reply. However, nothing came of it. His Thai friend knew right from the start that this temple stool was not for sale and that he would not even try to oblige the German teacher by inquiring about the object. He might have thought that his German friend would understand his behaviour. In another example, some servants who do not wish to continue working in a household for various reasons pretend to have a sick aunt or grandmother somewhere else in the country, take leave for a couple of days and never return to the old place.

Leech mentions in his book the neglected study of cultures and languages with a view on the Politeness Principle. He assumes that certain communication strategies are more valued in the Far East than in Western countries (1983: 150). In Thai special weight is put upon operations in the field of socio-pragmatics with a highly differentiated hierarchy of personal relations.The ways of communicating in Thai, which seem to be garnished by signs of politeness, are, in fact, the means of norm and convention, typical of the language and culture group.

In Thai, the communicative partners are constrained by the variables of sex, age, kinship, education and profession. It is on the basis of such norms that Thai people will distribute sets of expressives with care. If the respective scales of sender and recipient are not in balance this can mean that the sender wishes to upgrade his/her partner and wishes to downgrade himself/herself. If expressives are incoherently distributed, this may signal emotional involvement (or the influence of drugs, mental illness and other distortions).

Since the early days of Thailand, the ideal of statesmanship was a benevolent monarch in charge of his people. The hierarchy of the society is preserved in the system of pronominal and referential forms. Figure 2 (p. 330) depicts the Thai order of society in the shape of a pyramid with the King and the Buddhist Supreme Patriarch at the top. Understandably, this system cannot comprise all of the classes, levels and various professions (Kimsuvan 1984: 121). In addition to the categories of profession and education, there are further criteria which modify the expressives, i.e.,

(1) sex (with no priority order),
(2) age (the elderly have precedence),
(3) kinship (elders rank above youngsters).

There can be conflicting situations when a boss or head of a section has to deal with an official of lower rank who may be older and be his/her uncle, for example.

Apart from reference forms, exclamations and illocutionary indicators, there is a special vocabulary of verbal expression such as to "eat", "go" and "die", reserved for the use by and with members of the Royal Family and of the Sangha, the community of Buddhist priests.

It is controversial to label these words as "polite", "respectful", "rude" or "vulgar", and it is misleading to foreigners, who may be inclined to think that "formal speech" is "polite language" and words used in a loose way and jokingly among good friends and college students are "vulgar".

The Tables 1–3 illustrate the pragmatic differences in word usage within the framework of the Thai social order. The Thai language is written with an alphabet of Indic origin. The IPA provides the basis for the representation of the examples given, but some of the symbols have been modified slightly according to the specific Thai qualities. In Thai the final plosives which are rendered as [b'], [d'], [g'] are pronounced very *lenis* as in English *rib, lid, rug*. The semantically distinctive tones in Thai are carried by the kernel vowels of the syllables which are marked by diacritics:

a: normal
ā: high, slightly raised (as if spoken in pain)
a̲: low (reproachful)
á: rising (interrogative, unsure)
à: falling (imperative).

Of the referential forms for persons as shown in Table 1, the most numerously differentiated ones are reserved for the speaker and the addressee, i.e., for the *I/you* references. The table depicts the possible expressives of *I* and *you* concerning gender, status level and social mood. Words available for this purpose are pronouns, titles, kinship nouns, nicknames and general nouns. The examples given are restricted to commonly used frequent forms only. In addition to Table 1,

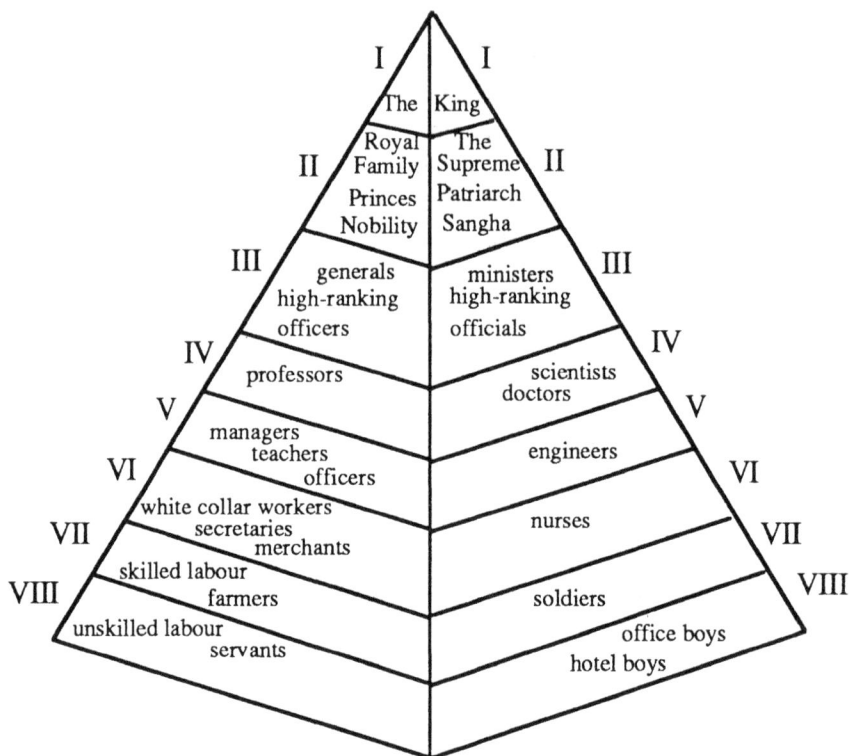

Figure 2. The hierarchy of Thai society.

Table 2 explains the extent to which pronominal pairs correspond when used by male–female couples (adapted from Cooke 1969: 60, Chart 15).

As previously mentioned, conflicting situations which make it difficult for a speaker to choose a satisfactory form from the available alternatives can occur. Cooke (1969: 63) gives a few examples which illustrate this. In one case, a democratic minded young Thai man finds it difficult to address an elderly pedlar. Finally, he abandons all the pronouns which he considered unsuitable and avoids pronouns altogether (which is possible in Thai since one can say "will come" or simply "come" if it is clear who is meant "to come").

There is another story about a Thai diplomat who had just returned home to Bangkok after a lengthy assignment in Washington and who

Table 1. Thai pronouns

I
m.   f.

social mood	status level (role)			status level (role)	social mood
formal	generally high (I<partner)	phɔm	dichan	generally high (I<partner)	formal
neutral	equals	phɔm	dichan	equals	neutral
informal	generally low (I>partner)	chan	chan	generally low (I>partner)	informal
		kan			
		kuu			
		ai	ai		
		muu	tùm	(nicknames)	

YOU
m.   f.

social mood	status level (role)			status level (role)	social mood
formal	generally high (I<partner)	thân	thân	generally high (I<partner)	formal
		khun	khun		
neutral	equals	khun	khun	equals	neutral
informal	generally low (I>partner)	(thəə)	thəə	generally low (I>partner)	informal
		mɨŋ			
		yuu	yuu		
		muu	tùm	(nicknames)	
		luy	pâa	(kinship names)	
		('uncle')	('aunt')		

ordered his meal in an open-air restaurant in a rather stilted way, using *high* forms in addressing the Chinese boy who served him the food. His order in Thai is said to have sounded like "Dear waiter, tell your respected father to kindly oblige me with a dish of rice and vegetable." The boy was flabbergasted and stared at the guest. He had not understood the message and the friends accompanying the diplomat translated the order laughingly and jokingly into simple Thai to the waiter.

Table 2. The correspondence of pronominal pairs in Thai

	I	**YOU**		**I**	
social mood	male → female			male ← female	
formal	pʰɔm	kʰun		kʰun	dichan
neutral/intimate	chan	kʰun		kʰun	chan
intimate	chan	tʰəə		kʰun	chan
	chan	reenuu		banyaa	chan
		(first names)			
	chan	tùm		mùu	chan
		(nicknames)			
very intimate	pʰîi	nɔɔŋ		pʰîi	nɔɔŋ
	elder	younger	/	elder	younger
	sibling	sibling			sibling
parental	pʰɔɔ	mɛ̀ɛ		pʰɔɔ	mɛ̀ɛ
	father	mother		father	mother
very intimate	kan	kɛɛ		kɛɛ	chan

Concerning the use of the pronominal pairs listed Cooke (1969: 63) gives an example about a situation which may occur.

> A young woman wishes to address a man of about her own age that she has just met, or one who is a rather casual acquaintance. Among the possible first person forms, /dichan/ is too deferential; /chan/ on the other hand is not deferential enough – particularly for young women of the rising generation who tend not to use /chan/ as a neutral or more general term; and even the nickname may appear a little too informal or intimate in such a situation. It therefore turns out that, for some speakers, there is no term that is completely acceptable. A woman in this situation therefore attempts to avoid using any first person form at all. But in a conversation where she must repeatedly refer to herself this may be impossible.

It is not surprising that misunderstandings arise concerning the choice of the pronouns (Cooke 1969: 63):

> One informant, for example, cites an occasion in which a high (female) official from the Ministry of Education [...] addressed a young Thai female student in the United States as /tʰəə/, a somewhat patronizing term used speaking to inferiors, especially teacher to pupil. The

student was then upset because she considered herself to be an adult
and therefore due proper respect.

Cooke also refers to a Thai Prime Minister (Phibulsongkram) who
was planning to abolish the elaborate system of pronoun forms. After
the 1932 coup, when democratic reforms were favoured by some
politicians in Thailand who had formerly studied in France and other
foreign countries, the Prime Minister advocated a reduction of the
available pronouns to one set for *I* and *you* only. However, the Thai
population considered these attempts "an assault on freedom and
democracy" and, like other plans for reforms in the 1930s, this plan
had to be abandoned.

There are three groups of particles in Thai which have communicative functions (Kummer 1984: 72–79):

(1) The *emotives*, which can be compared to the class of exclamations
 (as in English: *well, oh!, mmh!*);
(2) The *illocutionary particles* indicating speech acts, as in interrogative and imperative sentences (in English rising intonation, word
 order);
(3) *Appellatives*, which have the illocutionary quality of doubting,
 hesitating, and, in addition, show the status and social mood of
 the acting communicative partners (as in English: *please?, yes,
 sir!*)

Of these three groups, the last group (3) is of the most interest for
the subject of this chapter (see Table 3). In correspondence with the
pronominal forms, one can choose these particles, which are placed at
the end of an utterance or which appear in isolation (in place of a syntactic utterance). These expressives can be compared to tags as in "...
will you?", "well?", "...is it?". However, in Thai they carry the following information:

(1) gender
(2) status level
(3) social mood
(4) semantic-pragmatic elements, i.e., underlining or adding to the
 illocutionary indicators as in
 – answering questions
 – responding to persuasions, requests, statements
 – asking questions.

These forms, illustrated in Table 3, are short (monosyllabic) and have
tones which are, in some cases, situational and not distinctive in a

lexical sense. Thus, the falling tone is reserved for decisive, affirmative utterances: /hà ?/, whereas the high, lingering tone goes with questions and uncertain expressions: /hā?/ (doubting, suggesting, supposing). Between fifteen particles (Kummer 1984: 72) and twenty particles (Phukphasuk 1976: 4) are listed in this class. Kummer (1984) puts them in a descending order from respectful (formal) to very intimate (see Table 3). Phukphasuk makes a distinction between "polite" particles and "impolite" particles. It is claimed, however, that this is inaccurate as far as more subtle shades are concerned and misleading on account of the problematic use of the word on a communication level with its interpersonal factors. In fact, the particles can be thought of as being on a continuum between "formal" at one end and "very intimate" at the other, omitting the extreme and suggestive undertones of definitions which have the "snobbish/arrogant" and "vulgar/low-class" connotations.

It is interesting to note that the last three forms shown in Table 3 are close to the emotives (e.g., /ōi/ 'boy!', 'wow!', 'oh!') which refer solely to the speaker rather than to a communicative partner addressed by the speaker.

Referring to Table 3, these final particles correlate directly with the pronouns listed. When addressing Tum, who is female, another Thai woman may say:

/kʰun tù kʰā?.../

Without being present and without seeing the partners, one can assume that Tum is higher in social status than the speaker because of the added /kʰun/ = Miss, Mrs. Two more examples are

/chan tʰam raaiŋan sɛd' lɛ̄o yà?/ = I've finished my report; and
/pʰɔ́m caʔ pai siŋkʰapoo kʰrāb/ = I shall go to Singapore.

The first sentence contains the personal pronoun /chan/ that indicates equal status of sender and recipient and the final particle /yà?/ which suggests that the two (female) partners are good acquaintances and on intimate terms. The other sentence states an intention in a reserved but friendly mood.

The foreign reader may wonder if the Thai system of communication confines the communicative partners, so that they feel suppressed or hampered by the network of forms. One has to consider that the Thai people have lived with their verbal inventory for centuries. There is room for the special use of forms in special situations. If a Thai person of high status wants to be kind to a taxi driver or a housekeeper,

Table 3.

APPELLATIVES

Thai forms	speaker recipient	illocutionary force			social mood
		affirmative	imperative	interrogative	
kʰrab'	m. ⌐→	x	x	x	reserved, but friendly
kʰaʔ	f. ⌐→	x		x	reserved, but friendly
kʰàʔ	f. ⌐→	x	x		reserved, but friendly
haʔ	m. + f. ⌐→	x		x	affable
hàʔ	m. + f. ⌐→	x	x		affable
caʔ	m. + f. ⌐→	x		x	intimate
càʔ	m. + f. ⌐→	x		x	intimate
cáa	m. + f. ⌐→	x	x		intimate
kʰáa	f. ⌐→	x	x		intimate
yaʔ	f. ⌐→	x	x	x	intimate
yàʔ	f. ⌐→	x	x		intimate
waʔ	m. →	x	x	x	very intimate
wàʔ	m. →	x	x		very intimate
wŏi	m. →	x	x	x	very intimate

Key: speaker ⌐→ recipient   (higher than speaker)

speaker → recipient   (equals)

speaker ⌐_→ recipient   (lower than speaker)

he/she can, for instance, employ kinship terms, such as /luŋ/ or /pàa/ when addressing the partner (see Table 1). There remains ample opportunity for individual as well as pluralistic use. The Thai people are likely to go on with their diversified system of communication forms as long as these serve their intentions in accordance with the social values and interpersonal relations of Thai culture.

References

Ackroyd, Peter
    1985   *T. S. Eliot*. London: Abacus.
Adamzik, Kirsten
    1984   *Sprachliches Handeln und sozialer Kontakt*. Tübingen: Narr.
Adorno, Theodor
    1944   *Minima Moralia. Reflexionen aus dem beschädigten Leben.* (Reprinted 1982). Frankfurt: Suhrkamp.
Agar, Michael
    1986   *Speaking of Ethnography*. Beverly Hills: Sage.
Altman, G. and A. Riska
    1986   Towards a typology of couretesy in language. *Anthropological Linguistics* 8(1), 1–10.
Anderson, B.
    1966   *Imagined Communities: Reflections on the Origin and Spread of Nationalsim*. London: Verso Editions and NLB.
Arndt, Horst and Richard Janney
    1979   Interactional and linguistic models for the analysis of speech data: An integrative approach. *Sociologia Internationalis* 17, 3–45.
    1980   The clanger phenomenon: The nondeviant nature of deviant utterances. *International Review of Applied Linguistics* 18, 41–57.
    1981a   An interactional linguistic model of everyday conversational behaviour. *Die Neueren Sprachen* 80, 435–454.
    1981b   Intuitive linguistic knowledge as a problem of nonautonomous linguistic reserach: The verbal coordination of group role identities. *Forum Linguisticum* 6, 95–116.
    1983   Towards an international grammar of spoken English. In Morreall, J. (ed.), *The Ninth LACUS Forum 1982*. Columbia, SC: Hornbeam, 367–381.
    1984   Interpersonal factors in intercultural (mis)understanding. *Nagoya Gakuin University Round Table* 10, 13–29.
    1985a   Politeness revisited: Crossmodal supportive strategies. *International Review of Applied Linguistics* 23, 281–300.
    1985b   Improving emotive communication: Verbal, prosodic, and kinesic conflict avoidance techniques. *Per Linguam* 1, 21–33.
    1986   Neurological parameters of human multimodal communication. *Sociologia Internationalis* 24, 143–169.

1987a   The biological and cultural evolution of human communication. In Lörscher, W. and R. Schulze (eds.), *Perspectives on
Language in Performance*. Tübingen: Narr, 19–45.

1987b   *Intergrammar: Toward an Integrative Model of Verbal, Prosodic, and Kinesic Choices in Speech*. Berlin: Mouton de
Gruyter.

Arndt, H., R. Janney and H. Pesch
1984   Trimodale   Interaktion: Grundlagen   zur   integrierten
Interpretation von Sprache, Prosodie und Gestik. *Die
Neueren Sprachen* 83, 489–512.

Arndt, H., R. Janney and G. Schaffranek
1986   A neurological view of prosody and its importance in human
communication. *Die Neueren Sprachen* 85, 581–609.

Assman, J.
1990   *Ma'at. Gerechtigkeit und Unsterblichkeit im Alten Ägypten*.
München: Beck.

Atkinson, John and John Heritage
1984   *Structures of Social Action*. Cambridge: Cambridge University Press.

Atkinson, M. and V. Allen
1983   Perceived structure of non-verbal behaviour. *Journal of Personality and Social Psychology* 45, 458–463.

Austen, Jane
1816   *Emma*. Republished in *The Novels of Jane Austen*, Vol. IV,
1933, edited by R. W. Chapman. London: Oxford University
Press.

Axia, G. and M. Baroni
1985   Linguistic politeness at different age levels. *Child Development* 56, 918–927.

Bach, Emmon and Robert Harms (eds.)
1968   *Universals of Linguistic Theory*. New York: Holt, Rinehart
and Winston.

Bally, Charles
1909   *Traité de stylistique française*, Vol. 1, Heidelberg. Third edition 1951, Geneva/Paris: Klincksieck.

1913   *Le langage et la vie*. Geneva/Paris: Klincksieck.

1927   La contraint sociale dans le langage. *Revue Internationale de
Sociologie* 35, 209–217.

Basso, K.
1979   *Portraits of "the Whiteman"*. London: Cambridge University
Press.

Bates, Elizabeth
　　1976　　*Language and Context: The Acquisition of Pragmatics.* New York: Academic Press.
Bateson, Gregory
　　1954　　*A Theory of Play and Fantasy: Steps to an Ecology of Mind.* New York: Ballantine.
Beetz, M.
　　1990　　*Frühmoderne Höflichkeit. Komplimentierkunst und Gesell-schafts-rituale im altdeutschen Sprachraum.* Stuttgart: Metzler.
Beinhauer, Werner
　　1930　　*Spanische Umgangssprache.* Bonn: Dümmler.
Beninca, P., G. Cinque, E. Fava, P. Leonardi and P. Piva
　　1977　　101 modi per richiedere. In Simone, R. and G. Ruggiero (eds.), *Aspetti sociolinguistici dell' Italia contemporanea.* Rome: Bulzoni, 500–532.
Bennett, J.
　　1976　　*Linguistic Behaviour.* London: Cambridge University Press.
Berger, C.
　　1979　　Beyond initial interaction: Uncertainty, understanding and the development of interpersonal relationships. In Giles, H. and R. St. Clair (eds.), *Language and Social Psychology.* Oxford: Blackwell, 112–144.
Berger, C. and R. Calabrese
　　1975　　Some explorations in initial interaction and beyond: Toward a development theory of interpersonal communication. *Human Communication Research* 1, 99–112.
Bigelow, B.
　　1977　　Children's friendship expectations. *Child Development* 48, 246–253.
Blickle, Gerhard
　　1986a　　Höflichkeit als symbolisch generalisiertes Medium der Achtungs-kommunikation. Manuscript.
　　1986b　　Höflichkeit und rationale Argumentation. Manuscript.
Blum-Kulka, Shoshana
　　1982　　Learning to say what you mean in a second language: A study of the speech act performance of learners of Hebrew as a second language. *Applied Linguistics* 3, 29–59.
　　1987　　Indirectness and politeness: Same or different? *Journal of Pragmatics* 11, 147–160.
　　1989　　Playing it safe: The role of conventionality in indirectness. In Blum-Kulka, Shoshana, Juliane House and Gabriele Kasper (eds.), 37–70.

Blum-Kulka, S., B. Danet and R. Gerson
　1985　The language of requesting in Israeli society. In Forgas, J. (ed.), *Language and Social Situation*. New York: Springer Verlag, 113–141.
Blum-Kulka, Shoshana, Juliane House and Gabriele Kasper (eds.)
　1989　*Cross-Cultural Pragmatics: Requests and Apologies*. New Jersey: Ablex.
Blum-Kulka, S. and T. Katriel
　1991　Nicknaming practices in families: A cross-cultural perspective. In Ting-Toomey, S. and F. Korzenny (eds.), *Cross-cultural and Interpersonal Communication*. London: Sage, 58–77.
Blum-Kulka, S. and E. Olshtain
　1986　Too many words: Length of utterance and pragmatic failure. Studies in *Second Language Acquisition* 8, 47–67.
Blum-Kulka, S. and E. Weizmann
　1988　The inevitability of misunderstandings: Discourse ambiguities. *Text* 8, 219–241.
Boesch, E. and L. Eckensberger
　1975　Methodische Probleme des interkulturellen Vergleichs. In Graumann, C. F. et al. (eds.), *Handbuch der Psychologie*, Vol. 7: Sozialpsycho-logie. Göttingen: Hogrefe, 515–566.
Bogen, K.
　1969　*Gesten in Begrüßungsszenen auf attischen Vasen*. Bonn: Habelt.
Bolinger, Dwight
　1977　*Meaning and Form*. London: Longman.
　1982　Intonation and its parts. *Language* 58, 503–533.
Bourdieu, Pierre
　1972　*Esquisse d'une théorie de la pratique (précédé de trois études d'ethnologie kabyle)*. Genève: Droz.
　1991　*Language and Symbolic Power*, edited by J. Thompson and translated by G. Raymond and M. Adamson. Cambridge: Polity Press.
Boyer, Abel
　1702　*The English Theophrastus, or, The Manners of the Age*. London. (Originally printed 1695 with the title *Characters of the virtues and vices of the age, or, Moral reflexions, and thoughts upon men and manners*. London.)
Bradac, J., J. Bowers and J. Courtright
　1979　Three language variables in communication research: Intensity, immedicay and diversity. *Human Communication Research* 5, 257–269.

1980   Lexical variations in intensity, immediacy, and diversity: An axiomatic theory and causal model. In Giles, H. and R. St. Clair (eds.), *The Social and Psychological Contexts of Language*. Hillsdale, NJ: Erlbaum, 193–223.

Braun, Friederike
1988   *Terms of Address: Problems of Patterns and Usage in Various Languages and Cultures*. Berlin: Mouton de Gruyter.

Braun, F., A. Kohz and K. Schubert
1986   *Anredeforschung. Kommentierte Bibliographie zur Soziolinguistik der Anrede*. Tübingen: Narr.

Braun, Friederike and Klaus Schubert
1986   Von unhöflichen Höflichkeitsformeln, und was Höflichkeit eigentlich ist. *SAIS Arbeitshefte aus dem Seminar für Allgemeine und Indogermanische Sprachwissenschaft, Kiel* 9, 1–29.

Brooks, Cleanth
1939   *Modern Poetry and the Tradition*. Republished 1965. Chapel Hill: University of North Carolina Press.

Brown, G. and G. Yule
1983   *Discourse Analysis*. London: Cambridge University Press.

Brown, Penelope
1976   Women and politeness: A new perspective on language and society. *Reviews in Anthropology* 3, 240–249.
1980   How and why women are more polite: Some evidence from a Mayan community. In McConnel-Ginet, Sally, Ruth Borker and Nelly Furman (eds.), *Women and Language in Literature and Society*. New York: Praeger, 111–136.

Brown, Penelope and Stephen Levinson
1978   Universals in language usage: Politeness phenomena. In Goody, Esther (ed.), *Questions and Politeness: Strategies in Social Interaction*. Cambridge: Cambridge University Press, 56–289. Reissued 1987 as *Politeness: Some Universals in Language Usage*. Cambridge: Cambridge University Press.

Brown, Roger and Marguerite Ford
1961   Address in American English. *Journal of Abnormal and Social Psychology* 62, 375–385.

Brown, R. and A. Gilman
1960   The pronouns of power and solidarity. In Sebeok, T. (ed.), *Style in Language*. New York: Wiley, 435–449.
1989   Politeness theory and Shakespeare's four major tragedies. *Language in Society* 18, 159–213.

Bruner, Jerome
   1986   *Actual Minds, Possible Worlds.* Cambridge, Mass.: Harvard
             University Press.
Brunner, Hellmut
   1977   Höflichkeit und Etikette. *Lexikon der Ägyptologie, Bd. 2.*
             Wiesbaden: Harrassowitz, 1229–1230.
Brunot, Ferdinand
   1986   *La pensée et la langue.* Paris: Masson.
Bublitz, Wolfram
   1978   *Ausdrucksweisen der Sprechereinstellung im Deutschen und
             Englischen.* Tübingen: Niemeyer.
Buck, R.
   1984   *The Communication of Emotion.* New York/London: Guil-
             ford.
Bühler, Karl
   1965   *Sprachtheorie.* Stuttgart: Fischer. First edition 1930.
Byrnes, H.
   1986   The interactional style in German and American conversa-
             tions. *Text* 6, 189–206.
Callan, H.
   1970   *Ethology and Society. Towards an Anthropological View.* Ox-
             ford: Clarendon Press
Caminos, Ricardo
   1977   Gruβformeln. *Lexikon der Ägyptologie, Bd. 2.* Wiesbaden:
             Harrassowitz.
Castiglione, B.
   1986   *Das Buch vom Hofmann.* München: dtv. First edition 1528.
Chomsky, Noam
   1963   Formal properties of grammars. In Luce, R., R. Bush and E.
             Galanter (eds.), *Handbook of Mathematical Psychology,*
             Vol. 2. New York: Wiley, 323–418.
   1961   *Lectures on Government and Binding: The Pisa Lectures.*
             Dordrecht: Foris Publications.
Chomsky, N. and G. Miller
   1963   Finitary models of language users. In Luce, R., R. Bush and
             E. Galanter (eds.), *Handbook of Mathematical Psychology,*
             Vol. 2. New York: Wiley, 419–491.
Clark, H. and W. French
   1981   Telephone goodbyes. *Language and Society* 10, 1–19.
Clark, Herbert and Dale Schunk
   1980   Polite responses to polite requests. *Cognition* 8, 111–143.
   1981   Politeness in requests: A rejoinder to Kemper and Thissen.
             Cognition 9, 311–315.

Claus, M.
1982   *Lessing und die Franzosen: Höflichkeit–Laster–Witz.* Rheinfelden: Schäuble.
Conte, H. and R. Plutchik
1981   A circumplex model for interpersonal personality traits. *Journal of Personality and Social Psychology* 40, 701–711.
Cooke, J.
1968   *Pronominal Reference in Thai, Burmese, and Vietnamese.* Berkeley: University of California Press.
Coulmas, Florian
1979   Riten des Alltags. Sequenzierungsbedingungen in präfigurierter Rede. In van de Wege and van de Felde (eds.), *Bedeutung, Sprechakte und Texte.* Tübingen: Niemeyer, 171–180.
1980   Zur Personaldeixis im Japanischen. *Papiere zur Linguistik* 23, 3–19.
1981a   *Routine im Gespräch. Zur pragmatischen Fundierung der Idiomatik.* Wiesbaden: Athenaion.
1989   Democracy and the crisis of normative linguistics. In Coulmas, Florian (ed.), *Language Adaptation.* London: Cambridge University Press, 177–193.
1990a   Language adaptation in Meiji Japan. In Weinstein, B. (ed.), *Language Policy and Political Development.* Norwood, N.J.: Ablex, 69–86.
1990b   Bare Münze. Zur Ökonomie der Sprache. *Merkur* 492, 107–120.
Coulmas, Florian (ed.)
1981b   *Conversational Routine: Explorations in Standardized Communication Situations and Prepatterned Speech.* The Hague: Mouton.
Couper-Kuhlen, E.
1986   *An Introduction to English Prosody.* Tübingen: Niemeyer.
Couroyer, B.
1978   BRK et les formules égyptiennes. *Revue biblique* 85, 575–585.
Dalman, G.
1928   *Arbeit und Sitte in Palästina. Bd. 1: Jahreslauf und Tageslauf.* 2. Hälfte: Frühling und Sommer. Gütersloh: Bertelsmann.
Daly, E., W. Lancee and J. Polivy
1982   A conical model for the taxonomy of emotional experience. *Journal of Personality and Social Psychology* 45, 443–457.

Darwin, C.
1872   *The Expression of the Emotions in Man and Animals.* London: Murray.
Dauzat, Albert
1912   *La défense de la langue française.* Paris: Colin.
Davies, E.
1987   A contrastive approach to the analysis of politeness formulas. *Applied Linguistics* 8(1), 75–88.
de Vos, George A. and Orin Borders
1989   A comparison of delinquent and nondelinquent families. In de Vo, George A. and L. Bryce Boyer (eds.), *Symbolic Analysis Cross-Culturally: The Rohrschach Test.* Berkeley, Ca.: University of California Press, 149–167.
Dickens, Charles
1857   *Little Dorrit.* Republished 1967. John Holloway (ed.), Harmondsworth: Penguin Books.
Ducrot, Oswald
1980   *Dire et ne pas dire: principes de sémantique linguistique.* 2nd edition. Paris: Herman. First edition 1972. Paris: Herman.
Dupin, Henri
1931   *La courtoisie au Moyen Age.* Paris: Picard.
Duranti, Alessandro
1974   Cortesia e rispetto: un aspetto poco studiato della competenza linguistica. *Rassegna Italiana di Sociologia* 15, 311–322.
Eco, Umberto
1972   *Einführung in die Semiotik.* München: Fink.
Edelstein, W. and M. Keller
1982   Perspektivität und Interpretation. Zur Entwicklung des sozialen Verstehens. In Edelstein, W. and M. Keller (eds.), *Perspektivität und Interpretation. Beiträge zur Entwicklung des sozialen Verstehens.* Frankfurt/M.: Suhrkamp.
Edmondson, Willis
1980   *Spoken Discourse: A Model for Analysis.* London: Longman.
Egawa, K., K. Nomoto, F. Minami and S. Sugito
1985   Language change in a local community. *International Journal of the Sociology of Language* 58, 59–71.
Ehlich, Konrad and Jochen Rehbein
1972   Zur Konstitution pragmatischer Einheiten in einer Institution: Das Speiserestaurant. In Wunderlich, Dieter (ed.), *Linguistische Pragmatik.* Frakfurt/M: Athenäum, 209–254.

Ehrich, V. and G. Saile
1972   Über nicht direkte Sprechakte. In Wunderlich, Dieter (ed.), *Linguistische Pragmatik*. Frankfurt/M: Athenäum, 255–287.
Eibl-Eisbesfeldt, I.
1978   *Grundriß der vergleichenden Verhaltensforschung*. München: Piper.
1984   *Die Biologie des menschlichen Verhaltens*. München: Piper.
Ekman, P.
1965a   Communication through nonverbal behavior: A source of information about an interpersonal relationship. In Tomkins, S. and C. Izard (eds.), *Affect, Cognition and Personality*. New York: Springer, 390–442.
1965b   Differential communication of affect by head and body cues. *Journal of Personality and Social Psychology* 2, 726–735.
1972   *Emotions in the Human Face*. New York: Pergamon.
Faerch, Claus and Gabriele Kasper
1989   Internal and external modification in interlanguage request realization. In Blum-Kulka S., J. House and G. Kasper (eds.), 221–248.
Fatke, R. and R. Valtin
1988   Wozu man Freunde braucht. *Psychologie Heute* 4, 22–29.
Fehn, E. O., P. Rabe and C. Ritterhoff
1977   *Ob Baron Knigge auch wirklich tot ist?* Eine Ausstellung zum 225. Geburtstag des Adolph Freiherrn Knigge. Wolfenbüttel: Ausstellungskatalog der Herzog August Bibliothek.
Ferguson, C. A.
1976   The structure and use of politeness formulas. *Language in Society* 5, 137–151.
Fielding, Henry
1903   *The Writings of Henry Fielding*. Edited by William Ernest Henley. London: Heinemann.
Franck, Dorothea
1980   *Grammatik und Konversation*. Kronberg: Skriptor.
1984   Stil und Interaktion. In Spillner, B. (ed.), *Methode der Stilanalyse*. Tübingen: Narr, 121–135.
Fraser, Bruce
1990   Perspectives on politeness. *Journal of Pragmatics* 14, 219–236.
Fraser, Bruce and William Nolen
1981   The association of deference with linguistic form. *International Journal of the Sociology of Language* 27, 93–109.

Frevert, Ute
    1988   Bürgerlichkeit und Ehre. Zur Geschichte des Duells in England und Deutschland. In Kocka, J. (ed.), *Bürgertum im 19. Jahrhundert*. München: Deutscher Taschenbuchverlag, Vol. 3, 101–140.

Friedrich, P.
    1966   Structural implications of Russian pronominal usage. In Bright, W. (ed.), *Sociolinguistics*. Amsterdam: Mouton.

Fromkin, Victoria (ed.)
    1973   *Speech Errors as Linguistic Evidence*. The Hague: Mouton.

Gabelentz, Georg von der
    1969   *Die Sprachwissenschaft*. Tübingen: Narr.

Gardner, Helen T.
    1947   *Four Quartets: A Commentary*. Quoted in Cox, C. and A. Hinchcliffe (eds. 1968), *T. S. Eliot: The Waste Land. A Casebook*. London: Macmillan.

Garelli, P.
    1972–   *Hofstaat. Reallexikon der Assyriologie und Vorderasiatischen Archäologie*,
    1975   Vol. 4. Berlin: Mouton de Gruyter, 446–452.

Garfinkel, Harold
    1967   *Studies in Ethnomethodology*. Englewood Cliffs, NJ: Prentice-Hall.

Garrett, M., T. Bever and J. Fodor
    1966   The active use of grammar in speech perception. *Perception and Psychophysics* 1, 30–32.

Garvey, C.
    1975   Requests and responses in children's speech. *Journal of Child Language* 2, 41–63.

Gengo Kenkyu 93
    1988   Special issue: *Shinpojium shakaigengogaku no riron to hōhō* ['Theory and method of sociolinguistics'], 96–184.

Giddens, Anthony
    1984   *The Constitution of Society: Oultine of the Theory of Structuration*. Cambridge: Polity Press.

Gluckman, M.
    1962   *Essays on the Ritual of Social Relations*. Manchester: Manchester University Press.

Goffman, Erving
    1955   On face work: An analysis of ritual elements in social interaction. Psychiatry 18, 213–231 (Reprinted in Laver, J. and S. Hutcheson (eds.), 1972, *Communication in Face to Face Interaction*. Harmondsworth: Penguin, 319–346).

1959   *The Presentation of Self in Everyday Life*. New York: Doubleday.
1963   *Behavior in Public Places*. New York: Free Press.
1967   *Interaction Ritual: Essays on Face to Face Behavior*. New York: Anchor.
1981   *Forms of Talk*. Oxford: Blackwell.
Goodenough, W.
1965   Rethinking "status" and "role": Toward a general model of the cultural organization of social relationships. In Banton, M. (ed.), *The Relevance of Models for Social Morphology*. London: Tavistock, 1–24.
Goody, Esther
1978   *Questions and Politeness*. Cambridge: Cambridge University Press.
Gordon, D. and G. Lakoff
1971   Conversational postulates. *Papers from the Seventh Regional Meeting of the Chicago Linguistics Society*, 63–84.
Gordon, Lyndall
1977   *Eliot's Early Years*. Oxford. Oxford University Press.
Grabowski-Gellert, Joachim and Peter Winterhoff-Spurk
1988   "Your smile is my command": Interaction between verbal and nonverbal components of requesting specific to situational characteristics. *Journal of Language and Social Psychology* 7(3/4), 229–243.
Grant, Michael
1982   *T. S. Eliot: The Critical Heritage* (2 vols.). London: Routledge and Kegan Paul.
Grapow, H.
1960   *Wie die alten Ägypter sich anredeten, wie sie sich grüßten und wie sie miteinander sprachen*. Berlin: Akademie-Verlag.
Green, G.
1975   How to get people to do things with words: The whimperative question. In Cole, P. and J. Morgan (eds.), *Syntax and Semantics. Vol. 3: Speech Acts*. New York: Academic Press, 107–141.
Greenberg, Joseph (ed.)
1963   *Universals of Language*. Cambridge, Mass: MIT Press.
Grice, H. P.
1975   Logic and conversation. In Cole, P. and J. Morgan (eds.), 41–58.
Griffin, P. and H. Mehan
1981   Sense and ritual in classroom discourse. In Coulmas, F. (ed.), *Conversational Routine*. The Hague: Mouton, 187–213.

Grootaers, W.
1982   Soto kara mita nihongo ['Japanese viewed from the out-side']. *Kodensha zeminaru.* Tokyo: Kodansha, 163–207.
Gross, H.
1960   Gruβ. *Lexikon für Theologie und Kirche, Bd. 4.* Freiburg: Herder, 1255–1256.
Gu, Yueguo
1990   Politeness phenomena in modern Chinese. *Journal of Pragmatics* 14, 237–257.
Gülich, Elisabeth
1970   *Makrosyntax der Gliederungssignale im gesprochenen Französisch.* München: Finck.
Gülich, E. and K. Henke
1979   Sprachliche Routine in der Alltagskommunikation. *Die neueren Sprachen* 78, 513–530.
1980   Sprachliche Routine in der Alltagskommunikation. *Die neueren Sprachen* 79, 2–33.
Gumperz, John J. (ed.)
1982   *Language and Social Identity.* Cambridge: Cambridge University Press.
Gutknecht, C. and W. Mackiewicz
1977   Prosodische, paralinguistische und intonarische Phänomene im Englischen. In Gutknecht, C. (ed.), *Grundbegiriffe und Hauptströmungen der Linguistik.* Hamburg: Hoffmann, 95–132.
Habermas, Jürgen
1981   *Theorie des kommunikativen Handelns.* 2 volumes. Frankfurt: Suhrkamp.
Haga, Yasushi
1988   Gengo seikatsu ['The life of language']. In Kindaiti, H., O. Hayasi and T. Sibata (eds.), *Nihongo hyakka daijiten* ['An encyclopedia of the Japanese language']. Tokyo: Taishukan, 673–722.
Halliday, Michael
1973   *Explorations in the Functions of Language.* London: Arnold.
1978   *Language as a Social Semiotic.* London: Arnold.
Harada, Shin-ichi
1976   Honorifics. In Shibatani, M. (ed.), *Syntax and Semantics, Vol. 5: Japanese Generative Grammar.* New York: Academic Press, 299–561.
Harré, Rom and P. Second
1972   *The Explanation of Social Behaviour.* Oxford: Blackwell.

Hartmann, Dieter
1973   Begrüßungen und Begrüßungsrituale. Überlegungen zu Ver-
         wendungsweisen sprachlicher Symbolik in kommunikativen
         Handlungsmustern. *Zeitschrift für germantistische Linguistik*
         1, 133–162.
Haverkate, Henk
1987   La cortesia como estrategia conversacional. *Diálogos
         Hispánicos* 6, 27–65.
Havers, Wilhelm
1931   *Handbuch der erklärenden Syntax*. Heidelberg: Carl Winter.
Heeschen, Volker
1980   Theorie des sprachlichen Handelns. In Althaus, H., E. Wie-
         gand and H. Henne (eds.), *Lexikon der germanistischen Lin-
         guistik*. Tübingen: Niemeyer, 259–267.
Held, Gudrun
1988a   Danken – semantische, pragmatische und soziokulturelle
         Aspekte eines höflichen Sprechakts (gezeigt am Beispiel des
         Französischen). *Klagenfurter Beiträge zur Sprachwissen-
         schaft* 13–14.
1988b   Italienisch: Partikelforschung. In Holtus, G., M. Metzeltin
         and C. Schmitt (eds.), *Lexikon der romanistischen Linguistik,
         Bd. IV*. Tübingen: Niemeyer, 63–75.
1989   On the role of maximization in verbal politeness. *Multilingua*
         8, 167–206.
1992   Aspekte des Zusammenhangs zwischen Höflichkeit und
         Sprache in der vorpragmatischen Sprachwissenschaft.
         Zeitschrift für Romanische Philologie 108(1/2), 1–34.
Helt, R.
1982   Developing communicative competence: A practical model.
         Modern Language Journal 66, 255–262.
Hendry, J.
1992   Honorifics as dialect: The expression and manipulation of
         boundaries in Japanese. *Multilingua* 11.
Hersey, John
1946   *Hiroshima*. Harmondsworth: Penguin.
Hill, B., S. Ide, S. Ikuta, A. Kawasaki and T. Ogino
1986   Universals of linguistic politeness: Quantitative evidence
         from Japanese and American English. *Journal of Pragmatics*
         10, 347–371.
Holly, Werner
1979   *Imagearbeit in Gesprächen*. Tübingen: Niemeyer.

Hough, Graham
    1960   *Image and Experience*. London: Duckworth.
House, Juliane
    1989   Politeness in English and German: The function of "please"
                and "bitte". In Blum-Kulka, S., J. House and G. Kasper
                (eds.), 96–123.
House, Juliane and Gabriele Kasper
    1981   Politeness markers in English and German. In Coulmas, F.
                (ed.), *Conversational Routine*. The Hague: Mouton, 157–
                185.
Hymes, D.
    1972a   On communicative competence. In Pride, John and Janet
                Holmes (eds.), *Sociolinguistics*. Harmondsworth: Penguin.
    1972b   Models of the interaction of language and social life. In
                Gumperz, J. and D. Hymes (eds.), *Directions in Sociolin-
                guistics: The Ethnography of Communication*. New York:
                Holt, Rinehart and Winston, 35–71.
Ide, Sachiko
    1979   *Onna no kotoba otoko no kotoba* ['Female speech and male
                speech']. Tokyo: Nihon Keizai Tsuushinsha.
    1982   Japanese sociolinguistics: Politeness and women's language.
                Lingua 57, 357–385.
    1987   Strategies of "discernment" and "volition" for linguistic
                politeness. Paper delivered at the International Pragmatics
                Conference, Antwerp.
    1988   Introduction. *Multilingua* 7(4), 371–374.
    1989   Formal forms and discernment: neglected aspects of linguis-
                tic politeness. *Multilingua* 8(2), 223–248.
Ide, S., M. Hori, A.Kawasaki, S. Ikuta and H. Haga
    1986   Sex differences and politeness in Japanese. *International
                Journal of the Sociology of Language* 58, 25–36.
Israel, Joachim
    1979   *Der Begriff Dialektik. Erkenntnistheorie, Sprache und
                dialektische Gesellschaftswissenschaft*. Hamburg: Rowohlt.
Izard, C.
    1972   *Patterns of Emotion*. New York: Academic Press.
Jacob, G.
    1897   *Altarabisches Beduinenleben*. Berlin: Meyer und Müller.
Jaffe, J. and S. Feldstein
    1970   *Rhythms of Dialog*. New York: Academic Press.
Jain, Danesh Kumar
    1969   Verbalization of respect in Hindi. *Anthropological Linguis-
                tics* 11(3), 79–97.

James, S.
1978   Effects of listener age and situation on the politeness of chil-
            dren's directives. *Journal of Psycholinguistic Research* 7,
            307–317.

Janney, Richard W.
1988   Politeness. Paper delivered at the Societas Linguistica Eu-
            ropaea Annual Meeting, Freiburg, Workshop on Politeness.

Jhering, R. von
1883   *Der Zweck im Recht*. Bde. 1 und 2. Leipzig: Breitkopf und
            Härtel. (Third edition of Vol. 1, 1893; second edition of Vol.
            2, 1916).

Jucker, Andreas
1987   The relevance of politeness. *Multilingua* 7(4), 375–384.

Jugaku, Akiko
1979   *Nihongo to onna* ['Japanese and women']. Tokyo: Iwanami.

Kainz, Friedrich
1941–   *Psychologie der Sprache, 5 Bde*. Stuttgart: Enke.
1965

Katriel, T.
1986   *Talking Straight: Dugri Speech in Israeli Sabra Culture*.
            Cambridge: Cambridge University Press.
1991   *Communal Webs: Culture and Communication in Contempo-
            rary Israel*. Albany: State University of New York Press.

Keats, John
1954   *Letters of John Keats*. Edited by Frederick Page. London:
            Oxford University Press.

Keil, Regina
1987   Pour vos yeux – Augen wie Oliven: Das Kompliment in der
            Literatur. Paper delivered at the GAL-Tagung, Heidelberg.

Keller, Monika
1984   Rechtfertigungen. Zur Entwicklung pragmatischer Erklärun-
            gen. In Edelstein, W. and J. Habermas (eds.), *Soziale In-
            teraktion und soziales Verstehen*. Frankfurt: Suhrkamp, 253–
            300.

Kelz, H. and M. Kummer
1989   *Beiträge zur Phonetik des Thailändischen*. Hamburg: Buske.

Kemper, Susan and David Thissen
1981   How polite? A reply to Clark and Schunk. *Cognition* 9, 505–
            509.

Kendall, M.
1981   Toward a semantic approach to terms of address: A critique
            of deterministic models in sociolinguistics. *Language and
            Communication* 1, 237–254.

Kerbrat-Orecchioni, Catherine
1987   La description des échanges en analyse conversationelle:
        l'exemple du compliment. *Revue de Linguistique DRLAV*
        36/37, 1–53.
Kerbs, D., C. Müller and H. Krumteich
1970   *Das Ende der Höflichkeit. Für eine Rveision der Anstand-
        serziehung.* München: Juventa.
Khuri, F.
1979   The etiquette of bargaining in the Middle East. *Journal of the
        American Anthropologist* 70, 698–705.
Kiddle, L.
1953   Some social implications of the voseo. *Modern Language
        Forum* 37, 50–54.
Kimsuvan, A.
1984   Verstehensprozess bei interkultureller Kimmunikation. Am
        Beispiel Deutsche in Thailand. Unpublished PhD thesis,
        University of Heidelberg.
Kindaichi, H.
1957   *Nihongo* ['The Japanese Language']. Tokyo: Iwanami.
Kindaichi, H., O. Hayashi and T. Shibata
1988   *Nihongo hyakka daijiten* ['An Encyclopedia of the Japanese
        Language']. Tokyo: Taishukan.
Kishitani, Shoko
1969   Der japanische Honorativ und seine Verwendung in der
        Sprache der Gegenwart. In Lewin, B. (ed.), *Beiträge zum in-
        terpersonalen Bezug im Japanischen.* Wiesbaden: Harras-
        sowitz, 1–17.
KKK
1983   Keigo to keigoshiki ['Honorific speech and consciousness
        thereof']. *Kokuritsu kokugo kenyūjo hōkoku* 77 ['The 77th re-
        port of the National Language Research Institute']. Tokyo:
        Sanseido.
Klausner, T.
1950   Akklamation. *Reallexikon für Antike und Christentum, Bd. 1.*
        Stuttgart: Hiersemann, 216–233.
Klausner, W. and K. Klausner
1978   Conflict of communication. *Business Information Research*
        2.
Knapp, Karlfried and Annelie Knapp-Potthoff
1985   Sprachmittlertätigkeit in der interkulturellen Kommunika-
        tion. In Rehbein, J. (ed.), *Interkulturelle Kommunikation.*
        Tübingen: Narr, 450–463.

1986   Interweaving two discourses: The difficult task of the non-professional interpreter. In House, J. and S. Blum-Kulka (eds.), *Interlingual and Intercultural Communication: Discourse and Cognition in Translation and Second Language Acquisition Studies*. Tübingen: Narr, 151–168.

1987   The man (or woman) in the middle: Discoursal aspects of non-professional interpreting. In Knapp, K., W. Enninger and A. Knapp-Potthoff (eds.), *Analyzing Intercultural Communication*. Berlin: Mouton de Gruyter, 181–211.

Knapp, K., W. Enninger and A. Knapp-Potthoff (eds.)
1987   *Analyzing Intercultural Communication*. Berlin: Mouton de Gruyter.

Knapp-Potthoff, Annelie
1987   Speaking for others – on a neglected aspect of using a foreign language. In Lörscher, W. and R. Schulze (eds.), *Perspectives on Language in Performance*, Vol. 2. Tübingen: Narr, 1125–1142.

Köhler, L.
1922   Hebräische Gesprächsformen. *Zeitschrift für alttestamentliche Wissenschaft* 40, 36–46.

Kohz, A.
1982   Linguistische Aspekte des Anredeverhaltens. Untersuchungen am Deutschen und Schwedischen. Tübingen: Narr.

Koshal, S.
1987   Honorific systems of the Ladakhi language. *Multilingua* 6(2), 149–168.

Kraut, R. and R. Johnston
1979   Social and emotional messages of smiling. *Journal of Personality and Social Psychology* 37, 1539–1553.

Kremos, Helga
1955   *Höflichkeitsformeln in der französischen Sprache: Aufforderungs- und Bittformeln, Dankesbezeichnungen*. Zürich: Schippert.

Krings, H.
1961   Die Geschichte des Wortschatzes der Höflichkeit im Französischen. PhD thesis, University of Bonn.

Krumrey, H. V.
1984   *Entwicklungsstrukturen von Verhaltensstandarden*. Frankfurt: Suhrkamp.

Kummer, M.
1984a   *Grundlagen einer kommunikativen Grammatik für das Thailändische*. Wiesbaden: Harrassowitz.

1984b   *Grammatische   Übungen   für   Fortgeschrittene.*   Bonn:
         Dümmler.

Labov, William
1968   The reflection of social processes in linguistic structures. In
        Fishman, J. (ed.), *A Reader in the Sociology of Language.*
        The Hague: Mouton.
1969   Contraction, deletion, and inherent variability of the copula.
        Language 45, 715–762.

Labov, W. and D. Fanshel (eds.)
1977   *Therapeutic Discourse.* New York: Academic Press.

Laidler, D. and N. Rowe
1980   Georg Simmel's philosophy of money: A review article for
        economists. *Journal of Economic Literature* 18, 97–105.

Lakoff, Robin
1973   The logic of politeness: or, minding your p's and q's. *Papers
        from the Ninth Regional Meeting of the Chicage Linguistics
        Society*, 292–305.
1975   *Language and Woman's Place.* New York: Harper and Row.
1977   What you can do with words: Politeness, pragmatics, and
        performatives. In Rogers, A., B. Wall and J. Murphy (eds.),
        *Proceedings of the Texas Conference on Performatives, Pre-
        suppositions, and Implicatures.* Arlington: Center of Applied
        Linguistics, 79–105.
1989   The limits of politeness: Therapeutic and courtroom dis-
        course. *Multilingua* 8(2/3), 101–129.

Lande, I.
1949   *Formelhafte Wendungen der Umgangssprache im Alten
        Testament.* Leiden: Brill.

Lange, Willi
1984   *Aspekte der Höflichkeit. Überlegungen am Beispiel der
        Entschuldigungen im Deutschen.* Frankfurt: Lang.

Lavandera, Beatriz
1989   The social pragmatics of politeness forms. In Ammon, U., N.
        Dittmar   and   K.   Mattheier   (eds.),   *Sociolinguis-
        tics/Soziolinguistik: An International Handbook of the Sci-
        ence of Language and Society/Ein internationales Handbuch
        zur Wissenschaft von Sprache und Gesellschaft*, Vol. 2. Ber-
        lin: de Gruyter, 1196–1205.

Law, Howard
1948   Greeting forms of the Gulf Aztecs. *Southwestern Journal of
        Anthropology* 4, 43–48.

Leach, E. R.
1976   *Culture and Communication: The Logic by which Symbols are Connected.* Cambridge: Cambridge University Press.

Leavis, F. R.
1932   *New Bearings in English Poetry.* Republished 1963 and reissued 1972. Harmondsworth: Penguin.
1936   *Revaluation: Tradition and Development in English Poetry.* Republished 1964. Harmondsworth: Penguin.
1955   *D. H. Lawrence: Novelist.* Republished 1964. Harmondsworth: Penguin.

Lebra, Takie S.
1976   *Japanese Patterns of Behavior.* Honolulu: The University Press of Hawaii.

Leech, Geoffrey
1977   Language and tact. *L.A.U.T. Paper 46.* Reprinted as *Language and Tact.* Amsterdam: Benjamins.
1980   *Explorations in Semantics and Pragmatics.* Amsterdam: Benjamins.
1983   *Principles of Pragmatics.* London: Longman.

Lerch, Erwin
1933   *Französische Sprache und Wesensart.* Frankfurt: Diesterweg.

Levinson, Stephen
1983   *Pragmatics.* Cambridge: Cambridge University Press.

Lewin, Bruno
1969   Honorative Sprachformen des Japanischen im Zeitalter der Demokratisierung. In Lewin, B. (ed.), *Beiträge zum interpersonalen Bezug im Japanischen.* Wiesbaden: Harrassowitz, 167–184.

Lewis, D.
1969   *Convention.* Cambridge, Mass: Harvard University Press.

Lévi-Strauss, C.
1950   Introduction. In Mauss, M. (ed.), *Sociologie et Anthropologie.* Paris: Presses Universitaires de France, 9–64.

Lock, A. (ed.)
1978   *Action, Gesture and Symbol.* London: Academic Press.

Lucas, F.
1923   Review of *The Waste Land. New Statesman*, 3. November.

Luhmann, Niklas
1982   *Liebe als Passion. Zur Codierung von Intimität.* Frankfurt: Suhrkamp.

Machwirth, E.
1970   Höflichkeit, Geschichte, Inhalt, Bedeutung. PhD thesis, University of Trier.

MacLean, P.
   1973   *A Triune Concept of the Brain and Behavior.* Toronto: To-
           ronto University Press.
Malinowski, B.
   1930   The problem of meaning in primitive languages. In Ogden,
           C. and I. Richards, *The Meaning of Meaning.* London:
           Routledge.
Manes, J. and N. Wolfson
   1981   The compliment formula. In Coulmas, F. (ed.), *Conversa-
           tional Routine.* The Hague: Mouton, 115–132.
Mathiot, M.
   1983   Toward a meaning-based theory of face-to-face interaction.
           International Journal of the Sociology of Language 43, 5–56.
Matsumoto, Yoshiko
   1987   Universality of pragmatics: Evidence from Japanese polite-
           ness phenomena. Paper delivered at the International Prag-
           matics Conference, Antwerp.
   1988   Reexaminations of the universality of face: Politeness
           phenomena in Japanese. *Journal of Pragmatics* 12, 403–426.
   1989   Politeness and conversational universals – observations from
           Japanese. *Multilingua* 8(2/3), 207–221.
Mauss, Marcel
   1950   *Essai sur le don.* Paris: Presses Universitaires de France.
Mead, George H.
   1934   *Mind, Self and Society: From the Standpoint of a Social Be-
           haviorist.* Chicage: Chicago University Press.
Miller, G. and P Johnson-Laird
   1976   *Language and Perception.* Cambridge, Mass: Harvard
           University Press.
Miller, Roy A.
   1982   *Japan's Modern Myth: The Language and Beyond.* New
           York: Weatherhill.
Minami, Fujio
   1987   *Keigo.* Tokyo: Iwanami.
Miyaji, Yutaka
   1957   Keigo no konran ['The confusion of honorific speech'].
           Gengo Seikatsu 70(7).
Miyake, Takeo
   1961   "Kore kara no keigo" sono go – tokuni keishō ni tsuite ['Af-
           ter "kore kara no keigo" – especially about titles'] *Gengo
           Seikatsu* 115.

Mizutani, Osamu
1979 *Nihongo no seitai* ['The Ecology of Japanese']. Tokyo: Sotakusha.
Monbushō ['Ministry of Education']
1941 Reihō yōkō ['The essential points of etiquette']. *Gendai keigohō* ['The Rules of Present-day Honorific Language']. Tokyo: Nihongoyōiku shinōkai, 5–31.
1952 Kore kara no keigo ['Honorific language from now on']. *Kokugo Nenkan* 1854/2.
Moore, T. and C. Carling
1982 *Understanding Language*. London: Macmillan.
Morris, C.
1946 *Signs, Language and Behavior*. New York: George Braziller.
Müller, C.
1975 Anrufe an Lebende. *Lexikon der Ägyptologie, Bd. 1.* Wiesbaden: Harrassowitz.
Müller, Klaus
1979 Partnerarbeit in Dialogen. *Grazer Linguistische Studien* 10, 183–216.
1980 Interaktionssemantik. *Deutsche Sprache* 2, 289–303.
Nash, Manning
1961 The social contxet of economic choice in a small society. *Man* 61, 186–191.
Neisser, U.
1976 *Cognition and Reality*. San Francisco: Freeman.
Neuendorff, Dagmar
1987 Indicating politeness: A study into historical aspects of complex behavioral strategies. In Sajavaara, K. (ed.), *Discourse Analysis: Openings*. Jyväskylä: Department of English, 51–65.
Neustupný, J.
1972 Remarks on Japanese honorifics. *Linguistic Communications* 7, 78–117.
1974 Keigo wa Nihonga dake no mono dewa nai ['The language of politeness is not peculiar to Japanese']. In Hayashi, S. and F. Minami (eds.), *Keigo kooza 8: Sekai no keigo*. Tokyo: Meiji shoin, 6–7.
Nojiri, E.
1987 Practical aspects of cross-cultural problems in international commercial aviation. *Minutes of the Fifth International Airlines' Language Conference*. Buenos Aires: International Airlines' Council on the Teaching of Foreign Languages to Airline Personnel, 6–7.

O'Connor, J. and G. Arnold
1972   *Intonation in Colloquial English*. London: Longman.
Oksaar, Els
1981   Situationale Interferenzen und Kommunikationskonflikte. In Pöckl, W. (ed.), *Europäische Mehrsprachigkeit*. Tübingen: Niemeyer, 105–115.
1988   *Kulturemtheorie*. Göttingen: Vandenhoeck and Ruprecht.
Olshtain, Elite and Leora Weinbach
1987   Complaints: A study of speech act behavior among native and nonnative speakers of Hebrew. In Verschueren, J. and P. Bertalucci (eds.), *The Pragmatics Perspective*. Amsterdam: Benjamins, 195–211.
Osing, J.
1975   Anreden. *Lexikon der Ägyptologie, Bd. 1*. Wiesbaden: Harrassowitz, 292–293.
Østrup, J.
1929   *Orientalische Höflichkeit. Formen und Formeln im Islam. Eine kulturgeschichtliche Studie*. Leipzig: Harrassowitz.
Owen, Marion
1980   *Apologies and Remedial Interchanges: A Study of Language Use in Social Interaction*. Berlin: Mouton de Gruyter.
Palakornkul, A.
1975   A sociolinguistic study of pronominal usage in spoken Bangkok Thai. *Linguistics* 165, 11–41.
Parsons, Talcott
1980   *Zur Theorie der sozialen Interaktionsmedien*. Opladen: Westdeutscher Verlag.
Patterson, M.
1983   *Nonverbal Behavior*. New York: Springer.
Pearl, R.
1985   Children's understanding of others' need for help: Effects of problem explicitness and type. *Child Development* 56, 735–745.
Peng, Fred C. (ed.)
1975   *Language in Japanese Society: Current Issues in Sociolinguistics*. Tokyo: University of Tokyo Press.
Peterson, C., J. Peterson and D. Seeto
1983   Developmental changes in ideas about lying. *Child Development* 54, 1529–1535.
Phukphasuk, P.
1976   Variations in the use of particles in male and female speakers of the Thai language. Unpublished project paper. Singapore: SEAMEO RELC.

Piaget, J.
1973   *Das moralische Urteil beim Ki*nde. Frankfurt: Suhrkamp.
Pierini, Patrizia
1983   Struttura e uso di alcune formule di cortesia. In Orletti, F. (ed.), *Communicare nella vita quotidiano*. Bologna: Il Mulino, 105–117.
Pitt-Rivers, William
1966   Honor and social status. In Peristiany, J. (ed.), *Honor and Shame: The Values of Mediterranean Society*. Chicago: University of Chicago Press.
Plutchik, R. and H. Kellerman (eds.)
1980   *Emotion 1*. New York: Academic Press.
Polanyi, K.
1944   *The Great Transformation*. New York: Rinehart and Co.
Pomerantz, Anita
1978   Compliment responses. In Schenkein, J. (ed.), *Studies in the Organization of Conversational Interaction*. New York: Acadamic Press, 79–112.
Prator, C. H.
1982   Instruction in culture. *Nagoya Gakuin University Round Table 7*, 1–9.
Press, John
1958   *The Chequer'd Shade: Reflections on Obscurity in Poetry*. London: Oxford University Press.
Prideaux, Gary
1984   *Psycholinguistics: The Experimental Study of Language*. London: Croom Helm.
Rabin, Chaim
1976   Acceptability in a revived language. In Greenbaum, S. (ed.), *Acceptability in Language*. The Hague: Mouton, 149–167.
Raible, Wolfgang
1987   Sprachliche Höflichkeit. Realisationsformen im Deutschen und im Französischen. *Zeitschrift für französische Sprache und Literatur* 97, 145–168.
Reese, Hayne W. and Willis F. Overton
1979   Modelle der Entwicklung und Theorien der Entwicklung. In Baltes, P. (ed.), *Entwicklungspsychologie der Lebensspanne*. Stuttgart: Klett-Cotta. (First published in Goulet L. and P. Baltes (eds.), *Life-Span Developmental Psychology: Research and Theory*. New York: Academic Press.)
Renger, J.
1972–   Hofstaat. *Reallexikon der Assyriologie und Vorderasiati-*

1975   *schen Archäologie. Bd. 4.* Berlin: Mouton de Gruyter, 435–446.

Reiss, K. and H. Vermeer
1984   *Grundlegung einer allgemeinen Translationstheorie.* Tübingen: Niemeyer.

Richards, I. A.
1926   *Principles of Literary Criticism* (2nd edition). London: Routledge and Kegan Paul.

Roche, Reinhard
1965   Floskeln im Gegenwartsdeutsch. *Wirkendes Wort* 15, 385–405.

Rosengren, I. (ed.)
1984   *Sprache und Pragmatik.* Lund: CLEERUP.

Roulet, Eddy
1981   Echanges, interventions et actes de langage dans la structure de la conversation. *Etudes de Linguistique Appliquée* 44, 7–39.

Sacks, H., E. Schegloff and G. Jefferson
1974   A simplest systematics for the organization of turn-taking in conversation. *Language* 50, 696–735.

Sager, Sven
1981   *Sprache und Beziehung.* Tübingen: Niemeyer.

Sahlins, Marschall
1965   On the sociology of primitive exchange. In Banton, M. (ed.), *The Relevance of Models for Social Anthropology.* A.S.A. Monogarphs.
1976   *Culture and Practical Reason.* Chicago: University of Chicago Press.

Sakazume, Rikiji
1985   *Keigo. Omoiyari no komyunikeishon* ['Honorific Speech: Considerate Communication']. Tokyo: Yuhikaku.

Salonen, E.
1957–   Gruß. *Reallexikon der Assyriologie und Vorderasiatischen*
1971   *Archäologie, Bd. 3.* Berlin: Mouton de Gruyter, 668–670.
1967   *Die Gruß- und Höflichkeitsformeln in babylonisch-assyrischen Briefen.* Helsinki: Suomalainen Tiedeakademia.

Sampson, E.
1977   Psychology and the American ideal. *Journal of Personality and Social Psychology* 35, 767–782.

Sarles, H.
1977   *After Metaphysics.* Lisse: De Ridder.

Schaff, Adam
    1974   *Sprache und Erkenntnis und Essays über die Philosophie der Sprache.* Reinbeck: Rowohlt.

Scheflen, A.
    1973   *Communication Structure.* Bloomington: University of Indiana Press.

Schegloff, E.
    1979   Identification and recognition in telephone conversation openings. In Psathas, G. (ed.), *Everyday Language: Studies in Ethnomethodology.* New York: Irvington, 23–78.

Scherer, K.
    1979   Nonlinguistic vocal indicators of emotion and psychopathology. In Izard, C. (ed.), *Emotions in Personality and Psychopathology.* New York: Plenum, 495–525.
    1980   The functions of nonverbal signs in conversation. In St.Clair, R. and H. Giles (eds.), *The Social and Psychological Contexts of Language.* Hillsdale, NJ: Lawrence Erlbaum.

Schiffer, S.
    1971   *Meaning.* Oxford: Oxford University Press.

Schiffrin, Deborah
    1981   Meta-talk: Organizational and evaluative brackets in discourse. *Sociological Inquiry: Language and Social Interaction* 50(3/4), 199–236.

Scholtens, A. and J. Stalpers
    1982   *Episodeovergangen in diskussies: Een poging tot verduidelijking van het begrip dominantie in diskussies.* Amsterdam: Publikaties van het Instituut voor Algemene Taalwetenschap, Universiteit van Amsterdam.

Scholz, F.
    1956   Gruß und Anruf. *Zeitschrift für vergleichende Sprachforschung auf dem Gebiet indogermanischer Sprache* 70, 129–145.

Schönbach, Peter
    1974   Soziolinguistik. In Koch, W. A. (ed.), *Perspektiven der Linguistik, Bd. 2.* Stuttgart: Kröner, 156–178.

Schönrich, Gerhard
    1981   *Kategorien und transzendentale Argumentation: Kant und die Idee einer transzendentalen Semiotik.* Frankfurt: Suhrkamp.

Schroeder, O.
    1938   Briefe. *Reallexikon der Assyriologie, Bd. 2.* Berlin: de Gruyter, 62–68.

Schulze, Rainer
    1985   *Höflichkeit im Englischen.* Tübingen: Narr.
    1986   Strategic indeterminacy and face-work. *Studia Anglica Posnaniensia* 19, 75–89.
Schunk, D. and H. Clark
    n.d.   Extended requests and politeness. Unpublished manuscript.
Scollon, R. and S. Scollon
    1981   *Narrative, Literacy and Face in Interethnic Communication.* Norwood, NJ: Ablex.
Scott, M. and S. Lyman
    1976   Praktische Erklärungen. In Auwärter, M., E. Kirsch and K. Schröter (eds.), *Seminar: Kimmunikation, Interaktion, Identität.* Frankfurt: Suhrkamp, 73–115.
Searle, John R.
    1975   Indirect speech acts. In Cole, P. and J. Morgan (eds.), *Syntax and Semantics, Vol. 3: Speech Acts.* New York: Academic Press.
Seel, P.
    1983   Sprache und Kultur. Fragen zum Fremdsprachenunterricht in der "dritten Welt": Bedingungen und Grenzen einer "Interkulturellen Kommunikation". In Gerighausen, J. and P. Seel (eds.), *Interkulturelle Kommunikation und Fremdverstehen.* München: Goethe-Institut, 9–13.
Sell, Roger D.
    1985a   Tellability and politeness in the Miller's Tale: First steps in literary pragmatics. *English Studies* 66, 496–512.
    1985b   Politeness in Chaucer: Suggestions towards a methodology for pragmatic stylistics. *Studia Neophilologica* 57, 175–185.
    1986   The drama of fictionalized author and reader: A formalist obstacle to literary pragmatics. *REAL: The Yearbook of Research in English and American Literature* 4, 291–316.
    1989   Disciplinary fragmentation and integration: Grammatology and literary pragmatics. Parlance: The Journal of the Poetics and Linguistics Association 2, 5–24.
    1991   The politeness of literary texts. In Sell, R. (ed.), *Literary Pragmatics.* London: Routledge, 208–224.
Sell, Roger (ed.)
    1991   *Literary Pragmatics.* London: Routledge.
Selman, R.
    1980   *The Growth of Interpersonal Understanding.* New York: Academic Press.

1981   The child as friendship philosopher. In Asher, S. and J. Gott-man (eds.), *The Development of Children's Friendships.* New York: Cambridge University Press.

Sheffer, Hadas
    1987   Nicknaming practices in American and Israeli Jewish fami-lies. Unpublished paper, Hebrew University, Jerusalem.

Shotter, John
    1973   Prologemena to an understanding of play. *Journal for the Theory of Social Behaviour* 3, 47–89/
    1976   Acquired powers: The transformation of natural into personal powers. In Harré, R. (ed.), *Personality.* Oxford: Blackwell, 25–43.

Silbereisen, R. K.
    1986   Soziale Kognition. Entwicklung von sozialem Wissen und Verstehen. In Oerter, R. and L. Montada (eds.), *Entwick-lunspsychologie.* München: Psychologie Verlagsunion.

Silver, M., J. Sabini and W. G. Parrott
    1987   Embarrassment: A dramaturgic account. *Journal for the The-ory of Social Behviour* 17, 47–61.

Silverberg, William
    1940   On the psychological significance of *du* and *Sie. Psychoana-lytic Quarterly* 9, 509–525.

Silverstein, Michael
    1976   Shifters, linguistic categories and cultural description. In Basso, K. and H. Selby (eds.), *Meaning in Anthropology.* Al-buquerque: University of New Mexico Press.
    1988   Demeanor indexicals and honorific registers. Paper delivered at the Hebrew University, Jerusalem.

Simmel, G.
    1901   Philosophie des Geldes. Taken from G. Simmel, *Das freie Wort.* Reprinted in Frisby, D. and K. Söhnke (eds.), *Gesam-tausgabe, Bd. 6.* Frankfurt, 1989, 719–723.
    1916   Wandel der Kulturformen. *Berliner Tagblatt*, 27. August.

Simpson, C. and E. Weiner (eds.)
    1989   *The Oxford Dictionary, Vol. 7.* (2nd edition). Oxford: Claren-don Press.

Slobin, Dan
    1963   Some aspects of the use of pronouns of address in Yiddish. *Word* 19, 193–202.

Smith, Olivia
    1984   *The Politics of Language 1791–1819.* Oxford: Clarendon Press.

Sombart, Werner
    1902   *Der moderne Kapitalismus.* Leipzig.
    1913   *Luxus und Kapitalismus.* München/Leipzig: Duncker und Humblot.
Sperber, D. and D. Wilson
    1986   *Relevance.* Oxford: Blackwell.
Spitzer, Leo
    1922   *Italienische Umgangssprache.* Bonn: Schröder.
    1961   *Stilstudien, Bd. 1 & 2.* München: Huener. First edition 1928.
Stanitzek, Georg
    1989   *Blödigkeit. Beschreibung des Individuums im 18. Jauhrhundert.* Tübingen: Niemeyer.
Stankiewicz, E.
    1964   Problems of emotive language. In Sebeok, T. et al. (eds.), *Approaches to Semiotics.* The Hague: Mouton, 239–264.
Stati, Sorin
    1982   *Il dialogo.* Napoli: Liguori.
    1983   Tre dimensioni pragmatiche delle repliche oppure come si reagisce agli imperativi. *Grazer Linguistische Studien* 20, 153–169.
Strecker, Ivo
    1988   *The Social Practice of Symbolization: An Anthropological Analysis.* London: Athlone Press.
    1989   Cultural variations of "face". Mimeo.
Streeck, Jürgen
    1983   Konverstaionsanalyse. Ein Reparaturversuch. *Zeitschrift für Sprachwissenschaft* 2, 72–104.
Sucharowski, Wolfgang
    1982   Ich wollte dich noch etwas fragen, aber du wirst es nicht wissen. *Diskussion Deutsch* 13, 213–232.
Sugito, Seiju
    1976   Shokuba de no keigo ['Honorific speech at the work place']. *Gengo Seikatsu* 295, 30–41.
    1987   Doitsujin to nihonjin no keiikōdo ['Politeness behavior of Germans and Japanese']. *Gengo* 16(8), 50–55.
Sullivan, H.
    1953   *The Interpersonal Theory of Psychiatry.* New York: Norton.
Sussman, H. and H. Rosenfeld
    1982   Influence of culture, language, and sex on conversational distance. *Journal of Personality and Social Psychology* 42, 66–74.
Tannen, Deborah
    1986   *That's Not What I Meant.* New York: Ballantine Books.

Tannen, D. and P. Oeztek
1981   "Health to our mouths": Formulaic expressions in Turkish and Greek. In Coulmas, F. (ed.), *Conversational Routine*. The Hague: Mouton, 37–54.
Terasaki, A.
1976   Pre-announcement sequences in conversation. *Social Science Working Papers* 99. University of California at Irvine: School of Social Science.
Thurnwald, Richard
1926   Gruß. *Reallexikon der Vorgeschichte, Bd. 4*. Berlin: Walter de Gruyter, 571–576.
Toyama, Shigehiko
1978   Bunka to keigo ['Culture and honorific language']. In Kokubungaku (ed.), *Anato mo keigo ga tadashiku tsukaeru* ['You Too Can Use Honorific Language Correctly']. Tokyo: Gakuchōsha, 627.
Treitinger, O.
1956   *Die oströmische Kaiser- und Reichsidee nach ihrer Gestaltung im höfischen Zeremoniell. Vom oströmischen Staats- und Reichsgedanken*. Darmstadt: Gentner.
Trosborg, Anna
1987   Apology strategies in natives/non-natives. *Journal of Pragmatics* 11, 147–167.
Turiel, E.
1977   Distinct conceptual and developmental domains: Social convention and morality. In Keasey, C. (ed.), *Nebraska Symposium on Motivation, Vol. 25*. Lincoln: University of Nebraska Press, 77–116.
1978   The development of concepts of social structure: Social convention. In Glick, J. and K. Clarke-Stewart (eds.), *The Development of Social Understanding*. New York: Gardner, 25–107.
Valtin, R.
1982   Probleme der Erfassung sozial-kognitiver Fähigkeiten – analysiert am Beispiel der Perspektivenübernahme und der verbalen Kommunikation. In Geulen, D. (ed.), *Perspektivenübernahme und soziales Handeln*. Frankfurt: Suhrkamp, 270–297.
Valtl, Karlheinz
1986   Erziehung zur Höflichkeit. PhD thesis, University of Regensburg.
Verschueren. J.
1985   *What People Say They Do With Words*. New Jersey: Ablex.

Vollmer, H. and E. Olshtain
1989   The language of apologies in German. In Blum-Kulka, S., J. House and G. Kasper (eds.).

Waller, M. and J. Schoeler
1985   Die Entwicklung des Verständnisses der situativen Variationsbreite untersciedlich höflicher Fragen. *Zeitschrift für Entwicklungspsychologie und Pädagogische Psychologie* 17, 27–40.

Walper, S. and R. Valtin
1988   Development of the understanding of white lies and the concept of politeness. Lecture held at the *Third European Conference on Developmental Psychology*, Budapest, Hungary, June 15–19, 1988.

Walters, John (ed.)
1981   The sociolinguistics of deference and politeness. Special issue of *The International Journal of the Sociology of Language* 27.

Watanabe, Yūsuka
1977   Kaisō to gengo ['Social class and language']. In Susumu, Ono and Shibata Takeshi (eds.), *Iwanami kōsa nihongo 2. Gengo seikatsu.* Tokyo: Iwanami.

Watts, Richard J.
1989a   Relevance and relational work: Linguistic politeness as politic behaviour. *Multilingua* 8(2/3), 131–166.
1989b   "Taking the pitcher to the well": Native speakers' perceptions of their use of discourse markers in conversation. *Journal of Pragmatics* 13(1), 203–237.

Weber, Max
1905   Die protestantische Ethik und der Geist des Kapitalismus. *Archiv für Sozialwissenschaft und Sozialpolitik, Bd. XX und XXI.* Reprinted in Winckelmann, J. (ed.), 1984, *Die protestantische Ethik I.* Tübingen: Mohr, 27–278.

Weijdema, Willy
1985   Meta-uitingen in formele meerpartijen-discussies. Mimeo.

Weilner, I.
1960   Höflichkeit. *Lexikon für Theologie und Kirche, Bd. 5.* Freiburg: Herder, 425.

Weinrich, Harald
1966   *Linguistik der Lüge.* Heidelberg: Lambert Schneider.
1976   *Sprache in Texten.* Stuttgart: Ernst Klett.
1986   Lügt man im Deutschen, wenn man höflich ist? *Duden-Beiträge* 48. Mannheim: Bibliographisches Institut.

Weizman, Elda
1989 Requestive hints. In Blum-Kulka, S. J. House and G. Kasper (eds.), 71–96.
Werkhofer, K. T.
1984a Zur Symboltheorie der Sprachentwicklung: Eine Art Meta-Theorie. In Großmann, K. und P. Lütkenhaus (eds.), *Bericht über die 6. Tagung Entwicklungspsychologie*. Regensburg.
1984b Ist Höflichkeit skalierbar? Unpublished manuscript.
1985 Four views on politeness. Unpublished manuscript.
1986a Politeness and money: Two symbolic media. Unpublished manuscript.
1986b The development of politeness in children. Unpublished manuscript.
1986 Politeness and affect. Unpublished manuscript.
1989a Politeness and money. Unpublished manuscript.
1989b Models and methods in politeness. Unpublished manuscript.
Werlen, I.
1983 Vermeidungsritual und Höflichkeit. *Deutsche Sprache* 3, 193–218.
1984 *Ritual und Sprache: Zum Verhältnis von Sprechen und Handeln in Ritualen*. Tübingen: Narr.
Wetzel, Patricia J.
1985 In-group/out-group deixis: Situational variation in the verbs of giving and receiving in Japan. In Forgas, J. (ed.), *Language and Social Situations*. New York: Srpinger, 141–156.
White, D. and D. Carlston
1983 Consequences of schemata for attention, impressions, and recall in complex social interaction. *Journal of Personality and Social Psychology* 45, 538–550.
Wierzbicka, Anna
1985 Different cultures, different languages, different speech acts: Polish vs. English. *Journal of Pragmatics* 9, 145–178.
Wilkins, D.
1974 *Second Language Learning and Teaching*. London: Arnold.
Wimmer, H., S. Gruber and J. Perner
1984 Young children's concept of lying: Lexical realism – moral subjectivism. *Journal of Experimental Child Psychology* 37, 1–30.
Winter, W. (ed.)
1984 *Anredeverhalten*. Tübingen: Narr.
Winters, Yvor
1959 *On Modern Poets*. New York: Meridian.

Wittgenstein, L.
1967   *Philosophische Untersuchungen*. Frankfurt: Fischer.
Wolfson, N. and J. Manes
1980   The compliment as a social strategy. *International Journal of Human Communication* 13, 391–410.
1981   The compliment formula. In Coulmas (ed.), 115–133.
Wunderlich, D.
1984   Was sind Aufforderungssätze? In Stickel, G. (ed.), *Pragmatik in der Grammatik. Jahrbuch 1983 des Instituts für Deutsche Sprache*. Düsseldorf: Schwann.
Wundt, Wilhelm
1900   *Völkerpsychologie, Bd. 1: Die Sprache, Teil 1*. Leipzig.
1922   *Völkerpsychologie: Eine Untersuchung der Entwicklungsgesetze von Sprache, Mythos und Sitte*. 4th edition, Vol. 2. Stuttgart: Alfred Kröner.
Yoshizawa, Norio
1981   Hanasu ['Speaking']. In Kokubungaku (ed.), *Anato mo keigo ga tadashiku tsukaeru* ['You Too Can Use Honorific Language Correctly']. Tokyo: Gakuchōsha, 59–97.
Youniss, J.
1982   Entwicklung und Funktion von Freundschaftsbeziehungen. In Edelstein, W. and M. Keller (eds.), *Perspektivität und Interpretation. Beiträge zur Entwicklung des sozialen Verstehens*. Frankfurt/M.: Suhrkamp, 78–109.
Zaehle, B.
1933   *Knigges Umgang mit Menschen und seine Vorläufer. Ein Beitrag zur Gesellschaftsethik*. Heidelberg: Winter.
Zilliacus, H.
1949   *Untersuchungen zu den abstrakten Anrederformen und Höflichkeitstiteln im Griechischen*. Helsingfors: Centraltrykkeriet.
1953   Selbstgefühl und Servilität. Studien zum unregelmässigen Numerusgebrauch im Griechischen. Helsingfors: Centraltrykkeriet.
1964   Anredeformen. *Jahrbuch für Antike und Christentum 7*. Münster: Aschendorff.
1983   Gruβformeln. *Reallexikon für Antike und Christentum. Sachwörterbuch zur Auseinandersetzung des Christentums mit der antiken Welt* 7, 1204–1232.
Zimmermann, Klaus
1979   Indirekte Sprechakte im sozialen Kontext. In Bergenfurth, W., E. Dickmann und O. Winkelmann (eds.), *Festschrift für R. Rohr zum 60. Geburtstag*. Heidelberg: Gross.

1984   Die Antizipation möglicher Rezipientenreaktionen als Prin-
          zip der Kommunikation. In Rosengren, I. (ed.), *Sprache und
          Pragmatik*. Lund: CLEERUP, 131–159.
1985   Bemerkungen zur Beschreibung der interaktiven Funktion
          höflichkeitsmarkierender grammatikalischer Elemente. In
          Gülich, E. and T. Kotschi (eds.), *Grammatik, Konversation,
          Interaktion*. Tübingen: Niemeyer, 67–81.

References from the new "Introduction" and a selected bibliography from 1992 to 2005

Agha, Asif
1994   Honorification. *Annual Review of Anthropology* 23, 277–
          302.
Ajiboye, Tunde
1992   Politeness marking in Yoruba and Yoruba learners of French.
          Language Learning Journal 6, 83–86.
Allsopp, Richard
1994   Some parallels to Swift's "Polite Conversation" in current
          Caribbean English. *English Today* 10(1), 35–40.
Ambady, Nalini, Jasook Koo, Fiona Lee and Robert Rosenthal
1996   More than words: Linguistic and nonlinguistic politeness in
          two cultures. *Journal of Personality and Social Psychology*
          70(5), 996–1011.
Arundale, Robert
1999   An alternative model and ideology of communication for an
          alternative approach to politeness theory. *Pragmatics* 9(1),
          119–153.
Aston, Guy
1995   Say "Thank you": Some pragmatic constraints in conversa-
          tional closing. *Applied Linguistics* 16(1), 57–86.
Axia, Giovanna
1996   How to persuade Mum to buy a toy. *First Language* 16(3),
          301–317.
Bamgbose, Ayo
1994   Politeness across cultures: Implications for second language
          teaching. *Georgetown University Round Table on Languages
          and Linguistics*, 117–127.
Bargiela-Chiappini, Francesca and Sandra Harris
1996   Requests and status in business correspondence. *Journal of
          Pragmatics* 28, 635–662.

1997a   *Managing Language: The Discourse of Corporate Meetings.*
Amsterdam: Benjamins.

Bargiela-Chiappini, Francesca and Sandra Harris (eds.)
1997b   *The Language of Business: An International Perspective.*
Edinburgh: Edinburgh University Press.

Bayraktaroğlu, Arin
1992   Disagreement in Turkish trouble-talk. *Text* 12, 317–342.

Beebe, Leslie M.
1995   Polite fictions: Instrumental rudeness as pragmatic competence. *Georgetown University Round Table on Languages
and Linguistics*, 154–168.

Beeching, Kate
2004   Pragmatic particles – polite but powerless? Tone-group *hein*
and *quoi* in contemporary spoken French. *Multilingua*
23(1/2), 61–84.

Bergman, M. L. and G. Kasper
1993   Perception and performance in native and nonnative apology.
In Kasper, G. and S. Blum-Kulka (eds.), *Interlanguage
Pragmatics*. Oxford: Oxford University Press, 82–107.

Bermingham, Ann and John Brewer (eds.)
1995   *The Consumption of Culture, 1600-1800: Image, Object,
Text*. New York, NY: Routledge.

Bilbow, G.
1995   Requesting strategies in the cross-cultural business meeting.
Pragmatics 5(1), 45–55.

Blum-Kulka, Shoshana
1994   Review of *Politeness Phenomena in England and Greece: A
Crosscultural Perspective* by Maria Sifianou. *Pragmatics
and Cognition* 2(2), 349–356.
1997   *Dinner Talk: Cultural Patterns of Sociability and Socialization in Famil Discourse*. London: Lawrence Erlbaum Associates.

Bogoch, Bryna
1994   Power, distance and solidarity: Models of professional client
interaction in an Israeli legal aid setting. *Discourse and Society* 5(1), 65–88.

Boxer, D.
1993   Social distance and speech behavior: The case of indirect
complaints. *Journal of Pragmatics* 19, 103–125.

Brown, Penelope
1994   Gender, politeness, and confrontation in Tenejapa. In Tannen, Deborah (ed.), *Gender and Conversational Interaction*.
New York: Oxford University Press, 144-162.

Buck, R. A.
1993   Politeness theory as a model of discourse: A theoretical reconsideration. *Northwestern University Working Papers in Linguistics* 5, 1–9.
Buck, R. A. and Timothy R. Austin
1995   Dialogue and power in E. M. Forster's *Howards End*. In Verdonk, Peter and Jean-Jacques Weber (eds.), *Twentieth-Century Fiction: From Text to Context*. London: Routledge, 63–77.
Bustamante Lopez, Isabel and Mercedes Nino Murcia
1995   Impositive speech acts in Northern Andean Spanish: A pragmatic description. *Hispania: A Journal Devoted to the Interests of the Teaching of Spanish and Portuguese* 78(4), 885–897.
Carré, Jacques
1994   Ethique et politesse des élites foncières anglaises (1750-1850). *QWERTY: Arts, Littératures et Civilisations du Monde Anglophone* 4, 339–345.
Carré, Jacques (ed.)
1994   *The Crisis of Courtesy: Studies in the Conduct-Book in Britain, 1600–1900*. Leiden: Brill.
Chang, H. and G. R. Holt
1994   A Chinese perspective on face as inter-relational concern, In Ting-Toomey, S. (ed.), *The Challenge of Facework*. Albany NY: University of New York Press, 95–132.
Chen, Rong
2001   Self-politeness: A proposal. *Journal of Pragmatics* 33, 87–106.
Christie, Christine
2002   Politeness and the linguistic construction of gender in Parliament: An analysis of transgressions and apology behaviour. In Linguistic Politeness Research Group (ed.), *Working Papers on the Web*, www.shu.ac.uk/wpw
Christie, Christine (ed.)
2004   *Tensions in Current Politeness Research*. Special Issue of *Multilingua* 23(1/2).
Conlan, Christopher J.
1996   Politeness, paradigms of family, and the Japanese ESL speaker. *Language Sciences* 18(3/4), 729–742.
Cook, Haruko Minegishi
1996   Japanese language socialization: Indexing the modes of self. *Discourse Processes* 22(2), 171–197.

1997   The role of the Japanese *masu* form in caregiver–child
              conversation. *Journal of Pragmatics* 28(6), 695–718.
Copley, Stephen
1995   Commerce, conversation and politeness in the early eight-
              eenth-century periodical. *British Journal for Eighteenth
              Century Studies* 18(1), 63–77.
Coupland, N., K. Grainger and J. Coupland
1988   Politeness in context: Intergenerational issues. *Language in
              Society* 17(2), 253–262.
Culpeper, Jonathan
1996   Towards an anatomy of impoliteness. *Journal of Pragmatics*
              25(3), 349–367.
Dzameshie, Alex K.
1993   The use of politeness strategies as solidarity and deference
              moves in Christian sermonic discourse. *The SECOL Review:
              Southeastern Conference on Linguistics* 17(2), 113–126.
de Kadt, Elizabeth
1992   Politeness phenomena in South African Black English. *Prag-
              matics and Language Learning* 3, 103–116.
1994   Towards a model for the study of politeness in Zulu. *South
              African Journal of African Languages/Suid Afrikaanse Ty-
              dskrif vir Afrikatale* 14(3), 103–112.
1995   "I must be seated to talk to you": Taking nonverbal polite-
              ness strategies into account. *Pragmatics and Language
              Learning. Monograph Series* 6.
1998   The concept of face and its applicability to the Zulu lan-
              guage. *Journal of Pragmatics* 29, 173–191.
Dillard, James Price, Steven R. Wilson, Kyle James Tusing and Terry A.
Kinney
1997   Politeness judgments in personal relationships. *Journal of
              Language and Social Psychology* 16(3), 297–325.
DuFon, Margaret, Gabriele Kasper, Satomi Takahashi and Naoko Yoshinaga
1994   Bibliography on linguistic politeness. *Journal of Pragmatics*
              21(5), 527–578.
Eckert, P. and S. McConnell-Ginet
1992   Think practically and look locally: Language and gender as
              community-based practice. *Annual Review of Sociology* 21,
              461–490.
Eelen, Gino
1999   Politeness and ideology: A critcial review. *Pragmatics* 9(1),
              163–173.
2001   *Critique of Politeness Theories*. Manchester: St. Jerome
              Press.

Eisenstein, M. and J. W. Bodman
1993   Expressing gratitude in American English. In Kasper, G. and S. Blum-Kulka (eds.), *Interlanguage Pragmatics*. Oxford: Oxford University Press, 64–81.

Enomoto, Sanae and Helen Marriott
1994   Investigating evaluative behavior in Japanese tour guiding interaction. *Multilingua* 13(1/2), 131–161.

Escandell Vidal, Maria Victoria
1995   Cortesía, formulas conversacionales y estrategías indirectas. *Revista Espanola de Linguistica* 25(1), 31–66.
1996   Towards a cognitive approach to politeness. *Language Sciences* 18(3/4), 629–650.

Farghal, Mohammed and Ahmed Borini
1996   Pragmalinguistic failure and the translatability of Arabic politeness formulas into English: A case study of Mahfouz's "Awlad Haritna". *Interface: Journal of Applied Linguistics/ Tijdschrift voor Toegepaste Linguistiek* 11(1), 3–23.

France, Peter
1992   *Politeness and its Discontents: Problems in French Classical Culture.* Cambridge: Cambridge University Press.

Francesconi, Daniele
1997   Politeness: Una parola chiave del vocabulario di Hume. *Pensiero Politico: Rivista di Storia delle Idee Politiche e Sociali* 30(3), 551–559.

Fukushima, Saeko
1996   Request strategies in British English and Japanese. *Language Sciences* 18(3/4), 671–688.
2000   *Requests and Culture: Politeness in British English and Japanese.* Bern: Peter Lang.

Galliker, Mark and Margot Klein
1993   Knigges "Umgangsbuch". Zur Entwicklung der bürgerlichen Kom-munikationsregeln. In Sonntag Michael and Gerd Jüttemann (eds.), *Individuum und Geschichte. Beiträge zur Diskussion um eine "Historische Psychologie".* Heidelberg: Asanger, 74–88.

Goffman, Erving
1974   *Frame Analysis: An Essay on the Organization of Experience.* Cambridge, Mass.: Harvard University Press.

Gough, David H.
1995   Some problems for politeness theory: Deference and directness in Xhosa performative requests. *South African Journal*

of African Languages/Suid-Afrikaanse Tydskrif vir Afrikatale 15(3), 123–125.

Graham, Margaret Baker and Carol David
1996   Power and politeness: Administrative writing in an "organized anarchy". *Journal of Business and Technical Communication* 10(1), 5–27.

Grainger, Karen
2002   Politeness or impoliteness? Verbal play on the hospital ward. *English Studies: Working Papers on the Web*, http://www/shu.ac.uk/wpw.wpw. htm
2004   Verbal play on the hospital ward: Solidarity or power? *Multilingua* 23(1/2), 39–59.

Grosperrin, Jean-Philippe
1997   La Politesse des premiers ages: Un Aspect du primitivisme chrétien sous Louis XIV. In Wild, Francine (ed.), *Regards sur le passé dans l'Europe des XVIe et XVIIe siècles*. Berlin: Peter Lang, 397–406.

Haastrup, Niels
1994   The courtesy-book and the phrase-book in modern Europe. In Carré, Jacques (ed.), *The Crisis of Courtesy: Studies in the Conduct-Book in Britain, 1600–1900*. Leiden: Brill, 65–80.

Haroche, Claudine
1993   Civility and politeness: Neglected objects in political sociology/ La civilité et la politesse: des objets "négligés" de la sociologie politique. *Cahiers Internationaux de Sociologie* 40(94), 97–120.

Harris, Sandra
2001   Being politically impolite: Extending politeness theory to adversarial political discourse. *Discourse and Society* 12(4), 451–472.

Haugh, Michael
2004   Revisiting the conceptualisation of politeness in English and Japanese. *Multilingua* 23(1/2), 85–109.

Haverkate, Henk
1994a   The dialogues of Don Quixote de la Mancha: A pragmalinguistic analysis within the framework of Gricean maxims, speech act theory, and politeness theory. *Poetics* 22(3), 219–241.
1994b   Review of *Politeness Phenomena in England and Greece: A Crosscultural Perspective* by Maria Sifianou. *Language in Society* 23(4), 584–587.

Hayashi, Takuo
   1996   Politeness in conflict management: A conversation analysis of dispreferred message from a cognitive perspective. *Journal of Pragmatics* 25(2), 227–255.

Held, Gudrun
   1992   Aspekte des Zusammenhangs zwischen Höflichkeit und Sprache in der vorpragmatischen Sprachwissenschaft. *Zeitschrift für Romanische Philologie* 108(1/2), 1–34.

   1995   *Verbale Höflichkeit: Studien zur linguistischen Theorienbildung und empirische Untersuchung zum Sprachverhalten französischer und italienischer Jugendlicher in Bitt- und Danksituationen.* Tübingen: Gunter Narr.

   1996   Two polite speech scts in contrastive view: Aspects of the realization of requesting and thanking in French and Italian. In Hellinger, Marlis and Ulrich Ammon (eds.), *Contrastive Sociolinguistics*. Berlin: de Gruyter, 363–384.

   1999   Submission strategies as an expression of the ideology of politeness: Reflections on the verbalization of social power relations. *Pragmatics* 9(1), 21–36.

Hendry, Joy
   1992   Honorifics as dialect: The expression and manipulation of boundaries. *Multilingua* 11(4).

   1993   *Wrapping Culture: Politeness, Presentation and Power in Japan and Other Societies.* Oxford: Clarendon Press.

Henry, Alex
   1995   Raising awareness of politeness in business writing. *Language Awareness* 4(4), 179–188.

Hernández-Flores, N.
   1999   Politeness ideology in Spanish colloquial conversations: The case of advice. *Pragmatics* 9(1), 37–49.

Hernández-Sacristan, Carlos
   1995   Deixis social y cortesia en textos cientificos: Un estudio contrastivo. *Verba: Anuario Galego de Filoloxia* 22, 477–500.

Hinkel, Eli
   1996   When in Rome: Evaluations of L2 pragmalinguistic behaviors. *Journal of Pragmatics* 26(1), 51–70.

   1997   Appropriateness of advice: DCT and multiple choice data. *Applied Linguistics* 18(1), 1–26.

Holmes, J.
   1993   New Zealand women are good to talk to: An analysis of politeness strategies in interaction. *Journal of Pragmatics* 20(2), 91–116.

1995   *Women, Men and Politeness.* London: Longman.

Holmes, Janet and Maria Stubbe

1997   Good listeners: Gender differences in New Zealand conversation. *Women and Language* 20(2), 7–14.

2003   *Power and Politeness in the Workplace.* London: Pearson Education.

Holtgraves, Thomas

1992   The linguistic realization of face management: Implications for language production and comprehension, person perception, and cross-cultural communication. *Social Psychology Quarterly* 55(2), 141–159.

1997a   "Yes, but ...": Positive politeness in conversation arguments. *Journal of Language and Social Psychology* 16(2), 222–239.

1997b   Politeness and memory for the wording of remarks. *Memory and Cognition* 25(1), 106–116.

Holtgraves, Thomas and Joong-nam Yang

1992   Interpersonal underpinnings of request strategies: General principles and differences due to culture and gender. *Journal of Personality and Social Psychology* 62(2), 246–256.

Hong, Min Pyo

1992   A contrastive study of politeness consciousness of Japanese and Korean. *Keiryo Kokugogaku/Mathematical Linguistics* 18(7), 324–335.

Hu, H.

1944   The Chinese concepts of "face". *American Anthropologist* 46(1), 45–64.

Hutter, Otto

1993   Zur Pragmatik wissenschaftlicher Texte: Höflichkeit. In Ickler, Theodor (ed.), *Studien zu Deutsch als Fremdsprache, I: Beiträge zur Linguistik und Didaktik des Deutschen als Fremdsprache.* Hildesheim: Olms, 129–149.

Ide, Sachiko (ed.)

1993   *Linguistic Politeness, III: Linguistic Politeness and Universality.* Special issue of *Multilingua* 12(1).

Janney, Richard W. and Horst Arndt

1993   Universality and relativity in cross-cultural politeness research: A historical perspective. *Multilingua* 12(1), 13–50.

Jary, Mark

1998   Relevance theory and the communication of politeness. *Journal of Pragmatics* 30, 1–19.

Jaworski, Adam

1994   Apologies and non-apologies: Negotiation in speech act realization. *Text* 14(2), 185–206.

Jaworski, Adam (ed.)
  1997   *Silence: Interdisciplinary Perpectives.* Berlin: Mouton de Gruyter.
Johnson, Donna M.
  1992   Compliments and politeness in peer-review texts. *Applied Linguistics* 13(1), 51–71.
Johnson, Donna M. and Duane H. Roen
  1992   Complimenting and involvement in peer reviews: Gender variation. *Language in Society* 21(1), 27–57.
Johnstone, Barbara, Kathleen Ferrara and Judith Mattson Bean
  1992   Gender, politeness, and discourse management in same sex and cross-sex opinion-poll interviews. *Journal of Pragmatics* 18(5), 405–430.
Jucker, Andreas H.
  1994   Review of Politeness in Language: Studies in Its History, Theory and Practice, edited by Richard J. Watts, Sachiko Ide, and Konrad Ehlich. *Multilingua* 13(3), 329–334.
Jucker, Andreas H. (ed.)
  1995   *Historical Pragmatics: Pragmatic Developments in the History of English.* Amsterdam: Benjamins.
Kakavá, Christina
  1997   Review article: Politeness and the particularities of requests (Review of Sifianou 1992). *International Journal of the Sociology of Language* 126, 181–198.
  2002   Opposition in Modern Greek discourse: Cultural and contextual constraints. *Journal of Pragmatics* 34, 1537–1568.
Kallia, Alexandra
  2004   Linguistic politeness: The implicature approach. *Multilingua* 23(1/2), 145–169.
Kamisli, S. and S. A. Dogançay
  1997   Gender differences in conveying embarrassing information: Examples from Turkish. Women and Language 20(2), 25–33.
Kasper, Gabriele
  1990   Linguistic politeness: Current research issues. *Journal of Pragmatics* 14(2), 193–218.
Kienpointner, Manfred
  1997   Varieties of rudeness: Types and functions of impolite utterances. *Functions of Language* 4(2), 251–287.
Kienpointner, Manfred (ed.)
  1999   *Ideologies of Politeness.* Special issue of *Pragmatics* 9(1).

Kingwell, Mark
   1993a   Is it rational to be polite? *Journal of Philosophy* 90(8), 387–404.
   1993b   Politics and polite society in the Scottish Enlightenment. *Historical Reflections/Réflexions Historiques* 19(3), 363–387.

Klein, Lawrence E.
   1992   Courtly politesse and civic politeness in France and England. *Halcyon: A Journal of the Humanities* 14, 171–181.
   1994   *Shaftesbury and the Culture of Politeness: Moral Discourse and Cultural Politics in Early Eighteenth-century England.* Cambridge: Cambridge University Press.
   1995   Politeness for plebes: Consumption and social identity in early eighteenth century England. In Bermingham, Ann and John Brewer (eds.), *The Consumption of Culture, 1600-1800: Image, Object, Text.* New York, NY: Routledge.

Kleiner, Brian
   1996   Class ethos and politeness. *Journal of Language and Social Psychology* 15(2), 155–175.

Klotz, P.
   1999   Politeness and political correctness: Ideological implications. *Pragmatics* 9(1), 155–161.

Koike, D. A.
   1992   *Language and Social Relationship in Brazilian Portuguese: The Pragmatics of Politeness.* Austin TX: University of Texas Press.
   1994   Negation in Spanish and English suggestions and requests: Mitigating effects? *Journal of Pragmatics* 21, 513–526.

Kopytko, Roman
   1995   Linguistic politeness strategies in Shakespeare's plays. In Jucker, Andreas H. (ed.), *Historical Pragmatics: Pragmatic Developments in the History of English.* Amsterdam: Benjamins, 515–540.

Kotthoff, Helga
   1993   Disagreement and concession in disputes: On the context sensitivity of preference structures. *Language in Society* 22(2), 193–216.
   1996   Impoliteness and conversational joking: On relational politics. *Folia Linguistica: Acta Societatis Linguisticæ Europeæ* 30(3/4), 299–325.

Koutsantoni, Dmitra
   2004   Relations of power and solidarity in scientific communities: A cross-cultural comparison of politeness strategies in the

writing of native English speaking and Greek engineers. *Multilingua* 23(1/2), 111–143.

Kurzon, Dennis
    2001   The politeness of judges: American and English judicial behaviour. *Journal of Pragmatics* 33, 61–85.

Kwarciak, B. J.
    1993   The acquisition of linguistic politeness and Brown and Levinson's theory. *Multilingua* 12(1), 51–68.

Lambert, Bruce L.
    1996   Face and politeness in pharmacist-physician interaction. *Social Science and Medicine* 43(8), 1189–1198.

Lakoff, Robin
    1979   Stylistic strategies within a grammr of style. In Orosanu, J., K. Slater and L. Adler (eds.), *Language, Sex and Gender: Does la différence make a difference.* New York: The Annals of the New York Academy of the Sciences, 53–80.

Lee-Wong, Song-Mei
    1994a   Imperatives in requests: Direct or impolite: Observations from Chinese. *Pragmatics* 4(4), 491–515.
    1994b   *Qing/Please*: A polite or requestive marker? Observations from Chinese. *Multilingua* 13(4), 343–360.
    1999   *Politeness and Face in Chinese Culture.* Frankfurt: Pater Lang.

Li Wei
    1995   Code-switching, preference marking and politeness in bilingual cross-generational talk: Examples from a Chinese community in Britain. *Journal of Multilingual and Multicultural Development* 16(3), 197–214.

Liao, Chao-chih and Mary I. Bresnahan
    1996   A contrastive pragmatic study on American English and Mandarin refusal strategies. *Language Sciences* 18(3/4), 703–727.

Lim, Tae-Seop
    1994   Facework and interpersonal relationships. In Ting-Toomey, Stella (ed.), *The Challenge of Facework: Cross-Cultural and Interpersonal Issues.* Albany: State University of New York Press, 209–229.

Locher, Miriam
    2004   *Power and Politeness in Action: Disagreements in Oral Communication.* Berlin: Mouton de Gruyter.

Locher, Miriam and Richard J. Watts
    2005   Politeness research and relational work. *Journal of Politeness Research* 1(1), 9–33.

Lodge, A.
1999   Colloquial vocabulary and politeness in French. *Modern Language Review* 94(2), 356–365.
Longcope, Peter
1995   The universality of face in Brown and Levinson's politeness theory: A Japanese perspective. *University of Pennsylvania Working Papers in Educational Linguistics* 11(1), 69–79.
McIntosh, Carey
1998   *The Evolution of English Prose, 1700-1800: Style, Politeness, and Print Culture.* Cambridge University Press.
Magli, Patrizia
1992   Mediocrità e bon ton passionale. In Montandon, Alain (ed.), *Etiquette et politesse.* Clermont-Ferrand: Association des Publications de la Faculté des Lettres et Sciences Humaines de Clermont-Ferrand, 43–55.
Magnusson, A. Lynne
1992   The rhetoric of politeness and Henry VIII. *Shakespeare Quarterly* 43(4), 391–409.
Maier, Paula
1992   Politeness strategies in business letters by native and non-native English speakers. *English for Specific Purposes* 11(3), 189–205.
Mao, LuMing Robert
1994   Beyond politeness theory: "Face" revisited and renewed. *Journal of Pragmatics* 21(5), 451–486.
Marquez-Reiter, Rosina
1997   Politeness phenomena in British English and Uruguayan Spanish: The case of requests. *Miscelanea* 7, 159–167.
Marriott, Helen
1995   Acquisition of politeness patterns by exchange students in Japan. In Freed, Barbara F. (ed.), *Second Language Acquisition in a Study Abroad Context.* Amsterdam: Benjamins, 197–224.
Matsumoto, Yoshiko
1993   Linguistic politeness and cultural style: Observations from Japanese. In Clancy, Patricia M. (ed.), *Japanese/Korean Linguistics, II.* Stanford, CA: Center for Study of Language and Information, 55–67.
Mehrotra, Raja Ram
1995   How to be polite in Indian English. *International Journal of the Sociology of Language* 116, 99–110.

Meier, A. J.
    1992   Brown and Levinson's legacy of politeness. *Views* 1(1), 15–35.
    1995   Defining politeness: Universality in appropriateness. *Language Sciences* 17(4), 345–356.
    1996a   Two cultures mirrored in repair work. *Multilingua* 15(2), 149–169.
    1996b   Passages of politeness. *Journal of Pragmatics* 24, 381–392.
    1997   Teaching the universals of politeness. *ELT Journal* 51(1), 21–28.

Mey, Jacob
    2001   *Pragmatics: An Introduction.* 2nd edition. Oxford: Blackwell.

Mills, Margaret H.
    1992   Conventionalized politeness in Russian requests: A pragmatic view of indirectness. *Russian Linguistics: International Journal for the Study of the Russian Language* 16(1), 65–78.

Mills, Sara
    2002   Rethinking politeness, impoliteness and gender identity. In Sunderland, J. and L. Litoselliti (eds.), *Discourse Analysis and Gender Identity.* Amsterdam: Benjamins.
    2003   *Gender and Politeness.* Cambridge: Cambridge University Press.
    2004a   Class, gender and politeness. *Multilingua* 23(1/2), 171–190.
    2004b   Review of *Politeness*, by Richard J. Watts. Multilingua 23(1/2), 194–197.

Montandon, Alain (ed.)
    1992   *Etiquette et politesse.* Clermont-Ferrand: Association des Publications de la Faculté des Lettres et Sciences Humaines de Clermont-Ferrand.

Moore, Patrick
    1992   When politeness is fatal: Technical communication and the Challenger accident. *Journal of Business and Technical Communication* 6(3), 269–292.

Morand, David A.
    1996a   Politeness as a universal variable in cross-cultural managerial communication. *International Journal of Organizational Analysis* 4(1), 52–74.
    1996b   Dominance, deference, and egalitarianism in organizational interaction: A sociolinguistic analysis of power and politeness. *Organization Science* 7(5), 544–556.

Morisaki, S. and J. Gudykunst
    1994   Face in Japan and the United States. In Ting-Toomey, S. (ed.), *The Challenge of Facework: Cross-Cultural and Interpersonal Issues*. Albany: State University of New York Press, 47–93.

Mullany, Louise
    2004   Gender, politeness and institutional power roles: Humour as a tactic to gain compliance in workplace business meetings. *Multilingua* 23(1/2), 13–37.

Mursy, A. and J. Wilson
    2001   Towards a definition of Egyptian complimenting. *Multilingua* 20(2), 133–154.

Nevalainen, Terttu and Helena Raumolin-Brunberg
    1995   Constraints on politeness: The pragmatics of address formulae in early English correspondence. In Jucker, Andreas H. (eds.), *Historical Pragmatics: Pragmatic Developments in the History of English*. Amsterdam: Benjamins, 167–181.

Nevalainen, Terttu and Helena Raumolin-Brunberg (eds.)
    1996   *Sociolinguistics and Language History: Studies Based on the Corpus of Early English Correspondence*. Amsterdam: Rodopi.

Nwoye, Onuigbo G.
    1992   Linguistic politeness and socio-cultural variations of the notion of face. *Journal of Pragmatics* 18(4), 309–328.

Obeng, Samuel Gyasi
    1996   The proverb as a mitigating and politeness strategy in Akan discourse. *Anthropological Linguistics* 38(3), 521–549.

O'Driscoll, Jim
    1996   About face: A defence and elaboration of universal dualism. *Journal of Pragmatics* 25(1), 1–32.

Okamoto, S.
    1999   Situated politeness: Coordinating honorific and non-honorific expressions. *Pragmatics* 9(1), 51–74.

Pan, Yuling
    1995   Power behind linguistic behavior: Analysis of politeness phenomena in Chinese official settings. *Journal of Language and Social Psychology* 14(4), 462–481.

Pavlidou, Theodossia
    1994   Contrasting German-Greek politeness and the consequences. *Journal of Pragmatics* 21(5), 487–511.

Peng, Guoyue
    1993   Polite expressions in early-modern Chinese and their prag-
matic strategies. *Gengo Kenkyu: Journal of the Linguistic
Society of Japan* 103, 117–140.
    1995   The polite expressions and the speech act of asking about age
in "Golden Lotus": From the approach of sociolinguistics.
Gengo Kenkyu: Journal of the Linguistic Society of Japan
108, 24–45.

Penman, Robyn
    1994   Facework in communication: Conceptual and moral chal-
lenges. In Ting-Toomey, Stella (ed.), *The Challenge of
Facework: Cross-Cultural and Interpersonal Issues.* Albany:
State University of New York Press, 15–45.

Person, Natalie K. et al.
    1995   Pragmatics and pedagogy: Conversational rules and polite-
ness strategies may inhibit effective tutoring. *Cognition and
Instruction* 13(2), 161–188.

Piirainen, I. T.
    1996   Вежливость как категория языка. *Вопросы языкознания*
G-19, 100–105.

Pilegaard, M.
    1997   Politeness in written business discourse: A textlinguistic per-
spective on requests. *Journal of Pragmatics* 28, 223–244.

Placencia, Maria E.
    1996   Politeness in Ecuadorian Spanish. *Multilingua* 15(1), 13–34.

Rathmayr, R.
    1996   Sprachliche Höflichkeit. Am Beispiel expliziter und im-
pliziter Höflichkeit im Russischen. In Girke, W. (ed.), *Slav-
istische Linguistik 1995.* München: Verlag Otto Sagner, 362–
391.
    1999   Métadiscours et réalité linguistique: L'exemple de la poli-
tesse russe. *Pragmatics* 9(1), 75–95.

Raumolin-Brunberg, Helena
    1996   Forms of address in early English correspondence. In
Nevalainen, Terttu and Helena Raumolin-Brunberg (eds.),
*Sociolinguistics and Language History: Studies Based on the
Corpus of Early English Correspondence.* Amsterdam: Ro-
dopi, 167–181.

Roberts, Jo
    1992   Fact-threatening acts and politeness theory: Contrasting
speeches from supervisory conferences. *Journal of Curricu-
lum and Supervision* 7(3), 287–301.

Sanderson, Linda
    1995   Linguistic contradiction: Power and politeness in courtroom discourse. *Technostyle* 12(2), 1–24.

Sasagawa, Y.
    1995   Cultural studies on politeness. *International Journal of Pragmatics* 5, 1–25.

Scannell, Paddy
    1998   Media – language – world. In Bell, Allan and Peter Garrett (eds.), *Approaches to Media Discourse*. Oxford: Blackwell, 251–267.

Schank, Roder C. and Roberst P. Abelson
    1977   *Scripts, Plans, Goals and Understanding: An Inquiry into Human Knowledge.* Erlbaum: Hillsdale.

Scheuermann, Larry and Gary Taylor
    1997   Netiquette. *Internet Research* 7(4), 269–273.

Schmelz, Matthias P.
    1994   *Psychologie der Höflichkeit. Analyse des höflichen Aufforderns im betrieblichen Kontext am Beispiel von Arbeitsanweisungen.* Frankfurt a. M.: Peter Lang.

Schmidt, R.
    1980   Review of Esther Goody, ed., *Questions and Politeness: Strategies in Social Interaction. Regional English Language Centre Journal* 11, 100–114.

Schreier, Margrit, Norbert Groeben and Gerhard Blickle
    1995   The effects of (un-)fairness and (im-)politeness on the evaluation of argumentative communication. *Journal of Language and Social Psychology* 14(3), 260–288.

Shibamoto, Janet
    1994   Review of *Wrapping Culture: Politeness, Presentation, and Power in Japan and Other Societies* by Joy Hendry. *Contemporary Sociology* 23(4), 608.

Shu Dingfang and Hong Wang
    1993   Complimenting and belittling acts in interpersonal rhetoric and politeness principle. *Waiguoyu* 3(85), 7–13.

Sifianou, Maria
    1992a   *Politeness Phenomena in England and Greece.* Oxford: Clarendon.
    1992b   The use of diminutives in expressing politeness: Modern Greek versus English. *Journal of Pragmatics* 17, 155–173.
    1993   Off-record indirectness and the notion of imposition. *Multilingua* 12(1), 69–79.

1995a   Do we need to be silent to be extremely polite? Silence and FTAs. *International Journal of Applied Linguistics* 5(1), 95–110.

1995b   Indirectness and politeness: The case of English and Greek. *Reading Working Papers in Linguistics* 2, 241–253.

1997a   Politeness and off-record indirectness. *International Journal of the Sociology of Language* 126, 163–179.

1997b   Silence and politeness. In Jaworski, Adam (ed.), *Silence: Interdisciplinary Perpectives.* Berlin: Mouton de Gruyter, 63–84.

Smart, Barry
1996   (Mis)understanding Japan. Review article on *Wrapping Culture: Politeness, Presentation, and Power in Japan and Other Societies* by Joy Hendry. Theory, Culture and Society 13(3), 179–192.

Smith, Janet S.
1992   Linguistic privilege: "Just stating the facts" in Japanese. In Hall, Kira, Mary Bucholtz and Birch Moonwomon (eds.), *Locating Power, I & II.* Berkeley: Berkeley Women and Language Group, University of California, 540–548.

Smith, Janet Shibamoto
1997   Review of Joy Hendry, *Wrapping Culture. Language in Society* 26(2), 312–317.

Spencer-Oatey, Helen
1993   Conceptions of social relations and pragmatic research. *Journal of Pragmatics* 20, 27–47.

1996   Reconsidering power and distance. *Journal of Pragmatics* 25, 1–24.

Spencer-Oatey, Helen (ed.)
2000   *Culturally Speaking: Managing Rapport through Talk Across Cultures.* London: Continuum.

Spencer Oatey, H., P. Ng and D. Li
2000   Responding to compliments: British and Chinese evaluative judgements. In Spencer-Oatey, Helen (ed.), *Culturally Speaking: Managing Rapport through Talk Across Cultures.* London: Continuum, 98–120.

Spencer-Oatey, H. and X. Jianyu
2000   A problematic Chinese business visit to Britain: Issues of face. In Spencer-Oatey, Helen (ed.), *Culturally Speaking: Managing Rapport through Talk Across Cultures.* London: Continuum, 272–288.

Steppat, Michael
    1994   Social change and gender decorum: Renaissance courtesy. In
                Carré, Jacques (ed.), *The Crisis of Courtesy: Studies in the
                Conduct-Book in Britain, 1600–1900.* Leiden: Brill.
Strecker, Ivo
    1993   Cultural variations in the concept of "face". *Multilingua*
                12(2), 119–141.
Sunderland, J. and L. Litoselliti (eds.)
    2002   *Discourse Analysis and Gender Identity.* Amsterdam: Benja-
                mins.
Tannen, Deborah
    1993   Waht's in a frame?: Surface evidence for underlying expecta-
                tions. In Tannen, Deborah (ed.), *Framing in Discourse.* Ox-
                ford: Oxford University Press, 14–56.
Terkourafi, M.
    1999   Frames for politeness: A case study. *Pragmatics* 9(1), 97–
                117.
Ting-Toomey, Stella
    1994a   Face and facework: Theoretical and research issues. In Ting-
                Toomey, Stella (ed.), *The Challenge of Facework: Cross-
                Cultural and Interpersonal Issues.* Albany: State University
                of New York Press, 307–340.
Ting-Toomey, Stella (ed.)
    1994b   *The Challenge of Facework: Cross-Cultural and Interper-
                sonal Issues.* Albany: State University of New York Press.
Tirkkonen-Condit, Sonja
    1996   Explicitness vs. implicitness of argumentation: An intercul-
                tural comparison. *Multilingua* 15(3), 257–273.
Tuleja, Tad
    1995   Review of Language and *Social Relationship in Brazilian
                Portuguese: The Pragmatics of Politeness*, by Dale Koike.
                Language in Society 24(2), 294–298.
Turner, Ken
    1996   The principal principles of pragmatic inference: Politeness.
                Language Teaching 29(1), 1–13.
Usami, Mayumi
    2002   *Discourse Politeness in Japanese Conversation: Some Impli-
                cations for a Universal Theory of Politeness.* Tokyo: Hituzi
                Syobo.
van de Walle, Lieve
    1993   *Pragmatics and Classical Sanscrit: A Pilot Study in Linguis-
                tic Politeness.* Amsterdam: Benjamins.

Watts, Richard J.
  1999   Language and politeness in early eighteenth century Britain. *Pragmatics* 9(1), 5–20.
  2002   From polite language to educated language: The re-emergence of an ideology. In Watts, Richard J. and Peter Trudgill (eds.), *Alternative Histories of English*. London: Routledge, 155–172.
  2003   *Politeness*. Cambridge: Cambridge University Press.
Watts, Richard J. and Peter Trudgill (eds.)
  2002   *Alternative Histories of English*. London: Routledge.
Wenger, Etienne
  1998   *Communities of Practice. Learning, Meaning and Identity*. Cambridge: Cambridge University Press.
Wetzel, Patricia J.
  1993   The language of vertical relationships and linguistic analysis. *Multilingua* 12(4), 387–406.
  1994   Contemporary Japanese attitudes toward honorifics (*keigo*). *Language Variation and Change* 6(2), 113–147.
  1995   Japanese social deixis and the pragmatics of politeness. *Japanese Discourse: An International Journal for the Study of Japanese Text and Talk* 1, 85–105.
Wood, Linda A. and Rolf O. Kroger
  1994   The analysis of facework in discourse: Review and proposal. *Journal of Language and Social Psychology* 13(3), 248–277.
Woodhouse, John R.
  1994   The tradition of Della Casa's Galateo in English. In Carré, Jacques (ed.), *The Crisis of Courtesy: Studies in the Conduct-Book in Britain, 1600–1900*. Leiden: Brill, 11–23.
Yahya-Othman, Saida
  1994   Covering one's social back: Politeness among the Swahili. *Text* 14(1), 141–161.
Yeung, L. N. T.
  1997   Polite requests in English and Chinese business correspondence in Hong Kong. *Journal of Pragmatics* 27, 505–522.
Yli-Jokipii, Hilkka
  1994   *Requests in Professional Discourse: A Cross-Cultural Study of British, American and Finnish Business Writing*. Helsinki: Suomalainen Tiedeakatemia.

Author index

Ackroyd, P. 128
Abelson, R. P., xliii, 150, 183
Adamzik, K. 143
Adler, A. 112
Agar, M. 50
Aiken, C. 124
Aldington, R. 128
Allen, V. 32
Altman, G. 59, 151
Arndt, H. xiii–xvi, xviii–xix, xxv,
   xxxix, xlvi, 5, 13, 21–26, 28–
   32, 34–36, 39, 135, 147, 152–
   153, 258, 261, 267
Arnold, G. 31
Arnold, M. 121
Assmann, J. 92
Atkinson, J. 153
Atkinson, M. 52
Austen, J. 111, 115
Axia, G. 232
Bach, E. 53
Bally, C. 79, 132–133, 138, 145
Bargiela-Chiappini, F. xlv, xlvii
Baroni, M. 232
Basso, K. 265
Bates, E. 260
Bateson, G. xliii
Beetz, M. 96–99, 105
Beinhauer, W. 132–133, 138
Bellegarde, Abbé de 96
Bennett, J. 23
Berger, C. 35, 38, 40
Bergson, H. 107
Benincà, P. 152
Bever, T. 54
Bigelow, B. 250
Blake, W. 129

Blickle, G. 159
Blum-Kulka, S. xii–xiii, xxv, 15,
   21, 133, 153, 197, 256, 262–
   270, 273, 275
Bolinger, D. 27, 35, 37
Bourdieu, P. xlii, xlv–xlvi
Bowers, J. 29, 35
Bradac, J. 29, 35
Braun, F. 17, 46, 58–61, 82, 152,
   175
Brooks, C. 124–125
Brown, G. 219–220, 224, 229
Brown, P. xi–xii, xiv–xviii, xxiii,
   xxv, xxvii–xxxiii, xxxv–xxxix
   1–2, 7–10, 14, 23, 29, 44, 46,
   51, 54–55, 57, 79, 107, 115,
   117, 129, 131–132, 135, 137,
   139–141, 144–145, 148, 152,
   155, 158–159, 161–162, 164–
   171, 174–176, 178–182, 196–
   197, 203, 210–212, 216–217,
   219–220, 229, 231–232, 255,
   260, 267, 270, 272–273, 277,
   281
Brown, R. 17, 59–61, 165, 273,
   278, 327
Brown, S. 46
Bruner, J. 270
Brunot, F. 132–133, 138
Bublitz, W. 132, 141
Buck, R. 26
Bühler, K. 133
Byrnes, H. 217
Calabrese, R. 36, 40
Callan, H. 149
Carling, C. 30
Carlston, D. 32

Subject Index

.